Intermodal Maritime Security

Intermodal Maritime Security
Supply Chain Risk Mitigation

Edited by

Gary A. Gordon

Richard R. Young

**Foreword by Michael Chertoff, Secretary,
U.S. Department of Homeland Security (2005-2009)**

ELSEVIER

Elsevier
Radarweg 29, PO Box 211, 1000 AE Amsterdam, Netherlands
The Boulevard, Langford Lane, Kidlington, Oxford OX5 1GB, United Kingdom
50 Hampshire Street, 5th Floor, Cambridge, MA 02139, United States

Notices

Knowledge and best practice in this field are constantly changing. As new research and experience broaden
our understanding, changes in research methods, professional practices, or medical treatment may become
necessary.

Practitioners and researchers must always rely on their own experience and knowledge in evaluating and using
any information, methods, compounds, or experiments described herein. In using such information or
methods they should be mindful of their own safety and the safety of others, including parties for whom they
have a professional responsibility.

To the fullest extent of the law, neither the Publisher nor the authors, contributors, or editors, assume any
liability for any injury and/or damage to persons or property as a matter of products liability, negligence or
otherwise, or from any use or operation of any methods, products, instructions, or ideas contained in the
material herein.

Library of Congress Cataloging-in-Publication Data
A catalog record for this book is available from the Library of Congress

British Library Cataloguing-in-Publication Data
A catalogue record for this book is available from the British Library

ISBN: 978-0-12-819945-9

For information on all Elsevier publications visit our website at
https://www.elsevier.com/books-and-journals

Publisher: Joe Hayton
Acquisitions Editor: Brian Romer
Editorial Project Manager: Naomi Robertson
Production Project Manager: Selvaraj Raviraj
Cover Designer: Mark Rogers

Typeset by TNQ Technologies

Contents

Contributors

Bennett C. Abrams Tulane University, New Orleans, LA, United States

James J.F. Forest University of Massachusetts, Lowell, MA, United States

Aleksander Gerson Wydra Division for Shipping and Ports Research, Maritime Policy & Strategy Research Center, University of Haifa, Haifa, Israel

Gary A. Gordon, PhD, PE, MEMS, LTC USA (Ret.) Department of Civil & Environmental Engineering, University of Massachusetts Lowell, Lowell, MA, United States

Jon S. Helmick Maritime Logistics & Security Program, United States Merchant Marine Academy, Kings Point, NY, United States

Tomer May Wydra Division for Shipping and Ports Research, Maritime Policy & Strategy Research Center, University of Haifa, Haifa, Israel

Andrew B. Morrow Cybersecurity, School of Business Administration, Capital College, The Pennsylvania State University, Middletown, PA, United States

Matthew R. Peterson Supply Chain Solutions, LMI, Mechanicsburg, PA, United States

James H. Schreiner Department of Systems Engineering, United States Military Academy, West Point, NY, United States

Richard R. Young School of Business Administration, Capital College, The Pennsylvania State University, Middletown, PA, United States

Combined Cameo Bios

Editors

Gary A. Gordon, PhD, PE, MEMS, LTC USA (Ret.)

Senior Adjunct Professor, Department of Civil & Environmental Engineering, University of Massachusetts Lowell, Lowell, MA, United States

Gary A. Gordon holds a Ph.D. and B.S. in Civil Engineering, and MBA from the University of Massachusetts Lowell, and M.S. in Civil Engineering from the University of Maryland and is a Registered Professional Engineer and Military Emergency Management Specialist. Prior to academia, Dr. Gordon had a lengthy career in transportation operations, security, and infrastructure, to include the U.S. Army Reserve. This includes positions as former Assistant Federal Security Director—Surface Transportation for Department of Homeland Security (DHS)/Transportation Security Administration and Assistant Chief Engineer—Design and Construction of a former Class I Northeast Railroad. Militarily, his assignments included the U.S. Transportation Command, 7th Transportation Group (Terminal), 313th Transportation Battalion and predecessor of the U.S. Army Military Surface Deployment and Distribution Command. He is experienced and published in multimodal transportation operations and security, is a co-author of *Railway Security: Protecting Against Manmade and Natural Disasters* and is on the editorial board of the *Journal of Transportation Security*.

Richard (Rich) R. Young, Ph.D., FCILT

Distinguished Professor Emeritus of Supply Chain Management, School of Business Administration, The Capital College, The Pennsylvania State University

Richard R. Young holds a B.S. in Operations Management from Rider University, M.B.A. from the University at Albany, and Ph.D. in Business Logistics from the Pennsylvania State University. He is a fellow of the Chartered Institute of Logistics and Transport of the

United Kingdom, senior research fellow of the Institute for Supply Management, and he is accepted to practice before the U.S. Federal Maritime Commission. Prior to academia, Dr. Young held various supply chain management positions in industry including the U.S. subsidiary of Hoechst AG, the erstwhile German chemical giant. He has consulted with a wide range of transportation providers and industrial firms as well as the U.S. Marine Corps and has spoken before audiences worldwide. Dr. Young serves on the editorial boards of *Transportation Journal*, *Journal of Supply Chain Management*, and the *South African Journal of Transport and Supply Management*, and is a Fulbright German Research Scholar. He co-authored the book, *Railway Security: Protecting Against Manmade and Natural Disasters.*

Contributing authors (in chapter order)

Bennett C. Abrams, BA Political Science/Homeland Security (May 2021)

School of Liberal Arts, Tulane University

Bennett C. Abrams is pursuing a Bachelor of Arts degree in Political Science and Homeland Security Studies at Tulane University. His relevant courses taken include emergency management, introduction to homeland security, domestic terrorism, and Middle East security. Mr. Abrams has written several academic papers focusing on emergency response, homeland security, and terrorism, to include "A.Q. Kahn: The Success and Consequences of His Nuclear Proliferation." Bennett's career objectives are in the security of national defense.

James J.F. Forest, Ph.D.

Professor, School of Criminology and Justice Studies, University of Massachusetts Lowell

James J.F. Forest received his graduate degrees from Boston College and Stanford University, and his undergraduate degree is from Georgetown University. In addition to being a Professor at the University of Massachusetts Lowell, Dr. Forest is a Visiting Professor at the Fletcher School of Law and Diplomacy at Tufts University and coeditor of the scholarly journal *Perspectives on Terrorism*. He has published dozens of academic journal articles and over 20 books including *The Terrorism Lectures* (Nortia Press, 2019), *Essentials of Counterterrorism* (Praeger, 2015), and *Intersections of Crime and Terror* (Routledge, 2013). Dr. Forest has previously served as a senior fellow with the Joint Special Operations University and as Director of Terrorism Studies at the United States Military Academy, and has provided expert testimony for terrorism-related court cases and Congressional hearings.

Captain Aleksander Gerson (MSc)

Senior Research Fellow and Head, Wydra Division for Shipping and Ports Research, Haifa Research Center for Maritime Policy and Strategy, Haifa University

Aleksander Gerson holds a B.Sc. from the Israel Institute of Technology (Technion) in Industrial Management and an M.Sc. in International Maritime Sciences, Shipping, and Environment from the Southampton Solent University, UK. He is a graduate of the Israel Maritime Officers College, served 3 years in the Israeli Navy commanding a patrol boat and sailed in the Israeli Merchant Marine for 30 years, of which over 20 years as Captain. From 1998 to 2016, he served as a Senior Shipping Inspector and later as a Deputy Director General of the Israeli Maritime Administration. During his service in the Israeli Maritime Authority, represented the State of Israel in the International Maritime Organization (IMO) and various International Organizations such as REMPEC, EMSA, and Italian Coast Guard. Since his retirement from government service, he shares his time between Haifa University and sailing as Merchant Marine Captain.

Jon S. Helmick, Ph.D.

Captain, United States Maritime Service, Professor and Director, Maritime Logistics and Security Program, United States Merchant Marine Academy

CAPT Helmick holds a Ph.D. from the University of Miami and a U.S. Coast Guard license as MASTER OF OCEAN STEAM, MOTOR, AUXILIARY SAIL, AND SAIL VESSELS OF ANY GROSS TONS. He led the development of U.S. maritime security education and training standards and curricula and was the lead author for multiple IMO model maritime security courses. He chaired the interagency committee that developed a federal maritime security training certification program. He has testified before Congress and served as a member of U.S. delegations to IMO meetings. His research has been published in such journals as *Transportation Quarterly*, *Transportation Journal*, and the *Journal of Transportation Security*. He serves on numerous editorial boards, task forces, and committees. CAPT Helmick has received the U.S. Department of Transportation Gold Medal, the U.S. Maritime Administration Bronze Medal, and the U.S. Department of Homeland Security "Secretary's Award for Excellence" for his work.

Tomer May (MA)

Security Officer Israeli Ministry of Transport

Mr. Tomer May earned a Bachelor of Arts degree in Political Science and most recently a Master of Arts in International Political Science focusing on National Security and Maritime Strategy from Haifa University. He served as an artillery officer (Lieutenant) in the

Israeli Defense Force (IDF) and, upon completion of his service in the IDF, he joined the Ministry of Transport as a security officer and gained 10 years of experience in the security of shipping (especially passenger ships), marinas, and ports.

Andrew (Andy) B. Morrow, M.B.A., M.S.

Lecturer of Cybersecurity, School of Business Administration, The Capital College, The Pennsylvania State University

Andrew B. Morrow holds a B.S. in Management and a B.S. in Information Systems, an M.B.A. and a M.S. in Information Systems and is currently pursuing a Ph.D. in Public Administration with a specialization in Homeland Security from The Pennsylvania State University. He is a member of both (ISC)^2 and ISACA and holds numerous security-related certifications including Certified Information Systems Security Professional (CISSP) and Certified Information Systems Auditor (CISA). He is also a member of the Project Management Institute (PMI) and holds the Project Management Professional (PMP) and PMI-Agile Certified Practitioner (PMI-ACP) certifications in project management. Prior to academia, Mr. Morrow held various information technology and senior management positions including experience as a systems administrator, data base administrator, chief security officer, chief technology officer, chief information officer, and vice president of information technology in both public and private sectors. He currently consults on technology and cybersecurity topics for several firms in addition to his full-time teaching role.

Matthew R. Peterson, MBA, CSCP, SCOR-P

Principal, Supply Chain Solutions, LMI, Mechanicsburg, PA

Matt Peterson is a Principal, Supply Chain Solutions with LMI, a consultancy dedicated to improving the business of government. Matt leverages nearly 30 years of logistics and consulting experience to lead projects and advise military, federal, and state government clients. He has an extensive background in supply chain management, including warehousing and distribution, supply chain planning and risk management, emergency management logistics, business process improvement, and data analysis. Before joining LMI, he worked for the General Services Administration. Matt has an M.B.A. from George Mason University and a B.S. in business logistics from Penn State University. He holds a Certified Supply Chain Professional (CSCP) designation from APICS and is a Certified Supply Chain Operations Reference (SCOR) Model Professional. He has written several peer-reviewed supply chain management articles published in academic journals that documented opportunities for a new application of the SCOR model to emergency management logistics.

James H. Schreiner, Ph.D., PMP, CPEM, LTC USA

Associate Professor, Department of Systems Engineering, United States Military Academy, West Point

James H. Schreiner holds a B.S. in Mechanical Engineering from Marquette University, Milwaukee, an M.E. in Engineering Management from the University of Colorado, Boulder, and a Ph.D. in Systems and Entrepreneurial Engineering from the University of Illinois, Urbana-Champaign. He is a registered Project Management Professional (PMP) since 2004 and Certified Professional in Engineering Management (CPEM) since 2017. He has served for over 24 years, including over 36 months deployed in support of global war on terrorism (GWOT), in command and staff positions within the U.S. Army Corps of Engineers (USACE) including as Strategic Planner to the Chief of Engineers, USACE and as Deputy Commander of Chicago USACE. Most recently, he served at West Point as Director of the Operations Research Center in the Department of Systems Engineering and is now serving as the Program Director for the Systems and Decision Sciences Program. He is experienced and published in systems thinking and systems engineering disciplines to include work in the fields of water resources, cognitive engineering, and decision analysis. He serves as President Elect for the American Society for Engineering Management and is coeditor of the *SISE Industrial and Systems Engineering Review Journal*.

Foreword

The attacks of September 11, 2001 catalyzed a fundamental reassessment of global supply chain security. In particular, the hijacking of passenger airplanes and the targeting of the World Trade Center profoundly illustrated that global commerce was an ideological target of Al-Qaeda and its sympathizers abroad. As the US Department of Homeland Security sought to rein in the constellation of threats facing the United States in this post−9/11 era, a critical task of this effort was reevaluating the threats and vulnerabilities associated with the intermodal maritime supply chain.

Intermodal maritime operations have evolved significantly in the years following September 11. This is not altogether surprising. One of the hallmarks of globalization has been the proclivity of supply chains to reach outward in search of new suppliers and efficiencies, often with security as a secondary or peripheral concern. Advancements in technology, the economic, and infrastructural development of emerging markets, and international trade agreements have collectively broadened the touch points of the global supply chain to include insecure, opaque operating environments. For its part, the United States has enacted an array of policies and initiatives designed to better manage this dynamic risk landscape. The Maritime Transportation Security Act, the National Strategy for Maritime Security, the Customs-Trade Partnership Against Terrorism (CTPAT), the Secure Freight Initiative, and the Container Security Initiative are but a few examples of US-led initiatives designed to address intermodal supply chain security. The evolutionary nature of the global supply chain and the rapid growth of containerization mean that these initiatives will require continued recalibration from policymakers and vigilance from enforcement entities in the years ahead.

The COVID-19 pandemic poses yet another multifaceted challenge to the intermodal maritime supply chain. At various points during the pandemic, supply chains have been snarled by a patchwork of lockdowns, crossborder transportation restrictions, and business closures. At home, the commercial maritime industry has kept the nation running during the deepest points of the crisis, ensuring that logistical needs continue to be met and medical supplies like ventilators reach resource-strained hospitals. The security of these critical goods relies in no small part on the Jones Act. Over a century later, the Jones Act of 1917 keeps the tether between economic security and national security intact by mandating that only American-owned, flagged, and operated vessels carry maritime cargo between two US points. In addition to the visibility and control advantages, the Jones Act secures the United States against foreign manipulation of US waterways for geopolitical purposes. The Jones Act also empowers US mariners to serve as citizen sentinels on America's coasts, working closely with the US Coast Guard to report criminal behavior and suspicious activity.

The importance and timeliness of this book cannot be overstated. The arrival of this book comes at a time when global cooperation and a shared understanding of the risk landscape are needed to confront both enduring and emergent threats to maritime security and the global supply chain. The COVID-19 pandemic promises to be a protracted challenge to intermodal maritime operations, which will almost certainly be compounded by bad actors seeking to exploit the turbulent international environment. "Intermodal Maritime Security: An Approach to Supply Chain Efficiency and Risk Mitigation" offers a comprehensive education for stakeholders across industry, government, and academia. It is essential reading for anyone who seeks to advance US maritime security and expand the benefits of a global supply chain.

Michael Chertoff

Secretary, U.S. Department of Homeland Security (2005–2009)

Preface

Intermodal maritime transportation is an extremely complex undertaking meaning that one must appreciate the specific expertise required to understand its specific component parts. This book is an edited volume whereby the editors have sought to access the in-depth knowledge of a range of notable experts that hail from the shipping industry, insurance, government, and academia. Many are very senior in their organizations; hence, there are chapters where anonymity has been necessary in order that any attribution will be precluded. Rather than taking a strictly esoteric approach, several chapters will open with a vignette portraying a realistic albeit fictional situation from which the remainder of the chapter will be able to expand.

Chapter 1 discusses the Maritime Transportation Security Act and the component plans found within the National Strategy for Maritime Security established by the National Security Presidential Directive 13 and the Homeland Security Presidential Directive 41. Collectively, these form the regulatory framework for securing international maritime trade. To provide the reader with a basic understanding of intermodal operations, Chapter 2 provides some history of the technology as well as a working knowledge of the infrastructure and assets employed. Inasmuch as intermodal transportation requires a substantial investment in landside assets, Chapter 3 differentiates waterside from landside whereas Chapter 4 underscores the necessary interaction between maritime, trucking, and rail modes. Collectively, these three chapters can be deemed the *operational primer* in the book.

Throughout many chapters, the issue of risk and vulnerability will be repeated numerous times; hence, Chapters 5 and 6 examine these from the standpoint of a major marine casualty insurer. Chapter 7 reviews some of the background of the threats posed by terrorists and nonstate actors whereas Chapters 8 and 9 address the physical and technological considerations needed from an engineering perspective for protecting landside infrastructure. A growing concern, and certainly one where there are new developments nearly weekly, is the problem of cyberthreats, which Chapter 10 focuses on many of the facets that are of present concern plus some consideration of those anticipated for the future.

Earlier in Chapter 1, there is an emphasis placed on the multinational role of protecting international trade. Consequently, Chapter 11 provides a valuable taxonomy of the various initiatives put into play since the end of World War II, but highlights the cumulative effect that these have had where today there are several international agreements that endeavor to vet the chain of custody of the merchandise trade, some with a particular focus on containerization. Lest this volume have a solely US-centric approach, Chapter 12 provides the Israeli perspective with its unique situation and security issues that must be recognized and overcome. Chapters 13—15 endeavor to address the respective specifics of assessing risk at foreign ports of loading, issues for goods in transit on the high seas, and the matter of risk at US ports. With the need to be able to assess risk in an expeditious manner, Chapter 16 proposes a potentially useful model that examines multiple facets of the intermodal journey. Dubbed the Maritime CARVER Model, it is based on a U.S. Army CARVER targeting model, but clearly has been adapted for intermodal maritime shipping.

Chapter 17 endeavors to apply systems theory to the problem recognizing that maritime shipping in general, and intermodal shipping in particular, is a complex undertaking where not only an understanding of the operating environment is concerned but also how all of those elements fit together into a comprehensive process. The application of systems theory can then be used to pinpoint the relevant vulnerability and, therefore, provide guidance for where prevention, enforcement, and interdiction efforts need to be focused. Chapter 18 provides background on public policy, but then establishes a compelling case for the use of public—private, private-private, and public-public partnerships for providing a comprehensive approach to security.

Finally, Chapter 19 combines many of the key thoughts advanced by the many chapter authors and provides some insights for the where and the how intermodal maritime security efforts may evolve moving forward. We do not wish to leave the impression that this is any manner a perfect vision of the future given the number of operative variables and the dynamic nature of the political-economic landscape. Still, our objective is to raise the collective consciousness of the many and varied participants that by definition includes industry practitioners, government officials at all levels, academics conducting relevant research, and students. We are living in a time of increased international economic interdependency; therefore, as the primary mode of transportation, it is intermodal maritime transportation, as the enabler of that interdependency, that must be secured.

Acknowledgments

Undertaking a book having such far-reaching issues as well as implications has required the involvement of many individuals, both directly and indirectly. Our immediate appreciation extends to our various named chapter authors that include Dr. James Forest from the Homeland Security Program at the University of Massachusetts Lowell; Captain Alexander Gerson, Senior Research Fellow, and Mr. Tomer May, Israel Ministry of Transport Security Officer and Graduate Student, both of the Wydra Division for Shipping and Ports Research, Maritime Policy, and Strategy Research Center, University of Haifa; Captain Jon Helmick of the U.S. Merchant Marine Academy; Andrew Morrow from the Information Systems Program at Penn State University; Matt Peterson of LMI, Inc.; and Lieutenant Colonel James Schreiner, Ph.D., of the U.S. Military Academy at West Point. There are also those individuals who were unable to author chapters, but nevertheless provided us with important leads for others. Hence, thank you to Dominic O'Leary of PhilaPort, Mike Ford of BDP International, and James Drogan from State University of New York—Maritime.

Of special note, there are several authors who were willing to share their extensive expertise but found it preferable to remain anonymous. Their contributions can be so extensive only because they have chosen to forego attribution for both themselves and the organizations that they represent.

Providing important guidance for the editorial work and production of the book, we thank Naomi Robertson from Elsevier, who despite being half a world away in London, kept us on track and focused as we labored on. During summer 2020, we were privileged to have Bennett Abrams, a student at Tulane University, who was dual majoring in Homeland Security and Political Science take an independent study under our supervision to assist us with some of the research and chapter writing. He contributed extensively to Chapters 8, 9, and 13, where he is also listed as a coauthor but was also an active participant in our weekly online conferences.

A special thanks goes to Mr. Lee Kair, Principal at The Chertoff Group, for arranging for Secretary Michael Chertoff to write the Foreword. Lee and Gary collaborated in the past when they both worked together at the Transportation Security Administration. Gary was the Assistant Federal Security Director-Surface Transportation for the South Central Region under the leadership of Lee who was the Assistant Administrator for Security Operations, and this was during Michael Chertoff's tenure as the Secretary of Homeland Security.

Finally, no such work could ever have been undertaken without the ongoing support of our loving wives, Bobbie and Mary. They endured the endless hours of our working in solitude often making for delayed meals and getting together with family and friends, our frequent telephone and online conferences, and our nonstop thinking about secure maritime transportation. They encouraged us when we needed it most, often with just the right measure of humor to lighten our mood as well as the tasks at hand.

Gary Gordon

Rich Young

PART I

Introduction

9/11, Maritime Transportation Security Act (MTSA), and how we got to where we are?

Richard R. Young Ph.D., FCILT [1], Gary A. Gordon PhD, PE, MEMS, LTC USA (Ret.) [2]

[1]School of Business Administration, Capital College, The Pennsylvania State University, Middletown, PA, United States; [2]Department of Civil & Environmental Engineering, University of Massachusetts Lowell, Lowell, MA, United States

During World War II, the United States was protected by the size of the country as well as two great oceans that would have made any potential invasion an extraordinarily difficult undertaking. The supply lines necessary to execute such an invasion, whether from the Pacific or the Atlantic sides, would have been thousands of miles long and be devoid of any Axis-friendly nation that could function as a forward staging area (aka logistics base) such as the role played by Britain for the European Front.

Fast forward 50+ years to 2001 when hijacked planes were used to attack the high-profile targets of the Pentagon and the World Trade Center Towers. Many in the media as well as industry had uttered "It was a day that changed the transportation industry, not just aviation, forever." The worry was that foreign enemies and the wide expanses of ocean that have protected US shores would no longer be able to provide the same degree of protection as they had only 60 years prior. Arguably, the underlying cause for concern was the intermodal container, but to understand this thinking requires one to decompose what intermodalism has provided us. For one, fewer eyes are able to observe the goods because they are sealed inside a metal box, but the second reason is that the transit time from origin to final destination is substantially compressed when compared with break-bulk shipping—the standard practice of only a half century prior. Finally, and perhaps, the most compelling reason is the quantum increase in the volume of imported goods—since World War II world economies have become far more interdependent.

In the months following September 11, 2001, steps had quickly been implemented worldwide to inspect both passengers and cargo intending to board commercial aircraft. In

Intermodal Maritime Security. https://doi.org/10.1016/B978-0-12-819945-9.00005-8

the United States, the Transportation Security Administration (TSA) was established under the Department of Transportation, but soon transferred to the newly formed Department of Homeland Security. If there were to be further jihadist attacks on the United States using the aviation mode, it had just gotten more difficult. With the number of international flights arriving in the United States daily totaling less than the number of containers that can be loaded aboard even a modest size vessel, it becomes readily apparent that future attempts to attack US commerce, if not the soil, could potentially come from the maritime transport mode. Assessing the many facets of maritime transportation, or what has become known as Maritime Domain Awareness (MDA) was summarized by President Bush in the 2002 State of the Union Address:

> *The heart of the Maritime Domain Awareness program is accurate information, intelligence, surveillance, and reconnaissance of all vessels, cargo, and people extending well beyond our traditional maritime boundaries.*
>
> **NSMS (2005g).**

Later that year, Congress passed the Maritime Transportation Security Act (MTSA) that began the process of improving the security over all of those elements that President Bush had articulated. MTSA required the formation of Area Maritime Security Committees (AMSC) within each of the U.S. Coast Guard (USCG) Captain of the Port (COTP) jurisdictions.[1] An AMSC consists of experienced maritime local stakeholders that advise the COTP, but are also instrumental in the development of their respective Area Maritime Security Plans (AMSP) (U.S. Coast Guard, 2002).

MTSA is considered the cornerstone for all of the initiatives that were to follow and often the reference to MTSA is intended to include the elements of the National Strategy for Maritime Security (NSMS) which is far more detailed (Borchert, 2014; Department of Homeland Security, 2003). Appendix A to this chapter contains the findings that served as the underlying rationale for US regulation of maritime transportation moving forward (USC 2101, 2002).

Ultimately, eight supporting implementation plans were developed as components of the NSMS as provided for under the National Security Presidential Directive—41/Homeland Security Presidential Directive—13 (NSPD-41/HSPD-13) (White House, 2004). This chapter will address not only the specifics of the NSMS components, but also consider: (1) the traditional components that comprise the activities of the maritime trade, and (2) the global supply chain as best described by the Supply Chain Operations Reference (SCOR) Model (National Strategy for Maritime Security, 2005; Supply Chain Council, 2010).

---

[1] A Captain of the Port (COTP) is a senior U.S. Coast Guard officer that is empowered with far-reaching federal authorities—the power to control vessels, facilities, activities, and people on America's navigable waterways in order to safeguard the marine transportation system. See also *Proceedings of the Marine Safety and Security Council*, 75:2 (Fall, 2018) for a comprehensive discussion of the COTP position.

Although the NSMS seeks to link a multiplicity of otherwise discrete activities, many of these have continued to function independently albeit with cognizance of the larger security issue.

Maritime trade and the Supply Chain Operations Reference model

One of the most useful contemporary models for explaining supply chains is the SCOR model. Originally created during the late 1990s, it has gone through several iterations; however, the basic premise remains intact: supply chains consist of multiple entities each one conducting source, make, and deliver activities, but there also being an overarching plan activity as is depicted in Fig. 1.1. The total supply chain extends from that point that a material is either harvested or mined from the Earth to when its finished product is totally consumed by the final customer and there is disposition of the residual.

Between those two events, there are a myriad of activities performed by numerous participants, but between those activities, or links if the example of a chain is to continue, lie transportation that some have referred to as the glue that holds the supply chain together. Moreover, there are three principal flows that transcend the total length of the supply chain: physical, information, and financial (as shown in Fig. 1.2).

Firms do not have just a single supply chain, but rather multiple ones that may or may not have components in common. Consider, for example, the basic supply chains of an automobile assembler where steel body stampings, tires, windshield and window glass, seating, paint, electronics, and lighting components by necessity all have different sources, hence each has its own discrete supply chain. Whether goods are sourced internationally

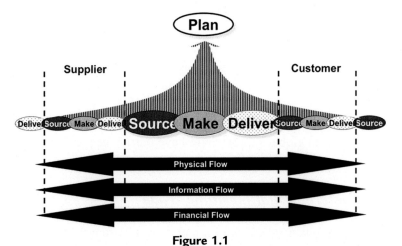

Figure 1.1
Supply chain operations reference model. *Supply Chain Council, 2010. Supply Chain Operations Reference Model: Overview, Version 10.0. Cypress, TX.*

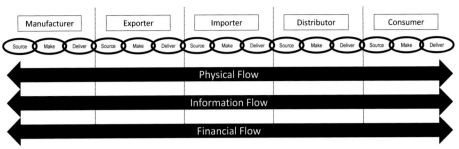

Figure 1.2

Supply chain parallel flows: physical, information, and financial. *Adapted from Supply Chain Council, 2010. Supply Chain Operations Reference Model: Overview, Version 10.0. Cypress, TX.*

or domestically, the main drivers are: (1) continuity of supply, (2) conformance to established specifications, (3) economic viability, and (4) timely availability.

Why this is important is that each of those supply chains represents vulnerability with respect to national security, especially if any respective supply chain originates offshore because each entity as discussed in the previous section of this chapter needs to be vetted when the chain of custody is documented. The term supply chain is often attributed to Chrysler Corporation because during the early 1980s financial rescue its management realized that it was the most vulnerable to disruption because of the high dependency that they had on outside sources of supply when compared to both Ford and General Motors as well as the Japanese competition.

With the repeated source-make-deliver activities representing an actual chain, the other element of the SCOR model that adds clarity to the discussion is its identification of the principal flows: physical, information, and financial. Physical flow has always been at the core of supply chain management from even before that moniker had been devised. The interest was in obtaining the right goods at the right time, but also at the right place and of the right quality (e.g., specification). Years later, there came the realization that there was a robust information flow that existed between buyers and sellers which was the key enabler of the physical flow. Finally, there is the financial flow, or the flow of payments for goods and services rendered, which was either enabled or impeded by the performance of the physical flow. Why this discussion appears here is to explain that various participants in the global supply chain have particular primary roles vis-à-vis one of these flows.

Components of international maritime trade

International maritime trade can be termed a complex and often thought of as a messy affair that has lots of moving parts managed by a plethora of specialist entities. It is a complex endeavor that bears some similarity to a domestic land-based counterpart but contains numerous unique components intended to protect the interests of sellers, buyers, exporters, importers, governments, shipowners, land and sea transportation service providers, and financial institutions. Moreover, there are alternative combinations of these entities depending upon: (1) the international commercial terms agreed upon,[2] (2) the location of the seller and exporter, (3) the relationship between buyer and seller, (4) particular capabilities or expertise of the importer and the exporter, and (5) the nature of the goods themselves.

When considering all of the combinations possible, it is the complexity that makes international maritime trade so challenging to manage. It was the advent of containerization, a topic that will be discussed at length in Chapter 2, that endeavored to at least simplify transportation because it readily accepted a wide range of goods and when it became a ubiquitous technology largely removed the nature of the goods as a key variable. For ease of explanation, Fig. 1.3 addresses some of this complexity through the lens of maritime transportation.

Importers may not be the same party as the ultimate consignee for several reasons, but perhaps the most significant is that the consignee may not have the expertise needed to

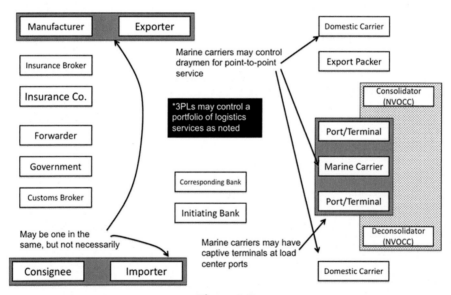

Figure 1.3

International maritime trade: significant combinations. *Young, R., Peterson, M., Novak, L., Flannery-Hayes, M., Tillotson, F., 2011. Proliferation Security Initiative Maritime Industry Study Final Briefing, (unpublished). Applied Research Laboratories project for Defense Threat Reduction Agency.*

---

[2] Incoterms, or International Commercial Terms, are defined by the International Chamber of Commerce, Paris, France. These are updated every 10 years, but given their complexity specific details will not be provided in this book.

effect international trade. A similar situation exists with the exporters and manufacturers, which might be one in the same, but not necessarily. It has been a longstanding practice that Japanese manufacturers have relied on trading companies to both represent and handle their international shipping needs. Often there is a trading company as a member of a Japanese kieretsu, or group of related firms.

Although container lines began offering solely port-to-port services, this changed in the mid-1980s when point-to-point options appeared where lines would include inland transportation at one or both ends of the transaction. When goods are not of sufficient volume to warrant the use of an entire container, the role of a consolidator comes into play, specifically the nonvessel operating common carrier (NVOCC) as shown with the alternate flow in Fig. 1.4. These are also employed for the movement of household goods, which remain shipments of interest with regard to smuggling in general and terrorist activity specifically.

Depending upon the size of the container line and the scale of business in particular ports, some port locations will be either owned or operated by the lines, or conversely the line will be just one of several smaller tenant lines making that port call.

Finally, the 1990s saw the advent of the third-party logistics providers, or 3PL, where the services for the physical and information flows could be bundled and offered to importers and exporters.

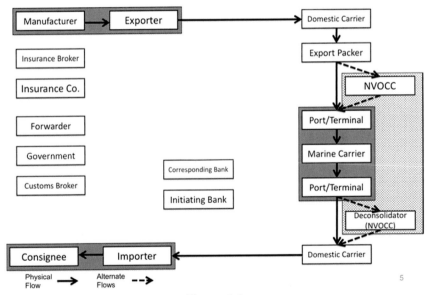

Figure 1.4

Physical flows: primary and alternate. *Young, R., Peterson, M., Novak, L., Flannery-Hayes, M., Tillotson, F., 2011. Proliferation Security Initiative Maritime Industry Study Final Briefing, (unpublished). Applied Research Laboratories project for Defense Threat Reduction Agency.*

International trade is a regulated activity for several reasons: (1) historically customs duties were a key revenue source for most nations, but with the liberalization of trade has become less of an issue; (2) many goods may be prohibited or subjected to quotas in order to protect domestic industry; and (3) many goods may be barred outright depending on the nature of the goods and/or country of origin. Illicit drugs clearly fall into this category, but there might also be a prohibition on some animal and agricultural products where invasive species might be a concern, and even Cuban cigars.

The information flow is critical to the regulatory effort given that many large importers with regular arriving shipments are known entities and their cargoes are frequently not physically inspected. Documentation is the primary method whereby shipment particulars are disclosed, whether to Customs and other regulators or to the container lines for devising stowage plans such as where dangerous goods will be stowed onboard ships. With as many entities as has been suggested so far, the documentation activities need to touch many different parties each with different interests. To follow the process in order of occurrence, Fig. 1.5 begins with the exporter's activities.

For ease of discussion, activities have been bifurcated between importers and exporters. Depending upon the size of the exporter, activities may be performed in-house or as is often the case with smaller firms, most likely outsourced to the freight forwarder. Many of these activities are the passing of documentation where the goods are described including

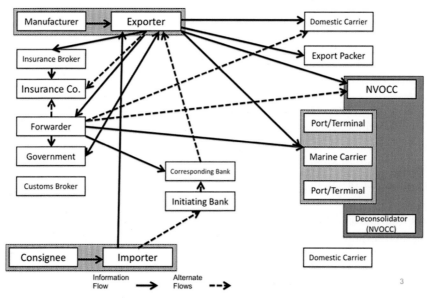

Figure 1.5

Information flows: exporter activities. *Young, R., Peterson, M., Novak, L., Flannery-Hayes, M., Tillotson, F., 2011. Proliferation Security Initiative Maritime Industry Study Final Briefing, (unpublished). Applied Research Laboratories project for Defense Threat Reduction Agency.*

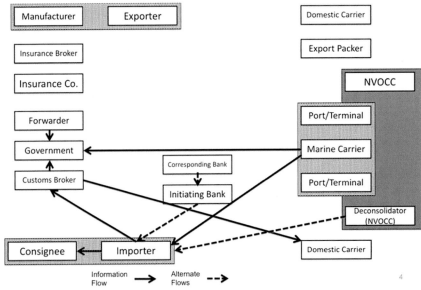

Figure 1.6

Information flows: importer's activities. *Young, R., Peterson, M., Novak, L., Flannery-Hayes, M., Tillotson, F., 2011. Proliferation Security Initiative Maritime Industry Study Final Briefing, (unpublished). Applied Research Laboratories project for Defense Threat Reduction Agency.*

their weight and physical dimensions, the importer identified, and value declared. Moreover, where banks are involved in the transaction, the exact performance including time will be stipulated by the importer. By comparison, as shown in Fig. 1.6, the information flows of the importer may be significantly less, however note that government plays a key part whether included as an exporter's flow or that of the importer.

There are two significant classifications of financial flow: that as actual payment for the goods and the payment for the various services required to facilitate the sale. The former is quite straightforward where the importer either pays the exporter directly on an open account basis, or alternatively payment is effected through the initiating and corresponding banks as on a letter of credit. The payment for those services provided by the carriers and the various intermediaries can be significantly more involved, as shown in Fig. 1.7, where the various International Commercial Terms (Incoterms) as well as the other elements of the commercial arrangements will dictate who pays whom for which.

The complexity becomes obvious where not only the activities of the importer are combined with those of the exporter, but when the physical, information, and financial flows are also taken into consideration. It becomes obvious, as shown in Fig. 1.8, that the permutations of participants and data elements can number in the hundreds. Some parties will possess all of the details of a particular shipment, while others will have only scant or limited knowledge.

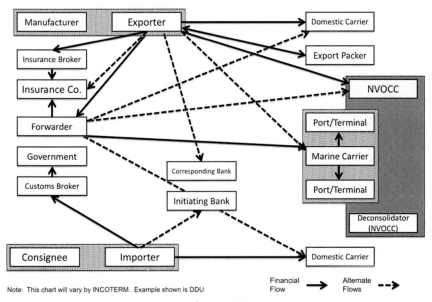

Figure 1.7

Financial flows: payment for transportation, intermediary services, and duties and taxes. *Young, R., Peterson, M., Novak, L., Flannery-Hayes, M., Tillotson, F., 2011. Proliferation Security Initiative Maritime Industry Study Final Briefing, (unpublished). Applied Research Laboratories project for Defense Threat Reduction Agency.*

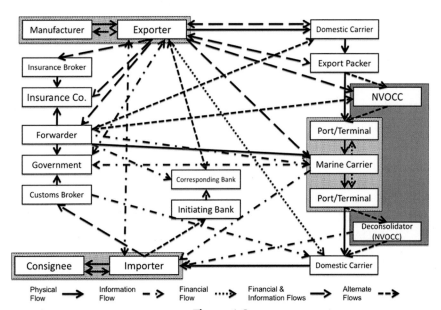

Figure 1.8

Combined flows: physical, information, and financial. *Young, R., Peterson, M., Novak, L., Flannery-Hayes, M., Tillotson, F., 2011. Proliferation Security Initiative Maritime Industry Study Final Briefing, (unpublished). Applied Research Laboratories project for Defense Threat Reduction Agency.*

Nevertheless, it is also a key point that the importer and the exporter are those two parties that will have the most knowledge of the shipment, a point that will be raised in later chapters when knowledge of the chain of custody is an important key to security.

Supporting implementation plans of the NSMS

With the eight component parts of NSMS understanding, the particular focus of each and how it relates to the key elements of maritime trade in general is very instructive given the already established fact that the maritime domain is already complex but made more so with the ongoing development of multinational regulations and industry practices. As this book will discuss in the following chapters, intermodalism has both added to, but in some respects, assuaged that complexity.

Maritime Domain Awareness

Echoing the discussion above that labeled the maritime domain as complex, the NSMS Implementation Plan for Domain Awareness (NSMS-DA) defines MDA as "[T]he effective understanding of anything associated with the global maritime domain that could impact the security, safety, economy or environment of the United States." Moreover, MDA requires the nation to collect, fuse, analyze, display, and disseminate actionable intelligence to an array of interested public and private sector stakeholders. As such, the Global Maritime Intelligence Integration Plan (IIP) provides the necessary framework identifying what information needs to be collected and what its sources may be. The MDA therefore becomes the basis for the formulation of the Maritime Operational Threat Response Plan.

The MDA Plan is based on obtaining persistent and extensive intelligence from a range of US agencies, the private sector, and foreign government sources that could be deemed a new era in that those approaches of the past half century are no longer adequate for the task at hand. The plan advocates employing innovative and enhanced means of collecting intelligence and to be able to combine it with what might otherwise be disparate information, whether publicly or privately sourced in order to provide a more comprehensive and informed picture. The MDA remains cognizant of the necessity of improving analytical techniques, but then names the National Maritime Intelligence Center[3] as the focal agency which is charged with cutting across organizational boundaries in order that the MDA be developed and shared by means of the Common Operating Picture (COP) in near real time (Vance and Vicente, 2006; NSMS, 2005g).

---

[3] The National Maritime Intelligence Center, located at the Suitland Federal Center outside Washington, DC, is operated by the U.S. Coast Guard.

Global Maritime Intelligence Integration Plan

Just as the events of 9/11 were not foreseen because an array of government agencies were not able to "connect the dots" represented by nonintegrated intelligence, the IIP endeavors to leverage all of the available intelligence regarding threats to the maritime domain. With 95,000 miles of coastline and millions of square miles of ocean within the Exclusive Economic Zone (EEZ) of the United States, there are numerous ports containing countless pieces of infrastructure such as container terminals, bridges and tunnels, aids to navigation, ship channels, and fueling facilities. Moreover, with better than three quarters of the population residing within 200 miles of a coastline, the US citizenry also remains at significant risk from terrorist actions coming from the sea. That maritime domain that serves the nation's economic activities also poses considerable risk because of the ease of movement and relative anonymity also facilitates criminal action.

The IIP concerns itself not just with terrorist activities, but a range of undesirable criminal ones that include smuggling of drugs, weapons and their components, money, and human trafficking, many of which could benefit from exploiting natural disasters and their diversion of law enforcement assets (see sidebar for an example of such a potential event). The concept of a layered defense is employed by the military but is also useful for protecting infrastructure. The importance of the IIP rests with augmenting a layered defense and keeping untoward activities at the greatest distance from the US homeland as possible. The detection, location, and tracking of potential threats to US maritime interests and providing for community sharing of information are the primary intent of the IIP. The objectives articulated in the IIP documents are fourfold: (1) prevention of terrorist attacks and criminal or hostile acts; (2) protection of maritime-related population centers and critical infrastructure; (3) minimize damage and expedite recovery after any incident; and (4) safeguard the oceans and their resources (NSMS, 2005c).

Example of potential exploiting of natural disasters

When preparing for Hurricane Katrina, railcars carrying toxic/poison inhalation hazards (T/PIH) were evacuated from New Orleans and taken west and inland toward Houston. As a result, the rail yards and available storage tracks were at or near capacity as Hurricane Rita approached Texas about a month later. The evacuation or protection of the T/PIH railcars from Houston and the surrounding areas was complicated by the interception of chatter about terrorists possibly exploiting the disaster by targeting the hazmat railcars as Hurricane Rita approached and made landfall. The TSA contacted the many railroads along the Gulf Coast alerting them of the potential and to take appropriate actions to secure infrastructure and equipment to protect against the possible attack. Fortunately, nothing materialized, however, a successful attack would have exceeded Houston's ability to respond and recover. This occurrence hints of how transportation operations and infrastructure can be exploited for terrorist purposes during a natural disaster. In the port environment, hurricanes, especially along the

Continued

Example of potential exploiting of natural disasters—cont'd

East and Gulf Coasts, could expose operations and infrastructure to exploitation opportunities as hurricanes approach and make landfall. Therefore, the potential for this should be considered when security and emergency planning is conducted.

Maritime Operational Threat Response Plan

This plan endeavors to establish the mechanism whereby the nation can respond to threats in a prompt and decisive manner. This is largely a combination of law enforcement and military[4] activities. Given the dynamics of advancing technology as well as the origins of threats, the types of responses are varied and the manner in which they are deployed is fluid thereby making further expansion of this discussion inappropriate.

International outreach and coordination strategy

We live in a global economy with interdependency being its cornerstone. That being the case, the protection of the maritime domain therefore equates to protecting the sea lanes for ocean transportation. The United States shares a mutual dependency with the other nations of the world. This strategy is best summed up as the following goals and objectives taken verbatim from its text.

Strategic Goal 1: A coordinated policy of US government maritime security activities with foreign governments, international and regional organizations, and the private sector.
Strategic Objective 1.1: Establish unified, consistent US positions on maritime security programs and initiatives for US bilateral and multilateral exchanges.
Strategic Objective 1.2: Emphasize the importance of maritime security as a key priority in US international policy.
Strategic Objective 1.3: Ensure the full integration of international law in the advancement of global maritime security at international meetings and exchanges.
Strategic Objective 1.4: Optimize the use of meetings and other exchanges with countries, international and regional organizations, and private sector groups to advance maritime security.
Strategic Goal 2: Enhanced outreach to foreign governments, international and regional organizations, private sector partners, and the public abroad to solicit support for improved global maritime security.

---

[4] One of the five US military services, the Coast Guard is unique in that it has both law enforcement and military roles. It is the sole military service that is not a part of the Department of Defense, but rather the Department of Homeland Security.

Strategic Objective 2.1: Build relationships with other countries and the maritime community to identify and reach out to regional and international organizations in order to advance global maritime security.

Strategic Objective 2.2: Coordinate US and international technical assistance to promote effective maritime security in developing nations and critical regions.

Strategic Objective 2.3: Coordinate a unified message on maritime security for public diplomacy.

Strategic Objective 2.4: Provide US missions abroad with guidance to enable them to build support for US maritime security initiatives with host governments, key private-sector partners, and general public abroad (National Strategy for Maritime Security, 2005).

Maritime Infrastructure Recovery Plan

Maritime activities are replete with significant landside infrastructure that is necessary for the movement of both passengers and cargo. The Maritime Infrastructure Recovery Plan (MIRP)[5] serves to establish a comprehensive approach whereby the maritime industry can recover from a transportation security incident. A key element is restoration of those capabilities and capacities affecting the flow of commerce with a minimum impact of the US economy.

Landside infrastructure is that which affects the loading and unloading of vessels, the provisioning and fueling to those vessels, and related vessel support activities. The MIRP provides recovery management procedures for decision-making at the incident site as well as those sites providing necessary support. In doing so, it articulates the roles and responsibilities of government at all levels plus the private sector and is specific to the needed functional responsibilities related to the recovery of maritime transportation capabilities (National Strategy for Maritime Security, 2005).

Maritime Transportation System Security Plan

The Maritime Transportation System (MTS) Security Plan is not so much about information systems as it is about adjusting everyone's perception emphasizing that it is a complex system of many critical components that function as a whole. It is geographically dispersed, consists of many different types of assets that include vessels, landside infrastructure, rights of way, and related aids to navigation. Moreover, it employs different assets depending on whether it is providing passenger or cruise ship services; bulk cargo

---

[5] It is not by coincidence that the Maritime Infrastructure Recovery Plan closely mirrors those elements that can be found in the National Infrastructure Protection Program which has *recovery* as one its five basic activities.

transportation, whether liquid or dry; vehicle transport as in roll-on/roll-off services; or intermodal container transportation. Various elements of interest within the MTS may be operated by private sector; federal, state, or local government; or quasi-governmental authorities. Note that the AMSP promulgated by the AMSC as provided for under MTSA are important components of the MTS.

The MTS is envisioned as a systems-oriented security regime built upon layers of protection and defense in depth that effectively mitigates critical system security risks, which preserving the functionality and efficiency of the MTS. Understanding the most effective security risk management strategies involves cooperation and participation of both domestic and international stakeholders acting at strategic points in the system, the United States seeks to improve security through a cooperative and cohesive effort involving all stakeholders. With multiple systems comprising the portfolio of applications, the MTS is a comprehensive approach to managing the many facets of transportation security as depicted in Fig. 1.9 (NSMS, 2005f).

Maritime Commerce Security Plan

This is the plan that endeavors to provide a comprehensively secure international maritime supply chain. Much of the content of the Commerce Security Plan (CSP) focuses on containerized cargo, that transportation innovation that has led maritime transportation to no longer be an impediment to effecting global supply chains. The intermodal container is

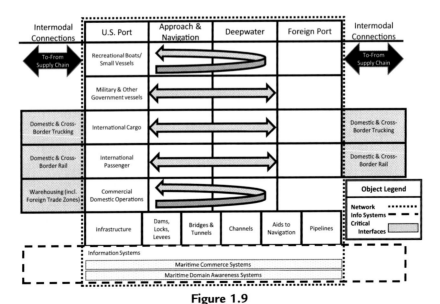

Figure 1.9

Maritime transportation systems: a system of systems. *Adapted from NSMS Transportation Systems Security Plan.*

the primary mode for moving a huge range of goods and in some cases may be the only practical one available. It is relatively inexpensive thereby making it attractive for moving a wide range of goods, but improving its security is a challenge because of the complex nature of such supply chains.

Because of the pervasive nature of containerized shipping, any disruption to that system has immediate and significant global economic impact. Every nation has an interest in seeing the oceans of the world being made more secure, but in doing so the responsibility cannot be left up to single nations—it is a multinational effort and has been for some decades already. The container, because of its intermodality, provides a vulnerability to every city and town whether they are near the ocean or not. They can represent hidden threats that the other forms of maritime commerce cannot. This is why layered defense is central to the discussion: threats must be held off and intercepted long before they reach US shores. The several USCG and Customs and Border Protection (CBP) initiatives found within the CSP is the Container Security Initiative (CSI) where US officials and host nation partners examine US-bound containers prior to their being loaded aboard ships at foreign ports; the Customs-Trade Partnership Against Terrorism (C-TPAT) where importers are encouraged to vet and document their international supply chains; and the Advance Manifest System where vessels must file details of their cargo in advance of arriving at a US port (NSMS, 2005a).

Domestic Outreach Plan

Continuing the discussion from the CSP, the Domestic Outreach Plan (DOP) uses a systems approach to link the interests of a broad range of stakeholders that include port infrastructure, industry, and populations adjacent to port areas, but because of the ready access as represented by the intermodal container, the inland communities as well as inland industries are by necessity a part of those conversations. Supply chain management, as described earlier in this chapter, has a dependency not only on one's immediate suppliers, but those that are second and third tier and beyond. While some stakeholders may have more economic interest than others, every single person by virtue of their being consumers, residents of a community, employees of an industry, and even travelers on the road systems are, indeed, stakeholders (NSMS, 2005b).

Summary

This chapter began with an overview of the nature of supply chain management whereby it was emphasized that every firm has multiple supply chains; each firm in the chain conducting source, make, and deliver activities; and that every supply chain has three flows: physical, information, and financial. To that we added the roles of the various international trade participants inclusive of importer, exporter, transportation service providers, financial institutions, and various intermediaries that serve to coordinate shipments as well as prepare documentation. It is imperative to emphasize that some variation may occur due to the size of the importer and/or exporter, the nature of the goods, the origin and destination, and the applicable commercial terms.

If the events of September 11th are the game changer for international transportation, the role of government and its relationship with the private sector, state and local governments, and other nations was clearly articulated by the MTSA of 2002 and the establishment of the NSMS authorized by the National Security Presidential Directive 13 and Homeland Security Presidential Directive 41. While this chapter provided an overview of the component plans of the NSMS, in summary these are comprehensive and touch every possible aspect of maritime transportation.

Appendix A: Title I—Maritime Transportation Security, Section 101: findings

The Congress makes the following findings:

(1) There are 361 public ports in the United States that are an integral part of Nation's commerce.
(2) United States ports handle over 95% of United States overseas trade. The total volume of goods imported and exported through ports is expected to double over the next 20 years.
(3) The variety of trade and commerce carried out at ports includes bulk cargo, containerized cargo, passenger transport and tourism, and intermodal transportation systems that are complex to secure.
(4) The United States is increasingly dependent on imported energy for a substantial share of its energy supply and a disruption of that share of supply would seriously harm consumers and our economy.
(5) The top 50 ports in the United States account for about 90% of all cargo tonnage. Twenty-five United States ports account for 98% of all container shipments. Cruise ships visiting foreign destinations embark from at least 16 ports. Ferries in the United States transport 113,000,000 passengers and 32,000,000 vehicles per year.
(6) Ports often are a major locus of federal crime, including drug trafficking, cargo theft, and smuggling of contraband and aliens.
(7) Ports are often very open and exposed and are susceptible to large-scale acts of terrorism that could cause a large loss of life or economic disruption.
(8) Current inspection levels of containerized cargo are insufficient to counter potential security risks. Technology is currently not adequately deployed to allow for the nonintrusive inspection of containerized cargo.

(9)   The cruise ship industry poses a special risk from a security perspective.

(10)   Securing entry points and other areas of port facilities and examining of inspecting containers would increase security at US ports.

(11)   Biometric identification procedures for individuals having access to secure areas in port facilities are important tools and prevent port cargo crimes, smuggling, and terrorist actions.

(12)   United States ports are international boundaries that—

(A)   Are particularly vulnerable to breaches in security;

(B)   May present weaknesses in the ability of the United States to realize its national security objectives; and

(C)   May serve as a vector or target for terrorist attacks aimed at the United States.

(13)   It is in the best interests of the United States—

(A)   To have a free flow of interstate and foreign commerce to ensure the efficient movement of cargo;

(B)   To increase US port security by establishing improving communication among law enforcement officials responsible for port security;

(C)   To formulate requirements for physical port security recognizing the different character and nature of US port facilities, and to require the establishment of security programs at port facilities;

(D)   To provide financial assistance to help the States and to provide the private sector to increase physical security of US ports;

(E)   To invest in long-term technology to facilitate the private sector development of technology that will assist in the nonintrusive timely detection of crime or potential crime at US ports;

(F)   To increase intelligence collection on cargo and intermodal movements to address areas of potential threat to safety and security; and

(G)   To promote private sector procedures that provide for in-transit visibility and support law enforcement efforts directed at managing the security risks of cargo shipments.

(14)   On April 27, 1999, the President established the Interagency Commission on Crime and Security in US Ports to undertake a comprehensive study of the nature and extent of the problem of crime in our ports, as well as the way in which governments at all levels are responding. The Commission concluded that frequent crimes in ports include drug smuggling, illegal car exports, fraud, and cargo theft. Internal conspiracies are an issue at many ports and contribute to Federal crime. Criminal organizations are exploiting weak security at ports to commit a wide range of cargo crimes. Intelligence and information sharing among law enforcement agencies need to be improved and coordinated at many ports. A lack of minimum physical and personnel

security standards at ports and related facilities leaves many ports and port users very vulnerable. Access to ports and operations within ports is often uncontrolled. Security-related and detection-related equipment, such as small boats, cameras, large-scale X-ray machines, and vessel tracking devices, are lacking at many ports.

(15)   The International Maritime Organization and other similar international organizations are currently developing a new maritime security system that contains the essential elements for enhancing global maritime security. Therefore, it is in the best interests of the United States to implement new international instruments to establish such a system.

References

46 USC 2101, 2002. Maritime Transportation Security Act. https://www.maritime.dot.gov/ports/deepwater-ports-and-licensing/maritime-transportation-security-act-2002. (Accessed 12 February 2020).

Borchert, H., 2014. Maritime Security at Risk: Trends, Future Threat Vectors, and Capability Requirements. Sandfire AG, Lucerne.

Department of Homeland Security, 2003. Protecting America's Ports: Maritime Transportation Security Act of 2002. Office of the Press Secretary, Washington, DC. https://www.aapa-ports.org/files/PDFs/mtsa_press_kit.pdf. (Accessed 21 March 2020).

National Strategy for Maritime Security, 2005a. Maritime Commerce Security Plan. Department of Homeland Security, Washington, DC. https://www.dhs.gov/sites/default/files/publications/HSPD_MCSPlan_0.pdf. (Accessed 14 April 2020).

National Strategy for Maritime Security, 2005b. Domestic Outreach Plan. Department of Homeland Security, Washington, DC. https://www.dhs.gov/sites/default/files/publications/HSPD_DomesticOutreach.pdf. (Accessed 14 April 2020).

National Strategy for Maritime Security, 2005c. Global Maritime Intelligence Integration Plan. Department of Homeland Security, Washington, DC. https://fas.org/irp/offdocs/nspd/gmii-plan.pdf. (Accessed 14 April 2020).

National Strategy for Maritime Security, 2005d. International Outreach and Coordination Strategy. Department of State, Washington, DC https://www.dhs.gov/sites/default/files/publications/HSPD_MIRPPlan_0.pdf.

National Strategy for Maritime Security, 2005e. The Maritime Infrastructure Recovery Plan. Department of Homeland Security, Washington, DC. https://www.dhs.gov/sites/default/files/publications/HSPD_MIRPPlan_0.pdf. (Accessed 14 April 2020).

National Strategy for Maritime Security, 2005f. Maritime Transportation System Security Recommendations. DC Department of Homeland Security, Washington. https://www.dhs.gov/sites/default/files/publications/HSPD_MTSSPlan_0.pdf. (Accessed 14 April 2020).

National Strategy for Maritime Security, 2005g. National Plan to Achieve Maritime Domain Awareness. Department of Homeland Security, Washington, DC. https://www.dhs.gov/sites/default/files/publications/HSPD_MDAPlan_0.pdf. (Accessed 14 April 2020).

Supply Chain Council, 2010. Supply Chain Operations Reference Model: Overview, Version 10.0. Cypress, TX.

U.S. Coast Guard, 2002. Area Maritime Security Committees (AMSC). Brochure. https://www.dco.uscg.mil/Portals/9/CG-FAC/Documents/AMSC%20Brochure%202019.pdf?ver=2019-05-22-080513-100. (Accessed 9 June 2020).

Vance, G., Vicente, P., 2006. Maritime domain awareness. In: Proceedings of the Marine Safety and Security Council, vol. 63, pp. 6—9, 3 (Fall).

White, H., 2004. National Security Presidential Directive 13/National/Homeland Security Presidential Directive 41. https://www.hsdl.org/?view&did=470301. (Accessed 14 February 2020).

Young, R., Peterson, M., Novak, L., Flannery-Hayes, M., Tillotson, F., 2011. Proliferation Security Initiative Maritime Industry Study Final Briefing, (unpublished). Applied Research Laboratories project for Defense Threat Reduction Agency.

PART II

Overview of intermodal maritime operations

CHAPTER 2

Intermodalism history, advantages, and disadvantages

Richard R. Young, Ph.D., FCILT
School of Business Administration, Capital College, The Pennsylvania State University, Middletown, PA, United States

Intermodalism, or the carrying of the vehicles of one mode upon another, has been around for nearly 175 years. One of the first examples was the carriage of wheeled baggage carts on flatcars by the Camden and Amboy Railroad, a forerunner of the Pennsylvania Railroad, in 1830s—just a few years after the introduction of the railroad in the United States. The experiment was limited to passenger trains and offered some flexibility in interchange between railroads and steamboats, but the practice was short lived due to the inefficient handling of the carts at origin and destination (Cunningham, 9).

There have been many advantages to intermodal maritime transportation, but that is not to say that it does not come without some disadvantages. The major theme of this chapter is to explore both the advantages as well as the disadvantages, but most importantly to understand how these have shifted over time. Moreover, it is necessary to understand that further advantages and disadvantages may appear and that responsible management processes will need to be sufficiently flexible in order to accommodate these.

Intermodalism: maritime and rail

The movement of railcars by ship was not new as the railroads had been ferrying freight cars across rivers for many years—even today the New York New Jersey Rail (formerly the New York Cross Harbor Railroad) still transports railcars between New Jersey and Long Island, New York. Ferrying over longer distances had been done for many years beginning in 1892 with the Ann Arbor Railroad's operations on the Great Lakes between Michigan and Wisconsin where the objective was to avoid the traffic congestion in and around Chicago. The service lasted until 1990 when deregulation under the Staggers Act[1]

---

[1] The Staggers Act of 1980 removed most of the economic regulation of the railroad industry.

Intermodal Maritime Security. https://doi.org/10.1016/B978-0-12-819945-9.00003-4

allowed for more competition and negotiated freight rates meaning that the poor economics doomed the service.

Years later, Seatrain Lines was launched with the concept of transporting loaded railroad freight cars from New York to Havana, Cuba. Beginning with two special-built ships, the operation was a success and two additional ships were ordered. Seatrain survived World War II and even contributed to the war effort by using their ships to transport tanks and other armored vehicles to the Africa Campaign. The 1950s offered continued success, but at the beginning of the 1960s, two events would eventually spell Seatrain's demise: the Cuban Revolution and the advent of the ocean container (Kendall, 236; Garrison and Levinson, 251−255).

Seatrain like all ferry operations operated with impaired economic advantages because the tare weight of the railcars was being carried as well as the weight of the cargo. Where Seatrain differed was that it was not a ferry operation per se, but rather using ocean-going ships where railcars were loaded and unloaded using a gantry that is not unlike those employed for ocean containers today. Moreover, any opportunities for expanding the concept with trade from the United States would have been limited to those markets where there is standard gauge railroads and US-style knuckle coupling systems.

Intermodalism: maritime and truck

Where previous efforts to provide intermodal service were limited by railroad equipment technology, this all changed due to the efforts of a trucker from North Carolina, namely Malcolm McLean. McLean's objective was to reduce the expense of transloading freight between trucks and ships because the practice at the time incurred expensive handling, the potential for loss and damage, the delay of trucks waiting to load and unload at the piers, and the nonproductive time that vessels needed to remain in port (Nocera, C1; Kendall, 192−199).

McLean began by converting a former World War II tanker and with the first sailing of the *SS Ideal-X* in 1956 launched an initial service between Port Elizabeth, New Jersey and Houston, Texas. Despite having only 58 containers onboard, the concept took hold and in the following year the new line, Pan-Atlantic Steamship, was calling at other ports on the Atlantic and Gulf coasts and inaugurating service to Puerto Rico. Pan-Atlantic changed its name to Sea-Land Service and 10 years later began hauling significant quantities of military cargo to Vietnam as well as instituting regular transatlantic sailings to Rotterdam and Bremerhaven (Kendall, 194).

In addition to the ships, there are two other equipment components necessary for operating maritime intermodal services: chassis and the containers themselves. As a trucker, McLean saw the disadvantages to moving entire trailers. The result was removing the road wheels and undercarriage, which removed approximately four tons of tare weight as well as reduced the height and enabled stacking onboard ship. Other advantages accrued from this action, but were not to be realized for a couple of decades (Kendall, 223−224; DuBoer, 56−57).

Advantages to containerization
Fleet size

Perhaps the most significant advantage for the shipping line is the reduced size of the fleet necessary to transport a given volume of cargo. Inasmuch as container operations are characterized by the carriage of general cargo, that will be the constant used for comparing break-bulk with containerized traffic meaning that roll-on/roll-off shipments and homogeneous materials such as steel, lumber, and other forest products. All comparisons shall be for liner services and purposely exclude the tramp sector (Garrison and Levinson, 253).

Ships earn money when they are at sea and not in port conducting loading and unloading operations. If comparing a 500 TEU vessel with each container holding an average net weight of 20,000 lbs., the overall net weight for a vessel, therefore, is 10,000 tons. While container port gantry cranes have different cycle times depending upon specific age and technology, such a ship could take 1.5 days to work. By comparison, a comparably sized break-bulk ship without a tween deck configuration could take 8 days. As an example, Table 2.1 shows a fictitious simple rotation beginning in Hamburg, Germany, and subsequently calling at Antwerp, Belgium, New York, and Norfolk, Virginia, before sailing east back to Hamburg. Table 2.1 provides both the sailing times and vessel working times in port showing total times for each rotation cycle as 65 and 39 days for break-bulk and container vessels, respectively (Rodrigue, 116–118).

Number of annual sailings if a fortnightly service: 26.

Number of sailings per ship for break-bulk vessels: 365/65 = 5.6.

Fleet size of break-bulk ships required: 26/5.6 = 4.6 ships rounded to 5.

Number of sailings per container ship: 365/39 = 9.4.

Fleet size of containerships required: 26/9.4 = 2.76 rounded to 3.

Table 2.1: Sailing and loading time comparison example.

	Sailing time	Break-bulk ship working time	Break-bulk cumulative total time	Container ship working time	Containerized cumulative total time
Hamburg	Start	8 days	8 days	1.5 days	1.5 days
Antwerp	1.5 days	8 days	17.5 days	1.5 days	4.5 days
New York	13.5 days	8 days	39 days	1.5 days	19.5 days
Norfolk	2.5 days	8 days	49.5 days	1.5 days	23.5 days
Hamburg	15.5 days	End	65 days		39 days

While the fixed cost of an investment in ships, their crews, provisioning, and bunkering is lower for a container operation, there is an offsetting investment required in containers and their chasses.

Cargo stowage

With break-bulk cargo, especially with general merchandise, vessel stowage was nearly as much of an art as a science given the different sized cargo of different weights that had to be positioned both fore and aft as well as from port to starboard in order that the ship maintain balance, or *trim*. Heavy, dense freight had to be stowed low in the holds to assure that vessels were not top-heavy and unstable. Hazardous freight would be stowed high to allow for possible jettisoning if need be. This is what made loading such a time-consuming endeavor.

Conversely, intermodalism placed loading of the container a responsibility of the shipper. To the ocean line, the gross weight and knowledge of the contents were important for overall stowage considerations, but the manner in which goods were generally distributed within a container was not nearly as important. Consequently, the new stowage plans still needed to assure that heavy weight containers were low in the hold and lighter weight containers plus those containing hazardous materials were stowed higher. Since all containers were either 20 or 40 feet long, the art-like effort of stowing different shaped cargos was removed thereby making loading a far simpler and less time-consuming task.

The reduction in stowage effort also reduced the demand for stevedore labor and a contentious labor relations issue that lasted for decades. This will be discussed further in Chapter 3: Water and Landside Operations.

Reduced inventory carrying costs

All modes of transportation are a demand-derived activity meaning that the demand for transportation does not occur unless there is a demand for the goods that need to be transported. The time that goods are undergoing transport are owned by someone, whether that party is the buyer or the seller. Cargoes in transit are, therefore, to be considered inventory and while the International Commercial Terms (INCOTerms) dictate who exactly is the owner, inventory in transit is not available for beneficial use.[2]

For example, if an importer should have only one container on each of the sailings shown in Table 2.1 and for the illustrative purposes, those goods have a transaction price of

---

[2] INCOTerms are updated every 10 years. A general discussion can be found in Jimenez, G. (1997). ICC Guide to import-Export Basics. Paris: ICC Publishing. The newest version is available online at https://iccwbo.org/resources-for-business/incoterms-rules/incoterms-2020/.

US\$1.00 per unit and an inventory carrying cost factor of 10% then the increased velocity within the supply chain created by containerization could be calculated as:

(65−39 days)/365 × 20,000 lbs. × \$1.00 × 10% = \$142.46 savings per container.

\$142.46 per container × 26 sailings = \$3704.

While \$3704 may appear modest, then consider the impact that this would have on my former employer that imported some 12,000 containers annually. Their inventory savings would be \$142.46 × 12,000 = \$1,709,520 (Coyle, Bardi and Langley, 270−274).

Reduced cargo loss and damage

Whenever cargo is handled, there is the potential for loss and damage. Taken individually, loss can mean disappearance or in the extreme condition of damage deemed total destruction. Some may be intentional, but most loss and damage is not. The generalized categories of loss and damage are relatively few as shown in Table 2.2.

Considering the impacts of containerization when compared to break-bulk for general merchandise, the ability to pilfer goods and/or tamper with them has been significantly reduced. Notice that we use the word reduced and not eliminated. The ocean container becomes the equivalent of a low security vault that is not impenetrable as there are many recorded instances of illegal entry and removal of contents or even of tampering with contents to make them worthless or to taint them for subsequent use. (See Chapters 6 and 8 which provide useful actions to protect against illegal entry.)

The container did much to reduce the amount of handling required between modes and thereby reduce the potential loss and damage incurred. Where loss and damage may occur is in the loading and unloading of containers from vessels, railcars, and chassis for over-the-road movement. Where break-bulk required the services of an export packer to devise

Table 2.2: Taxonomy of loss and damage factors.

Intentional	Handling	Stowage
Pilferage Tampering	Inadequate packaging Improper handling equipment selection Inappropriate equipment operation	Inadequate packaging Inappropriate stowage location (environment) Incompatibility with adjacent cargo
	Impact	
Disappearance Destruction Damage	Destruction Damage	Destruction Damage

transport damage resistant packaging, containerization largely reduced if not totally eliminated the need for incurring such expense because much of the packaging acceptable for over-the-road domestic transport would suffice. Blocking and bracing of loads, much the same as that required for domestic highway transport, will often be all that is needed. That said, however, there is little chance that a full container dropped a hundred or so feet from a gantry will come through the experience unscathed.

Stowage onboard is more secure with each container load limited in movement to its own 20 or 40 foot cell. Goods will generally be more compatible with each other in that they originate from a single shipper, except when they are being dispatched by a consolidator or nonvessel operating common carrier (NVOCC), but see a discussion of that issue later in this chapter.

Packaging, a term that covers a wide range of options, can be an issue with either break-bulk or containerized cargo. In an era where packaging is seen as a major source of solid waste pollution, its minimization can mean even more waste in the form of damaged goods. Containerization is better likely to accommodate lighter forms of packaging such as corrugated cartons as opposed to wooden boxes and crates. Handling damage, when it does occur, will frequently come from forklifts engaged in the container loading or unloading process.

Pilferage, a major issue when shipping break-bulk cargo, was substantially reduced by containerization. One of the major vulnerabilities was whenever goods transitioned from one mode to another. It was not uncommon for break-bulk cargo to sit unattended on the pier waiting to be loaded onboard ship, or having just been unloaded, cleared through customs, and awaiting pickup. When in a sealed container pilferage, while not impossible, is much more difficult. Once a container is loaded and sealed by the shipper, it moves as a single unit to the port.

Disadvantages of containerization

No innovation can be implemented without incurring some disadvantages, and the intermodal maritime container is no exception. Oftentimes, innovations come with disadvantages that are externalities borne by the public at large. Economic dislocations essentially means that costs are transferred from one party to another. Such is the case with the beneficiaries of the intermodal container because much of the infrastructure necessary becomes an investment, one often borne by the port authorities and by the adjacent communities (Rodrigue, 118—119).

Port infrastructure

With the advent of the intermodal container came the need for acreage for portside container yards where containers are received from trucks and railcars, staged and sequenced, and loaded onboard ships. The reverse is also true inasmuch as the container yard serves as a warehouse for inbound containers offloaded waiting for customs clearance and ultimately pickup for inland movement. The container yard replaced the finger piers that had been the standard landside infrastructure for centuries. Port activities were often relocated because container yards required significantly more land. The old finger piers quickly became stranded assets as the break-bulk traffic rapidly dwindled.

Break-bulk cargo was typically loaded using ship's tackle—those integral cranes typically found on most break-bulk vessels. In contrast, container operations require gantry cranes with sufficient reach to be able to access containers stowed anywhere across the beam of a vessel. As containerships have increased in size, so have the reach and working height of gantries. Although there are container yards owned and/or operated by individual shipping companies, most are owned by quasi-governmental units, usually port authorities.

Where containerization provided efficiencies for the shipping companies, much of the investment required shifted to others. The argument can be made that the higher efficiency provided by intermodalism required significant investment that can be justified by the higher volume of traffic that is attracted. Those higher volumes stimulate other investment with the result being further overall economic development of a region.

Where break-bulk vessels had upper limits placed on their size due to the port times needed time to load and unload cargo, containerships could spend considerable less time in port, but the rapid discharge of vessels produced "lumpy demand" for access infrastructure. At first, access was provided by road, but as intermodalism grew and containers moved greater distances from port areas, the benefits of rail became evident. One of the noteworthy developments was that of the landbridge where containers were not unloaded in port, but rather transported sometimes great distances inland. Landbridges are characterized in three ways (Table 2.3):

A landbridge uses the advantages of the container and is employed to reduce transit times which reduce inventory holding costs (Coyle et al., 241; Rosenberg, 176; Cavinato, 120, 137–138). See the map in Fig. 2.1 below.

When first developed, container services relied heavily on trucks to move containers to and from port areas. As landbridge schemes became more popular so did the use of

---

[3] Panamax denotes the largest ship that could transit the canal. Post-Panamax means a ship too big for the canal prior to its recent expansion. Some newer ships are still too big for the enlarged canal and are labeled post-neopanamax.

Table 2.3: Taxonomy of landbridge options.

Landbridge	Containers arrive at a port, transported to another port where they are loaded aboard another vessel. One example would be containers arriving in Philadelphia, transported to Seattle, and thence by ship to Japan. The examples need not be US-centric because technically the Panama Canal Railroad traditionally moved containers across the isthmus for shipping lines with vessels too large for the canal (Post-Panamax).[3]
Mini landbridge	Containers arrive at a port and transported overland to another port where they may be cleared by customs and delivered to the consignee. Containers arriving in Charleston that are destined for a consignee in Houston would be a good example.
Micro landbridge	Containers arrive at a port and transported to a consignee deep inland. Containers arriving in Hampton Roads, Virginia, and transported to Omaha is but one example.

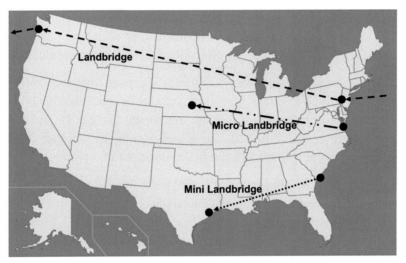

Figure 2.1
Variations of landbridges.

the railroads. Initially, containers were moved on their chassis as a trailer-on-flatcar (TOFC) arrangement that was identical to that of highway trailers.

The subsequent development of double-stack service eliminated the unnecessary movement of the container chassis and utilized railcars where containers could ride closer to the rails thereby providing the necessary overhead clearance. Initially, many railroad intermodal yards were located a few miles from the port thereby requiring the use of short over-the-road drays such as was the case with both the Conrail Oak Island rail yard and the New York, Susquehanna, and Western/Sea-Land facilities serving the port of New York—New Jersey.

Eventually, on-pier (or container yard) rail facilities were built, but port area congestion continued to build. Some railroads established inland ports some hundreds of miles away and staged unit trains of containers to specific ports coordinated with vessel arrival times, or in the case of exports, with vessel sailing times. A more aggressive approach was adopted by the Ports of Los Angeles and Long Beach where an Alameda Corridor was built as a dedicated multiple rail link with rail yards located miles inland (Hubler and Meek, 47).

In short, the plethora of ports offering containership berthing and the double digit growth over a long period of time has created many benefits to shippers, but also major costs the accrue to port operators in the form of continuing major investments in infrastructure.

Container security

Mention was previously made of how containerization improved the security and safety of goods transported by sea. Clearly, goods stowed and sealed in a container were handled by far fewer persons between points of origin and destination. There was little need for export packers; and parcels, denominated as drums, crates, boxes, and bundles, did not need to be individually chosen and grouped by size and weight to effect a stowage plan[4] that would enable maintaining vessel trim. All containers were the same sizes and the stowage considerations were generally limited to weight, designated port of unloading, and whether the contents were deemed hazardous or not (Szyliowicz, 538–540).

With less handling, goods had a higher probability of reaching their destinations with less damage, but also pilferage, which had been a common problem in port areas, was significantly reduced. In short, shippers found containerization to be very attractive. If there was additional handling, it could be when customs elected to do a physical examination of the contents and ordered a container stripping[5] where the entire contents were removed, had to be reloaded after examination, and often required new blocking and bracing. Still, by the old standards, the amount of handling from origin to destination was drastically reduced.

No technology can be less than a double-edge sword as the container posed new and different safety and security issues that in many respects are still evolving. One downside is the hidden from sight nature of the goods meaning that generally only the shipper knows the contents of the container, which is true unless there has been some in route

---

[4] A stowage plan seeks to establish where goods are located onboard whereby the vessel will not list to either port or starboard, be too top-heavy, and is neither bow nor stern heavy. All are considerations for safe operation in a range of sea states and weather conditions.

[5] The cost of restowing as well as the requisite blocking and bracing of cargo within the container is borne by the shipper or the consignee depending upon the Incoterms employed.

tampering with the goods or introduction of other goods. When only the shipper knows the contents, the potential exists for intentional misdeclaration—at one time this was done to obtain a lower freight rate, but with the increasing use of FAK (freight all kinds) rates this has diminished. Misdeclaration to avoid disclosure of hazardous materials tends to be much more common despite the significant penalties attached to such an infraction. Where there is a concern, and certainly within the scope of this book, is either the introduction of additional items into a container in route by others for nefarious purposes. Moreover, the tampering or outright theft of the contents of a container may go unnoticed until it is delivered to the consignee (see the appended material in Chapter 6 for more details on this latter eventuality).

Comparing and contrasting the issues of safety and security of break-bulk versus containerized cargo, the key points can be summarized in the following table (Table 2.4).

Needs of the small shipper and consignee

In the break-bulk era, little differentiation would be made between shipments for large shippers and consignees and smaller ones. The major change that came with containerization was the requirement for small shipments being consolidated into containers. NVOCC filled this consolidation need by providing booking services as well as physical locations for consolidation and deconsolidation. Use of an NVOCC meant that many small shipments were contained within a single unit for more efficient loading and unloading from ships; however, the true knowledge of the contents was one more step removed as the relationships between carrier and the shipper, or carrier and the consignee.

Table 2.4: Loss and damage of goods comparison.

	Break-bulk	**Containerized**
Goods damaged in handling	Exterior packaging reveals damage; hidden interior damage still possible	Less likely, but not impossible depending on how the container might have been handled in transit
Good pilfered in transit	Not detected until arrival for customs clearance	May not be detected until container delivered to consignee
Goods tampered with in transit	May or may not be obvious from inspection of exterior packaging	May not be detected until container delivered to consignee
Illicit goods added to container in transit	Less likely with individually packaged goods	May not be detected until container delivered to consignee

Where a full container may be transported for a single shipper, the goods can be assumed to be of a similar nature if not an exact one. One example could be machinery and related components and parts. By similar example, a container may be transporting drums of chemicals; there may be various types, but drums just the same. When transporting by an NVOCC, the contents could range from clothing to pistachio nuts to machinery spare parts. The differences in the goods and that these represent several shippers and several consignees suggests that other goods could be added by nefarious parties while in transit.

A final variant of the multiple goods within a single container could stem from the movement of household goods where there could be a great dissimilarity that ranges from clothing to furniture to office contents and kitchenware. Moreover, when the contents of multiple households are combined in a single container, identification becomes even more difficult. Yet, while the number of containers carrying household goods tends to be a relatively small part of the overall container volume, the need for inspections cannot be overstated.

Shifts over time

At the outset containerized shipments occurred between a relatively few ports worldwide, the main reasons being the general lack of container handling equipment and the availability of chassis to facilitate inland movement. Over time, however, more ports added capacity and the container lines made chassis available. Such developments were usually based on customer-driven demand as the economic benefits of intermodal containers became evident to an ever-larger number of shippers.

Many of the larger early ports continued to expand their capacity while simultaneously smaller ports began handling containerized shipments. The result was that the larger ports became load centers receiving from and sending to the smaller ports in a manner that paralleled the development of hub-and-spoke airline networks. Not unlike the infrastructure preblems of smaller airports, the smaller seaports lacked dredged deep-water berths, long reach container cranes, and myriad sophisticated intermediary services. Government agencies also did not staff such ports with large regulatory staffs.

As trade volumes grew, however, the container lines kept increasing the vesselsize thereby limiting the number of ports able to accommodate them. Competition between ports during the past 10 years has focused on which had the deepest channels, the longest berths, the largest container yards, and the greatest access to port areas by road and rail. Table 2.5 shows the timeline and growth of container ship size.

Table 2.5: Evolution of vessel size.

Year	Category	Ship LOA	Ship draft	TEUs	Examples
1956	Early types (sea-land)	137 m	9 m	650	
1985	Panamax (Hapag Lloyd)	294 m	12 m	5,000[a]	Stuttgart Express
1990	Post-Panamax (Maersk)	300 m	12 m	8,000	Susan Maersk
2014	Neopanamax (Maersk)	366 m	15.2	11,000	Emma Maersk
2015	Post-Neopanamax (Mediterranean)	400 m	16 m	18,000	MSC Oscar

[a]Some of the earliest of this type were the 12 E-Con class ships of United States Lines with 4,300 TEUs each. By some estimates, the amount of port time required to work these vessels adversely impacted shipper appeal and U.S. Lines ultimately went bankrupt.
Source: Geography of Transport Systems.

Other developments

Although the innovation of the container was focused upon the movement of general cargo, a short time later advantages were seen for other goods. In particular, there are two major additions to the standard dry box container: the flat rack and the liquid bulk (ISO tank). Table 2.6 shows the evolution of these along with major variants.

Much of the discussion in this chapter remains focused on the standard dry box; however, cognizance of the variants is necessary because all can and will be comingled onboard ship.

Table 2.6: Dry box container types.

Initial design	Variation	Variation	Variation	Variation	Notes
Standard dry box *General cargo use*	**High cube dry box** *For lighter density cargoes*	**Open top dry box** *Useful for difficult loadings*	**Reefer container** *Requires compressor, major use for food*	**Dry bulk in dry box** *Standard dry box with a bulk liner bag*	**All available as 20 and 40 ft.**
Tank container *a.k.a. ISO tank for liquids*	**Dry bulk tank** *Chemicals and polymers*	**Cryogenic tank (cryotank)** *Refrigerated gases; requires compressor*			**Mostly 20 ft, but some 40 ft cryotanks**
Flat rack *Smaller machinery where roll-on/roll-off (RORO) may not be economic*	**Bulkhead flat** *A more flexible alternative to the open top dry box*				**All available as 20 and 40 ft.**

Summary

The intermodal maritime container provided major economic advantages to shippers and consignees because it significantly reduced both lead times for globally sourced goods and loss and damage incurred during transit. A key result was that it became the driver for the prodigious long-term growth in international trade. Conversely, it required port authorities to spend vast sums on waterfront acreage and expensive gantry cranes for working the ships. For the container lines it meant investing in all new ships, thousands of chassis, and the containers themselves.

The primary takeaways from this chapter, however, are the safety and security concerns given that containerization on the one hand significantly improved both, but over time presented another set of issues that have evolved into compelling challenges and, in fact, the overall theme of this book.

References

Cavinato, J., 1989. Transportation Logistics Dictionary. International Thompson Transport Press, Washington, DC.

Coyle, J., Bardi, E., Langley, J., 2003. The Management of Business Logistics, seventh ed. Thomson South-western, Mason, OH.

Coyle, J., Bardi, E., Novack, R., 2006. Transportation, sixth ed. Thomson South-Western, Mason, OH.

Cunningham, J., 1951. Railroading in New Jersey. Association of New Jersey Railroads, Newark.

DuBoer, D., 1992. Piggyback and Containers: A History of Rail Intermodal on America's Steel Highway. Golden West Books, San Marino, CA.

Garrison, W., Levinson, D., 2014. The Transportation Experience, second ed. Oxford University Press, London.

Hubler, P., Meek, J., 2007. Beyond the waterfront: ports as leaders of intermodal trade. In: Plant, J.F. (Ed.), Handbook of Transportation Policy and Public Administration. Taylor and Francis, Boca Raton, FL.

Jimenez, G, 1997. ICC Guide to Import-Export Basics. ICC Publishing, Paris.

Kendall, L., 1986. The Business of Shipping, fifth ed. Cornell Maritime Press, Centerville, MD.

Nocera, J., May 13, 2006. A Revolution that Came in a Box. The New York Times. (Accessed 9 January 2020).

Rodrigue, J., 2013. The Geography of Transport Systems, third ed. Routledge, New York.

Rosenberg, J., 1994. The Dictionary of International Trade. John Wiley and Sons, New York.

Szyliowicz, J., 2007. Globalization and transport security. In: Plant, J.F. (Ed.), Handbook of Transportation Policy and Public Administration. Taylor and Francis, Boca Raton, FL.

Further reading

Fremont, A., 2010. Maritime networks: a source of competitiveness for shipping lines. In: Cullinae, K. (Ed.), International Handbook of Maritime Business. Edward Elgar, Northampton, MA.

CHAPTER 3

Water and landside components

Richard R. Young, Ph.D., FCILT

School of Business Administration, Capital College, The Pennsylvania State University, Middletown, PA, United States

In the previous chapter, the discussion focused on intermodal transportation as it applies to maritime trade in general. Beginning with the concept of intermodalism and how it was ultimately applied by Malcolm McLean and how it developed into the ubiquitous mode for transporting a huge range of goods thereby largely displacing the break-bulk shipping industry (Nocera, C1). The dramatic change to vessel design, however, is only a small part of the story. This chapter will endeavor to examine the various component activities currently found in ports, how they evolved, and what are the implications for the future. The chapter ends with an examination of supply chain theory using the Supply Chain Operations Reference (SCOR) Model as a template, but then overlaying port activities to underscore their importance in the global supply chain.

Shipping has always required the investment in improved harbors for the safe movement of ships and extensive landside infrastructure to accommodate the efficient handling of cargo. This chapter shall explore the historical developments including those of up to the present time including the aspects of ownership and technology and the evolution of global trade. Specifically, the topic of ocean vessels is excluded from the discussion in this chapter.

To enhance understanding of the evolution, developments can be categorized as: (1) the nascent era, (2) the trading company period, (3) global trading system, and (4) intermodal era. Note, too, that the developments surrounding e-commerce can be lumped into the last of these. Table 3.1 attempts to sort specific components by when they first occurred.

At this juncture, a brief definition and explanation of the characteristics that made each of these elements important to international trade is in order. However, be ever mindful that at the outset each was located either within a port or in an area immediately adjacent in order that efficient trade could be effected.[1]

---

[1] A useful reference source for international trade-related terminology is J. M. Ropsenberg (1994). Dictionary of International Trade. New York: John Wiley and Sons.

Intermodal Maritime Security. https://doi.org/10.1016/B978-0-12-819945-9.00016-2

Table 3.1: Chronological taxonomy of components of global maritime trade.

	Nascent era	Trading company	Global trading	Intermodal
Physical services	• Ship brokers • Dockside labor (stevedoring)	• Export packers (coopers) • Marine surveyors		• Nonvessel operating common carriers • Landbridge services • Point-to-point service
Information services	• Banking • Customshouse brokers • Freight forwarders • Ship brokers • Insurance underwriters	• Trading companies		
Operating supplies providers	• Ships stores/chandlers		• Bunkering	
Infrastructure-related	• Barge and lighterage services • Warehousing • (Vessel) berthing	• Dredged channels • Finger piers	• On-pier railroads	• Chassis pools • Container lessors • Inland ports • Container yards

Physical service providers

• Dockside labor (stevedore services): As ports grew and the number of vessels making port calls increased, shipowners wanted a reliable workforce for working their vessels. Stevedore services emerged as the outsource for dockworkers. The trade became more specialized given the relative expertise that such laborers were required to have concerning the not only safe and efficient stowing cargo, but safely handling it.

• Export packing (coopering) services: Handling during vessel loading and unloading had great potential for incurring loss and damage, hence specialized packing was required. Originally, this took the form of barrels, but even in modern times, blocking and bracing of goods inside intermodal containers can be an issue and cooperage services still exist.

• Landbridges: Containers can be moved intact from the port of entry to the ultimate consignee without being unload. There are several versions of the landbridge that include mini and micro. A pure landbridge is when the goods arrive at one port and moved overland to another port where it is reloaded for a continuing voyage. Philadelphia to Seattle and thence to Juneau would be one such example. A mini-landbridge is when the ultimate destination is within the land mass such as Philadelphia to New Orleans. Finally, a micro-landbridge is where the ultimate destination is inland such as Philadelphia to Omaha (Coyle et al., 241−242).

- Marine surveyors: Vessels needed to be inspected for seaworthiness, but such assessment had to be performed by an objective independent party. Today, surveyors determine such matters as to whether a barge is sufficiently clean prior to taking on a bulk cargo.
- Nonvessel operating common carrier (NVOCC): With the rapid decline of break-bulk vessels as ushered in by the equally rapid rise of intermodal containers, there remained a need for continuing less-than-container services to meet the needs of the smallest shippers. The NVOCC came about as an entity that could purchase the use of a whole container and sell off portions to small shippers at a markup (Coyle et al., 241).
- Point-to-point service: Shipping lines began quoting services from the point of origin to the point of destination whereby inland moves on both ends were built into a single rate. This offered convenience to consignees who might not wish to arrange the various transportation legs on a piecemeal basis. An example could be the Ford's movement of engines from Cologne, Germany, to Kansas City (Coyle et al., 154).
- Repair facilities: Shipyards and an array of specialty services emerged from the very beginning of maritime transportation. Many of these were natural outgrowths of ship-building and the term shipwright was coined.
- Banking: A major enabler of international trade, initiating banks, and corresponding banks were formed into a network whereby buyers could efficiently pay sellers. The system that evolved into the letters of credit process established sufficient safeguards to both parties (Rosenberg, 127, 179).

Information service providers

- Customshouse brokers: Not long after parties from different nations began trading nation states sought to both protect their own merchants from the actions of others, but to also financially benefit through the levying of tariffs. The customshouse broker was created as an outsourced service with expertise for navigating the increasingly complex labyrinth of trade regulations.
- Freight forwarders: Merchants required expertise for completing export documentation, arranging transportation, and much like the customshouse broker, a source of knowledge concerning the export regulations. Not surprisingly, freight forwarding and customs brokerage were activities likely carried out by a single firm (Rosenberg, 133).
- Insurance underwriters: At the outset shipping was an inherently risky endeavor and the loss of goods and the vessels transporting them was a very real prospect. The most famous of the underwriters was actually formed as a consortium, Lloyd's of London.
- Ship brokers: Transportation has always had the age-old problem of matching supply with demand. In the maritime domain, this matching of supply and demand was accomplished early by the establishment of ship brokers that probably grew out of the presence of one or two persons sitting in either a pub or a coffeehouse engaged in matching loads with vessels.

Suppliers of goods

- Bunkering services: With steam powered vessels came the demand for coal with the place where it was stored onboard being referred to as a bunker. As diesel replaced coal as the fuel of choice, the suppliers continued to be referred to as bunkering services. Even at the present when there appears to be a trend toward liquefied natural gas (LNG) powered vessels, the moniker lives on.
- Ships stores and chandlery: While the chandlers were some of the earliest suppliers of ship parts and supplies, namely sails, the range of goods required for ever-longer voyages grew and included crew provisioning.

Infrastructure-related

- Barge and lighterage services: Another version of intermodalism is the transfer of goods to and from domestic water modes. Barge and lighterage services probably predated international shipping, but soon became an important adjunct to it. See *feeder services* below for another more recent development (Cavinato, 126).
- Berthing: Some of the earliest port-related infrastructure was berth or dock space. It secured a vessel to land where unloading and loading could be accomplished in an efficient manner. As time went on, berthing acquired specialized materials handling equipment. While some vessels would carry their own cranes, these took up space that could be more productively used for holding cargo. Fast forward to the present where berths for intermodal containers at load center ports require multiple specialized gantry cranes to accommodate timely working of the largest vessels.
- Cargo handling equipment: Handling equipment continues to evolve. Since this book is about intermodal shipping, that equipment is designed for long reach across the beam of ships, accommodate the gross weight of containers, and have a cycle time that enables timely working of the vessel.
- Chassis pool: Containers require chassis, or those sets of wheels that enable highway transport. Chassis pools are maintained in port areas, and various carriers can draw equipment in order to facilitate container movement. In recent years, these pools are also operated by inland carriers such as railroads and major drayage firms.
- Container yards: The same idea behind container chassis also applies to containers themselves. In many port areas, individual lines do not have the volume to warrant their own facilities; hence, the third party operation provides the necessary efficiency.
- Dredged channels: Where natural channels do not exist, they need to be dredged in order that vessels have access to harbor facilities that would include piers, wharfs, and ship repair providers.
- Inland port: Although discussed later in this chapter, inland ports were developed by the railroads as a rationale for assembling intermodal trains to and from specific ports. They

were a ready means for relieving container congestion in port areas. Some of the earlier examples of inland ports was Norfolk Southern Railway's Front Royal, Virginia operation.

• Inland transportation providers: From the beginnings of the maritime trades when goods would generally be consumed in markets in relative proximity to the ports, the situation now is one of markets being thousands of miles from the port and served by truck or increasingly by container-on-flatcar rail transportation. See also landbridge.

• On-pier railroads: In the era of the finger piers, having on-pier railroad access was not always common. With the advent of the intermodal container, it soon became obvious that there were efficiencies to be had if container-on-flatcar configurations could be assembled shipside. Recent years have seen such capacities built at those ports where they might not have been initially provided.

• Tugboat services: As vessels became larger, they required assistance when docking or otherwise in port with auxiliary power. Thus, was born the tugboat, which is also a means of propulsion for barges.

• Warehousing: As trade grew, facilities were needed for holding goods either: (1) until they were to be loaded aboard a vessel or (2) when they had been unloaded and were awaiting inland movement. Moreover, specialized warehouses, including bonded facilities, were established to hold goods that had not yet cleared customs (Coyle et al., 172).

Historical perspective

At the outset, most of the functions of international trade were probably undertaken by a relatively few participants who likely shared a close working relationship with one another. As volume grew, the demand for specialists emerged, and Table 3.1 can be thought to be trifurcated between vessel operations, landside operations, and information services.

With the transition from individual traders to the era of the trading companies, the latter evolved as large firms with key outposts scattered across the globe organized to facilitate trade. Those organizations included ownership of vessels, operation of port facilities, the employment of trade specialists by which is meant those engaged in buying and selling, and related staff specialties. Perhaps, the earliest forerunner of the trading company was the Hanseatic League that operated on multiple edges of the Baltic Sea beginning in the mid-1100s: clearly international in scope, but nowhere near being as global as was the case with the leading British and Dutch firms that followed some half century later. Not really a single firm per se, the Hanseatic League could be better described as a geographic cooperative or perhaps consortium (Garrison and Levinson, 71−76).

Because of the wealth that these firms created, their interests became congruent with those of the national interest and respective foreign policies evolved that furthered the interest of such firms as the Dutch East India Company, the Dutch West India Company and its English equivalents, the British East India Company, and the British West India Company. The history of the growth of the British Commonwealth had clear parallels with the expansion of the British East India Company. Other European nations had less well-known trading organizations and the Portuguese, Danish, and Swedish can be added to the list. Yet, whether well-known or not, the basic structure was all similar (Garrison and Levinson, 74).

During the 20th century as imperialism waned, trade continued to grow, particularly in the post-WWII era, much in concert with both the newly found independence of former colonies as well as the postwar rebuilding of Asian and European economies. We have dubbed this era global trade, and it spans the middle of the century until the advent of the intermodal maritime container.

From the above, it also becomes apparent that the intermodal container was a revolutionary concept that over a relatively short period of time upended the industry. Finger piers were no longer efficient landside infrastructure given the accommodate the volumes of containers awaiting loading aboard ships or just having been discharged and awaiting inland transportation. Whereas the previous growth of ports had been incremental—merely adding more peers and some occasional dredging, the intermodal container ushered in period of increasingly stranded assets in the form of the old finger piers, a demand for broad expanses of waterfront property to accommodate berths, and the ever-growing container yards.

The landside traffic that had created major congestion in such cities as New York, Boston, Philadelphia, and Baltimore would have evolved into impassible obstacles that had the old finger piers not been replaced in situ by container yards. The advantages of the intermodal container meant better asset utilization for the shipping companies, improved safety and security for the goods in transport, and more compressed lead times as goods were not tied up in port waiting to be loaded or unloaded from ships. See Fig. 3.1 for an example of finger piers in San Diego during the early part of the 20th century.

Technology, however, does have its costs; those costs are incurred by different parties and in the case of intermodal containerized transport meant that ports per se. The land use concerns of the intermodal container extend far beyond the immediate port area. In part, this was due to the prodigious growth whereby the economic and physical security aspects were readily available to shippers. While transportation is said to be a derived demand activity meaning that it is driven by the demand for the underlying goods, the economic advantages when coupled with postwar economic development elsewhere on the globe meant access to a great range of goods at affordable prices.

Figure 3.1
Broadway pier in San Diego, c.1913 (City of San Diego archives).

Congestion, a problem previously encountered with the old finger piers, became a growing concern with respect to highway and rail access to port areas. The US's largest ports, namely New York—New Jersey and Los Angeles—Long Beach, endured choking truck traffic on all of their respective access highways. On the west shore of the Hudson River where the bulk of New York—New Jersey's container traffic was focused, most container yards had no on-pier railroad service for several decades. Containers had to be drayed by truck albeit just a few miles to either the Conrail facility at Oak Island or the Delaware Otsego terminal (serving Sea-Land, but now Maersk).

On the west coast, the situation was even more dire and the solution prompted the creation of the Alameda Corridor, a dedicated 20-mile multitrack rail access to the Ports of Los Angeles—Long Beach as seen in Fig. 3.2. It was just one more instance where landside transportation companies, in particular the railroads, had established inland ports and operated through a multistakeholder authority in order to debottleneck the congestion in and around ports. There are others nationwide, but the Alameda Corridor represents the most extensive such asset. However, having only opened to traffic in 2002, it was already operating at capacity by 2006 meaning that further expansion was considered and under construction as this is written.

Figure 3.2
Alameda Corridor below grade rail operations. *Source: Alameda Corridor Transportation Authority.*

Recent years have seen an endless string of news items concerning the building of ever larger container ships (see Fig. 3.3 for a chronological comparison) as well as numerous load center ports dredging deeper harbors, seeking funding for such dredging, or contemplating a dredging project. It was the age-old story of ports competing with one another for a further driver of economic development.

Shipping lines continue to invest in larger vessels, but the number of ports where these can be accommodated at the outset are very limited. In the United States, the ability to increase the depth of the channel, expand the acreage of the container yard and invest in gantry cranes with greater reach and height is limited by the ability to raise the necessary funding, perform an acceptable environmental impact study, and comply with a range of land use requirements. A notable example of the latter would be the dimensions of those gantry cranes installed at Port Newark/Port Elizabeth, New Jersey, where the port is immediately adjacent to Liberty (Newark) International Airport where the height of nearby structures is subject to the Federal Aviation Administration restrictions.

With vessels having increased draft, beam, and length, the issues for the ports are more than just linear feet of berth space, although that is a major concern as well. Rather the landside infrastructure becomes an evermore compelling matter affecting acreage and access capacity. The growth in port throughput does not occur equally across all ports of entry. Not all ports are willing to invest in greater capacity meaning that the largest load centers will continue to grow whereas smaller ports become relegated to feeder status. With the United States seeing tens of millions of containers arrive at its shores annually, shippers look for ports of arrival that are efficient in their own right, but also are early on a container line's vessel rotation. There are some trade-offs to be considered here, including the following:

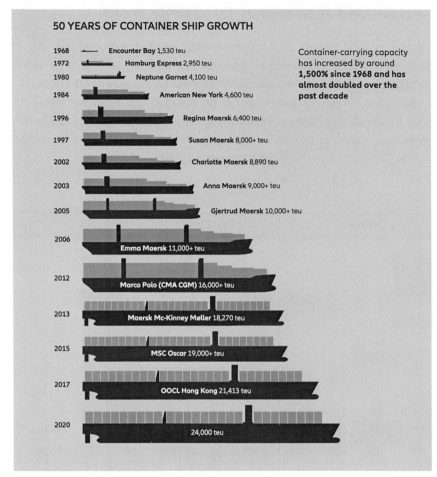

Figure 3.3
Chronological evolution of containership size. *Source: Allianz Global and Specialty.*

(1) Receive containers at the first port of discharge even if it means a longer inland dray. This will reduce the inventory hold time for goods in transit.

(2) Leave containers onboard until a later port of discharge if doing so allows the importer to avoid a congested port. Longer and more expensive drayage may be offset by a shorter overall lead time. Customs processing time may also be a factor.

(3) Receive containers at the first practical port of discharge, but move them in bond to a more convenient port with more efficient customs clearance. This was the approach that Eastman Kodak used for many years when it cleared a vast majority of its imports through the Port of Rochester, New York.

Port operations and opportunities for security breach

An often-quoted general rule of thumb is that cargo when at rest or sitting idly is most susceptible to theft. The same can be asserted for security tampering. Although tampering is normally thought to be an issue associated with the physical flow of goods, modern times have also seen tampering with both the information and financial flows.[2] Of the opportunities for goods to remain at rest, the handoffs from one supply chain entity to another offers the greatest potential. Fig. 3.4 depicts the physical flows in particular considering the various alternatives extant (Gordon, 2018).

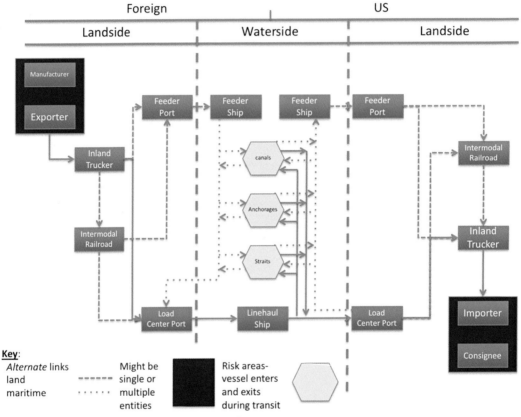

Figure 3.4

Point of origin to point of destination physical flow components. *Source: Gary A. Gordon, Ph.D., 2018. Intermodal Maritime Transportation Security: A Multifactor Framework for Assessing Routing Risk (Doctoral dissertation). University of Massachusetts—Lowell.*

---

[2] Supply chain theory, in particular as described by the Supply Chain Operational Reference Model or SCOR Model consists of three principal flows: physical, information, and financial. These are visually depicted elsewhere in this chapter.

As already established, global trade is a complex endeavor where considering just the transportation firms engaged there may be two or more inland trucking firms, two or more inland railroads, three or more seagoing vessels, and at a minimum two ports.

Information-related

A common methodology that logisticians use when describing or analyzing supply chain networks is known as links and nodes. Specifically, nodes are those fixed places of geography where goods are at rest, even if just momentarily. While the explanation of Fig. 3.4 mentioned only two ports, the end-to-end cataloging of nodes would include (1) the place of manufacture, (2) the respective distribution center or warehouse dispatching the goods, (3) one or more truck terminals controlled by the foreign inland trucker, (4) the two port terminals in a general sense, (5) a facility for export packing, (6) one or more intermodal rail yards depending on the ground modes selected, (7) a customs inspection facility at each the port of loading and the one of arrival.

Many of these nodes are by definition located within a port area, and here we must be careful to not just think of a port or even a terminal within a port as a single node because opportunities abound where goods can be either stolen or otherwise compromised. In the latter case, we mean either tampered with or having other goods, such as contraband, added to a legitimate shipment.

Evolution of port infrastructure

International trade began as overland commerce but realizing the relative efficiency of water-borne transportation quickly evolved. It was a small enough endeavor that was highly fragmented among individual merchants operating within a single port. Ports at that time began as simple affairs with their natural characteristics—water depth, protection from open seas, and access to land. With the wealth provided by trade, participants sought ways to improve their returns, the most obvious being to increase the size of the ships as well as the number of ships engaged in trade. The obvious economic trade-off was the size of ships where the relationship of their variable costs was not a linear one. However, the infrastructure was the constraint a key ship size up to a point (Rodrigue, 166).

Additional limiting factors were propulsion systems of the day and that larger ship sizes meant additional port time to accomplish loading and unloading. This latter issue is one that would continue to place a limit on ship design and persists even today.

Ports did continue to get larger and more sophisticated, yet the question of building ever more complex infrastructure persisted. Moreover, there was always the issue of who was going to pay for it. Municipalities made some investments as did individual merchants and consortia of merchants. As trade continued to grow, waterfront congestion became a reality and many ports, due to the inability to dock so many ships, had to rely on anchorages where vessels could wait for dock space. But a ship waiting at anchorage plus the time required for loading and unloading meant that many vessels spent more time idle than at sea, a prospect that ran counter to the concept of effective asset utilization.

One solution to the congestion problem was the advent of the finger pier which allowed vessels to dock perpendicular to land thereby dramatically increasing port capacity, at least insofar as ships were concerned. Finger piers (see previously shown Fig. 3.1) became ubiquitous in all ports of any consequence. Where they were able to relieve traffic congestion for ships, they magnified it for landside operations causing traffic jams of major proportions on those roadways adjacent to waterfronts.

The number of ships accommodated by a given port also had a bearing on the amount of warehouse space that was required to house goods having just been imported or awaiting loading for export. Inventory control processes of the time were not sophisticated with respect to reordering points and minimum/maximum levels. In relative terms, the most expensive component of imported merchandise was the transportation involved.

Given the complexity of shipping, specialist services emerged for accommodating the ordering processes, storage of goods, coordination of inland transportation, and the engagement of vessels. Customs brokers, as noted earlier, developed for effecting the efficient entry of goods in particular legal jurisdictions and banking evolved into a network representing buyers and sellers in order that goods were paid for in a secure manner.

The finger piers were either privately owned or built by the local or state government and leased to an operator, whether a stevedoring firm or a shipping line. In some port areas, such as New York, some piers were either owned or operated by the railroads, The Erie, Pennsylvania, and New York Central Railroads being three noteworthy examples.

As these became increasingly stranded assets sitting atop valuable real estate, they gave way to other land uses, but in the meantime container terminals continued to appear and grow in size as depicted in Fig. 3.5 aerial view of the expanding facilities at the Port of Philadelphia.

Significance to supply chains

Understanding the significance of internodal maritime transportation in general, and the necessary port infrastructure required to support it, specifically, finds the Supply Chain Operational Reference Model to be a useful template. It is presented here to emphasize how transportation, although not specifically named, is literally the glue that holds the supply chain together, an even more compelling case for the global supply chain.

Figure 3.5
New Gantries at the Port of Philadelphia *Source: Courtesy of PhilaPort.*

The brief explanation of the Supply Chain Operational Reference Model is that every firm from point of origin to that of consumption is engaged in source, make, and deliver activities. Sourcing is defined as obtaining goods from another firm whereas making is the transformation from a material or component into a finished good to be used by another entity, which may be the ultimate consumer. Delivering is that activity that puts one's products in the hands of the customer whether it is a final product for the consumer or an intermediate good to undergo further manufacturing. The key point is that one firm's source activity links to another's deliver activity. Transportation may occur wherever a link exists including those activities internal to the firm such as committing raw materials to some production process, the transfer from one production process to another, and the transport of finished product from the point of production to the distribution system (Association for Supply Chain Management, 2012).

The term supply chain is believed to have first been uttered by Thomas Stallkamp, a senior procurement executive at Chrysler Corporation in the early 1980s. Chrysler, being the smallest of the Big Three automakers, was the least vertically integrated meaning that it was the most heavily dependent upon the performance of its suppliers. Chrysler was painfully aware that it was dependent not only upon the first-tier suppliers, but those that extend to the second, third, and beyond. Finally, note that the SCOR Model speaks to the matter of three parallel flows: physical, information, and financial noting that historically the utmost attention was focused on physical flows because those are when sustained most firms (Stallkamp, 116). Information flows, concerned with both transactional data as well as other elements such as forecasts and long-term plans, were enablers of physical flows

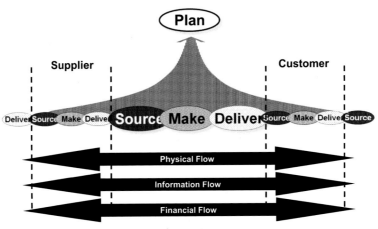

Figure 3.6

Original Supply Chain Operations Reference Model. *Courtesy of Association for Supply Chain Management, 2012. Supply Chain Operations Reference Model. Supply Chain Council, Chicago.*

meaning that the information flow had to be accurate or the physical flow would never be. Finally, the financial flow was the value exchanged as a result of the physical flows and if the physical flow was not properly functioning, then the financial flow would be adversely impacted. Fig. 3.6 depicts the basic SCOR Model as originally devised in the late 1990s, while Fig. 3.7 highlights where the transportation links occur along the supply chain.

The discussion of the SCOR Model is highly germane to that of ports because one needs to superimpose the diagram appearing in Fig. 3.4 into each of the intersections between links in Fig. 3.7 to understand the opportunities where goods in transit can be potentially compromised—the permutations with the global supply chain may well be counted in the

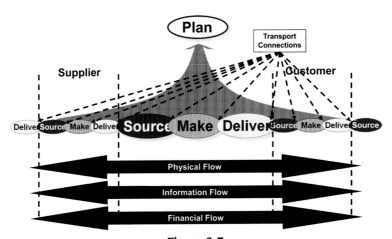

Figure 3.7

Supply Chain Operations Reference Model adapted to Highlight Transportation Activities.

hundreds, yet most global firms assume that their supply chains will repeatedly function in a flawless manner. The remainder of this book will highlight all of the potential opportunities extant suggesting that further diligence is required.

Port operations have significantly evolved, but also continue to do so. As was illustrated in Table 3.1 developments can be loosely attributed to four eras: nascent, international trade, global trade, and intermodal containerization. While the first two were driven by growth, the third was driven by a change in motive power, namely the transition from sailing ships to those propelled by machinery. The most radical change is clearly that brought about by containerization where it was not just the vessels themselves that were radically different, but all of the supporting services and infrastructure that those vessels required. Culturally, it has changed the way maritime labor is employed, patterns of land use, and the expansion of global trade whereby goods today travel many more miles throughout their supply chains than they ever have in recorded time.

References

Association for Supply Chain Management, 2012. Supply Chain Operations Reference Model. Supply Chain Council, Chicago.

Cavinato, J., 1989. Transportation Logistics Dictionary. International Thompson Transport Press, Washington, DC.

Coyle, J., Bardi, E., Langley, J., 2003. The Management of Business Logistics, seventh ed. Thomson South-Western, Mason, OH.

Coyle, J., Bardi, E., Novack, R., 2006. Transportation, sixth ed. Thomson South-Western, Mason, OH.

Garrison, W., Levinson, D., 2014. The Transportation Experience, second ed. Oxford University Press, London.

Gordon, G.A., 2018. Intermodal Maritime Transportation Security: A Multifactor Framework for Assessing Routing Risk (Doctoral dissertation). University of Massachusetts—Lowell.

Nocera, J., May 13, 2006. A Revolution that Came in a Box. The New York Times. (Accessed 9 January 2020).

Rodrigue, J., 2013. The Geography of Transport Systems, third ed. Routledge, New York.

Rosenberg, J., 1994. The Dictionary of International Trade. John Wiley and Sons, New York.

Stallkamp, R., 2005. Score: A Better Way to Do Business. Pearson Education, Upper Saddle River, NJ.

Further reading

Hubler, P., Meek, J., 2007. Beyond the waterfront: ports as leaders of intermodal trade. In: Plant, J.F. (Ed.), Handbook of Transportation Policy and Public Administration. Taylor and Francis, Boca Raton, FL.

CHAPTER 4

Other transportation modes

Gary A. Gordon, PhD, PE, MEMS, LTC USA (Ret.)
Department of Civil & Environmental Engineering, University of Massachusetts Lowell, Lowell, MA, United States

A transportation manager for a chemical manufacturer in Germany has learned that the contents of the containers being shipped are likely targeted. The first question that must be answered is the credibility of the information. Next, what is the safest and most expedient way of transporting the 40 intermodal containers to the Port of Bremerhaven? The transportation manager must now determine which mode of transportation is the least risky and should be used to transport the containers to the port. Should it be rail or truck?

The transportation manager is aware that the roadways along the route are subject to heavy traffic congestion and that a three-mile portion was under construction. For the most part, the rail lines to the port paralleled the roadway and, like the roadway, are easily accessible. The difference is that the rail line had a low freight density and simple signal system that allowed for a constant speed and relatively short transit time when compared to motor carrier.

Once the transportation manager determined that the targeting information is credible, he should consider the comparative risk of transporting the containers by rail versus truck. The risk he/she is considering is whether the tampering of the cargo in the containers jeopardizes the ability of the container to be loaded on a ship. The rail option would have the containers loaded at the manufacturing plant and could be handled in one train. The trucking option would require 40 separate trucks. If the cost of the rail and truck options were the same or not a consideration, the decision would be made primarily on the exposure to risk. Other factors that the transportation manager considered included the number of times the container would be handled for the rail option, would the 10 intermodal railcars be in a dedicated or general commodity train and the availability of sufficient trucks and reliability of the trucking firm. The decision is neither linear nor simple.

In this chapter, we will look at the transportation modes serving ports. The characteristics and issues associated with the modes will be addressed from both a domestic and international perspective. First, the transportation modes associated with the handling of intermodal containers will be identified and discussed. Then, we will look at several US and international ports to amplify the characteristics, operational components, and possible impacts if compromised. Then, risk and its components associated with the modes will be discussed with a discussion of risk assessment in a following chapter.

Intermodal means, as it indicates, between modes. In the previous chapter, the importance and need for highway and railroad access to port areas was introduced. Pipelines are also a transportation mode to and from ports, but not intermodal and, since they transport liquids and gaseous material in "bulk," it will not be considered herein. Truck and rail are also transporters of petrochemical and other chemical products and noncontainerized or bulk commodities into ports. For the purpose of this chapter and book, the discussion will focus on truck and rail, as they are the prime movers of intermodal freight to and from the ports.

In addition to rail and truck, smaller container ships transport intermodal containers from feeder to load center ports. This process is an extension of land-based transportation and consolidates and loads intermodal containers onto larger container vessels for the long-haul voyage (Gordon, 2018). The smaller container ships function much like rail and truck delivering a small number of containers to be consolidated and loaded onto larger ships. Feeder ship operations are short haul and often close to shore increasing the risk of compromise, but on the other hand is within coastal protection forces.

Major ports continue to find port access an ongoing challenge given that larger vessels have been stretching their capacities almost faster than they can be expanded. In 2002, the Alameda Corridor, a 20-mile long multiple rail corridor, was constructed to provide improved rail access to the Ports of Los Angeles and Long Beach (Alameda Corridor, 2020). Just over 15 years later, the Corridor is suffering from traffic congestion as 4.7 million twenty-foot equivalent units (TEUs)[1] traverse its length annually. While the Corridor took trucks off neighboring roadways, the need for more locally destined traffic has not diminished. Moreover, where ship-to-rail connections were present, there is a short dray between modes; many of them have been replaced by on-pier rail operations access.

Trucks entering ports, although essentially eliminated by the Alameda Corridor, truck traffic to and from ports is an issue elsewhere in the United States. The issue of truck traffic is twofold. First, it creates traffic in the surrounding roadway network often impacting residential and commercial areas. Second and based on the commodities carried, a safety and security risk may exist that must be mitigated. However, there is not as much of a risk with intermodal containers as there is with petrochemical and other products considered as hazmat. For example, the Everett, Massachusetts liquified natural gas (LNG) Marine Terminal and associated tanker truck traffic pose a risk, which

---

[1] TEU is a twenty-foot equivalent unit used to describe the capacity of container ships and terminals.

includes being used as material to make a weapon of mass destruction (WMD) (LeClair, 2019). On the other side of Boston Harbor is the Massachusetts Port Authority's (Massport) Conley Container Terminal, which handled 307,000 TEUs in Fiscal Year (2019). Located across the channel from the Flynn Black Falcon Cruise Terminal, the Conley Terminal, as shown in Fig. 4.1, is located within a residential and commercial area in the City of Boston and is subject to heavy traffic.

Given the proximity of intermodal container and cruise terminals, safety and security is an issue that could have significant consequences if a WMD or the components to make one are hidden in a container and deployed in the area (Gordon, 2018). Fig. 4.2 shows a container ship docked at Conley Container Terminal from the deck of a cruise ship departing Flynn Black Falcon Cruise Terminal in Boston, MA.

For the purpose of this chapter and book, truck and rail access to a container port will be discussed, as are combined ports, where LNG, petrochemical products, and hazmat are handled. Domestic and international ports will be discussed because the supply chain for this book is based on the containers originating from an overseas source, including the ground transportation to the port of debarkation. This is because research on the security of the intermodal supply chain indicates that the greatest risk originates at and from the manufacturer to the port of debarkation (Gordon, 2018).

Figure 4.1
Conley container (left) and Flynn Black Falcon Cruise (right) terminals, Boston, MA. *Source: Massachusetts Port Authority.*

Figure 4.2
Conley container terminal from the Norwegian Dawn departing Boston. *Courtesy of Gary Gordon, 2017.*

Trucks approach and enter ports via major highways and local roads. This is often in or near populated residential and commercial areas where many people live and gather to conduct business, partake in entertainment, or dine. The risk associated with trucking is potentially significant because the truck is not physically constrained to where it goes and when. It could carry a WMD to a target at any time of the day. Traffic restrictions, however, can prevent trucks from using certain roads and streets, but will a person with terror intent heed traffic regulations and restrictions? Rail operations are via a fixed guideway and are physically constrained by the track structure and defined route. The risk with rail is that they often operate in large trains with many railcars. Plus, a conspirator knows where a train will be and relatively when it will be there. If a container on a flat car (COFC) contains a WMD intended to be deployed in a populated area in the vicinity of a port, it would have deleterious consequences. And what if the train also contained flammable material? What if the train is stopped blocking roadway traffic in conjunction with another nefarious act? It could prevent people from evacuating and first responders from arriving in a timely manner.

There are physical and operational differences between truck and rail as they enter and exit ports, and in the port itself. Let us look at a couple of examples in both domestic and international ports.

Domestic ports

The three largest container ports in the United States are Los Angeles (9.5 million TEUs—#17 of the top 50 container ports in the world based on 2018 data), Long Beach (8.1 million TEUs—#20), and New York/New Jersey (7.2 million TEUs—#23) and will be discussed with regard to volumes and the associated rail and truck operations (World Shipping Council, 2020). The Ports of Houston and Boston (Everett LNG Terminal and Conley Container Terminal), although not in the top 50 container ports in the world, will also be discussed in this chapter because of the author's familiarity with them. The issues associated with the Boston and Houston ports are similar in nature to that of Los Angeles, Long Beach, and New York/New Jersey, where the sheer volumes in these ports will exacerbate and amplify the issues and risk associated with Boston and Houston.

The Port of Houston is located along a 25-mile segment of the 52-mile Houston Ship Channel and is the home to 200 private and eight public industrial terminals that include the Barbours Cut and Bayport Container Terminals. It is the largest port on the Gulf Coast (Port of Houston Authority, 2020). Located at the mouth of Galveston Bay, the Barbours Cut Container Terminal consists of six berths, provides for roll-on/roll-off (RORO) operations and has 230 acres of paved hardstand and four working railroad tracks and spurs to/from the terminal. Barbours Cut Container Terminal currently handles 1.2 million TEUs annually and is expected to grow to 2 million TEUs when the modernization project to better handle Panamax container ships is complete. Whether by truck or rail, access to Barbours Cut Container Terminal is via populated and commercial/industrial areas.

The Bayport Container Terminal, which is considered to be the most modern and environmentally sensitive container terminal on the Gulf Coast, will have seven container berths and capacity to handle 2.3 million TEUs when fully complete. It will have a 376-acre container yard and a 123-acre intermodal facility. Bayport also has an automobile terminal, and the former cruise terminal has been converted to handle RORO operations.

When fully developed, these two container terminals will have a combined throughput of 4.3 million TEUs. The Barbours Cut Container Terminal operations are contracted with rail service via the Burlington Northern Santa Fe (BNSF), Union Pacific (UP), and Port Terminal Railroad Association (PTRA). Truck access is via Texas Routes 146 and 225 with connections to I-45 and I-10 in the Houston Metropolitan area. Bayport Container Terminal is located off Texas Route 146 about 7 miles south of Barbours Cut Container Terminal. Truck access is via Texas Route 146 and Port Road and rail service via the BNSF and UP.

Truck and rail access to these container terminals is via roadways and rail lines that are in and around the City of Houston. Knowing traffic and the roadway system in and around Houston, there is much congestion resulting in slow and stopped traffic. It is not uncommon for cars and trucks to be stopped for lengthy periods of time or pressed to take a diversion to avoid the traffic. This diversion affords a perpetrator the opportunity to compromise or sabotage the container unnoticed. There is a similar dynamic for the rail traffic operating to and from these ports. The only exception is that the trains are restricted to the fixed right-of-way and operate on fixed guideways and, as a result, often must wait at wayside signals, passing sidings or secondary yards for clearance to proceed. These occurrences can also afford a perpetrator an opportunity to sabotage or compromise a container.

The Massport's Conley Container Terminal is much smaller (300,000 TEUs in 2019) than the Houston container terminals (Massport Conley Terminal, 2020). There is no rail service into the terminal, but the CSX has an intermodal rail yard that is 50 miles west and has about an hour-and-a-half dray time by truck. In 2017, MassPort constructed a dedicated haul road to the terminal; however, access to the haul road is via I-93 and I-90 onto local streets all of which are in the City of Boston. Through the City of Boston, I-93 is in a tunnel and I-90 is in a tunnel east of I-93 to Boston's Seaport District where it connects with local roads. Both the interstate highways, as well as the local roads, experience heavy traffic, and there are few escape routes to avoid it. While a risk in Houston is an incident on one of their many flyovers, the risk in Boston is in the tunnels. In the Seaport District, there is extensive residential and commercial development, as well as Boston's cruise port. Even though there is extensive traffic congestion, there is little opportunity for the container to be sabotaged or compromised unnoticed. A WMD attack would likely be by a device put in the container at the point of origin or in transit before it reaches the port. A similar scenario would be for an incoming container from a foreign port.

What does this all mean? It shows the exposure of a container is by way of the environment in which they are delivered to and taken from ports and opportunity to compromise the container or exploit as a WMD. It also shows the vulnerability of compromise and opportunity for smuggling drugs and other commodities. Even parts of a WMD to be assembled at a later time and different location, perhaps in America's heartland. Next, we will lay out similar scenarios and conditions from the foreign manufacturer to the foreign load port.

International ports

Internationally, the three largest container ports in the world will be discussed with regard to container volumes, the associated rail and truck operations, and vulnerabilities inherent to the mode. The three largest container ports in the world are Shanghai, China (42 million TEUs), Singapore (36.6 million TEUs), and Shenzhen, China (27.7 million TEUs) (World Shipping Council, 2020). The Port of Hamburg, Germany, (#19 with 8.7 million TEUs in 2018) will be discussed, as it is the port used in the development of the intermodal maritime container security framework for assessing routes (Gordon, 2018).

The Port of Hamburg is the largest port in Germany and third largest in Europe. It includes four state-of-the-art container terminals, as well as cruise terminals, break-bulk, and RORO operations (Port of Hamburg, 2020). It is located on the Elbe River about 68 miles from the North Sea. The Port is a large port covering about 29 square miles on both sides of the river. In 2019, it handled about 9.3 million TEUs with more than 2300 freight trains per week. The modal split of container traffic at the port is 51.3% by truck, 46.3% by rail, and the balance of 2.4% by barge. The import/export TEU split in 2019 was 48.8% export and 51.2% import equating to about 2.3 million TEUs that arrive in the port from inland locations by truck, 2.1 million TEUs by rail and 0.1 TEUs by barge.

Because of the size of the Port of Hamburg, rail and highway access appears to be complex with many access and egress points. Trains and trucks will have to traverse populated residential and commercial/industrial areas to access the port. Only a few short miles from the city center, the port likely experiences similar risks regarding traffic congestion on the roadways and freight density on the rail lines as with other ports in the world. Unlike Houston and to a lesser degree Boston, the freight and commuter and passenger train operations appear to share operating rights-of-way which further increases the exposure and risk. In 2019, the Port of Shanghai handled about 24 million TEUs (Ship Technology, 2020). Located at the mouth of the Yangtze River, the Port of Shanghai has three container handling facilities and hardstand areas totaling about 2.6 square miles along eight miles of the Baoshan Waterway. Each of the container terminals are operated by different companies. The port also handles bulk cargo, RORO operations, and cruise ships. Located within the densely populated City of Shanghai, there are many roadways serving the three container ports, but there does not appear to be rail service into or near the container terminals.

Containers constitute a small fraction of the total freight, which is primarily bulk cargo, representing about 2.2% in 2013 (Rail Transport in China Wikipedia, 2020). Further and in 2016, only about 8% of all cargo was transported by rail. From a review of available maps of the Shanghai metropolitan area, it appears that rail does not serve the container terminals, and trucking is used to dray the containers to and from pier side. Also and from the review of available maps, there is an intricate roadway network to and from the container terminals. Therefore, it can be concluded that the trucks moving to and from the container terminals would be subject to traffic congestion and "stop and go" traffic in and among densely populated residential areas, as well as commercial and industrial areas.

From the discussion of domestic and international ports, it is quite apparent that there is an inherent risk to transporting intermodal containers by truck and rail common to all ports whether domestic or international. The focus herein is to look at the risks associated with transporting the intermodal container from a foreign manufacturer to a foreign port. Domestically and because the greatest risk is on the outbound legs of the journey, the inland domestic transport will not be addressed (Gordon, 2018).

Risk to rail and trucking to ports

Risk

When looking at risk, there is a commonly accepted relationship among three factors: threat (T), vulnerabilities (V), and consequences (C), and is commonly shown in the following equation (Lewis, 2015):

$$R = T \times V \times C$$

This relationship can be used objectively or subjectively. It could be used to determine risk and compare one route or mode of transportation over another from the manufacturer to the port. Risk assessment frameworks will be discussed in Chapter 16, Routing Analysis, Risk and Resiliency. This relationship and approach are used by the U.S. Department of Homeland Security (DHS) and its partners, and has relevance and applicability to the intermodal maritime supply chain. The following sections will look at the components of risk in general and, then, specifically for rail and truck.

In general and whether domestic or international, the threats and vulnerabilities are essentially the same, but there will be differences based on, among other things, location of the nation and its rules, regulations and processes, and physical and technological mitigation measures. Truck and rail each have their own threats, vulnerabilities, and risk to operations and the robustness and resilience of the physical supporting infrastructure. Exposure to risk occurs throughout the supply chain, but this chapter will focus on operations to and from the port and within the port. The following will discuss the threats, vulnerabilities, and consequences in general terms and, then, modally specific to rail and truck.

Threats

The threats experienced in international versus US ports include a function of the proximity to "hotspots" with regard to terrorism and ease of access. Railroads operate on fixed guideways, and location, schedules, and operations that define to some degree as to when and where a train will be. This makes compromise comparatively easy. Trucks operate on roadways and the route that can be taken is only as fixed as the roadway options available. Operations and schedules are not as easily determined, as with rail, but trucks can be diverted to roadways that bring it through densely populated areas and areas that have commercial and industrial uses. The latter could involve areas that store or produce hazardous materials exacerbating an event or compromise.

When looking at railroads, the likely threats are derailment, bridge failures, equipment failure, or releasing hazardous material. These are often the result of unintentional acts, such as poor maintenance or operator error, or intentionally caused for terrorist purposes or vandalism. Also when trains operate at slow speeds (e.g., at wayside signals or when slow orders are in place), the contents of a railcar or intermodal container could be accessed and compromised. Hijacking a train or a runway train could cause a number of events that might compromise the neighboring area. The Lac-Megantic railway accident is an example of a railway accident that caused a disaster of major proportions that impacted the Town of Lac-Megantic, PQ and Lac-Megantic itself (Valcik and Tracy, 2017). Although an accident, it shows the vulnerability of parking a train and leaving it unattended and the resultant threat to a local community and body of water.

Threats to train operations can be physical and cyber related. Physical threats can be either natural or man-made occurrences, but cyber related will likely be man-made. Physically, railroad infrastructure and operations can be compromised. Locomotives and railcars as well as the infrastructure over which they operate can be sabotaged. By operating in remote, as a well as populated areas, it is easier to compromise railroad equipment and infrastructure unnoticed in rural areas rather than in urban areas unless in the middle of large rail yards. The remoteness of some locations makes the unnoticed tampering of intermodal containers easier. Sabotaging the track structure and roadbed, bridges, tunnels, and culverts could cause an accident, such as a derailment and bridge strike, but it could also cause the slowdown of trains permitting containers to be accessed and tampered with. Sabotaging the signal or train control system could also cause an accident (e.g., run-in) or, like tampering with the physical infrastructure, cause trains to slowdown and making it easier to tamper with.

Trucks are less predictable as to where they operate and when they will be at a given location, as there are few restrictions as to where they can operate. The vulnerability is that a truck operates among regular traffic and is subject to congestion often operating at slow speeds or even stopped. This allows for the potential of a truck to be hijacked or container tampered with. If the truck is hijacked, it could be driven to an unobserved location where the container could be tampered with or, based on the commodity carried, be driven to a populated area and used as a WMD. The threat is that intermodal maritime containers could be compromised introducing a WMD or the material for one, or the truck could be driven to a densely populated or industrial area and used as a WMD. However, "virtual fencing" can be used to detect deviations from planned routes.

Sabotaging roads, bridges, and tunnels could cause an accident with "unintended consequences" or cause a cessation or rerouting of traffic. The latter could result in the rerouting of traffic though populated or industrial areas that contain hazmat producing facilities. Either one could result in a major incident. Tampering with traffic signals and electronic advisory signs could have the same impact and result as compromising the roadway infrastructure, bridges, and tunnels.

The main concern of this book is the ability of accessing and tampering with the contents of intermodal containers in transit. Easy access to containers provides an easy avenue that could be used to introduce a WMD or its components, drugs, and other contraband during the move from the factory to the outload port. This, in turn, could have a cascading effect and, ultimately, risk to the maritime transportation system. Compromising containers in ports will be discussed in other chapters but could include what is brought in by the surface transportation modes and what can be introduced within the port. As a result, the ship's voyage or the intermodal container could be compromised during the voyage. This could have an impact on the US ports receiving the containers and/or to the domestic inland destinations. This impact could be exacerbated by the use of inland ports, which are logistics and distribution hubs away from the seaport to lessen the congestion.

Vulnerabilities

A vulnerability is a weakness or gap in a security program that can be exploited by threats to gain unauthorized access to an asset (Vellani, 2007) and is based on an assessment of the likelihood that an incursion could occur (Young et al., 2018). The weakness or gap could be infrastructure or systems related or operational. For railroads and highway or roadway systems for trucks, the infrastructure is linear, complex, and easily accessed, and in many instances, are in rural areas where monitoring and surveillance are minimal. In urban areas, bridges and tunnels can be accessed, but the chance of being noticed is greater because of the traffic. This vulnerability allows an unwanted intrusion that could result in tampering with cargo in a container or using it as a WMD.

When using rail to haul containers from a manufacturer to a port, transportation managers must realize the risk of operating on a fixed route and relatively fixed schedule. This aids a perpetrator in knowing when and where a train will be and where it could be easily compromised unnoticed. Trains operate via a signal or train control system that is increasingly cyber-based and dependent thus allowing a higher number of trains to occupy the rail line than would be the case with some of the older train signaling systems.

Train control systems are similar in purpose as roadway/intersection traffic signals, as they provide stop control for opposing or conflicting directions of traffic. This is accomplished by using wayside signals or interlockings to slow or stop trains. It is easy to access a train when it is operating at slow speeds or is stopped. Tampering with the train control system could create an accident that could be (1) the intended purpose of the incursion or (2) to stop the train so that a container could be compromised prior to reaching the port.

Other methods of slowing or stopping trains is to tamper with the track structure or put objects on the tracks. Bridges and tunnels could be compromised in a similar manner, but the repair would take much longer than for a section of track. If tampering is discovered prior to the train's arrival, the train could be delayed or rerouted based on the extent of the damage. Rerouting of the train could be the perpetrator's intent. The vulnerabilities are exacerbated when freight trains share track occupancy with passenger trains.

Trucks operate among regular traffic and are subject to traffic congestion, traffic signals, and roadway geometry.[2] Trucks stopped at accident sites or a traffic lights can have their cargo; containers in this case compromised. What about hijacking? Trucks that are stopped can easily be hijacked and (1) be brought to an unobserved location to be tampered with or (2) brought to a densely populated area to be used as WMD. A benefit is that trucks are not on a fixed guideway like railroads and can bypass traffic congestion or problem areas, such as accidents. A disadvantage is that they can operate most anywhere, to include in densely populated areas and industrial areas where hazardous material is manufactured.

An intermodal container's vulnerability is also based on the number of times it is handled, as well as the distance and transit time to the port. Most intermodal containers when transported by rail are loaded and reloaded between the manufacturing plant and port. Trucks on the other hand are only loaded once at the manufacturing plan and are not usually unloaded until it arrives in the port. The multiple handling of the intermodal container increases the risk of compromise (Gordon, 2018).

As shown in the photograph, below, containers are removed from chassis in the Port of Charleston, SC. (Fig. 4.3). If the container is loaded on the truck at the factory, it is handled twice. If rail is used to transport containers to the port, the container is often trucked to an intermodal yard and loaded onto the railcar. Then, the container is offloaded in another intermodal yard and trucked into the port unless there are pier-side tracks and cranes. So, the container could he handled as little as two times if it is trucked directly to the port having pier-side tracks. In a traditional rail move, the container could be handled as many as four times. Therefore, a consideration in selecting landside transportation, in addition to cost, should be to minimize the number of times the container is handled.

Consequences

As discussed in this chapter, the threats and vulnerabilities could lead to a wide range of consequences. Using rail to and from the port, the consequences of an incursion could result in a compromise of the contents of the container, an accident, whether purposeful or unintentional, or even a denial of a valuable transportation route supporting the supply chain. Compromising the contents of the container could have deleterious consequences either enroute or at its destination. The consequences could be physical damage,

---

[2] Roadway geometry often requires vehicles to operate at slow speeds because of safety concerns in horizontal curves and power requirements on grades.

Figure 4.3
Container Drayage in the Port of Charleston, SC. *Source: South Carolina Ports Authority.*

casualties, and loss of life or economic damage. Rail's exposure is high, on one hand, because it operates on fixed routes and schedules. On the other hand, the exposure limits the areas of potential damage to the immediate environs of the track.

Consequences, when trucking the container to the port, are somewhat different from that with rail because of the flexibility of routing. Although trucks operate on roadways that are fixed, there are easily accessible alternate routes that could be taken to avoid various situations. Unlike rail, this could create an uncertainty as to the route the container could take to the port theoretically minimizes the risk of an incursion. The consequences of an incursion, however, could be extended beyond the original route. Alternate routes could expose populated and industrial areas to unnecessary risk and consequences. The diversion from the original route could be planned nefariously to a remote and/or unmonitored area where the contents of a container could be tampered with. A hijacked truck could be used as a WMD in a densely populated area or industrial area where hazardous material is manufactured. It is far more likely that a truck would be hijacked than a train.

Addressing the Risk

Given the threats, vulnerabilities, and consequences, there are many ways of addressing risk and, hopefully, mitigating risk or minimize the consequences. US and international government rules, regulations, and policies can advance vet the cargo in the container, its shipper, and processes prior to loading on the ship. Hardening and protecting infrastructure and monitoring operations are essential. Cooperation and coordination, to include intelligence sharing, among all domestic and international governments, stakeholders, and partners in the intermodal maritime container supply chain (e.g., International Maritime Organization) are the cornerstones of a successful security plan that involves the surface transportation to and from a port. All of these will be discussed in other chapters in the book.

References

Alameda Corridor Transportation Authority, 2020. http://www.acta.org/projects/projects_completed_alameda_timeline.asp.

Gordon, G., 2018. Intermodal Maritime Container Security: A Multifactor Framework for Assessing Routing (Doctoral dissertation). University of Massachusetts Lowell.

LeClair, N., 2019. The Everett LNG Marine Terminal: A Risk Assessment. University of Massachusetts Lowell, CRIM 5660. Transportation Systems Safety & Security CRIM.

Lewis, T., 2015. Critical Infrastructure Protection in Homeland Security: Defending a Networked Nation, second ed. ISBN-13: 978-1118817636.

Massachusetts Port Authority Port of Boston Website, May 24, 2020. http://www.massport.com/conley-terminal/.

Port of Hamburg Website, May 24, 2020. https://www.hafen-hamburg.de/en.

Port of Houston Authority Website, May 23, 2020. https://porthouston.com/.

Rail Transport in China, Wikipedia, May 22, 2020. https://en.wikipedia.org/wiki/Rail_transport_in_China.

Ship Technology, May 24, 2020. https://www.ship-technology.com/projects/portofshnaghai/.

Valcik, N.A., Tracy, P.E., 2017. Lac-megantic rail disaster - Quebec, Canada, 2013 case study. In: Case Studies in Disaster Response and Emergency Management, second ed. Routledge.

Vellani, K., 2007. Strategic Security Management: A Risk Assessment Guide for Decision Makers. Butterworth-Heinemann.

World Shipping Council, 2020. http://www.worldshipping.org/about-the-industry/global-trade/top-50-world-container-ports.

Young, R., Gordon, G., Plant, J., 2018. Railway Security: Protection Against Manmade and Natural Disasters. Routledge/Taylor & Francis Group.

PART III

The nature of intermodal maritime security risk

CHAPTER 5

Nature of the intermodal maritime security risk?*

The supply chain encompasses the processes of sourcing, transporting, storing, and distributing raw materials, components, subassemblies, and finished goods. It involves logistics, warehousing, inventory management, quality control, production planning as well as other intrinsic subsets. Let us consider one discrete, yet not wholly separate, function—logistics, which the Council of Supply Chain Management Professionals[1] defines as that part of the supply chain process that plans, implements, and controls the efficient flow and storage of goods, services, and related information from the point of origin to the point of consumption in order to meet customer's requirements (CSCMP, 2020).

The supply chain comprises numerous stakeholders; some have a direct commercial and/or fiduciary relationship while others seem to be on the periphery but nonetheless play a role in ensuring goods move smoothly and safely from origin to destination. However, while these entities may be inextricably linked, they may have some inherent competing, if not downright, conflicting priorities as shown in Table 5.1. Let us look at how the focus on an entity and consider how operational and/or financial benefits can accrue to them will/can be at the expense of another.

These are sweetened generalizations, so it is necessary that we be more specific as to the how focusing on just one can yield suboptimal results. After 9/11, a true watershed for transportation security and that of cargo specifically, Customs officials were more closely scrutinizing imported goods; this heightened inspection regime would have resulted in some delay in releasing the goods to the beneficial cargo owner which in turn adversely affects the delivery to the consignee. However, there are other stakeholders that are impacted such as the shipper's need for speed or the terminal's focus on production. All of these considerations come down to asset utilization whether the assets are fixed, as

---

* *Anonymous. This chapter is written by a senior executive of a well-known insurer of marine cargo transportation. Anonymity was requested in order to assure that neither the author nor their employer could be associated with any statements made.*

   It is also suggested that the reader consider Chapters 5 and 6 as an intended pair. Whereas Chapter 5 provides ample background on the evolution of containerization within the modern supply chain replete with global sourcing, Chapter 6 offers a practical guide for reducing supply chain risk and vulnerability.

[1] Previously known as the Council of Logistics Management.

Intermodal Maritime Security. https://doi.org/10.1016/B978-0-12-819945-9.00008-3

Table 5.1: Trade stakeholder mindsets and metrics.

Links	Emphasis	Metric
Manufacturer	Outsource	Profit
Financial intermediary	Risk management	Contract certainty
Shipper	Speed	Time to market
Consolidator (CFS)[2]	Value added	Cube
Carrier	Efficiency	Resource (utilization)
Terminal	Throughput	Throughput.(TEU)
Consumer	Value for the money	Cost
Insurer	Safety	Asset protection
Government	Homeland security	Compliance
Environment	"Green"	Sustainability score

in equipment, or current, as is the case with inventory. In supply chain management, trade-offs are pervasive, and there are many more that enter the decision-making.

With that as a backdrop, let us consider the modern supply chain as truly global in scope; geographically dispersed and complex and thus inherently sensitive (fragile) and very much vulnerable to disruptions. Table 5.2 highlights some broad descriptors of today's supply chain and factors embedded them.

Table 5.2: Modern supply chain characteristics.

Descriptor	Characteristics	Outcomes
Global	Outsourcing, contract manufacturing	Locally concentrated risks become widely defused
Specialized	Geographical concentration of production	Processes can be easily disrupted by a single event
Complex	Reliance on multiple parties in diverse locations	Reduced visibility and latent ability of monitoring and reporting systems
Lean	Single sourcing and inventory reduction	Improved efficiency but with fewer options after disruptions
Information-reliant	"Track and trace" systems answering the question of "where is it?"	Increasing need for more timely flow of data
Legislatively bound	Knowledge of goods and trading partner identities	National and international supply chain security systems[3]; added protocols can impede efficient flow of goods

---

[2] CFS denotes containerized freight station.
[3] Registration and qualification of trade participants with such initiatives as Customs-Trade Partnership Against Terrorism (C-TPAT) and Authorized Economic Operator (AEO).

Before narrowing your view to specific situations and conditions, you would be well served to review the work entitled "New Models for Addressing Supply Chain and Transport Risk." Unveiled by the World Economic Forum (WEF) at the 2012 Annual Meeting in Davos, its findings still resonate today. This document which represents an amalgamation of ideas from supply chain risk management and resiliency thought leaders in the public and private sector also served as the precursor to the *National Strategy for Global Supply Chain Security* (The White House, 2012).

"New Models for Addressing Supply Chain and Transport Risk" is a notable work on so many levels. It is the first macro examination of supply chain exposures rightly positing that safety, reliability, and efficiency can only be gained through collaboration between industry and government. Moreover, it suggests that these goals need not be mutually exclusive. Toward that end, the WEF gathered supply chain and transport risk experts to explore systemic vulnerabilities and their respective external forces. They recognized that the increasingly global operating models and the growing interconnectivity and interdependence of supply chain and transport networks lead to new risk profiles and risk management priorities that supply chains, if they are to be resilient, need to have taken into consideration.

The work also rightly states that organizations must balance long- and short-term strategic decision-making and that risk must be analyzed against objective and transparent criteria with costs weighed against the benefits of potential risk mitigation methods. While corporate managements endeavor to achieve these objectives, the results are all too often suboptimal. Hence, the following five overarching recommendations are made by WEF:

1. Improve international and interagency compatibility of resilience standards and programs;
2. More explicitly assess supply chain and transport risks as key elements of top level management and governance processes bringing together those organizational components represented by Purchasing, Logistics, and Risk Management along with Operations, Quality Control, and Security;
3. Develop trusted networks of suppliers and customers and associated stakeholders all-embracing a focus on risk management;
4. Improve visibility through two-way information sharing and the collaborative development of standards, risk assessment, and quantification tools. This will be difficult to accomplish due to the reluctance of many organizations to share data (aka actionable intelligence); also, there are numerous groups, not to mention companies, that have established best practices and, yet to-date, no move has been undertaken to build a best of the best;

5. Improve pre- and postevent communications on systemic disruptions and between security and facilitation to bring a more balanced discussion between the public and private sectors. Customs has always had the task of juggling the trade-off between security and cargo movement. While these do not seem mutually exclusive, there will never be a level playing field, and depending on the flavor of the day, one will be favored at the expense of the other. Even the WEF realized that Post-9/11 efforts have failed to strike the right note between protecting against terrorist threats and facilitating the smooth flow of goods and people (World Economic Forum, 2012).

The United States in its *National Strategy*, referenced above, articulated two goals:

- To promote the timely, efficient, and secure movement of legitimate commerce while protecting and securing the supply chain from exploitation and reducing its vulnerability to disruption and to do so through strengthening the security of the physical infrastructure, conveyances, and information assets;
- To foster a resilient global supply chain that is prepared for and can withstand evolving threats and hazards and can rapidly recover from disruptions (The White House, 2012).

Admittedly, these are very broad and high-sounding goals and not unexpectedly one can find that the following five subsets are embedded therein:

- Understanding and addressing vulnerabilities by actors who seek to introduce harmful products or materials and disruptions stemming from international attacks, accidents, or natural disasters;
- Utilizing a multilayered defense to protect against or otherwise thwart the panoply of traditional and asymmetric threats. These layers by definition must encompass intelligence and information analysis; the appropriate use of technology; and the application of regulations and policies through the use of properly trained and equipped personnel and effective partnerships;
- Adapting a security posture to meet evolving threats through the development and implementation of a flexible risk management approach that prioritizes actions to address those risks having the greatest potential impact;
- Refining our understanding of the threats and risks associated with the global supply chain through updated assessments;
- Advancing technology research, development, testing, and evaluation efforts aimed at improving our ability to secure cargo in all modal environments (The White House, 2012).

World trade continues to grow in importance and virtually every company is part of today's truly global supply chain that is an interconnected and interdependent network—try to think of a firm that neither ships to nor receives a product or products from outside their borders? The International Transport Forum predicts that demand for goods and services worldwide will triple between now and 2050.

A dramatic shift in global trade

In 2000, a relatively small, and to be unnamed, manufacturer of automotive aftermarket products located in central Pennsylvania was interviewed concerning their import and export activities. At the time, they had no imports and less than 10% of their output was exported and that was only limited to customers within North American Free Trade Agreement (NAFTA). Just 10 years later the CEO was interviewed again, at that time he proudly disclosed that better than 25% of their raw materials and components were sourced offshore. Moreover, nearly 40% of that firm's output was exported to foreign customers, many in Europe and the Middle East.

Regardless of trade tensions, tariffs, nationalist sentiments, and the varying political winds, goods and services will continue to move freely between countries. This does not mean that these will have no effect because clearly actions by or reactions to these factors will cause or accelerate dislocations with the flow of merchandise shifting as a result. Additionally, new trade routes can be expected to emerge. Two prime and current examples now appearing regularly in the news are the opening up of Arctic waters and the northern sea passage as well as rail networks connecting Asia and Europe (e.g., China's Silk Road).

As depicted in Fig. 5.1, goods in international trade travel through a labyrinth passing through the hands of multiple service providers often representing one or more different modes of transportation. Not only are there handoffs at these logical interchanges but there are dwell times; periods when a shipment is waiting for transfer, transshipment, or transloading. For example, such may occur when goods for export are cross-docked from a highway trailer into a container or moved from an ocean container into a trailer for inward inland road transit.

For our purposes, we will concentrate on waterborne commerce as well as the attendant conveyances that support the longer ocean passage. Maritime trade, representing 71% of all goods shipped, is the lifeblood of the world with essential (and even frivolous) goods pulsing through its arteries from origins to destinations around the globe. Cargo transport by air pales in comparison; essentially limited to emergency/rush shipments and those commodities with the associated value to make the faster and more expensive routing cost-efficient. There are two elements we will address: security and disruptive events that may or may not be associated with security or lack thereof.

Let us first delve into the issue of supply chain risk and the accompanying disruptions they can cause using a holistic approach to risk and vulnerability—marrying traditional transportation risks with operational risks, financial risks, reputational risks, and strategic risks.

Supply chain disruptions, even those that appear to be isolated, can cascade across product lines and borders. Mismanaged exposures can cost money and shareholder value; it can also prevent firms from taking advantage of opportunities that drive innovation and growth. The more that one understands these exposures within its business, the better it

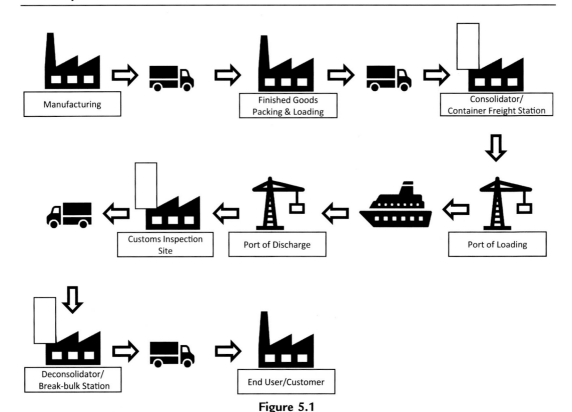

Figure 5.1
The physical flow of imported goods. *Source: Young, 2020.*

can make informed decisions and prepare for them. It is only then that one can finally understand the total cost of ownership for goods and hence can maximize performance.

BSI Supply Chain Solutions[4] offers a number of indicators that they have neatly, albeit with some overlap, placed into risk categories:

- Business Continuity Risk: Man-made disruptions, natural disasters, and political and economic stability.
- Environmental Risk: Environmental health and safety.
- Geopolitical Risk: Corruption, crime, and government ineffectiveness, employee screening practices, and political and economic stability.
- Security Risk: Anti-Western sentiment, cargo theft, counterfeit protection, terrorism, and unmanifested cargo.
- Social Responsibility Risk: Forced and child labor and human rights, environmental pollution from transportation mishaps (BSI, 2019).

---

[4] BSI was originally the British Standards Institute, one of several agencies that could perform ISO registrations.

There are disruptive triggers that are subsumed in each of these somewhat broad classifications; fire, extreme weather, cyberattacks, pandemics, price and currency volatility, energy shortage, and ownership or investment restrictions to name just a few.

Fig. 5.2 is a graphic display of a recent BSI Global Threat map that pinpoints transportation trouble spots that while not immutable does present a snapshot in time. Moreover, while for the sake of convenience, the countries and/or regions may be broad-brushed, realize that there are certainly pockets within that space where the risk may be more or less elevated. Clearly some could take the view that if it is never happened here; it never will. Conversely, as Stein's Law asserts: "if something cannot go on forever it will stop." Put somewhat more plainly, trends that cannot continue, will not.

While it may be useful to recognize the pitfalls that face any enterprise engaged in international trade, a company needs to create visibility of its goods as they flow throughout the supply chain involving all channel partners. One method to do this is through a mapping exercise upstream from raw material and component suppliers to your customers downstream, potentially even to the ultimate consumer.

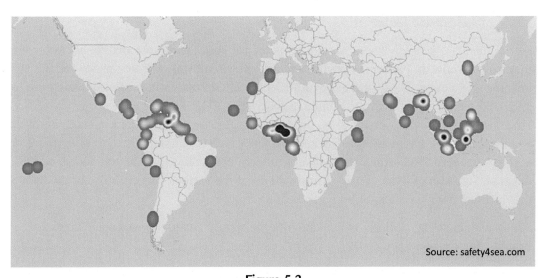

Source: safety4sea.com

Figure 5.2
Global threats and trouble spots. *Source: [The] State of Maritime Piracy (2018). One Earth Future. Bloomfield, CO. https://stableseas.org/sites/default/files/stateofpiracy2018_0.pdf. (Accessed August 30, 2020).*

Diagramming the flow of goods has to be augmented with an assessment that touches on the following questions that have been developed by Zurich Insurance Global Supply Chain Group:

- Do you know who your critical suppliers are and how much their failure would impact your company's profits?
- Have you integrated risk management processes[5] into your supply chain approach?
- Is supply chain risk management integrated into your enterprise risk management thinking?
- Do you have routine, timely systems for measuring the financial stability of critical suppliers?
- Do you understand your Tier1[6] production facilities and logistics hub exposures to natural catastrophes?
- Do you record the details of supply chain incidents and the actions you have put in place to avoid future such incidents?
- Do your Tier 1 suppliers have business continuity plans that have been tested in terms of their viability?
- Have you provided risk training to your supply chain management team?
- Is risk a topic on the agenda at performance meetings with your critical suppliers? (Boileau and Skow, 2016).

Just as there are people who know, those you do not know, and those that do not know that they do not know, in the supply chain there are known knowns, known unknowns, and unknown unknowns. To illustrate the pitfall of the latter condition, medieval maps were known to often contain the rather ominous inscription "Hic Sunt Dracones" or "There Be Dragons." The cartographers of those times had local knowledge of the nearshore but were warning mariners that there were uncharted areas which if entered that they were doing so at their own peril. The same can be said of modern companies that fail to understand the depth and breadth of their supply chains with all of the various participants, not the least of which are their suppliers of both goods and services.

Along with mapping, a closer examination of the supply chain provides some tangible benefits. For example, it can:

- Help protect profits, balance sheet, brand, and company valuation against the significant implication of supply chain disruptions;

---

[5] Identify risk, analyze risk, evaluate/rank risk (measure severity and frequency), treat the risk (accept, avoid, transfer, mitigate, prevent, share, exploit) and monitor and review the risk (decide which solution or solutions to use and implement).

[6] While one clearly needs to understand the risk and vulnerability of the Tier 1 or immediate suppliers, business history is replete with stories of how firms were almost cast into bankruptcy because they did not assess their Tier 2, Tier 3, or even Tier n suppliers.

- Provide greater understanding of the reliability and potential financial exposure of key suppliers;
- Quantify scenario-based financial impact figures for potential disruptions to your production;
- Review exposures and business continuity plans throughout the supply chain from tier 1 production facilities to the raw material level;
- Include a deeper analysis of the key suppliers beyond Tier 1. Note that the majority of supply chain failures do not occur at that level.

Additionally, this assessment, which military planners would label as "situational awareness," allows for the following benefits to be realized:[7]

- Recognition that suppliers may have different levels of maturity in supply chain risk management;
- Use of the same risk factors and thus both a detailed and repeatable approach;
- Identification of mitigation actions you can take to help reduce risks and estimate the potential payback on the investment;
- Benchmarking data against current best practices and integrate improvements into your standard sourcing and supplier management process;
- Presentation of supply chain exposure information in a single data model that can be combined with other financial/balance sheet modeling to fast track improvements in your business continuity plans;
- Enabling betterments in the way you factor risk into sourcing and supplier management and risk transfer decisions;
- Increased transparency in your supply chain which augments other efforts such as corporate responsibility and carbon footprint reduction.

If one now turns to cargo transport, the event that revolutionized it was the concept of containerization. However, talk about having to deal with a boatload (pardon the pun) of unintended consequences!

Throughout maritime history, cargo was essentially loaded on and unloaded from vessels piece-by-piece in what is commonly termed *break-bulk* fashion. That is until the mid-20th century when an enterprising trucking company owner from North Carolina, who often transported trailer loads of goods to a pier only to watch as stevedores had to manually handle casks, cartons, drums, or crates one at a time, wondered why one could not load an entire trailer as a single action onto the ship (Wikipedia, 2020).

---

[7] A comprehensive understanding of the risks facing investment in the firm is required to be disclosed under the Sarbanes—Oxley legislation.

The first use of containers in ocean transportation began almost 60 years ago when the brainchild of the legendary Malcom McLean came to fruition. The maiden voyage of containerized cargo took place on April 26, 1956 when 58, 35-foot "containers" were loaded aboard the *S/S Ideal-X* for a voyage between Port Newark, NJ, and Houston, TX. The use of ocean containers then moved into international commerce in the 1960s, and the industry has never looked back (Wikipedia, 2020).

As trade expanded, so did the size of the containerships carrying goods to the four corners of the globe. Measured based on container carrying capacity (a TEU or twenty-foot equivalent unit), Table 5.3 shows the dramatic growth over the past 50 years.

In conjunction, with the size of ships the number of seaports able to accommodate them has dwindled with the demand for increased channel dredging and various landside infrastructure. This has resulted in changes to trading patterns and an increased need to use feeder ships—smaller scale vessels that help disgorge these behemoth mother ships and able to serve smaller ports (Table 5.4).

Combining the larger volumes of goods on just a single ship and the limited options for ports with the probability of a disruptive event is a chilling prospect. Cargosmart (2019) tracks, among other things, ship, and port delays, and it is not unusual for a particular sailing to be several days behind schedule. This leads to accumulation of cargo at marine terminals, leaving them often stretched to maximum capacity whereby it not only represents a substantial concentration of risk with the tremendous aggregated values of goods but also the potential exposure to natural and man-made events. There is a definite seasonality for a number of trade lanes and coupled with historical weather patterns can place cargo at risk from cyclones, tsunamis, windstorms, and floods.

Table 5.3: Evolution of containership size.

Year	Vessel	Owner	TEU capacity
1968	*Encounter Bay*	P&O	1,530
1972	*Hamburg Express*	Hapag-Lloyd	2,950
1980	*Neptune Garnet*	Neptune Overseas	4,100
1984	*American New York*	United States Lines	4,600
1996	*Regina Maersk*	Maersk	6,400
1997	*Susan Maersk*	Maersk	8,600
2002	*Charlotte Maersk*	Maersk	8,890
2003	*Anna Maersk*	Maersk	9,310
2005	*Gjertrud Maersk*	Maersk	10,500
2006	*Emma Maersk*	Maersk	11,000
2012	*Marco Polo*	CMA CGM	16,000
2013	*Maersk McKinney Moller*	Maersk	18,270
2015	*MSC Oscar*	Mediterranean Shipping	19,000
2018	*OOCL Hong Kong*	Orient Overseas	21,413

Source: World Shipping Council, 2019a. Container Ship Design: 50 Years of Container Ship Growth. http://www.worldshipping.org/about-the-industry/liner-ships/container-ship-design. (Accessed October 9, 2019).

Table 5.4: Top 10 world container ports.

Port	Nation	Annual TEUs (millions)
Shanghai	China	42.0
Singapore	Singapore	36.6
Shenzhen	China	27.7
Ningbo-Zhoushan	China	26.4
Guangzhou	China	21.9
Busan	South Korea	21.7
Hong Kong	China	19.6
Qingdao	China	18.3
Tianjin	China	16.0
Jebel Ali	Dubai (UAE)	15.0

Source: World Shipping Council, 2018. Top 50 Container Ports. http://www.worldshipping.org/about-the-industry/global-trade/top-50-world-container-ports. (Accessed August 30, 2020).

Rough seas on the North Atlantic

Anyone who has been a regular importer or exporter of goods through U.S. Atlantic coast ports knows that the months of February and March each year see numerous storms producing extremely rough seas. It is not uncommon for containers to be swept overboard at these times, particularly those that are stowed on the top tier near the bow of the ship.

The growth of traffic in the major sea lanes is projected to grow as shown in Table 5.5 below (all figures are in millions of TEUs annually).

Superimposing a world map showing historical storm frequency and severity will prove the need for shippers to incorporate seasonal weather into logistics planning. Moreover, as cargo throughput is mismatched with more coming into port than what is leaving, storage facilities are taxed which can result in containers temporarily shifted to satellite yards away from the main terminal that may not offer the same level of security. Compared to the history of seaborne traffic, containerization at 65 years of age is still in its infancy. A great deal is yet to be learned, sometimes by hard and costly lessons.

Table 5.5: Container traffic on major sea routes.

Trade route	2019	2025
Transatlantic	7.6	8.7
Transpacific	28.9	36.5
US Atlantic—East Africa	8.4	10.4
Europe—East Asia	20.8	25.0
Intra East Asia	33.2	42.4
Total	163.4	206.3

Source: World Shipping Council, 2019b. Top Trade Routes (TEU Shipped). http://www.worldshipping.org/about-the-industry/global-trade/trade-routes. (Accessed October 10, 2019).

Containers and the concept of containerization came into being in an effort to minimize the physical handling of individual pieces of cargo and, thus, reduce damage and eliminate pilferage while paring manpower costs and improving vessel turnaround time in port. The containers added simplicity and productivity to cargo handling and led to the construction of purpose-built vessels, hence the containerships, specifically designed to carry them.

The anticipated labor efficiencies and economy have clearly been realized; however, the degree of cargo loss and damage, and one would add security, continues to be a function of several interrelated variables. One of those variables is the inspection of the container to ensure that it can adequately protect the goods it carries as well as being both sea- and roadworthy. Of course, security of the goods remains critical.

Although the first containerized services that was offered to shipper was port-to-port, over time this has evolved into two additional options.

Port-to-port (pier-to-pier)

This service is described as when the ocean carrier is simply providing transportation of the container from the port of loading to the port of discharge and the shipper and/or consignee has to arrange for inland transit both to and from the port. This can take place when cargo volume does not provide for a full container load or when the shipper, or the consignee, does not have the facilities to load or unload the cargo at their premises. When the shipment so requires, shippers can use the services of freight forwarders, cargo consolidators or the actual ocean carrier at a Container Freight Station (CFS) to load the goods in a container at the port of departure. Since the cargo is not in the container for the entire journey, it is subject to virtually the same degree of exposure to weather, physical handling and stowage damage and theft/pilferage as traditional break-bulk cargo. This transport method also requires deconsolidating or transloading the shipment at the destination port for inland transit.

Door-to-port/port-to-door

Combinations of Door-to-Door and Port-to-Port service are possible depending on the desires of the shipper and the facilities available. While these hybrids are more advantageous than Port-to-Port service, the cargo will still be exposed to attendant hazards during part of its journey.

Regardless of which service is selected, the integrity of the container can be breached at any point along its transit. While the entire unit can be stolen, the more likely scenario is that someone can enter the container and pilfer some of the goods or insert something surreptitiously into the cargo space. The only thing preventing this is a security seal.[8] Historically, shippers and their supply chain partners were concerned about the security of the goods in ocean containers while in transit; namely the potential for someone gaining access to the cargo space and remove items. Post-9/11 the script was flipped with now the issue being the possibility of entry in order to place something into the box. This vulnerability requires that there be clear visibility and control of the products far upstream in the supply chain.

Door-to-door (house-to-house)

The greatest benefits of containerization are realized when the shipper uses the container to carry goods directly from its premises to a customer's location. Perhaps, the only time the container will be opened en route is for Customs inspection. Reduced susceptibility to pilferage and theft and exposure to the elements are all attractive features of this service. However, the shipper accepts the additional responsibility of ensuring that its cargo is properly loaded and secured in the container. That being said, as was pointed out previously, the container will pass through several hands along its journey. To illustrate, a shipment from Asia Pacific to the US Midwest can mean cargo loaded in Vietnam can be sent to a regional mega containership hub[9] in Singapore; transported by vessel to a west coast port such as Los Angeles or Long Beach. Then after discharge taken by truck to a railhead, moved via rail (intermodal landbridge) to perhaps Chicago and then drayed the "last mile" to its final destination.

This chapter has discussed the evolution of containerized shipping including the growth of ships, expansion of ports, and what it has meant for the industry in terms of competitiveness, security, and investment. While more secure than break-bulk shipping, containerized cargo does have its limits, included with these are risks and vulnerabilities that shippers need to remain cognizant of when constructing their respective supply chain networks.

References

Boileau, J., Skow, A., 2016. Your Supply Chain at Risk: The Value of a Strong Resiliency Program. Zurich American Insurance Company. https://www.zurichna.com/knowledge/articles/2016/12/your-supply-chain-at-risk. (Accessed 2 October 2019).

CargoSmart, 2019. CargoSmart Tracking. https://www.cargosmart.ai/en/. (Accessed 10 October 2019).

---

[8] A comprehensive discussion of the various types of cargo seals and their relative advantages can be found in Chapter 6.

[9] Also referred to as a load center port.

Council of Supply Chain Management Professionals, 2020. Supply Chain Management Definitions and Glossary. https://cscmp.org/CSCMP/Educate/SCM_Definitions_and_Glossary_of_Terms.aspx. (Accessed 18 June 2020).

[The] State of Maritime Piracy, 2018. One Earth Future. Bloomfield, CO. https://stableseas.org/sites/default/files/stateofpiracy2018_0.pdf. (Accessed 30 August 2020).

[The] White House, 2012. National Strategy for Global Supply Chain Security. Department of Homeland Security, Washington, DC. https://obamawhitehouse.archives.gov/sites/default/files/national_strategy_for_global_supply_chain_security. Downloaded June 18, 2020.

Wikipedia, 2020. Malcolm McLean. https://en.wikipedia.org/wiki/Malcom_McLean. (Accessed 23 May 2020).

World Economic Forum, 2012. New Models for Addressing Supply Chain and Transport Risk. http://www.weforum.org/reports/new-models-addressing-supply-chain-and-transport-risk. (Accessed 8 October 2019).

World Shipping Council, 2018. Top 50 Container Ports. http://www.worldshipping.org/about-the-industry/global-trade/top-50-world-container-ports. (Accessed 30 August 2020).

World Shipping Council, 2019a. Container Ship Design: 50 Years of Container Ship Growth. http://www.worldshipping.org/about-the-industry/liner-ships/container-ship-design. (Accessed 9 October 2019).

World Shipping Council, 2019b. Top Trade Routes (TEU Shipped). http://www.worldshipping.org/about-the-industry/global-trade/trade-routes. (Accessed 10 October 2019).

Young, R., 2020. Physical flow of imported goods. (unpublished) PowerPoint for graduate school lecture. The Pennsylvania State University, Capital College (Penn State Harrisburg).

CHAPTER 6

Components of intermodal maritime security risk*

The container: it is just a big box, right?

Ocean containers require careful inspection to ensure no contraband has been secreted within the cargo space. Actually, it is always good practice to affix a seal on all empty containers. The best guidance on this comes from U.S. Customs and Border Protection (CBP) as part of the Customs-Trade Partnership Against Terrorism (C-TPAT) Initiative.

The following is a Seven Point Inspection Checklist to determine if the integrity of the container is compromised and/or if areas are being concealed so as to serve as possible hiding places for contraband. Fig. 6.1 depicts a typical steel 40-foot container commonly found in international service.

A detailed inspection could reveal some telltale signs of possible tampering:

- Different color material or parts appearing much newer than others.
- Unusual repairs.
- Interior repairs are visible on the outside.
- Sidewalls and ceiling produce a hollow sound when tapped.
- Vents are visible.
- Length, width, and height of the container disagree with those marked externally.
- Floor is raised and not flat.
- Locking hardware is not in good working condition.

Container doors should close completely. For the sake of good order and while not directly related to in-transit security, other complementary steps should be taken to prevent damage to the goods from physical movement such as shifting, water contact, or infestation. Essentially the goal is to only load cargo in a container that is clean, dry, odor-free, and devoid of defects.

---

* This chapter is intended to be a series of detailed explanations of where potential risk lies for the intermodal shipper. Of particular value, there are also several checklists that provide the practitioner with a guide for their tactical day-to-day activities.

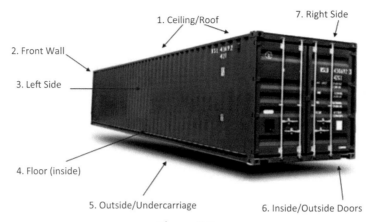

Figure 6.1

Intermodal maritime 40-foot container with seven point checklist. *Source: Customs and Border Protection, 2019a. Seven-Point Container Security Checklist. https://www.cbp.gov/sites/default/files/documents/7_pcic.pdf. (Accessed September 22, 2019).*

While this does provide some guidance to shippers, additional detail would not only assist in ensuring that the container inspection meets the C-TPAT requirements relating to the security of the cargo but also can enable detecting a structural problem or operational issues that could potentially result in damage to the contents of the container. With that in mind, we offer these steps:

(1) Know who is delivering the empty container to your facility. Prior to allowing the driver access, he/she should present government-issued photo identification.[1] Take an image of the identification for further reference.

(2) Walk around the outside of the container checking for obvious holes, punctures, or other defects. While small dents and scrapes are considered normal wear and tear, look for:

- Structural defects such as weld fractures, particularly at corner posts.
- Heavily bulged or dented side panels or corrugations.
- Deformed, fractured, or heavily corroded crossmembers on the undercarriage.
- Damaged, missing, or inadequate landing gear, lights, reflectors, and tire tread and inflation on the chassis.[2]

(3) Examine the doors and ensure that all hardware is operable. Check that the:

- Door hardware is original to the container. Examine closely the right-door inner locking bar, door handle, and locking hasp for any damage or unauthorized

---

[1] The Transportation Workers Identification Credential (TWIC) is now the common source of identification.

[2] A damaged container arriving at a container yard may potentially incur repair charges for the shipper.

modification. Make sure the handle is secured with a rivet that cannot be removed without leaving some evidence of tampering; for example, by drilling it out.

- Left-hand door cannot be opened unless the right side is opened first. There should be a steel plate (i.e., Customs plate) that overlaps the left-hand door. Inspect for any signs of bending and then restraightening such as flaked paint.
- Door hinge pins are intact and are not removable.
- Interior of the door hardware, especially the fasteners at the right-hand inner locking bars (top and bottom) and hasp are in place. There should be some tamper-evidence—the only way to remove these should result in destroying the fastener.

(4) Look inside the container. Check for:

- Any repairs that are not consistent with your external inspection.
- Evidence of false walls, floor, ceiling, or other concealed compartments (use a tape or other tool to measure the length, width, and height to make sure the dimensions are consistent with those of the type of container ordered—consult the steamship line for this information).
- Floors that are flush with the door threshold plate.

(5) Walk inside the container. Check that:

- It is clean, dry, free of any odor, and completely suitable to receive and transport your cargo.
- Doors close properly and are not bent or bowed. Check to see that the gaskets are intact and in good condition (not cut, torn, or cracked). Determine if any light enters through any undetected holes or other openings.
- Roof bows are not bent, deformed, or pulled free.
- Floor boards are not missing, buckled, or rotted.
- There are an adequate number of lashing fittings, such as pad eyes or other tie-down points, to allow for properly secured cargo.

(6) After loading. Check for:

- There are no void spaces that would allow cargo to shift during handling and transit.
- An ISO 17712/C-TPAT compliant security seal is affixed, noting the number on the shipping documents.
- The proper placard is attached if the cargo is a hazardous material.

The US government is assisting importers into the country through the Container Security Initiative (CSI), a CBP program is based on a single premise—the global trading system is more secure if containers are screened as early as possible by pushing borders and points of control to foreign ports. Underpinning this is more complete and accurate shipment information to support profiling, scanning, and screening.

The three core elements of CSI are:

- Identifying high-risk containers. CBP uses automated targeting tools to identify containers that pose a potential risk for terrorism based on advance information and strategic intelligence.
- Prescreening and evaluating containers before they are shipped. Containers are screened as early in the supply chain as possible, generally at the port of departure.
- Using technology to prescreen high-risk containers to ensure that screening can be done rapidly without impeding the flow of trade. This technology includes large-scale X-ray and gamma ray machines and radiation detection devices.

CSI is operational at 58 ports in North America, Europe, Asia, Africa, the Middle East, and Latin and Central America handling over 80% of all maritime containers set to enter the United States (CBP, 2019b).

Again, with the purpose of moving borders, the Maritime Transportation Security Act imposed the 24-Hour Rule requiring shippers to provide advance cargo declarations prior to loading. Moreover, carriers must transmit manifest information prior to arrival at a US port. Further, it eliminates the use of incomplete or vague descriptions of goods such as *Freight All Kinds* (FAK) or *Said to Contain* (STC) on shipping documents (CBP, 2004).

After the container has been selected, inspected, and sealed, the goods are now set to begin the transportation phase. However, before that the shipper needs to prepare the necessary documentation since it can be said that cargo moves on paper. From supply chain safety and security perspectives, the shipment must be properly and accurately described as misdeclarations can wreak havoc to all parties involved and, in fact, reportedly have resulted in significant casualties onboard vessels. When misdeclarations are discovered, they can also mean delays to shipments.

Seals: keeping the goods inside and intruders out

Every loaded ocean container is protected by some sort of seal. In the event of cargo theft or pilferage from a conveyance or any intrusion, the type used, how it was affixed and ultimately defeated will be the focus of the subsequent investigation. Security seals are generally passive, one-time devices used to detect tampering or entry of cargo spaces. There are numerous seal manufacturers and various types and models, any of which can be effective provided appropriate application, and proper procedures are followed. The reader is referred to Appendix B for a comprehensive glossary of seal-related terminology.

Security seal manufacturers incorporate four main features into their design:

- Tamper resistance: It should not be possible to manipulate the components of the seal without the use of tools;

- Resistance to rebuilding: The seal construction should not allow any component part of a used seal to be substituted into another seal of the same or similar design;
- Tamper-evidence: The materials used during the seal manufacturing process should ensure that once the seal has been fitted correctly to the container, any attempt to open the seal would leave visible evidence;
- Tamper-proof: *In our opinion, no seal is tamper-proof and one should be wary of any manufacturer who uses this phrase claiming otherwise.*

Manufacturing requirements can vary from company to company but generally the key criteria are pull strength, shear cutting strength, ability to maintain structural integrity during bending, and impact and in high and low temperature environments. For the more robust barrier seals, drill-resistant hardened metal bodies that contain no soft materials such as zinc are the norm.

Security seals fall into two rather broad categories: *indicative* and *barrier.* A newer development, electronic seals, can be either indicative or barrier but are coupled with radio frequency identification (RFID), Global Positioning System (GPS) or Assisted GPS technology to provide seal and conveyance integrity and location monitoring.

The selection of an appropriate security seal should not be based on cost alone. Relevant transport factors that play a part in the decision-making process include the nature of the cargo, its value and theft attractiveness, its routing and destination as well as the chosen mode of transportation. Other considerations include the duration or transit time, whether conveyance and cargo will be left unattended and, if so, for what length of time. For example, if cargo is low value and being shipped in a short, or interplant or other closed-loop transport system, then a simple, low cost *indicative* type seal will usually be suitable.

Indicative seals are designed to evidence any tampering or attempts at tampering. These are generally flat strap-type seals fabricated from flat tin or galvanized steel or plastic since strength is not a critical feature. They can be of fixed or adjustable lengths. These security seals incorporate some degree of protection but can be easily defeated with minimal time and effort, such as by hand or a simple shear or snipping tool.

For a higher value shipment or one transiting a high-risk area, the seal of choice should be one that combines greater protection with the tamper-evident characteristics of the less expensive types. Most cargo security professionals recommend the use of *barrier-type* seals for high valued loads transported over any distance. These seals are typically hardened, solid or cable alloy steel (not less than 3/16 inch thick) although they can be made from tough acrylic plastics as opposed to plated metal or polypropylene. Most have two pieces (a head and locking chamber or barrel) with self-locking mechanisms. They can be broken with bolt cutters or a specially made tool designed solely for that device. While, in fact, all seals can be removed, they largely act as a deterrent.

In the past few years, there has been a fair amount of interest in electronic security seals ("e-seals") since they can be part of a "smart" container. The electronic seal has embedded telematics. There is a covert tracking and sensing device within the seal that can be fixed to any locking aperture. While electronic seals have been used by the United States military to track/monitor military shipments, they have not yet achieved commercial traction, or widespread utilization primarily due to cost.

The main advantages of a seal are security and tamper-evidence. However, even with the most robust construction and ingenious positioning or application, security seals are still vulnerable to attack and can be successfully defeated often without detection. There are six areas of vulnerability: hasp area, rivet, vertical bar, retaining flap, retaining bracket and keeper/cam/header area. Note that perpetrators DO NOT remove the container door hinges.

The first and more common way of circumventing the seal has been by physically cutting it and then either replacing the original seal with a new seal or simply "repairing" the damaged one. Traditional metal and plastic indicative seals (designed to indicate that the seal had been tampered with) can be easily defeated. Even the barrier-type hardened models can be removed given enough time and the right tools.

There are various methods to physically attack the container by circumventing the security seal. These include:

- Cutting: This can range from the simple to more sophisticated. A power tool is employed in order to save precious time when hardened steel container latch assemblies are used. Many locations do not permit perpetrators from having the luxury of time given the possibility of security patrols or video observation.
- Ratcheting: Using pliers, the bolt seal barrel/locking mechanism is twisted and pulled at the same time in different directions. The seal will come apart but will still remain functional.
- Spinning: The pin/bullet of a bolt seal is cut just below the head and the top of the longer threaded piece so that it can be put together by screwing the two pieces together. The cut point can usually be hidden under the door hasp.
- Picking: Much like the technique for picking a lock, a pin is inserted into the seal aperture where the length of cable joins with the locking mechanism. The cable is then backed out. After the container is tampered with, it is easily reaffixed.
- Freezing: The interior or the locking mechanism is filled with water using a syringe. The mechanism is then frozen with a fire extinguisher or Freon causing the lock to retract. One method of defeating this would be to insert the 2-piece seals with the head in the down position and not the traditional upright orientation.

There is also at least one way to attack the left-hand side door, which is generally not protected in any way. The left-hand door is closed first after loading, and while the right-hand door does not overlap, there is a rubber gasket that does to provide a weather/ water seal. Also, on containers there is a Customs plate that is part of the right-hand door and is there to prevent anyone opening up the left-hand door first. Perpetrators have used a homemade device to bend the Customs plate back 90° in order to open up the left-hand door. To overcome this technique, some shippers have decided to place security seals on both the right and left doors.

As several seal manufacturers and a trade association, the International Seal Manufacturers Association (ISMA) have indicated another vexing issue facing the transportation industry is the counterfeiting of seals. Not only are these products of questionable quality but their presence raises the specter of twin or duplicate seals bearing the same identification. It is not a stretch of imagination to see the consequences.

Traditionally the market has dictated what seals and seal characteristics become de facto standards for shippers, their customers, transportation companies, and insurers. This comes down to the effectiveness of the security devices and their experience and track records. This approach may be supplanted, at least for shippers to the United States, by CBP that has established best practices for their certified containers as part of the C-TPAT program.

CBP has determined that for any seal to be C-PTAT compliant, it must meet physical and mechanical properties as set forth in ISO 17712. Seal manufacturers and vendors need to indicate which of their seals meet these requirements. Typically, the C-TPAT compliant seals will be marked with an "H" to signify they are high barrier seals and have at least an 18 mm (nearly ¾-inch) diameter shaft. Also, these seals must undergo physical testing to determine a seal's classification for strength.

There are two organizations that have developed standards for security seals: ASTM International, formerly known as the American Society for Testing and Materials, and the International Standards Organization (ISO). ASTM International,[3] through their F12.50 Subcommittee, has published standards relating to seals on classification (F83-90) and performance parameters (F1157-90). The latter entitled: "Standard Practice for Classifying the Relative Performance of the Physical Properties of Security Seals" covers pull, shear, bending, impact and temperature testing for *indicative* and *barrier* seals. A technical committee of the ISO established specifications, the aforementioned ISO 17712, for mechanical seals used to secure freight containers moving in commerce.

Although not a guarantee, implementation of the following can help prevent unauthorized entry into containers. These steps can also assist in detecting security seal or container door hardware tampering and in identifying the timing and nature of the security breach.

---

[3] See Appendix A for specific contact information.

Outbound shipments

- Seals should have legible markings that are unique to your company (However, it is not prudent to use the company name or other identifying information on the seal);
- Seals should be consecutively numbered;
- Store all seals in a controlled area to prevent unauthorized use;
- Maintain a logbook of all seal activity to facilitate seal inventory;
- Use heavy-duty barrier-type security seals that meet ISO specifications on all shipments since they provide a higher level of security with improved seal integrity;
- Use a seal device that will secure the two, right-door, vertical locking bars and protect the vulnerable rivet of the right-side door handle;
- Ensure that an employee or representative physically affixes the seal to the container. Supervisors should periodically check to ascertain that seals are being properly applied. An incorrect seal correctly fitted may provide adequate security, but a correct seal incorrectly applied will provide none;
- Note the seal number, including all alpha and numeric markings, on the shipping documentation so that seal integrity can be monitored throughout transit.

Inbound shipments

- Compare the seal number on the container at arrival with that noted on the shipping documentation;
- Ensure that receiving personnel or security representatives, not the driver, physically remove the seal. The seal should be maintained until the entire shipment has been unloaded and the contents have been verified;
- Inspect the seals, container, and container hardware for telltale signs of misuse, abuse, or tampering:
  - Seals: Pull and twist standard band seals, twist the barrel (bottom) of bolt seals (it should spin freely), and look for the residue of glue or other binder material;
  - Container: Look for obvious defects such as holes, sprung doors, and doors not properly seated;
  - Container hardware: Door handle rivets should be well anchored. Check for any differences in appearance such as a shiny rivet next to one that is heavily rusted, or one painted various colors. Door hinges should be examined for trueness and any evidence that they have been disturbed.

Thinking about your supply chain: important considerations

Arguably, the most important decision a shipper makes is choosing its transportation providers, carriers, and intermediaries, as they have care, custody, and control of your merchandise throughout transit. So, choose wisely. This selection process obviously is done prospectively, i.e., before you actually hire them but once selected, the carriers should be evaluated periodically to ensure they are fulfilling their part of the bargain.

The following is a list of criteria/requirements highlighting people, processes, and performance geared toward transportation providers. They are intentionally generic in nature and mostly North American–centric. Moreover, they can be modified to meet specific and local needs.

- *Organizational structure*: The carrier should have a dedicated point-of-contact specifically for you, a person with enough stature within their company who can not only respond to inquiries from you, but have the authority to make decisions on behalf of the carrier;
- *Professional reputation*: The carrier should be active in local, regional, national, or international trade or industry groups and be members in good standing;
- *Current customer contacts/references*: The carrier should be able to furnish a list of current customers (ask for at least three references) so that you can query them on the carrier's performance;
- *Fit*: Ideally, the carrier should be familiar with your industry and your company. However, as this is not always the case, the carrier must want to truly understand your business;
- *Financial stability*: The carrier should provide current financial data (balance sheet, income statement, etc.) contained in their Annual Report, 10-K or similar documents (Note that in the case of closely held firms such information may be difficult to obtain). Your Finance Department can use a number of short-run performance and long-term ratios, for example, acid test, debt-equity, debt-asset, and total assets turnover, to assess the carrier's ability to not only stay in business but also have the financial wherewithal to make necessary capital improvements to grow as needed to continue to serve your needs;
- *Quality of carrier staff*: The carrier should have solid preemployment screening practices and foster personnel improvements in general business and technical areas;
- *Operating philosophy*: The carrier should have a record of innovation, quality initiatives such as Continuous Improvement, and hold a current ISO 9000/1/2[4] registration. Ocean carriers and nonvessel operating common carriers (NVOCC) should be in compliance with the International Maritime Organization's (IMO), International Safety Management (ISM) Code, and International Ship and Port Facility Security (ISPS) Code. Participation in the C-TPAT, Authorized Economic Operator (AEO), or similar national supply chain security programs, although voluntary in nature, is strongly encouraged;
- *Workforce*: The carrier, whether they are union or nonunion, should have an in-force long-term labor contract. The carrier should have an acceptable history devoid of lengthy work stoppages, strikes, disputes, etc. Employee turnover rate should be at or below industry average;

---

[4] A quality standard developed and maintained by the International Standards Organization.

- *Geographical coverage*: The carrier should be able to handle traffic lanes that you need and with the transport frequency that you require;
- *Communications capability*: The carrier should have EDI (Electronic Data Interchange), satellite tracking (should cover both the tractor and the trailer), onboard computer linkage, bar coding, and other state-of-art technology. They should be able to provide ancillary services such as assistance with import/export documentation as well as Customs clearance and other related activities. In addition to real-time visibility of shipments, the carrier should proactively inform you of what is happening with your goods in transit and what, if any, changes have taken place;
- *On-time performance and target*: The carrier should meet your on-time performance target consistently;
- *Fleet size*: The carrier should have sufficient equipment of the type (e.g., dry containers, refer containers, tank containers, and chassis) that you require. This equipment should be readily available at/near the shipment point-of-origin in order to minimize subcontracting;
- *Intermodal linkages/partners*: The carrier should have partnerships with reputable intermodal transport providers in all areas where you do business. For example, they should be able to orchestrate a movement to the United States from the Pacific Rim as well as to/from mainland China, to/from Central America and any one of your worldwide markets;
- *Use of owner-operators and/or subcontractors*: The carrier should use subcontractors only when/if they provide you with prior notice and you give consent. The carrier should be responsible to ensure that use of subcontractors is minimal and that any subcontractor meets your requirements;
- *Fleet condition and maintenance*: The carrier's equipment should be periodically renewed and the average age of the equipment should be below the industry average. The carrier's maintenance schedule should meet or exceed industry standards. Trucking companies should have bona fide agreements with qualified repair facilities for emergency road service within the geographical areas they are traveling. Violation incidence and out-of-service records from the Department of Transportation (or its equivalent) can provide some clue as to how the truckers are performing where and when "the rubber meets the road." There is more information on source data below;
- *Cargo equipment inspection frequency and procedures*: The carrier's personnel should carefully inspect the structural integrity and condition of the equipment and security devices (alarms, seals, locks, etc.) to verify that they are suitable for use. Maintenance and repair shall be done on a preventative basis;
- *Experience in hauling cargo similar to yours*: They should understand your business; the carrier should have specific experience and expertise in handling your equipment and materials. The carrier should provide you with the list of products they carry, and special attention should be made to any that might pose a contamination potential to your shipments;

- *High value cargo handling and transport*: The carrier should have documented procedures in place for high value or cargo vulnerable to theft, pilferage, and hijacking. These procedures should be contained in the company's employee manual and updated periodically, but should also be auditable by you or your designated third party. The carrier should also have the physical tools to protect the high value shipments during the entire course of transit, including storage/staging periods between origin and destination;
- *Cargo security devices*: The carrier should use appropriate devices on their equipment, such as high quality seals and locks, kingpin or fifth wheel locks, and vehicle immobilizers. The carrier should also have available niche items (e.g., tracking technology sensors) that afford a greater degree on in-transit security;
- *Cargo information security*: The carrier should restrict knowledge of the identity of your cargo to those with "a need to know," to include documentation. Carrier equipment should not have markings that would indicate that they are carrying your cargo or other similarly attractive merchandise (an exception would be the appropriate use of hazardous material placards);
- *Cargo tracking*: The carrier should have the ability to provide real-time tracking/tracing of all of your shipments in their system. Ideally, they should be contacting you with updates on your shipments and advising you of any changes, issues, etc.;
- *Routing*: The carrier should offer direct routing with no stoppages en route (this also translates into more expeditious transit, and thus shorter transit times, as well as it minimizes physical handling of your cargo and the amount of time your cargo is at rest and therefore, most at risk). For example, transshipping, hub and spoke routing, and in-transit transfers at the carrier's terminals should be minimized, if not eliminated. If there must be stoppages, the carrier should be able to protect your cargo in a secure area. This guideline has to be tempered with common sense. If the cargo is high value and the anticipated transit is of long duration, the carrier should consider using a two-driver team;
- *Preemployment*: The carrier should conduct thorough background checks of all perspective employees, including direct contact with previous employers and references, and also perform periodic updating of driver records/traffic violations, criminal record search, credit and financial ratings, and other relevant data. Screening should also incorporate a prehire medical exam including drug and alcohol testing. Once a person is hired, random drug testing, even if not mandatory, is also a positive loss prevention step. Although not a preemployment issue, all truckers needing to enter a port area are required to possess a Transportation Worker Identification Credential (TWIC);
- *Testing*: The carrier should have job-specific preemployment competency testing and periodic developmental training curriculums for each category of employee that is involved in any aspect of cargo handling or transporting of your cargo. For trucking companies, each driver should pass a defensive driving course and be trained in hijack awareness and preparedness;

- *Discipline*: The carrier should have a formal written policy statement and take prompt and effective action against employees involved in cargo loss/damage or on-the-job accidents involving cargo;
- *Cargo inventory*: Carrier personnel perform a count and condition of all your shipments at each transport leg including delivery to final destination or ultimate consignee;
- *Loss/damage notification*: The carrier should immediately contact your designated representative should there be any evidence of loss or damage to a shipment. You should provide your transportation providers with the appropriate contact names and numbers. Carriers should also be in a position to assist in minimizing the extent of loss or damage through recoopering, segregating damaged from sound items and similar activities;
- *Insurance Coverage:* While the liability in most modes is established, you should ensure that any service provider transporting your goods has cargo liability limits commensurate with the value of the largest shipment anticipated. Depending on your relationship with the trucker (shipper vs. freight broker), consideration should be given to have you listed as a certificate holder/additional insured;
- *Limits of liability*: The carrier should be agreeable to negotiating a recovery rate for loss or damage that takes into account the average value per kilo of your product rather than simply relying on the terms of the standard ocean bill of lading (Carriage of Goods by Sea Act, or COGSA), or similar liability regimes. Ocean shipment bills of lading should not include foreign arbitration clauses as this may mean that any dispute must be settled overseas, making settlement more protracted, costly and unpredictable;
- *Loss and damage experience*: The carrier's actual performance is a key determinant in selection and retention;
- *Safety record and safety training for personnel*: The carrier should have an exemplary safety record as well as provide recurrent safety training to their staff.[5] For North American trucking companies, check sources such as the Federal Motor Carrier Safety Administration rating (FMCSA), other national transportation safety data, and/or Compliance Safety Accountability scores as well as Equasis, the Chemical Distribution Institute, for ocean-going vessels.

This is a dynamic list and should be revisited regularly. Also, one may wish to develop numerical ratings for each carrier by "weighting" each criteria/requirement depending on its importance to your firm. This may be a useful approach when attempting to choose among several potential providers.

Securing the global supply chain is integral to maintaining the stability of the world's economy and any disruption either accidental or malicious can have major implications. Companies, large and small, play a part and should work to promote the efficient and

---

[5] See also First Observer at https://www.firstobserver.com.

secure movement of legitimate goods as well as foster a global supply chain that is resilient to both natural and man-made disruptions.

We advocate solutions that combine physical and procedural controls. We also endorse a layered approach to cargo loss control—one that factors in (1) Threat (identifying potential adverse events); (2) Vulnerability (identifying weaknesses in present processes and procedures); (3) Criticality (identifying and evaluating important operations and/or assets); and (4) Risk (determining the likelihood, severity, and impact of an adverse event) assessments. The best approach is akin to one adopted in physical security starting at the perimeter and moving inwards (aka layered defense). Another term for this tactic is "Defense in Depth": Deter, Deflect, Detect, Delay, and Defeat.

Some final words of advice to shippers

There can be no substitute for information because it forms the basis for management action. Therefore, there are a range of topics that practitioners need to not only be familiar with, but update on an ongoing basis:

- Your supply chain environment versus assuming, guessing, or worse yet not caring;
- Transport infrastructure (roads, rail, air, and sea), handling equipment, and regulatory hurdles both at origins and destinations versus simply delegating/abrogating this to a third party;
- Door-door (house-house) shipments versus pier-pier or any hybrid arrangements that necessitate the breakdown of goods prior to, during, or after the actual ocean transport segment;
- Direct routing versus transshipment;
- Direct transit versus en route stoppages in the hub and spoke environment;

The difference between all-water service versus intermodal/landbridge cross-country moves.

On dock railcar loading versus truck moves miles inland:

- Partnerships with carriers and intermediaries versus simple business transactions;
- Continuous monitoring of supply chain partners and carrier performance versus annual rate review;
- Hired transport carriers versus subcontractors assigned by someone else;
- Secure cargo facilities versus open gates, open dock doors, open information;
- Expedited Customs clearance versus added dwell time at cargo terminals;
- The importance of limiting the number of people with knowledge of your shipment versus broadcast messaging;
- Accountability during cargo handoffs versus undocumented transfers;
- Real-time tracking versus after-the-fact tracing.

If there is one point that this chapter seeks to convey, it needs to be that the risks producing vulnerabilities for any supply chain are constantly changing as the underlying technologies, legal environment, cultural norms, political landscape, and macroeconomic conditions continue to evolve. Remaining dutifully cognizant is neither an activity for amateurs nor those thinking it is only part-time. Moreover, it is an endeavor for the constantly curious as well as enjoying constant variation to the daily routine.

Appendix A: directory for standards associations for seals

There are numerous manufacturers of security seals that publish technical specifications as well as guidelines and recommended practices relating to the selection and application of these devices. Contact information for the two major standards organizations:

ASTM International:	100 Barr Harbor Drive
	P.O. Box C700
	West Conshohocken, PA 19428-2959;
	610-832-9500 or www.astm.org
International standards	1, ch de la Voie-Creuse CP 56,
Organization (ISO):	CH-1211 Geneva 20, Switzerland
	Ph.: 41-22-7490111
	Fax: 41-22-7333430
	www.iso.org

Appendix B: glossary of terms regarding seals

Audit trail	The checking and recording of seal numbers and characteristics during transit.
Barrier seal	A seal with indicative features combined with high tensile strength.
Bolt seal	A two-piece seal composed of a male pin and a female locking body.
Electronic reusable seal	A multiuse two-part seal using electronic protocol to generate a new seal number each time it is used.
Indicative seal	Normally a low strength seal designed to leave evidence of attempted removal and refitting.
Mechanical reusable seal	A multiuse, two-part seal using mechanical principles to generate a new seal number for each time used.
Metal seal	A seal fabricated from tinplate or other similar material.
Plastic seal	A seal made from thermoplastic materials.
Pull through seal	A seal with a variable length that allows the one end of the seal to be pulled through the closure to varying lengths.
Seal numbers	The unique alphanumeric code that is applied by the seal manufacturer or are generated by electronic or mechanical means. This number is used to track the seal during transit.
Strap seal	Also known as the strip seal. A seal designed with a metal or plastic strip as one of its main construction features.

Substitution	Removing the original security seal and replacing with another one.
Tampering	Compromising of the security seal after it has been applied.
Tamper-evident	The property of a security seal that provides proof of evidence that the seal integrity has been compromised.
Tamper-proof	A seal that claims it can effectively resist tampering.
Tamper-resistant	A seal that can resist attack and reassembly.
Two-piece seal	A seal that consists of two separate parts.
Variable length seal	A one-piece seal that provides variable length sealing options through one fixed locking head.

References

Customs and Border Protection, 2004. Required Advance Electronic Presentation of Cargo Information. https://www.cbp.gov/bulletins/37genno52.pdf. (Accessed 22 September 2019).

Customs and Border Protection, 2019a. Seven-Point Container Security Checklist. https://www.cbp.gov/sites/default/files/documents/7_pcic.pdf. (Accessed 22 September 2019).

Customs and Border Protection, 2019b. CSI: Container Security Initiative. https://www.cbp.gov/border-security/ports-entry/cargo-security/csi/csi-brief. (Accessed 22 September 2019).

CHAPTER 7

Threats from terrorists and other violent nonstate actors

James J.F. Forest

University of Massachusetts, Lowell, MA, United States

There are several avenues through which the strategic objectives of violent nonstate actors could intersect the intermodal shipping system. While we must keep in mind the vast differences in capabilities and intentions among terrorist networks, insurgents, local gangs, and transnational organized crime, some of the most common themes and scenarios in this realm of threat analysis include:

- Hijacking valuable cargo for monetary ransom or with the intent to sell the stolen goods on the black market;
- Utilizing containers to smuggle illicit goods like weapons, drugs, counterfeit products, etc. to a location where other members of the criminal or terrorist network can take possession of them;
- Attacking freight containers, trucks, trains, and ships mainly to damage the economy of a particular country;
- Utilizing containers for human trafficking, something that transnational organized crime networks (particularly those based in Asia) have done, but not terrorist groups;
- A terrorist-oriented "Trojan Horse" scenario involving potential weapons of mass destruction and their components.

More than 420 million containers move around the globe by sea every year, transporting 90% of the world's cargo (Container Control). Some of these containers are being used to smuggle drugs, weapons, counterfeit goods people, as will be described later in this chapter. In fact, it seems more likely for violent nonstate actors to engage in this kind of activity than to directly attack maritime targets. In fact, given the wide range of possible scenarios, there is only a limited history of violent nonstate actors attacking the intermodal container supply chain. As described later in this chapter, these have included direct assaults against cargo ships, as well as instances of hijacking ships and stealing cargo. Further, the historical record indicates that these attacks have been motivated far more often by criminal motives than by terrorism. The bottom line up front is that the threat to

Intermodal Maritime Security. https://doi.org/10.1016/B978-0-12-819945-9.00004-6

intermodal maritime security is far more likely to cause disruption than death and destruction and is increasingly focused on compromising containers for illicit purposes.

Of course, it is worth noting that violent nonstate actor attacks against intermodal shipping is not solely a maritime security problem. Trucks, trains, warehouses, etc. have also been attacked periodically. For example, container trucks have been attacked with arson and automatic gunfire in India and Pakistan, while containers of bananas and other produce have been repeatedly attacked in the Philippines by a terrorist group known as the New People's Army (NPA). Throughout the past half-century, hundreds of trains—mostly in Southeast Asia, Africa, and Latin America—have been attacked by terrorist groups with bombs, arson, and sabotaged rails leading to the loss of lives and cargo. Attacks against warehouses, truck depots, rail tracks, stations, and other infrastructure elements can certainly cause major disruptions and delays in the intermodal transportation system (Global Terrorism Database).

For the purposes of this *Intermodal Maritime Security* book, the discussion in this chapter will focus primarily on the maritime dimensions of the threat posed by terrorists and organized crime networks. During the past 2 decades, thousands of maritime vessels large and small—including hundreds involved in the intermodal shipping industry—have been the victim of piracy and armed robbery. Cargo ships, passenger ferries, private sailboat charters, and even naval warships have been attacked by both terrorist and criminal networks. Evidence indicates these attacks have been motivated by profit-seeking objectives far more often than by political ideologies.

But while the threat to maritime targets is real, this chapter highlights the need to keep a balanced perspective in our security policies and practices. Although there have been a number of prominent incidents, as described in this chapter, terrorist groups and other violent nonstate actors recognize that there are far more land-based targets to choose from, and which would be considerably easier to attack, in order to achieve their strategic objectives. Further, research on the decision-making of these kinds of organizations reveals a tendency to avoid unnecessary risks, conserve resources, maximize the likelihood of success, and minimize the chances of failure. From that perspective, the long-term investments made in strengthening the security of the intermodal maritime shipping industry will continue to play an important role, though nonmaritime intermodal assets require equal—if not greater—attention.

Maritime terrorism: a brief overview

When examining the terrorist threat to intermodal maritime security, we must first acknowledge the strategic nature of terrorist networks. Research indicates that clandestine organizations tend to be conservative when making decisions about tactics and targeting, particularly when there is high uncertainty about the potential benefits versus the costs involved (Crenshaw). They are particularly risk averse when it comes to decisions about managing and deploying their resources (which are always limited), and their leaders are highly concerned about return on investment. In this regard, terrorist groups are not much different from other organizations. Thus, our threat analysis benefits from understanding the challenges faced by these organizations, and the strategies they use to overcome those challenges.

For example, compared to planning terrorist attacks against unprotected land-based targets—which are more plentiful and much easier to attack, from the standpoint of logistical concerns like target surveillance, timing, escape routes, etc.—maritime targets pose significantly higher levels of difficulty and potential complications that must be ironed out. Additionally, specific skills are required to successfully attack maritime targets. Perpetrators must be adequately trained to navigate boats of various sizes and speed, and able to carry out basic operations such as boarding, subduing a crew, and taking over a ship. Before launching an attack, the more sophisticated pirates would want to have some idea of the ship's manifest, cargo value, skills of the crew and captain, and so forth. Without adequate intelligence gathering and analysis capabilities, they are unlikely to identify and infiltrate key areas of vulnerability in order to achieve their strategic objectives undetected. Violent nonstate actors cannot afford to blindly attack a ship on the open seas, hoping to cash in on being able to ransom some high value cargo. It could very well be a ship carrying industrial waste or scrap metal. Any risks associated with attacks against the intermodal maritime container supply chain must be worth the potential rewards. These and other layers of complexity increase the chances of failure for the terrorists—as any organizational leader knows, the more complexity a plan involves, the higher the chances will be of something not going according to plan.

Overall, when analyzing the dynamic threat to intermodal maritime security, we must acknowledge that the more sophisticated terrorist and criminal networks are largely "thinking enemies," always evolving and adapting to their environment (DHS National Small Vessel, 2007). Further, violent nonstate actors have substantial flexibility in choosing their targets and attack methods, and they are likely to be opportunistic in taking advantage of perceived security vulnerabilities of a target from which they could gain a strategic or financial benefit. This is a key reason why, compared to other targets of terrorism—like subway systems, commuter railways, bus terminals, airplanes, and airports—attacks against ships and seaports have been comparatively rare, representing only a small percentage of terrorist attacks in the last half-century. As of March 2020, the Global Terrorism Database—managed by the National Consortium for the Study of Terrorism and Responses to Terrorism—provides details of more than 190,000 terrorist incidents since 1970. Of the incidents recorded in the database, 499 (0.26%) were against maritime targets (Global Terrorism). Similarly, an earlier study by the RAND Corporation found that out of 40,126 terrorist cases between the year 1968 and 2007, only 136 (0.34%) were against maritime targets (Stepanova, 2008).

It is important to keep this in mind, not to diminish or underappreciate the threat to maritime security, which is certainly real, but to keep that threat in perspective. Surely, as a brief review of this historical record demonstrates, a few of these incidents have sometimes been quite dramatic and impactful. For example, the hijacking of an Italian cruise ship in October 1985 highlighted the potential threat of maritime terrorism. Before this incident—from the late 1960s through the early 1980s—terrorist attacks and hostage-taking incidents became all too frequent, with targets including airports, airplanes, a meeting of OPEC leaders in Vienna, and even the 1972 Summer Olympics in Munich, Germany. But, this was the first major incident involving a passenger cruise ship.

The *Achille Lauro,* a vessel owned by the Italian government, was a 23,629-ton cruise ship that was 643-feet long, capable of serving 900 passengers, having two swimming pools, a movie theater, and a discotheque (Anderson and Spagnolo, 2007). Some 748 passengers had boarded the ship at Genoa on October 3, 1985 for a 12-day Mediterranean cruise, with calls at Naples, Syracuse, Alexandria, Port Said, Ashdod (Israel), Limassol (Cyprus), and Rhodes (Greece). Passengers included tourists from about 20 nations, including, Belgium, Brazil, Britain, France, Holland, Italy, Spain, Switzerland, the United States, and West Germany (Anderson and Spagnolo, 2007).

Also boarding the ship that day were four members of Force 17, a faction of the Palestinian group Fatah, who carried with them Soviet-made Kalashnikov automatic rifles, grenades, and detonators—all in their uninspected baggage (Tagliabue, 1985). Research about this incident later describe surprisingly lax security measures on the ship. Only a passport was required; there were no checks of luggage, and very little observation of persons embarking other than to ensure they were paid passengers (Anderson and Spagnolo, 2007). The terrorists boarded the ship with passports issued from Norway, Argentina, and Portugal (Jenkins and John, 1988). On the fifth day of the cruise, October 7th, a majority of the passengers disembarked at Alexandria, Egypt, for a tour of the Pyramids, from which they would journey overnight by bus and rejoin the ship the next day at Port Said in order to continue the cruise. It was at that point—with only 97 passengers remaining on board, along with 350 members of the crew—that the terrorists launched their attack, storming into the dining room, firing their weapons into the air to frighten and subdue the passengers. Next, they ordered the captain of the ship to head for the port of Tartus, Syria, warning that any attempts by him or the crew to disobey their orders would result in harm to the passengers they now held hostage. They also radioed their demands in the name of the Palestinian Liberation Front for the release of 50 Palestinian prisoners in Israel. The ship's transponders were then turned off, allowing it to blend into the busy sea lanes of the Mediterranean. Thus, in spite of extensive tracking efforts by the United States, Egypt, Italy, Great Britain, and Israel, it disappeared for much of the next 36 hours (Anderson and Spagnolo, 2007).

During the next several hours, Jewish passengers were separated from the others; two were beaten, and one—Leon Klinghoffer, an elderly wheelchair-bound man from the United States—was killed and thrown overboard. As the ship approached Tartus, the Syrian authorities refused them permission to enter the port. The terrorists then ordered the captain back to Port Said, while Egyptian authorities contacted the ship and began negotiations. Eventually, Egyptian and Italian authorities agreed to grant the hijackers' demands of safe passage out of Egypt with no prosecution in exchange for their freeing all the hostages and their surrendering the ship, but only on the condition that no one had been harmed. The captain, unaware that a passenger had been killed and others assaulted, gave his assurance to the authorities that all passengers and crew were safe and unharmed, following which a boat dispatched by the Egyptians was used to take the terrorists and their weapons off to a destination unknown (Anderson and Spagnolo, 2007).

In the end, this incident was recorded as one of the many failed hostage-taking attempts by terrorists that occurred during this period of time. Notably, the tactic of hijacking a cruise ship was not replicated by other terrorist groups, who most likely realized it would be much easier logistically to grab and hold hostages at airports, airplanes, public venues, and other such targets. Meanwhile, passenger ships have also been attacked by terrorists using other methods. For example, in 1998, the Abu Nidal group was responsible for the bombing of a Greek day-excursion ship—the *City of Poros*—that killed nine passengers. Terrorists belonging to the Egyptian Al-Gamaa al-Islamiyya (also known as the Islamic Group) attacked cruise ships along the Nile River on four occasions from 1992 to 1994 (Sinai, 2006). On February 25, 2000, the Moro Islamic Liberation Front carried out a bomb attack against the passenger ferry *Our Lady Mediatrix* off the coast of the Philippines, killing 40 people and injuring 100 others. And in a similar type of incident, the jihadist-linked Abu Sayyaf Group carried out a bombing of the *Superferry 14* as it left Manila Bay on February 27, 2004, which killed 116 people.

Naval warships and facilities have also been targeted by terrorists. On January 3, 2000, the U.S. Navy destroyer *USS The Sullivans* (a ship named after the five Sullivan brothers who lost their lives on a ship sunk by Japan in WWII) was docked in the port of Aden, Yemen, when a terrorist cell of al-Qaeda members tried to carry out a suicide boat attack. However, their skiff was overloaded with explosives and sank shortly after leaving shore, thwarting the plot. But then on October 12, 2000—having assessed and corrected their earlier mistakes—the same tactic was used in the same location to attack the U.S. Navy destroyer *USS Cole*. The blast killed 17 sailors, injured 38 others, and blew a 40-foot hole in the port side of the ship (Beitler, 2007). Less than 2 weeks later, on October 23, 2000, four armored boats packed with explosives entered the Sri Lankan Trincomalee Naval facility at night, killing 24 people (including the attackers), destroying one ship and damaging another. Pakistani naval facilities were attacked by al-Qaeda operatives in 2009, and again in 2011 by members of the Pakistani Taliban (Naval HQ Foiled, 2009). A naval facility in the port of Derna, Libya, was bombed in June 2014, and the Yemeni Coast Guard base at al-Mukalla was attacked by three car bombs in May 2016 (Navy Inside the Port, 2014).

On November 7, 2000, the Palestinian group Hamas attempted a maritime terrorism attack against an Israeli patrol boat, but the suicide bomber exploded before reaching his target. Similarly, on November 23, 2002, a pair of suicide bombers from the Palestinian Islamic Jihad attempted to attack an Israeli Coast Guard patrol boat off the northern shore of the Gaza Strip. They had rigged a fishing boat to look normal, and then attracted the patrol's attention by entering an area where fishing was prohibited. However, as the patrol boat approached their vessel, they detonated their explosives prematurely, resulting in only minor wounds to four of the Israelis (Lorenz, 2007). And in 2002, Singapore foiled a terrorist plot in 2002 to hit U.S. naval vessels visiting the South China Sea using a small boat rigged with explosives (Piracy and Maritime Crime, 2010). The challenges posed by such a tactic are well-known. These small boats can duck under surface radar and are difficult to see from a distance in choppy seas. They can move around easily and dodge fire from a vessel's weapons. When such boats are packed with explosives and piloted by trained crews, they can become suicide torpedoes that are nearly impossible to stop.

While these attacks against passenger ships and military vessels have been dramatic and tragic, the much more frequent type of terrorist attack has been against commercial maritime vessels, as described in the next section of this chapter. However, the intentions behind those attacks differ. Few are instances of terrorism or destruction, while most are forms of piracy and criminality that just happen to be carried out by terrorist group members. This is where the real threat to intermodal maritime security is found.

Terrorist threats to intermodal maritime security

As noted earlier, physical attacks against specific elements of the intermodal container supply chain—including containers, ships, railways, trucks, ports, etc.— can lead to system disruptions and destruction or loss of transported cargo. As a result, significant investments have been made throughout the past several decades to prevent or deter such attacks, although these have some impact on operational costs. As a recent professional trade magazine noted:

"Increased security measures, while intended to mitigate the risk of additional attacks, have disrupted the typical flow of cargo, especially for cross-border shipments. These additional procedures often have slowed the movement of freight and increased shipping costs, and companies have frequently responded by rerouting cargo or modifying shipping arrangements, further driving up costs … Attempts to tamper with international cargo shipments can compromise the integrity of the load or result in the seizure or destruction of goods by customs authorities. When companies have to unexpectedly divert or reroute shipments, the costs can reach massive figures". (Global Supply Chain, 2017)

Thankfully, when looking specifically at the maritime dimensions of this threat, the historical record indicates only a very small number of significant terrorist attacks, including bombings, arson, and armed assaults. Examples include the 1973 bombing of the 573-ton transport freighter *Mereghan II*, originally from The Bahamas, while it awaited cargo loading at a dock in Miami. In a call to the news media, a man who identified himself as a spokesman for a Cuban liberation group in Miami said the action was directed against the Government of The Bahamas in retaliation for the murder of Cuban nationals (Jenkins, 1983). Similarly, in 1976, a Soviet cargo ship docked at Port Elizabeth, New Jersey, was damaged by a bomb apparently planted by an anti-Castro refugee group. No group took responsibility for blowing up a Lebanese cargo ship at the port of Tyre in 1982. In 1983, members of the Provisional Irish Republican Army seized a British cargo ship off the coast of Northern Ireland, and blew it up—after casting its crew adrift in a lifeboat (Incidents are recorded in Jenkins, 1983). More recent examples include the 2016 attack against the Iranian cargo ship *MV-Jouya-8*, in which seven crew members were killed by a rocket fired by unknown assailants off the coast of Yemen.

Other significant attacks against commercial maritime vessels—though not part of the intermodal supply system—include the October 2001 coordinated suicide attack by Tamil Tiger separatists against the *MV Silk Pride*, an oil tanker which was carrying more than 650 tons of diesel and kerosene to the port of Jaffna, in northern Sri Lanka. The attackers used five boats in the attack. One rammed the tanker, triggering an explosion on board, and three sailors died in the attack (Tamil Tigers Claim, 2001). A year later, in October 2002, an explosives-laden boat slammed into the French oil tanker *MV Limburg* in the port of Ash Shihr, off the coast of Yemen, splitting the vessel's hull. At the time of the blast, which killed one crew member and sent more than 90,000 barrels of Iranian crude oil pouring into the Gulf of Aden, the *Limburg* was picking up a pilot to guide it into the terminal (Tanker Blast, 2002). Similarly, in August 2010, the Japanese supertanker *M. Star* was attacked by a suicide boat bomb as it passed through the Strait of Hormuz, though it resulted in only limited damage (Robert, 2010).

There have also been some indications that terrorists may be looking for ways to use ships as weapons. For example, on March 26, 2003, armed hijackers commandeered the chemical tanker *Dewi Madrim* off the coast of Sumatra, Indonesia (Pirates Board, 2003). They had approached in the dark using a high-powered speedboat, and using ropes and grappling hooks, the team of approximately a dozen men quickly swarmed aboard. Armed with machine guns and machetes, they surprised and overpowered the crew, disabled the ship's radio, took the helm, and steered the vessel, altering course and speed, for about an hour. Then, they left in their speedboats, taking with them some cash, equipment, and technical documents, and the captain and first officer, who were held hostage for some time (Baumann, 2007).

Some analysts believe that the *Dewi Madrim* incident could have been a training run for terrorists or other violent actors seeking to acquire the skills to hijack a large vessel and use it for various means. For example, a hijacked ship's cargo, crew, or passengers could provide criminals and terrorist with negotiation leverage, or even a human shield if the intent is to pilot the ship at full speed into a land-based target like a bridge support column or a public wharf (a maritime version of the 9/11 attacks which converted commercial airplanes into guided weapons). There is also the possibility that a terrorist group would seek to destroy or disable ships in order to cause economic distress to their target countries. Bringing just a modest amount of explosives on board a captured vessel, the terrorists could choose to blow up the drive shaft in order to disable the ship or even destroy part of the hull from within and sink it.

There is also the possibility that terrorists could seek to hijack a supertanker transporting liquefied natural gas (LNG), with the intention of detonating it near a port terminal or harbor. To describe the potential impact of such an attack, experts point to the December 6, 1917 explosion that literally destroyed Halifax Harbor, Nova Scotia, when the French munitions carrier *Mont Blanc* collided with the merchant ship *Imo*. The resulting explosion killed over 1900 people and injured 900 more (Glass, 2004). This threat is compounded by the fact that in some coastal areas there are residential areas alongside the narrow channels and canals that some LNG tankers routinely navigate. No indications of such a plot have actually materialized in real life. But similar scenarios, described below, have envisioned a cargo ship being used to deliver a weapon of mass destruction (WMD) or its precursor components to a target country.

The Trojan Horse Scenario

Significant concern throughout the intermodal maritime shipping industry has focused on the "Trojan Horse Scenario," in which terrorist networks co-opt various elements of the intermodal transportation chain for their own lethal purposes. Hypothetically, terrorists could bribe, extort, or ideologically inspire individuals working within the system—for example, at a cargo warehouse, a customs inspection station, a shipping company, etc.—enabling the terrorist group to transport whatever they want from point of origin to eventual destination. Portrayals of this scenario often envision the most lethal outcomes possible. For example, from a U.S. perspective, the "Trojan Horse Scenario" refers to the notion that terrorists could somehow utilize the intermodal shipping system to transport chemical, biological, radiological, or nuclear (CBRN) weapons (or precursor materials and technologies) from overseas to the United States in support of a WMD terrorist attack against the homeland.

As these scenarios unfold, the idea is that an ordinary-looking shipping container would contain something undetected that would be transported legally through the intermodal transportation system. The shipping manifest would indicate something completely different and harmless was inside the container. Some scenarios even envision how an entire container could be "hijacked" or repurposed to suit the terrorist group's objectives. The container would then conceivably travel by rail, ship, and truck until it reaches its final destination, at which point another individual acting on behalf of the terrorist group would take delivery of the item(s). And from that point, any number of potential terrorist attacks could unfold.

Various books, movies, and television shows all feature some variation of this scenario. However, there are many faulty assumptions that are too often ignored when relying on these fictional scenarios to depict real-world possibilities. The first and most fault-ridden assumption is that terrorists would even need to do such a thing. The amount of precursor materials for CBRN weapons already available within the United States is truly staggering. Some are well-protected and secure, others not so much, offering an array of local opportunities for the terrorists to secure those materials locally.

In a brief essay published in a 2000 issue of *Chemical Engineering News*, James Tour—a well-known organic chemist at Rice University—described how his secretary was able to order and receive without difficulty all the chemicals needed to make Sarin, along with its nerve agent cousins Soman and GF (James, 2000). Chemical agents can be manufactured using 40-year-old production technologies and synthetic methods that have been published in publicly available scientific literature (Centers for Disease Control). Most of these agents are made from chemicals which have peaceful industrial applications. For example, Chlorine is a fairly common chemical found in industrialized societies, where it is used for a broad range of applications from municipal sewage treatment plants to plastics and other industries.

Further, the potential WMD threat is not limited to the repurposing of industrial chemicals. In 1981, cult members working at the Rajneeshee compound in Oregon obtained samples from a diagnostic kit of the Salmonella bacterium, a common cause of food poisoning, and cultivated the agent using their medical clinic's laboratory glassware. Then, they sprinkled it on salad bars around the area, causing hundreds of local residents to become seriously ill (WMD Terrorism and Forest, 2012). In March 1998, authorities at a Greensboro, North Carolina hospital, reported that 19 small tubes of cesium, meant for use in cancer treatment, had been stolen. In 2001, seven letters laced with spores of Bacillus anthracis (an organism that causes the anthrax disease) were mailed from New Jersey to news agencies in New York and Florida, and to Senate offices in Washington, DC. Five Americans were killed and 17 were sickened in what has been called "the worst biological attacks in U.S. history" (Anthrax Investigation). These and other incidents highlight the fact that the WMD terrorism threat faced by the United States has far more often had domestic origins, not foreign.

This oft-repeated assumption of "the foreign terrorist threat" continues to plague many threat analyses in politics and business and is often based on a nationalistic and prejudiced view of "others." Surely, it is assumed, it would be easier for terrorists and criminals to acquire CBRN materials in other countries than here in the homeland. Surely, it is assumed, the insider threat problem regarding access to WMD is far more likely—especially in a so-called "Muslim country"—than it is here in the United States. Surely, it is assumed, the largest and most serious terrorism threat to the United States involves foreigners, not U.S. citizens. And yet the facts do not support these assumptions. Instead, the data show that the overwhelming majority of terrorist attacks in any country, including the United States (Michael and McGarrity, 2019), have been carried out by citizens of that country, not by foreigners (Global Terrorism). Further, the predominant mode of operation in these terrorist attacks has been to utilize weapons—guns and explosives, for example—acquired locally, not from a foreign entity. And of course, the United States is not (and has never been) among the top 10 countries in which terrorist attacks occur (Dominic Dudley, 2019).

Additionally, as explained earlier, we have to account for the strategic decision-making of terrorist networks. A significant, complicated attack involving a WMD would necessarily involve careful strategic planning in order to minimize risks and maximize return on the group's limited resources. Thus, instead of all the risky challenges of transporting something undetected from one country to another, the far easier (and likely more successful) plan would be to steal those materials locally, often with the help of an ideologically inspired employed at a facility where such materials are stored. The terrorist group would then simply develop the weapon closer to the target that they intend to attack with it.

Worst-case "Trojan Horse" scenarios include smuggling a nuclear bomb aboard a cargo ship and then detonating it near a populated area or critical infrastructure, like a bridge or seaport, in the destination country. The impacts of such an attack would be surely be severe—and yet to date, no credible plot to do so has ever been reported. In fact, the consensus among nuclear weapons experts, terrorism experts, and many others is that the likelihood of terrorists acquiring and using a functional nuclear weapon is extremely low. And while it would be easier to acquire the components for a radiological dispersal device

(RDD, also called a "dirty bomb," which contains both regular explosives and radioactive material), the likelihood of terrorists doing this is very low as well. This underscores another faulty assumption built into these "Trojan Horse" scenarios: the notion that terrorist groups actually *want* to use WMD to attack their enemies. The historical facts do not support this assumption any more than the others.

In fact, of the thousands of terrorist groups that have come and gone over the past several hundred years, only a tiny fraction of them have shown any indication of interest in CBRN weapons of any kind. Further, only a handful of them have succeeded, or come close to succeeding, in using those weapons effectively. As John Parachini observed, even the rare incidents that involved the use of these kinds of weapons have hardly threatened mass destruction (Parachini, 2003). Further, reflecting the point made earlier, these rare incidents—like Aum Shinrikyo's attack on the Tokyo subways using Sarin nerve agent, or the Tamil Tigers use of chlorine against troops in Sri Lanka—have all been domestic in origin and target orientation. Meanwhile, some of the largest and most well-known terrorist groups have never sought—nor shown any interest in seeking—CBRN weapons. Examples include Hezbollah, Hamas, PIRA, ETA, FARC, PKK, and so forth. Former leaders of al-Qaeda have declared an interest in acquiring WMD but have failed to do so in over 30 years of existence (Rolf Mowatt-Larsen, 2010).

In recent years, the Islamic State is the only terrorist group to have successfully crossed the WMD threshold, using rudimentary chemical weapons against dozens of targets in Iraq and Syria, their primary region of operations. And yet, of the many Islamic State–inspired (or directly orchestrated) terrorist attacks outside that region (including Europe and the United States), none have involved WMD. Further, no known significant WMD terrorism plots—thwarted by authorities or simply unsuccessful due to the terrorist group's lack of capabilities—have been reported this decade. The culmination of all these facts lead some experts to suggest that the threat of WMD terrorism is largely inflated (John Mueller et al., 2012). To succeed in a WMD attack, a terrorist group would have to overcome a number of technical, tactical, strategic, and operational challenges—all requiring advanced levels of knowledge and skills among the group's members (Forest, 2012).

Adding to this are the many challenges associated with successfully compromising a cargo container, while governments (and private shipping companies) worldwide are clearly aware of the WMD terrorism threat associated with intermodal maritime security and are responding accordingly. The Container Security Initiative (described in this volume) plays a prominent role here, through bilateral partnerships with foreign authorities to identify high-risk cargo containers originating at ports throughout the world before they are loaded on vessels destined for the United States (Container Security). Electronic screening of shipping data using an Automated Targeting System is employed to detect anomalies and ensure the optimal deployment of inspection assets for containers arriving at U.S. ports. The data needed to conduct this screening are acquired in sufficient time because of the enforcement, since February of 2003, of a 24 hours rule that requires the submission of manifest data 24 hours before a container is loaded aboard a ship in a foreign port.

Similarly, the Container Control Program was launched jointly by the United Nations Office on Drugs and Crime (UNODC) and the World Customs Organization (WCO) to assist governments at selected seaports in minimizing the risk of shipping containers being exploited for illicit drug trafficking, transnational organized crime, and other forms of black market activity (Container Control). And while they rarely get the recognition they deserve, a critical role in maritime and port security is played by members of the many dockworker's unions (like the International Longshoreman's Association), long-haul truckers associations, railway engineers, and millions of other nongovernmental workers who serve as the eyes and ears that notice something suspicious and then report it to the authorities (Maritime Suspicious).

Meanwhile, we must ensure that focusing our attention on the intermodal maritime shipping dimension of this threat does not blind us to other possible threat scenarios. For example, according to a report by the U.S. Department of Homeland Security, it is equally plausible that a WMD (or the CBRN materials needed to build such a weapon) could be loaded on board a fishing boat or a recreational boat that transports it to the target virtually undetected (DHS National Small Vessel, 2007). Thus the nature of this threat lies far beyond the issue of securing elements of the intermodal container supply chain. Rather, the most effective response to this kind of threat requires broad international intelligence cooperation, particularly when identifying the capabilities and intentions of specific terrorist entities, and then exacerbating the inherent challenges and obstacles they would face in any kind of WMD-related endeavor.

To sum up, the Trojan Horse scenario may make for compelling Hollywood screenplays, but the cold hard evidence indicates that most terrorist groups really have no interest in weapons of mass destruction at all. This makes sense when we unpack the risk-averse nature of terrorist groups: if they were to invest the necessary resources to acquire weapons of mass destruction (or precursor materials), it would be too risky to transport those by means that are out of their direct control. Further, the combination of effective intelligence gathering and analysis, public—private collaboration on threat analysis and mitigation, and the use of technology to detect potential CBRN materials in cargo containers all pose elevated risks for any terrorist group who might even consider this type of operation. So while it would be foolish to dismiss the threat outright, members of the intermodal maritime container supply chain must view this type of scenario in the context of other, more likely—and evidence-based—kinds of potential terrorist attacks and respond accordingly.

Other dimensions of the terrorist threat to maritime security

Obviously, the threat to intermodal maritime security must be viewed in context of broader maritime threats. For example, instead of trying to orchestrate a complicated hostage-taking incident or WMD attack, a terrorist group may seek to cause economic disruption for a target country by disabling or sinking a vessel, although a significant amount of explosives would be needed to do so (Greenberg et al., 2006). A particularly impactful attack of this nature could target one of the well-known maritime choke points like the Strait of Malacca, where a 500-mile corridor separating Malaysia from Indonesia is used by several hundred ships each day. Similarly, the Strait of Hormuz, which connects the Arabian Sea and the Persian Gulf, is only a mile and a half wide at its most narrow point, similar to the entrance to the Red Sea, the Bab-el-Mandeb, and the Bosporus Strait—linking the Mediterranean and Black Seas—is even more narrow, not even a mile wide at some points. Terrorists seeking to have a major impact on the global economy could potentially derive a strategic benefit from attacking and sinking ships in these narrow waterways, or perhaps creating an oil spill that requires weeks of mitigation efforts before the passage can be used again by other ships. Prominent al-Qaeda ideologue Abu Musab al-Suri referred to this kind of attack in his 1600-page thesis on jihadist strategy, though to date no information about a plot to do so has emerged (al-Suri, 2004).

In addition to ships underway or at anchor, there are also concerns about terrorist networks targeting commercial ports. Several training manuals circulating online among jihadists describe how ports are key links in the global economy, and, thus, a significant attack against any major port would have second-order effects in many industrial, commercial distribution, and service sectors. Similarly, offshore oil platforms could be attractive targets for terrorists, either as a means to capture and hold hostages, steal oil to be sold on the black market, or blow up a platform and cause major economic, energy security, and environmental problems for target countries.

And finally, while much attention in the realm of maritime security has focused on passenger ships, commercial vessels, and port facilities, we also cannot overlook the potential threat of small vessels (vessels of under 300 tons, including recreational boating) being involved in a terrorist attack. As a Department of Homeland Security summit on this topic noted in 2007, the risk of terrorist exploitation of small vessels as a threat vector takes multiple forms, including:

- WMD transport: Possible terrorist use of small vessels to transport or deliver weapons of mass destruction.
- Conventional explosives delivery platform: Terrorist groups have demonstrated a clear interest and ability to use small vessels to deliver waterborne improvised explosive devices (WBIED) in attacks against larger ships, as was the case in the attack on the *USS Cole* in 2000.
- Smuggling people and material: Terrorists and criminal organizations might exploit small vessels to smuggle dangerous people and materials into the United States.
- Platform for weapon attack: Terrorists could use small vessels as platforms for stand-off weapon (e.g., Man-Portable Air Defense Systems [MANPADS] or surface-to-surface missile platforms) attacks. (DHS National Small Vessel, 2007)

Terrorists have also attacked maritime targets solely for profit-oriented goals, essentially mirroring the far more common acts of piracy by criminal networks, as described in the next section of this chapter. For example, the well-publicized attacks against ships off the coast of Somalia last decade were perpetrated mostly by criminal piracy gangs, but also by some jihadist groups. Meanwhile, the Abu Sayyaf Group, based in the Philippines, has been attacking cargo vessels and abducting foreigners from tourists resorts since the late 1990s. In these instances, even if the attackers happen to be members of a terrorist group, the attacks are typically categorized as criminal in nature (rather than acts of terrorism) because the motive is profit. That is, the attacks are meant to generate revenue (sometimes via ransom) rather than to achieve any sort of political or ideological objectives.

To sum up, the threat of maritime terrorism is real, but for various reasons—including logistical challenges—most terrorists have not focused on attacking maritime targets with any real frequency, preferring other, easier and more politically and ideologically meaningful targets instead. Meanwhile, the more common threat to intermodal maritime security is posed by nonideologically oriented criminal organizations.

Intermodal maritime security threats from nonideologically oriented criminals

As noted earlier in this chapter, a central aspect of the threat to intermodal maritime security involves violent nonstate actors infiltrating various points of the system, and then compromising a shipping container in order to move weapons, drugs, counterfeit products, and so forth to a location where other members of the criminal or terrorist network can take possession of them. This type of attack is far more commonly associated with nonideologically oriented criminals than with terrorist networks. But regardless of their motivations, these kinds of activities pose significant risks to the criminals—particularly the risk of their illicit cargo being detected somewhere along the way. For example, imagine the dismay of the drug cartel leaders who lost an estimated $1 billion when their 33,000 pounds of cocaine hidden in seven shipping containers were discovered and seized by authorities in Philadelphia in June 2019 (Rubinkam, 2019). Smaller interdictions of drug shipments are more routine, like the March 2019 seizure of 3200 pounds of cocaine (worth an estimated $77 million) at the Port of New York/Newark (U.S. Customs and Border, 2019), or the 110 pounds seized by authorities in June 2020 at the Port of Savannah, Georgia (U.S. Department of Justice, 2020).

Similarly, customs agents at the Port of Antwerp in Belgium seized around 50 tons of cocaine in 2018, 22% more than in 2017, and six times more than in 2013, and Brazil's Department of Federal Revenue revealed that cocaine seizures at its ports jumped 50% in the first 10 months of 2019 compared with the same period the year before (Paris, 2020). And in August, the UK's National Crime Agency seized a record 1.3 tons of heroin in a container aboard a cargo ship at the Port of Felixstowe, the country's largest seaport (Paris, 2020). U.S. Customs officials say traditional methods of drug smuggling—like small planes operating from private airstrips, speedboats, and mini-submarines—are still being used, but that criminal networks are apparently showing more faith in the intermodal supply chain (Paris, 2020).

Meanwhile, in August 2018, US government authorities announced the seizure of counterfeit luxury goods (including purses, handbags, belts) worth at least $500 million, that had been manufactured in China. Over 30 men and women were arrested—all of Chinese heritage and living in the United States illegally (Robbins, 2018). This was the culmination of a 6-year investigation, which found that 20 of the containers came into the United States through the Port of New York and New Jersey, and two through the Port of Los Angeles. In another of the largest counterfeit-goods cases ever prosecuted in the United States, 29 people were arrested in New York, New Jersey, Texas, and Florida for trying to smuggle $325 million worth of fake goods from China into the United States (Schweber, 2012).

But worse than drugs or counterfeit goods is the recent increase of human traffickers using compromised intermodal shipping containers. Illegal immigrants apprehended at ports in Britain, Canada and the United States (among other countries) after arriving inside shipping containers revealed that many of them had paid a criminal network large sums of cash for the dangerous journey inside a steel crate. For others, this journey ended tragically—like the 39 Vietnamese whose bodies were discovered in a cargo container at a British port in March 2020 (Lo, 2020). The same month, the bodies 64 Ethiopians were found in a shipping container in Mozambique (considered by some experts as a smuggling corridor for migrants seeking to make their way to South Africa) (More than 60 people found dead, 2020). In both instances, authorities believed the victims had suffocated to death.

Estimates of the scope and scale of these illicit smuggling activities are nearly impossible because all that is known for certain are instances where authorities successfully interdicted a compromised shipping container. And of course, these activities are not limited to the maritime arena, as numerous cases of drug and human trafficking across land borders have been widely reported. The Organisation for Economic Co-operation and Development (OECD) has recently suggested that the overall international trade in counterfeit and stolen goods amounts to as much as half a trillion dollars (Trends in Trade in Counterfeit and Pirated Goods, 2019).

Responding to the maritime dimensions of this criminal activity is clearly difficult. As maritime security expert Peter Cook notes, "The greatest challenge… is the sheer volume of container moving through the ports and the speed with which they have to processed" (Lo). The containers inspection programs described earlier do have some impact in thwarting attempts by criminal networks to compromise the intermodal shipping system. Some experts have also suggested that one way to approach the problem is to "change the risk calculation for smugglers by checking at least three of every 10 containers before they are loaded on ships, or three times more than the current checks" (Paris). And new technologies are being developed in order to improve the ability to detect the presence of human beings inside cargo containers arriving at ports. But thwarting the use of compromised shipping containers by smugglers will remain a challenge for the foreseeable future. And meanwhile, maritime security experts continue to grapple with the longstanding threat of piracy.

The primacy of piracy

A common type of intermodal maritime security incident involving violent nonstate actors is piracy, which takes many forms. In some cases, the perpetrators of the attack may seek to hold the crew and cargo for ransom. In other cases, the goal may be to steal whatever they can get their hands on, in order to then sell on the black market. For example, in 1982, armed pirates boarded a Swedish cargo ship off the coast of Lagos, Nigeria, and stole rolls of cloth (incidents are recorded in Jenkins, 1983). On May 5, 1998, armed pirates hijacked the Malaysia-based oil tanker *Petro Ranger* and siphoned off most of its cargo. Chinese authorities later detained 12 Indonesians on suspicion of the hijacking and theft. More recently, on February 25, 2020, armed robbers boarded the tanker *San Ramón* at an anchorage off Isla Borracha, Venezuela, and killed the vessel's master in an altercation. The victim was identified by Venezuelan media as Capt. Jaime Herrera Orozco, 58, a Colombian national. Six armed men in masks boarded the *San Ramón* on

Monday morning, intending to rob the vessel. Capt. Orozco reportedly attempted to resist and was shot and killed. The robbers proceeded to steal valuables from the ship, then fled in a boat. At the time of the attack, the *San Ramón* was anchored near the Venezuelan port of Barcelona, awaiting a decision from Venezuelan authorities on allegations of fuel smuggling (Pirate Attack off Venezuela, 2020).

The International Chamber of Commerce's International Maritime Bureau (ICC IMB) describes piracy as the act of attacking any vessel by boarding it in order to commit theft or any other crime by use of force (ICC International Maritime Bureau, 2020). Worldwide, according to the ICC IMB's Piracy Reporting Centre (IMB PRC), 406 cases of piracy and armed robbery were reported in 2009 (International Maritime Bureau, 2010). A decade later, that number had dropped by more than half. Further, as shown in Fig. 7.1, the overall frequency of piracy and armed attacks has declined in the past 5 years.

Meanwhile, the most significant decline has been seen in the waterways around Indonesia (including the Strait of Malacca), while Nigeria has seen an increase over that time period. In all other countries monitored by IMB over this 5-year period, the number of incidents has only rarely been 10 or more. Six countries accounted for 57% of all the attacks reported in 2019: Nigeria (35), Indonesia (25), Singapore Straits (12), Malaysia (11), and Peru (10). These are also the same countries that saw more frequent incidents targeting ports and anchorages during 2019. Overall, while attacks against maritime targets by violent nonstate actors are a global security challenge, there are distinct hotspots of

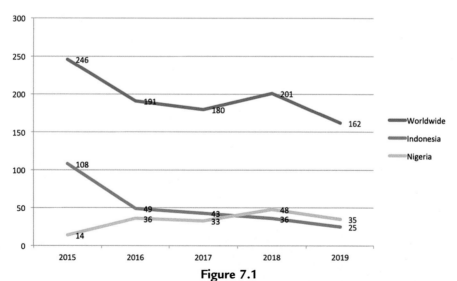

Figure 7.1

Piracy and armed robbery against ships, 2015–19. *ICC International Maritime Bureau, Annual Report, 2020. Available online at: https://www.icc-ccs.org/piracy-reporting-centre/.*

activity that are of major concern: (1) Southeast Asia (including waterways near Indonesia, Malaysia, and Singapore); (2) the Horn of Africa, particularly the coast of Somalia; and (3) West Africa, most notably the Gulf of Guinea.

In Southeast Asia, one of the most oft-cited areas of concern is the Strait of Malacca, a 550-mile narrow waterway between Indonesia and Malaysia. Piracy has been a problem in this important passageway between India and China for several centuries. As recently as 2006, Lloyd's of London declared the Strait a high-risk area (for insurance purposes) (Simon, 2006). However, over the past 2 decades, an increase in patrols and uses of technology has significantly diminished incidents of piracy here. Similarly, according to the IMB PRC, armed robbery attacks in Indonesian ports declined from 36 incidents in 2018 to 25 in 2019.

In contrast, however, the nearby Singapore Straits (a narrow 65-mile stretch of water) experienced a rise in armed robbery attacks against ships, with 31 reported incidents in 2019 compared to just a handful the year before. Of these, 17 occurred to ships while underway in the eastbound lane of the Singapore Strait and 14 occurred in the westbound lane (Piracy Incidents in Singapore, 2020). Three incidents were even reported on the same day (December 20, 2019), two involving bulk carriers and one involving a tanker. Two more attacks occurred on December 23 and another one on December 25. Further, in most of these incidents, the perpetrators successfully boarded the vessel, confronted crew members, and escaped—sometimes with items stolen from the ship. Bulk carriers and tankers have been targeted more frequently than other kinds of ships in this region, including intermodal cargo ships (More Piracy, 2019). The trend continued into the first months of 2020, with six incidents reported by the end of February. In fact, two incidents occurred on the same day—February 9, 2020—involving ships underway in the eastbound lane of Singapore Strait (Piracy Incidents in Singapore, 2020).

Elsewhere in Southeast Asia, the last 2 decades have seen a significant increase in the use of small boats by criminal gangs like the Abu Sayyyaf Group to kidnap people (from diving resorts, large ships, and even personal watercraft, including sailboats), and hold them hostage for ransom. Abu Sayyaf was originally classified as a terrorist group, when there was clear evidence that their acts of violence were motivated by jihadist ideology. Their original leader Abdurajak Janjalani even spent some time at an al-Qaeda training camp in Afghanistan, and allegedly fought against the Soviets alongside Osama bin Laden during the 1980s. However, during the first decade of the 21st century, the group came to be viewed as exclusively a violence-for-profit entity, mostly kidnapping foreigners for ransom and apparently having abandoned any purported religious or political ideology they once proclaimed (O'Brien, 2012). Experts have changed this perception recently, following a terrorist bombing on January 27, 2019 that killed 20 people attending a Sunday service at a cathedral in Jolo, Southern Philippines. The Abu Sayyaf Group claimed responsibility for the attack, indicating a resurgence of Islamist extremism, and also likely reflecting how the profits generated from their seaborne criminal activities have enabled the group to carry out new terrorist operations. As one report noted, "Although these activities were mainly profit-motivated, the ransoms were used to purchase weapons and other supplies for the group" (Curran, 2019).

Meanwhile, the Horn of Africa has also been a noteworthy hotspot of piracy. During the first decade of the 2000s, Somali pirates used various kinds of small fast boats in an increasing number of attempts to commandeer commercial vessels, and then hold the crew and pilot hostage until a ransom was paid. Some of the more publicized incidents include the June 2005 hijacking of the *MV Semlow,* a ship carrying United Nations (UN) food aid, which was held for 100 days. In October of that year, another UN ship carrying aid, the *MV Miltzow,* was hijacked and held for more than 30 hours. In April 2006, a South Korean cargo ship *Dongwon-ho 628* was seized, and the crew were held hostage until a ransom was (allegedly) paid 4 months later. In February 2007, another ship delivering UN food aid to Somalia, the *MV Rozen,* was hijacked, and the crew were held hostage for 40 days. In September 2008, a Ukrainian ship, the *MV Faina*—with a cargo of tanks, rocket launchers and small arms—was hijacked and held for over 5 months until a $3.2 million ransom payment was (allegedly) received by the pirates. In November of that year, an oil supertanker from Saudi Arabia, the *Sirius Star*, was hijacked off the coast of Kenya. The ship's crew and cargo—two million barrels of crude oil en-route to the United States—were held hostage until a multimillion dollar ransom was (allegedly) paid. And in perhaps the most publicized attack of that era, Somali pirates hijack the US-flagged cargo ship *Maersk Alabama* in April 2009. The captain, Richard Phillips, offered himself as a hostage in order to protect his crew, and he was rescued a few days later when US Navy SEAL snipers fatally shot three pirates and took the fourth into custody. Hollywood later made a movie about this incident, with Tom Hanks in the lead role.

Overall, acts of piracy off the coast of Somalia dominated maritime security concerns and headlines for nearly a decade. From 2007 to 2012 alone, more than 200 vessels were hijacked by Somali pirates in the Horn of Africa region. These incidents prompted an increasing number of powerful countries to dramatically increase their naval and air presence in the region. Ships and aircraft from European countries, the United States, China, India, and South Korea cooperated in a multinational effort that involved patrolling, protecting ships, and capturing would-be pirates. This in turn created a deterrence mechanism that eventually resulted in a rapid decrease in incidents. As noted above, there were only a few acts of piracy in this region in all of 2019.

However, just as piracy decreased on the eastern coast of Africa, it began to increase on the western coast, particularly in the Gulf of Guinea—which stretches 3500 miles from

Senegal to Angola. The region accounted for 64 incidents including all four vessel hijackings that occurred in 2019, as well as 10 out of 11 vessels that reported coming under fire. The number of crew members kidnapped in the Gulf of Guinea increased more than 50% from 78 in 2018 to 121 in 2019, accounting for over 90% of global kidnappings reported at sea that year (ICC International Maritime Bureau, 2020).

In previous decades, the region had been known mainly for pirate attacks involving the theft of fuel cargo, which was then resold on the black market (Onuoha, 2013). Hundreds of such attacks occurred off the coast of Nigeria alone (Murphy, 2010). Some of these incidents took place at the loading and anchorage facilities in the Nigerian port of Lagos (Piracy in West Africa, 2019). But more recently, the Gulf of Guinea has experienced an escalation of piracy, kidnapping, and armed robbery at sea incidents (Carafano, 2013). A 2018 report by the IMB noted that attacks in the region more than doubled from the year before, with six hijackings, 13 ships fired upon, 130 hostages taken, and 78 seafarers kidnapped for ransom (International Maritime Bureau, 2019). For example, in October 2018, 11 crew members were kidnapped from a container vessel 70 nautical miles off Bonny Island, Nigeria. Two days later, pirates in a speedboat hijacked a tanker underway 100 nautical miles off Pointe-Noire, Congo. Eight of the 18 crew members were kidnapped (From Sea to Land, 2020). In 2019, as noted above, the region—and particularly the coast of Nigeria—has become the number one hotspot for piracy worldwide. In December 2019, the IMB issued a special report expressing its heightened concern "at the unprecedented level of crew kidnapped in the Gulf of Guinea" and advising all ships to be extra vigilant when transiting through the region (International Chamber of Commerce). And this trend continued well into the following year. For example, the intermodal container cargo ship *Maersk Tema* was attacked by pirates off the coast of São Tomé in the Gulf of Guinea on February 14 (Boxship Maersk Tema, 2020). Two more piracy incidents occurred on March 6, 2020 in the Gulf of Guinea. A tanker *Minerva Virgo* was boarded by pirates off the coast of Benin, and hours later the Hong Kong—flagged vessel *Huanghai Glory* came under a similar attack (Two Pirate Boardings, 2020).

To sum up, we have seen dozens of attacks each month against maritime vessels, predominately involving criminals engaged in piracy for the main purpose of gaining profit either through kidnapping for ransom or direct theft of cargo. These patterns of attacks and likely motivations are reflected in the fact that, as indicated in Table 7.1, the two most common types of vessels attacked by criminals have been tankers and bulk carriers, with intermodal container cargo ships a distant third or fourth, depending on the year.

So, while the threat of terrorism against maritime targets cannot be ignored, it is far less predominant than the nonideological kinds of criminality described here. To fully

Table 7.1: Most frequent types of vessels attacked, 2015—19.

	2015	2016	2017	2018	2019
Bulk carrier	86	52	38	59	46
Container	30	10	23	18	14
Tanker chem/Product	62	56	42	50	45
Tanker oil	20	13	19	16	19
Tug/Offshore tug	10	14	11	11	7

ICC International Maritime Bureau, Annual Report, 2020. Available online at: https://www.icc-ccs.org/piracy-reporting-centre/.

understand why, it is important to analyze what is known about the strategic motivations of terrorist and criminal attacks against maritime targets, and why they are not attacked more frequently.

Attacking intermodal maritime targets: motivations and challenges

As noted above, a desire for material profit is the motivation behind most attacks against maritime targets, whether by terrorists or nonideologically motivated criminal groups. The fact that disruption, rather than destruction, is the predominant type of attack makes intuitive sense when we recognize that violent nonstate actors need a functioning intermodal transportation system just like the rest of us. Instead of attacking this system, they will look for ways to use it to their advantage. Those who have studied terrorism extensively understand several key reasons for this. First, terrorist organizations act strategically and choose targets that will help them achieve strategic goals and objectives. Thus, intermodal shipping containers pale in comparison to the myriad other potential targets that terrorists can (and often do) attack, like public transportation, hotels, office buildings, airports, and other public spaces. Second, terrorist groups need financial support, always. There has never been a terrorist group with unlimited funds at their disposal. Thus, the products shipped via the intermodal system could be hijacked and repurposed for financial gain. This is no different than how transnational criminal organizations have viewed the shipping containers as a potentially lucrative source of revenue. In that sense, terrorists either coordinate with criminal networks or simply cease to be terrorists and take on the mantle of organized crime themselves.

Successful acts of piracy can help facilitate the violent nonstate actors' operations in the future; cargo and hostages can be ransomed, or in some cases valuable cargo stolen in the operation can be sold on the black market. Imagine, for example, the amount of profit that could be generated by diverting a shipment of computers, cell phones, and other high tech consumer products bound for Europe or North America. Meanwhile, as Kent Baumann explains, "raiding ships and port facilities can provide logistical supplies, and in some cases specialized equipment that could facilitate follow-on, maritime terrorist operations" (Baumann, 2007).

Further, since both terrorists and criminals seek targets of opportunity, unarmed commercial vessels and cruise ships may seem to be a reasonably promising target, under the right conditions. In fact, successfully hijacking a passenger vessel in order to hold hostages could yield significant ransoms. In addition to kidnapping for ransom, terrorists have also taken hostages for the purpose of negotiating policy concessions, like the release of imprisoned comrades (the primary demands of the *Achille Lauro* hijackers). But the perpetrators face a risk that the country or company involved may respond with a rescue attempt rather than pay the ransom, further complicating matters. And while Hollywood movies have sometimes featured outlandish plots involving attacks against cruise ships, these are highly unlikely in real life. For example, the logistics of replicating the hijacking of the *Achille Lauro* would introduce monumental hurdles to overcome before the terrorist group could succeed. Today's cruise ships are larger, requiring the terrorists or criminals to provide considerably more manpower and weaponry in order to control large numbers of hostages (some of whom, in our post-9/11 era, may decide to fight back), as opposed to the four-man team deployed by the Palestinian terrorists in 1985. In sum, an attack against a cruise ship like the *Achille Lauro* is a very rare incident, and to date only terrorist groups have done so. Over the past several decades, we have not yet seen any credible attempts by a criminal organization to hijack a cruise ship and hold its passengers and crew hostage for ransom.

On the other hand, while a terrorist group may seek to destroy a ship in order to cause economic disruption, a criminal organization would see this as bad for business. Criminal networks need consumers of their products—whether drugs, weapons, counterfeit goods, or whatever—and major economic disruptions threaten their profits. The same logic would explain why, to date, we have not seen a criminal network attack an oil tanker in an attempt to sink it or cause a massive environment disaster. Instead, these choke points are much more likely to be viewed by nonideologically motivated attackers as a vulnerable access point to minimize the logistical challenges of approaching a ship at speed with the intent to board it. But with the increased security measures at these and other strategically important waterways have been put in place to reduce this perceived vulnerability.

Future projections of threat

To conclude, the projection of future trends and patterns appear consistent with previous years, in terms of hotspot locations, tactics, and perpetrators. For the most part, terrorist groups have remained a distinct minority when it comes to involvement in attacks against maritime targets. The motivations behind attacks against maritime targets of all kinds appear far more oriented toward criminal profiting than any sort of political ideology. And we know that there are a range of logistical hurdles that terrorists and criminals would need to overcome in order to successfully carry out an attack like the ones described in this chapter. Cruise ships in particular pose major hurdles for any group—criminal or terrorist—based on the size and scale of the target considered for such an operation. Given our understanding that most violent nonstate actors are concerned about things like return on investment and minimizing the risks of failure, it becomes clear that there are many potential targets to choose from that pose far fewer challenges.

And while much attention has been focused on WMD detection in maritime containers, there is virtually no evidence that terrorist groups have sought to carry out such an attack. There have been a few scares and false alarms. For example, in June 2017 authorities in the United States were notified that an RDD had been smuggled aboard the *Maersk Memphis*. When the ship approached the Port of Charleston, the crew were immediately evacuated, as was the port terminal and surrounding area. An investigation by the FBI and U.S. Coast Guard found no traces of any radiological weapon (Kristiansen, 2017). Further, there are no credible indications that nonideological criminal networks would view such an attack as having any strategic benefits, and in fact would very likely prove counterproductive to their illicit profit-seeking goals. As noted earlier, all kinds of violent nonstate actors need a functioning economy in order to generate the funds needed to carry out their operations.

Further, the increasing use of compromised shipping containers for smuggling drugs, weapons, counterfeit products, and people would seem to indicate that violent nonstate actors would rather utilize the intermodal supply chain to their advantage, rather than attacking it. In other words, violent nonstate actors appear more likely to view the intermodal maritime supply chains as a potential source of revenue, rather than a meaningful target to attack.

Of course, this conclusion is not meant to suggest we can dismiss altogether the threat of violent attacks. It is certainly true that terrorist groups have attacked maritime targets in the past, including Polisario, the Abu Sayyaf Group, al-Qaeda, the Moro Islamic Liberation Front, the Tamil Tigers, and Palestinian groups. We know that terrorists have attacked cruise ships, commercial vessels, and even naval warships. And we know that criminal organizations have been far more involved in piracy than terrorists, particularly within the last decade. For both kinds of groups, the tactical and logistical challenges they had to overcome in order to succeed in such attacks varied but were often daunting.

The examples of maritime attacks by nonstate actors described in this chapter are admittedly few in number, compared to the much greater numbers of terrorist attacks and criminal acts of violence that take place on land worldwide each year. That is the good news. We also see that particular regions of the world's waterways have attracted more of this activity than elsewhere. Specifically, there are ongoing terrorist and violent nonstate actor threats in at least two key regions: the Gulf of Guinea and the Singapore Strait. Others remain areas of concern—including the Malacca Straits and other coastal waterways of Indonesia, and the coast of Somalia/Horn of Africa—though we have seen major reductions of activity here in response to international efforts to improve security. In fact, the most recent data suggest that attacks by armed groups against commercial vessels worldwide are declining in frequency and severity.

Overall, in order to maintain a suitably balanced perspective about the threat against maritime targets posed by violent nonstate actors, we must take into account key differences in the intentions of potential attackers, as well as the internal and external influences on these actors' decision-making. To date, most attacks have been motivated by criminal profit not by political or ideological concerns. We must analyze the tactics of violent nonstate actors, study their attempts to attack maritime targets (the successes and the failures), and incorporate that learning into new security protocols and procedures to make things even more difficult for them to achieve. Certainly, the threat is real and should not be dismissed lightly, but it is also a manageable one.

References

al-Suri, A.M., December 2004. *Dawat al-muqawama Al-Islamiyaal-Alamiya* [Call for a Global Islamic Resistance], p. 1384.

Anderson, S.K., Spagnolo, P.N., 2007. The Achille Lauro Hijacking. In: Forest, J.J.F. (Ed.), Countering Terrorism And Insurgency In the 21st Century. Praeger, Westport, CT, pp. 54—59.

See "Anthrax Investigation," Federal Bureau of Investigation, online at: http://www.fbi.gov/about-us/history/famous-cases/anthrax-amerithrax/amerithrax-investigation.

Baumann, K., 2007. Red Sky in the morning: the Nexus between international maritime piracy and transnational terrorism. In: Forest, J.J.F. (Ed.), Countering Terrorism And Insurgency In the 21st Century. Praeger, Westport, CT, pp. 261—262.

Beitler, R.M., 2007. The attack on the USS Cole. In: Forest, J.J.F. (Ed.), Countering Terrorism And Insurgency In the 21st Century. Praeger, Westport, CT, pp. 145—146.

Boxship Maersk Tema attacked by pirates in Gulf of Guinea. Maritime Execut., February 14, 2020 Online at: https://www.maritime-executive.com/article/boxship-maersk-tema-attacked-by-pirates-in-gulf-of-guinea.

Carafano, J.J., November 14, 2013. Oil and Gas Attracts Pirates to Gulf of Guinea. The Heritage Foundation. Online at: https://www.heritage.org/africa/commentary/oil-and-gas-attract-pirates-gulf-guinea.

See the Centers for Disease Control's website on Chemical agents, http://www.bt.cdc.gov/chemical/, and the NTI Chemical Weapons tutorial, online at http://www.nti.org/h_learnmore/cwtutorial/chapter04_03.html.

Container Control", United Nations Office on Drugs and Crime. Online at: https://www.unodc.org/unodc/en/urban-safety/container-control.html.

Container Security Initiative, online at: https://www.hsdl.org/?view&did=29070.

Prominent examples of this research literature include Bruce Hoffman, "Modern Terror. Mind-set: Tact., Target., Tradecraft Technol.," Inside Terro., p. 242-268; M. Crenshaw, "Innovation: Decision Points in the Trajectory of Terrorism," pp. 35—50 in Terrorist Innovations in Weapons of Mass Effect: Preconditions, Causes and Predictive Behaviors, edited by Maria J. Rasmussen and Mohammed M. Hafez (August 2010 Workshop Report). (Washington, DC: Defense Threat Reduction Agency); and Paul Gill, "8 Things You Need to Know About Terrorist Decision-Making," Centre for Research and Evidence on Security Threats (January 4, 2018). Online at: https://crestresearch.ac.uk/comment/terrorist-decision-making/.

Curran, M., May 24, 2019. The Deadly Evolution of Abu Sayyaf and the Sea. The Maritime Executive. Online at: https://www.maritime-executive.com/editorials/the-deadly-evolution-of-abu-sayyaf-and-the-sea.

Report of the DHS National Small Vessel Security Summit, October 19, 2007. Homeland Security Institute. Online at: https://www.dhs.gov/xlibrary/assets/small_vessel_NSVSS_Report_HQ_508.pdf.

For example, see Dominic Dudley, "Terrorist Targets: The Ten Countries Which Suffer Most From Terrorism," Forbes (November 20, 2019), online at https://www.forbes.com/sites/dominicdudley/2019/11/20/ten-countries-terrorism/#33c0ce944db8.

Forest, J., 2012. A framework for analyzing the future threat of WMD terrorism. J. Strat. Secur. 5 (4), 51–68.

From Sea to Land: Tackling Maritime Crime in the Gulf of Guinea, 2020. UNODC. Online at: https://www.unodc.org/nigeria/en/from-sea-to-land_-tackling-maritime-crime-in-the-gulf-of-guinea.html.

Glass, C., January 8, 2004. The New Piracy. London Review of Books – Letters Page, p. 268. Cited in Baumann.

"Terrorist Attacks on Global Supply Chain Hit All-Time High," Supply & Demand Chain Executive, August 24, 2017. Online at: https://www.sdcexec.com/risk-compliance/news/12362711/terrorist-attacks-on-global-supply-chain-hit-alltime-high.

See Global Terrorism Database, online at: https://www.start.umd.edu/gtd/.

These and similar kinds of incidents are recorded in the Global Terrorism Database, available online at: https://www.start.umd.edu/gtd/.

Greenberg, M.D., et al., 2006. Maritime Terrorism: Risk and Liability. Rand, Santa Monica, CA, pp. 112–115.

ICC International Maritime Bureau, Annual Report, 2020. Available online at: https://www.icc-ccs.org/piracy-reporting-centre/.

These and Other Incidents Are Recorded in Jenkins, 1983 et al.

International Chamber of Commerce, International Maritime Bureau, "Gulf of Guinea Kidnappings." Online at: https://www.icc-ccs.org/index.php/1285-gulf-of-guinea-kidnappings.

International Maritime Bureau, 2010. Piracy and Armed Robbery against Ships Annual Report 01 January-31 December 2009. ICC International Maritime Bureau, Essex.

International Chamber of Commerce, International Maritime Bureau, "IMB Piracy Report 2018: Attacks Multiply in the Gulf of Guinea, January 16, 2019. Online at: https://www.icc-ccs.org/index.php/1259-imb-piracy-report-2018-attacks-multiply-in-the-gulf-of-guinea.

James, M., July 10, 2000. Tour, "do-it-yourself chemical weapons. Chem. Eng. News 78 (28), 42–45.

Jenkins, B., September 1983. details about the 1973 attack on the Mereghan II are found in Brian Jenkins, et al. "A Chronology of Terrorist Attacks and Other Criminal Actions Against Maritime Targets. RAND Corporation. Available online at: https://apps.dtic.mil/dtic/tr/fulltext/u2/a145248.pdf.

V. Jenkins, The Achille Lauro Hijacking. John F. Kennedy School of Government Case Program, 1988. This case was written by Vlad Jenkins at the John F. Kennedy School of Government for Professor Philip Heymann and the Project for the Study and Analysis of Terrorism, Harvard Law School. Funding was provided by the Central Intelligence Agency and the John D. and Catherine T. MacArthur Foundation. (0894). Cited in Anderson and Spagnolo, p. 54.

For example, see John Mueller, "The Atomic Terrorist?" in Weapons of Mass Destruction and Terrorism (second ed.), edited by J.J.F. Forest and R. Howard (New York: McGraw-Hill, 2012), p. 236-254;and M. Bunn and Anthony W., "The Seven Myths of Nuclear Terrorism," Belfer Center, Harvard University (April, 2005). Online at: http://belfercenter.ksg.harvard.edu/files/bunnwier.pdf.

Kristiansen, T., June 15, 2017. Shipping is a 'low priority' target for terrorism. Shipping Watch. Online at: https://shippingwatch.com/carriers/article9655187.ece.

C. Lo, "Human Trafficking at Ports".

C. Lo, "Human Trafficking at Ports," Ship Technology, Issue 69 (March 2020). Online at: https://ship.nridigital.com/ship_mar20/human_traffic_tackling_people-smuggling_at_ports.

For Details on These and Similar Instances, See Akiva J. Lorenz, September 24, 2007. The Threat of Maritime Terrorism to Israel, ICT. Online at. http://citeseerx.ist.psu.edu/viewdoc/download?doi=10.1.1.572.7338&rep=rep1&type=pdf.

Also, see the Maritime Suspicious Activity Reporting Initiative, described online at: https://www.dhs.gov/publication/maritime-suspicious-activity-reporting-initiative-msi.

For example, see: Michael C. McGarrity, "Confronting the Rise of Domestic Terrorism," Testimony before the House Homeland Security Committee by the Assistant Director, Counterterrorism Division, Federal Bureau of Investigation (May 8, 2019), online at: https://www.fbi.gov/news/testimony/confronting-the-rise-of-domestic-terrorism-in-the-homeland; Countering Violent Extremism: Report to Congress (April 2017), online at: https://www.gao.gov/assets/690/683984.pdf; Neil MacFarquhar, "As Domestic Terrorists Outpace Jihadists, New U.S. Law is Debated," New York Times (Feb. 25, 2020), online at: https://www.nytimes.com/2020/02/25/us/domestic-terrorism-laws.html; David Neiwert, et al. "Homegrown Terror" The Center for Investigative Reporting (June 22, 2017), online at: https://apps.revealnews.org/homegrown-terror/; Daniel Sipes, "Right-Wing Radicals a Higher Threat than Undocumented Immigrants Ever Were," Globe Post (November 9, 2018), online at: https://theglobepost.com/2018/11/09/right-wing-radicals-immigrants/.

More Piracy Incidents in the Singapore Strait, December 22, 2019. The Maritime Executive. Online at: https://www.maritime-executive.com/article/three-more-piracy-incidents-in-the-singapore-strait.

More than 60 People Found Dead in Cargo Container in Mozambique, March 25, 2020. Al-Jazeera. Online at: https://www.aljazeera.com/news/2020/03/60-people-dead-cargo-container-mozambique-200324104510678.html.

Murphy, M.N., 2010. Small Boats, Weak States, Dirty Money: Piracy and Maritime Terrorism. Columbia University Press, New York, p. 111.

Attack on Naval HQ Foiled; Two Killed," Dawn (December 3, 2009). Online at: http://www.dawn.com/news/856344/attack-on-naval-hq-foiled-two-killed; Salman Masood and David E. Sanger, "Militants Attack Pakistani Naval Base in Karachi," The New York Times (May 22, 2011). Online at: http://www.nytimes.com/2011/05/23/world/asia/23pakistan.html?_r=0.

An Explosion in a Building Belonging to the Navy Inside the Port of Derna," Al-Wasat (Libya), (June 9, 2014). Online at: http://www.alwasat.ly/ar/news/libya/21884; "13 Dead from the Attacks against the Yemeni Military in Al-Mukalla," Al-Arabiya TV (Abu Dhabi), 12 May 12, 2016). Online at: http://ww.alarabiya.net/ar/arab-and-world/yemen/2016/05/12/3.

Onuoha, F., 2013. Piracy and maritime security in the Gulf of Guinea: trends, concerns and propositions. Journal of the Middle East and Africa 4 (3). https://doi.org/10.1080/21520844.2013.862767.

O'Brien, M.K., 2012. Fluctuations between crime and terror: the case of Abu sayyaf's kidnapping activities. Terrorism Polit. Violence 24 (2), 320—336.

Parachini, J., 2003. Putting WMD terrorism into perspective. Wash. Q. 26 (4), 37—50.

C. Paris, "Global Shipping Faces Troubling New Smuggling Questions".

Paris, C., January 6, 2020. Global shipping faces troubling new smuggling questions. Wall St. J. Online at: https://www.wsj.com/articles/global-shipping-faces-troubling-new-smuggling-questions-11578330634.

Ellerman, B.A., Forbes, A., Rosenberg, D. (Eds.), 2010. Piracy and Maritime Crime: Historical and Modern Case Studies. Naval War College Press, Newport, RI, p. 84.

Piracy in West Africa: The World's Most Dangerous Seas?, June 19, 2019. BBC News. Online at: https://www.bbc.com/news/world-africa-48581197.

Two More Piracy Incidents in Singapore Strait, February 9, 2020. The Maritime Executive. Online at: https://www.maritime-executive.com/article/two-more-piracy-incidents-in-singapore-strait.

Tanker Captain Killed in Pirate Attack off Venezuela, February 25, 2020. The Maritime Executive. Online at: https://www.maritime-executive.com/article/tanker-captain-killed-in-pirate-attack-off-venezuela.

Pirates Board Indonesian Tanker," CBS News (March 29, 2003). Online at: www.cbsnews.com/stories/2003/03/29/world/main546695.shtml; also, Michael Richardson, "Terror at Sea: The World's Lifelines are at Risk," Straits Times (Singapore) (November 17, 2003). Online at: http://www.stevequayle.com/News.alert/03_Terror/031117.terror.at.sea.html.

Robbins, L., August 16, 2018. Investigators Seize Fake Luxury Goods Worth Half a Billion Dollars. The New York Times. Online at: https://www.nytimes.com/2018/08/16/nyregion/fake-luxury-goods-handbags.html.

Robert, F., August 6, 2010. Worth, "Tanker Damage Caused by Attack, Inquiry Finds. The New York Times. Online at: http://www.nytimes.com/2010/08/07/world/middleeast/07tanker.html?_r=0.

For more on this, see Rolf Mowatt-Larsen, January 2010. *Al Qaida Weapons of Mass Destruction Threat: Hype or Reality* Belfer Center for Science and International Affairs. Harvard University. Online at: http://belfercenter.ksg.harvard.edu/publication/19852/al_qaeda_weapons_of_mass_destruction_threat.html.

Rubinkam, M., June 19, 2019. Staggering Drug Bust Shows Traffickers Turning to East Coast. Associated Press. Online at: https://apnews.com/6f00e68e092243c88366fbb3afe57c75.

Schweber, N., March 2, 2012. Officials Tell of Fake Labels Hidden beneath Fake Labels. The New York Times. Online at: https://www.nytimes.com/2012/03/03/nyregion/officials-say-they-smashed-a-ring-smuggling-counterfeit-uggs.html.

Simon, M., October 30, 2006. "Hard Times for Piractes in Busy World Waterway," *Christian Science Monitor.* Online at: https://www.csmonitor.com/2006/1030/p01s04-woap.html.

Sinai, J., 2006. Terrorism and business: the threat and response," *counter terrorism.* Spring J. Counterterror. Homeland Secur. Int. 12 (1), 26–33. Cited in Baumann, p. 272.

Stepanova, E., 2008. Terrorism in Asymmetrical Conflict: Ideological and Structural Aspects. (SIPRI Research Report # 23). Oxford University Press, Stockholm.

Tagliabue, J., November 20, 1985. Italians Identify 16 in Hijacking of Ship. New York Times, p. 2. A3. Cited in Anderson and Spagnolo.

Tamil Tigers Claim Tanker Attack, October 31, 2001. BBC News. Online at: http://news.bbc.co.uk/1/hi/world/south_asia/1628218.stm.

Yemen Says Tanker Blast was Terrorism," *BBC News,* (October 16, 2002). Online at http://news.bbc.co.uk/1/hi/world/middle_east/2334865.stm; and "Craft 'Rammed' Yemen Oil Tanker," BBC News, (October 6, 2002). Online at http://news.bbc.co.uk/2/hi/middle_east/2303363.stm.

OECD, March 2019. Trends in Trade in Counterfeit and Pirated Goods. Online at. https://www.oecd.org/governance/risk/trends-in-trade-in-counterfeit-and-pirated-goods-g2g9f533-en.htm.

Two pirate boardings in one day. The Maritime Execut., March 6, 2020 Online at: https://www.maritime-executive.com/article/two-pirate-boardings-in-one-day-in-gulf-of-guinea.

U.S. Customs and Border Patrol, March 11, 2019. CBP, HSI, DEA, USCG, NYSP & NYPD Approximately 3,200 Pounds of Cocaine Seized. Online at: https://www.cbp.gov/newsroom/local-media-release/cbp-hsi-dea-uscg-nysp-nypd-approximately-3200-pounds-cocaine-seized.

U.S. Department of Justice, June 3, 2020. Hidden Cocaine Shipment Seized from Container," U.S. Attorney's Office. Southern District of Georgia. Online at: https://www.justice.gov/usao-sdga/pr/hidden-cocaine-shipment-seized-container.

For more on these and other examples, see James Forest, "Opportunities and Limitations for WMD Terrorism," in Weapons Of Mass Destruction And Terrorism *(second ed.),* edited by J.J.F. Forest and R. Howard (New York: McGraw-Hill, 2012) p. 55-72; and J. Forest, "A Framework for Analyzing the Future Threat of WMD Terrorism," Journal of Strategic Security 5(4) (2012), pp. 51–68.

CHAPTER 8

Physical and technological considerations

Gary A. Gordon PhD, PE, MEMS, LTC USA (Ret.) [1], **Bennett C. Abrams** [2]

[1]*Department of Civil & Environmental Engineering, University of Massachusetts Lowell, Lowell, MA, United States;* [2]*Tulane University, New Orleans, LA, United States*

There are a wide range of threats and associated vulnerabilities and consequences to the intermodal maritime container supply chain. Although the threats are a combination of operational, procedural, physical, and technological underlying causes, this chapter will look at the threats to the physical and technological security measures and vulnerabilities that exist. Physical security and its technology are dependent on and comingled with cyber systems. Therefore, the cyber system relationship will only be touched upon in this chapter as it relates to physical security, but it will be developed in further detail in Chapter 10.

These physical security measures are unique to each port and body of water whether it be an ocean, strait, canal, bay, or anchorage, but there are general categories that apply to all. They include, but are not limited to, fencing and access control, technological surveillance (e.g., CCTV [closed-circuit television], intrusion detection, infrared cameras, and motion sensing) in conjunction with human measures, lighting, X-ray, and radiation detection. These measures have both landside and waterside uses. During the voyage at sea, physical security measures are limited and are essentially cyber based (e.g., GPS tracking) and is the subject of further research.

The United States has robust physical security measures in its ports and within its territorial waters, which accompany its operational (e.g., U.S. Coast Guard's [USCG] 96-hour notice of arrival rule) and procedural (e.g., Customs and Border Protection's [CBP] Cargo Security Initiative [CSI]) security measures. Because of this, the greater risk to the intermodal maritime supply chain occurs from the foreign manufacturer to and through the port of origin and during the voyage. The differences between US and international physical and technological security measures will be addressed as to how they impact the security of intermodal maritime containers when they arrive on US shores.

Physical security measures

Physical security measures in ports are those resources and systems that provide deterrence in preventing crime and potentially dangerous persons, vehicles, and materials

Intermodal Maritime Security. https://doi.org/10.1016/B978-0-12-819945-9.00008-3

(Christopher, 2015). Whether at domestic or international ports, the security measures are relatively the same. Only the level of sophistication will differ. Fencing, access control, lighting, intrusion detection, and surveillance both human and aided by cameras are among the traditional measures. There is an overlap and dependency among the physical usually "low tech" security measures, technological, and the related cyber systems. These measures are primary for landside access to the port, but waterside security measures should also be considered.

Crime Prevention Through Environmental Design (CPTED) is a guideline that addresses the relationship between the physical and social environment to prevent crimes by minimizing risk through design of criminal activity (Fennelly and Crowe, 2013). It has wide applicability to the transit environment and has an application to the maritime environment in ports. In the transit environment, a major focus is to minimize spaces and locations where people can hide, or a backpack could be concealed. There is a particular application of the principles of CPTED to the maritime environment in ports. Keeping out unwanted people and eliminating places to hide things, such as materials for a weapon of mass destruction (WMD) that could be put in an intermodal maritime container, are just a couple of examples where the principles of CPTED can be applied.

Let us look at the physical security measures typically used in ports. First, layers of security must be determined to address the sensitivity of what is to be protected. In simple terms, less sensitive operations and assets require less in the way of security measures. The layers of security graphic, below (Fig. 8.1), shows how security is viewed at airports by the Transportation Security Administration (TSA) and in general (Rozin, 2012). This principle can be applied to the maritime environment.

When looking at the rings or layers of protection of assets and operations, there are four basic considerations: deter, deny, detect, and delay (Bennett, 2018). They are based on the importance and need to prevent or deter any unwanted aggression against the asset or operation being protected, deny unwanted access entirely, detect intrusion as early as possible so as to respond, and delay an unwanted access so as to deploy a proper response. These considerations are, in part, based on the security strategies of acceptance, avoidance, diversification, transference, and consolidation (Edwards and Goodrich, 2013). Diversification addresses the spreading out of assets so as to not "have all their eggs in one basket" ensuring the operations will not be adversely affected. This is not possible as the assets and operations in a port are essentially in one area. Transference is focused on transferring responsibility for security to another organization or location, which in principle is not acceptable and could result in unintended consequences impacting other entities, such as the adjacent commercial and residential communities. Therefore,

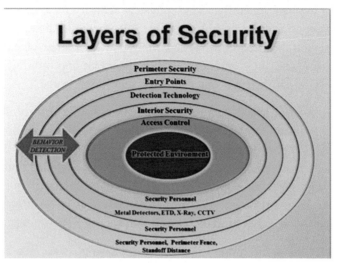

Figure 8.1

Transportation Security Administration layers of security. *Rozin, M., October 1, 2012. U.S. Security Shifting to Preventative Methods. Security Magazine. https://www.securitymagazine.com/articles/83537-us-security-shifting-to-preventative-methods.*

protecting assets in a port, and to some degree the land transportation to the port, will be viewed based on acceptance, avoidance, and consolidation strategies. This aligns well with the principles or deter, deny, detect, and delay as they relate to the port environment.

Now, let us turn our attention to the physical security measures by category. They are, in part, associated with processes and regulatory measures in place and include access control, lighting, intrusion detection, and infrastructure protection and hardening. The focus is to prevent unauthorized access to the port from both land and sea.

Access control

One of the main physical security measures used to achieve the four basic considerations of deter, deny, detect, and delay is access control. It refers to the selective restriction of access to restricted or operational areas of the port. The main goal of access control is finding the balance between securing the port and having an appropriate level of access to allow for operational efficiency (Christopher, 2015). In developing access points, port officials must be considerate of customers as well. Too few access points, while ideal from a security perspective, could impact operational efficiency to the point where customers are driven elsewhere (Christopher, 2015). Too many access points could result in the port being exposed to compromise and, thus, increasing the level of risk.

What the correct balance is and what types of access control are most effective are dependent upon the port and its natural environment, but there are some aspects of access control that can be applied generally. A key physical security measure of access control is fencing, which provides a visual and physical barrier preventing unauthorized and uncontrolled access into port facilities. When combined with other physical and technological security measures, such as intrusion detection and lighting, fencing is typically effective as a perimeter or outer layer of security at ports.

Another important layer of access control is parking and traffic control. Parking control is a physical security measure that allows for the management and identification of vehicles entering and exiting the port. Parking areas should be outside of fenced operational areas, especially restricted areas. This is because keeping personal vehicles out of cargo and operational areas minimizes the opportunity for an illegal transfer of any cargo or contraband (Christopher, 2015). In order for parking controls to be effective, parking regulations must be vigorously enforced by port and security personnel.

For access control to the port's more sensitive and high-value areas, the key physical security measure is gates, especially when combined with further technological and physical security measures, such as keypads, extra padlocks, and recording systems. Controlled gates provide another layer of security. For high-value cargo locations of the port (such as pharmaceuticals, consumer electronics, computers, or weapons systems), gates equipped with an alarm system provides a further layer of security (Christopher, 2015). Access control via gates allows for port and security personnel to effectively screen and identify ship crew members and personnel entering restricted operational areas. Some access gates will require manned gatehouses, which should at a minimum be equipped with the necessary technology to allow security personnel to do their jobs (Christopher, 2015).

Another physical security measure of access control is the use of barriers. Barriers provide an additional layer of security and can be utilized both on the perimeter and at more interior access points. There are two main categories of barriers: passive and active. Passive barriers, such as walls or heavy bollards, are fixed and do not allow vehicle entry. Passive barriers are typically placed along the perimeter and outer layers of a facility; the entire port area in this case. The other type is an active barrier, such as a retractable bollard or rotating wedge system.[1] An active barrier requires some action by equipment and/or personnel to either allow or deny entry of a vehicle, and these are typically placed near vehicle access points, such as parking garages (FHWA, 2018) and embassy gates, as shown in Fig. 8.2 below.

---

[1] Wedge barriers are hydraulically operated steel devices that angle upward from ground level to create an impregnable edge above the surface of the road. A retracted wedge barrier forms part of the road surface. Once deployed, a wedge barrier makes a 45° angle from the road surface facing the direction of vehicle movement and is coupled to a foundation pad to absorb the kinetic energy from an impact. These devices are very effective against an attempted vehicular breach. Retrieved from https://www.dhs.gov/sites/default/files/publications/ACT-HB_0915-508.pdf.

Figure 8.2
Typical US Embassy antiterrorism barrier. *Delta Scientific, February 23, 2007. U.S. Embassies Upgrading Physical Barriers. https://www.securityinfowatch.com/perimeter-security/physical-hardening/news/10558117/us-embassies-upgrading-physical-barriers.*

On the perimeter and within the port, barriers can be used to protect fencing and other areas (e.g., operational) from being rammed or penetrated by a vehicle. Concrete highway barriers or enhanced guardrails and combined with fencing can be used when roads are adjacent to fence lines. Fig. 8.3, below, shows concrete barrier and fencing at an exit gate in the Port of Seattle.

Figure 8.3
Concrete Barrier and Fencing at Exit Gate at Terminal 18 Port of Seattle, *Photo Courtesy of The Northwest Seaport Alliance.*

Barriers are particularly important to mitigate the risks that vehicles pose to a port. Vehicles can be used to penetrate access points or can be used as a vehicle-borne improvised explosive device (VBIED). Barriers help mitigate this risk by controlling how close a vehicle can get to operational and restricted areas of the port and establish a "standoff" distance separating the vehicle from the access point (FEMA, 2007). Bollards are particularly effective at helping to provide additional protection for access points because they can increase the standoff distance between a vehicle and the point of access, whether defined or via a gap or vulnerability in perimeter fencing and control. Bollards are vertical posts which can be utilized to direct and control vehicle movement at access points of the port, and more complex and technological bollard systems can be controlled electronically to be raised or lowered, which allows the facility or port to be flexible when varying levels of security may be needed (Christopher, 2015).

In addition to physically denying access into a port, technological measures such as CBP's VACIS (Vehicle and Cargo Inspection System) and radiation detection portal systems are used to detect radioactive and other illicit material from entering the port. Fig. 8.4, below, shows an access gate to one of Houston's container ports. Notice the radiation portals and VACIS systems affixed to the gate structure.

Figure 8.4

Container terminal entry gates. *Port of Houston. https://porthouston.com/terminal-toolbox/container-terminals/gate-information/. (Accessed 12 June 2020).*

As an adjunct to the physical and technological access control measures, the Transportation Worker Identification Credential, commonly referred to TWIC, is required in accordance with the Maritime Transportation Security Act or MTSA to vet workers who require unescorted access to operating areas within ports and the vessels berthed there.[2] This provides value added to the physical and technological access control measures.

Lighting

Another important physical security measure at ports is lighting. Lighting is an important physical security measure when it comes to preventative security and the principles of deter, deny, detect, and delay. The principles of CPTED can also be applied to lighting, as it helps minimize risk and prevent crime based on the design of the environment. Different areas of the port will require different lighting intensities. Lighting along the perimeter, and in work and parking areas, should be such that operational safety is maintained, and unwanted access is visibly and technologically detected.

On the perimeter, lighting should be placed to avoid any possible obstruction and should be directed at the roadside pavement or any other possible entrapment areas.[3] At a port, for areas intended for nighttime use (e.g., pedestrian walkways, access routes, parking areas, or pier side) should be sufficiently lit so that a person with normal vision could identify a face from about 10 meters away (CPTED Guidebook, 2003). For piers and waterfront lighting, high mast lighting provided for waterside operations supply adequate illuminance for security requirements (UFC 4-025-01, 2012). On the contrary, for paths or areas that are not intended for nighttime use, lighting and visibility can give a false sense of comfort during nighttime. One method to discourage gathering or nighttime use is to leave the area or path completely unlit. Lighting of different wattage, color temperature, sensitivity, and rendition can also make areas or paths less hospitable for gathering or nighttime use (CPTED Guidebook, 2003). Lighting near the entrances to buildings or access gates should be consistent and provide for clear visibility. Another important design aspect of lighting is consistency. Lighting should be consistently and sufficiently spread to lessen the contrast between shadows and illuminated areas.

---

[2] The Transportation Security Administration is responsible for issuance of the Transportation Worker Identification Credential (TWIC) and U.S. Coast Guard for enforcement. Before a TWIC can be issued, a background check of the individual is conducted to determine a person's eligibility and assessment of risk. Mariners licensed by the U.S. Coast Guard also require this credential.

[3] Entrapment areas are small, confined areas near or adjacent to well-traveled routes that are shielded on three sides by some barriers, such as walls or bushes. Examples are lifts, tunnels, or bridges, enclosed and isolated stairwells, dark recessed entrances that may be locked at night, gaps in tall vegetation.

Lighting alone is not enough to deter crime. Lighting must be combined with other physical and technological measures, as well as security personnel in order to prove effective. Further, lighting and proper visibility is critical to the function of other security measures at the port, in particular the technological security measures involved in surveillance. For example, most ports use CCTV as video surveillance around the port and its different areas. For CCTV and other methods of surveillance to be effective, other than infrared cameras, adequate lighting is necessary and must be maintained. Lighting fixtures must be maintained regularly if the bulb is burnt out, broken, or the fixture is obstructed, and the lighting fixtures themselves should be protected with vandal-resistant materials and design (Fennelly and Crowe, 2013). For the function of surveillance through CCTV where lighting is not desired, other technological measures can be used. To compensate for less than desirable lighting, motion sensing and alarm systems to detect intrusion and activate the cameras are used. Infrared cameras are also effective when lighting levels are low in a port.

Intrusion detection

The threat of intrusion is a serious security concern for port facilities, especially along the perimeter where intrusion detection systems (IDS) are critical to ensuring that any intrusion is detected. This is because a port perimeter is, in all likelihood, too large for conventional security patrols to practically or effectively cover, so they must rely on other security measures in tandem. This includes IDS and CCTV or a different method of identification, such as video content analysis (VCA) or biometrics to secure the perimeter and the port.

It should be understood that an intrusion can be via land or sea. Because of this, a further security measure at ports is intrusion detection, which is a critical aspect of the "detect" security principle outlined by Bennett (2018). This component includes physical and technological devices (e.g., regular and infrared cameras) used in conjunction with security forces monitoring the perimeter and site itself. Even though the term "Intrusion Detection System" can be used to describe a single, stand-alone system (i.e., a "sensor" unit), it is more often used to describe a complete and integrated system that defines, controls, and displays security areas and intrusion into those areas (Rowsham and Simonetta, 2003). Intrusion detection is an important measure in terms of the different layers of security. It is usually combined and integrated with access control to effectively secure the port and its operating and administrative areas. IDS can be used on the outer layers, such as along the perimeter fencing, but also can be utilized as an inner layer of security, such as at gates, doors, and locks (Accetturo, 2012). Intrusion detection is less a preventative method of security and more of a warning and response mechanism. IDS usually must be combined with other identification methods such as CCTV, which must be monitored and recorded to be effective. If not monitored, the recordings are used for investigations or simply evidence.

Intrusion detection provides an alert to on duty security personnel to look at a specific cameras (locations) and respond in a timely manner. IDS can have false alarms, such as with rodents; hence the use of CCTV and monitoring by security personnel are critical.

To get a flavor of how other transportation agencies and their associated fixed facilities address intrusion detection, especially since 9/11, the focus is and has been on developing better IDS capabilities and programs. Much of the technology and developments regarding intrusion detection is in the sphere of public transportation but is readily adaptable to a port environment. For example, TCRP (Transit Coopreative Research Program) Report 86 details the physical and technological measures that make up IDS for public transportation facilities. The most basic of these measures are physical, including fences, barriers, and lighting, which have all been adapted to a port environment. A further measure is video systems, such as CCTV or a pan–tilt–zoom camera or PTZ, to remotely monitor and assess security and controlled areas (Rowsham and Simonetta, 2003). The type of video system that could be used in a port would depend on both the cost of the system and the port's environment.

Access control systems, which could be anything from a key to a biometrics system, also can be considered part of a facility's IDS. The level and complexity of an access control system is dependent on the sensitivity of the area that it is controlling access or movement to/from. Sensor systems are a critical part of public transportation facilities' IDS and are adaptable to a port environment. Again, the type of sensor and its specific location are dependent on the port and its environment. Sensor systems technologies can range from simple push button switches to complex radar, but one thing to note is that in addition to sensing intrusion, some IDS and sensor systems can also provide historical data that can assist post-incident analysis (Rowsham and Simonetta, 2003).

Because of the large options of sensor systems and possible utilizations, sensors can be easily integrated into a port's IDS. Identification systems also play an important role in intrusion detection. Identification systems refer to technologies that are used to create a credential that can be used by both security personnel and electronic access control systems to uniquely identify authorized status (Rowsham and Simonetta, 2003). A low-cost example is a simple photograph identification, while a higher cost and more complex example is a biometrics data system, which can include fingerprints or an iris scan (Rowsham and Simonetta, 2003). The TWIC is an example of this.

Finally, the data collected from these different systems and technologies need to be analyzed and displayed, which is accomplished through a data fusion, display, and control system. A data fusion, display, and control system refers to a combination of either a single or multiple software application(s) and some type of computer hardware that can be used by security personnel to "see" real-time data from all aspects of a facility's IDS

(Rowsham and Simonetta, 2003). What system could be best adapted to a port environment is dependent upon the port itself (e.g., weather, wiring, and power concerns) and where such a system would be placed.

There are different types of IDS and deciding which one is most effective, is dependent on the port's operations, physical characteristics, and its environment. For example, there are motion sensing cameras, alarm systems, and infrared cameras that can be used individually or in combination. IDS can be stationary, such as a fixed infrared camera or can be active. An active IDS refers to a system or camera that relies on movement to detect—motion sensing. The clearest example of this would be motion-sensing detectors or cameras that can be utilized both on the perimeter as well as in the inner layers of the port's operations. In terms of cameras, the most significant distinction is between passive infrared versus active infrared technology. Passive infrared cameras/sensors detect an intrusion by sensing the temperature contrast between an intruder moving through the detection area and the background environment (Southwest, 2020). Active infrared technology employs a two-column sensor for detection of intruders—the transmitter unit emits invisible active infrared beams and the receiver unit receives and analyzes the beams and detects intruders passing between the two columns (Southwest, 2020).

The above systems and applications have a universal use in the transportation environment. Unlike most mass transportation systems and airports, the application of technology and intrusion detection in the port environment must address landside and waterside risk. The challenge and risk that the waterside poses to port security can hardly be overstated. Potential waterside attacks pose different challenges that the port must take into consideration, and intrusion detection plays a key role in waterside security. Threats to the waterside can either be surface threats (e.g., boats or swimmers) or subsurface threats (via scuba diver or submersible) (UFC 4-025-01, 2012).

To protect the waterside and waterfront assets, it is critical to establish and maintain a defined perimeter that is clearly marked off with signs, buoys, or a similar barrier. Once a clear perimeter is established, the waterside can be broken up into different security zones: the Waterside Assessment Zone, the Waterside Warning Zone, and the Waterside Threat Zone, which can be seen in Fig. 8.5 (UFC 4-025-01, 2012). In order to adequately protect the waterside, the Waterside Assessment Zone is where IDS should be set up to detect and assess any surface or subsurface threats approaching from the water.

One security system aimed at protecting the waterside and waterfront assets is an electronic harbor security system (EHSS). The EHSS integrates electronic sensors and video systems to detect, assess, track, and archive capabilities for waterside surface and subsurface threats. The type of system utilized shall be based on a port's different assets to be protected and levels of risk (UFC 4-025-01, 2012). In an EHSS, radar and video technology are the equipment and systems used for the detection, tracking, and assessment

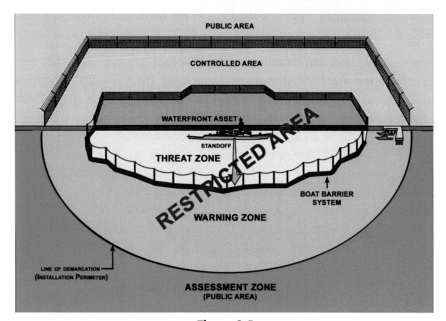

Figure 8.5

Waterfront security zones. *Fig. 5.1, U.S. Department of Defense, November 1, 2012. Unified Facilities Criteria, Security Engineering: Waterfront Security (UFC 4-025-01).*

of all surface threats approaching the waterside. The location of radar and video equipment is site-specific based on factors such as the waterside and landslide terrain, but typically the radar equipment should be placed on elevated surface locations (UFC 4-025-01, 2012). The video imaging system of the EHSS is a collection of cameras, recorders, switches, keyboards, and monitors that allow assessment and recording of security events and utilizes two different cameras: one low-light color PTZ camera for daytime assessment and one PTZ night vision camera or imaging device at each location. Multiple technologies must be deployed to ensure adequate coverage of the waterside area (e.g., low-light cameras, infrared cameras, thermal imagers) (UFC 4-025-01, 2012).

Potential subsurface threats present a different threat to the port waterside, and, thus, different technology is necessary for intrusion detection and assessment of underwater threats. Sonar technology (e.g., sonar transponder) and underwater soundheads[4] are the common intrusion detection technology utilized for underwater waterside security at ports. Submerged nonvisual sonar transponders are installed at various underwater locations feeding their inputs to a central display (e.g., operator workstation) (UFC 4-025-01, 2012). The soundhead can be bottom-mounted, side-mounted, or moored. The use of multiple

---

[4] The term "sound head" is used to designate the sonar transducer or hydrophone including its housing and mounting. https://maritime.org/doc/sonar/chap18.htm.

transponders helps eliminate holes and shadows in the nonvisual submerged surveillance picture (UFC 4-025-01, 2012).

The development of EHSS and its reliance on technology are indicative that the future of IDS, especially on the waterside, that are evolving away from physical security measures and toward complex, integrated technological systems that provide a level of detection, tracking, and assessment that physical measures, such as a swimmer net or boat barrier, simply cannot. One consideration in this continued development of IDS is that not every intrusion on the waterside is necessarily a direct threat. Any new waterside security system needs to be flexible enough to discriminate between the inadvertent, the deliberate but nonmalicious and those with hostile intent (Evans, 2008). One example of the technological developments in underwater protection and detection is the Integrated Swimmer Defense (ISD), which is a project developed by the US Navy in partnership with members of industry. ISD combines active sonar with radar and electro-optics/infrared and integrating software which links real-time datasets to provide speed and accuracy of detection (Evans, 2008).

The above information addresses US transportation facilities and ports. The challenge in securing foreign ports is the perceived higher level of threats and associated vulnerabilities, and physical and technological security measures in place. Do they meet minimum US security measures? Do they meet international or reasonable security measures given the threats and associated risk? The USCG's International Port Security Program (IPSP) is intended to minimize the risk to US maritime interests and enables secure maritime trade by: (1) instilling confidence in the effectiveness of a port state's implementation of security measures to include physical and technological as espoused by the International Ship and Port Facility Security (ISPS) Code,[5] (2) other international maritime security standards, and (3) to enhance port security measures beyond the minimum requirements of the ISPS Code (Brown, 2006).

Infrastructure protection and hardening

Infrastructure protection and hardening and system redundancy are also important steps to securing a port from adversaries, crime, and attacks. Although layered security is intended to keep the "bad actors" out, nothing is 100% effective. By identifying the critical infrastructure in the port and the physical security measures in place (e.g. fencing, gates, and barriers), protecting and hardening the infrastructure may also be necessary. This issue is one of the reasons that the Department of Homeland Security (DHS) has developed a

---

[5] The International Ship and Port Facility Security (ISPS) Code that sets minimum security standards and procedures for ships, ports, and government agencies prescribing the responsibilities of all parties involved in maritime operations and commerce detect security threats and take preventive measures against them in ports and at sea.

list of critical infrastructure vital to the United States and its economy, and the USCG has developed and implemented the Maritime Security Risk Assessment Model (MSRAM) to mitigate the risk in US ports and waterways, and prioritize resources for port security operations (Gordon, 2018).

Infrastructure protection and hardening, when combined with system redundancy through cyber-based supervisory controls and data acquisition (SCADA) and other control systems, provides for the resiliency and robustness of the port's facilities, buildings, and structures. SCADA is a computer and digital network that was developed to support the operations of the water, power, and energy sectors. Since the potential for an asymmetric attack on a port's SCADA-like systems has grown over recent years, hardening and system redundancy have become a key concern for both port officials and DHS. The Bioterrorism Act of 2002 makes recommendations to protect against a potential SCADA attack and recommends the hardening of targets by adding intrusion detection equipment (like motion sensors), installing fences, gates, locks, lighting, and making improvements to SCADA (Lewis, 2020).

The hardening of infrastructure refers to the hardening and protection of physical and technological systems. To protect physical infrastructure, the security measures previously discussed, such as fencing, lighting, barriers, IDS, and access control all play significant roles in hardening physical infrastructure. In a port environment, it is critical that this hardening is accomplished on both the landside and the waterside to protect from all potential intrusions and adversaries. What infrastructure needs to be most protected and hardened is dependent on the port, its different levels of risk, and the different costs associated with hardening infrastructure.

Hardening infrastructure can be from protecting the piers and associated roadways and craneways through protecting the bridges that provide access to the port to the administrative and maintenance buildings. This includes barriers, but also includes hardening the physical structure itself against man-made and natural disasters. Many agencies conduct security reviews of infrastructure and new construction and reconstruction projects during the preliminary stage of the design process. The purpose of the security review is to determine:

- The weakest structural members of the bridge, tunnel, building, etc.
- Via assault planners (e.g., ex-Navy SEALS and Army Special Forces) how the structure could be attacked and compromised.
- What measures could be put in place to deter, detect, delay, and degrade the magnitude of the attack.
- The risk reduction measures and associated costs of implementing them.
- The approach to reducing the risk appropriate for the structure and proceed to final design.

The above process appropriately modified can be used for existing infrastructure deemed critical.

Security review framework for port access roadway bridges

For example, and for the Port Newark Container Terminal, E. Port Road and North Avenue E. are major access roadways to and from the port. Both cross over the railroad tracks serving the port, as well as I-95/New Jersey Turnpike to the west. Also, the port is located immediately east of Newark International Airport (EWR) and in the flight path for Runway 11/29. Taking out either bridge would severely impact port access and could potentially impact operations at Newark International Airport and on the New Jersey Turnpike. As these are existing bridges, the security review of either bridge would first involve a review of the bridge design plans and calculations. Once the critical members[6] of the bridge are determined from the review, assault planners would be used to find ways to attack (usually by explosives) and take down the bridge(s) to deny access to the port. The method of delivery to compromise the bridge(s) could be by an improvised explosive device (IED), VBIED, or even via a train from the tracks underneath. What about a hijacked airplane on final approach to EWR Runway 29? Once the method of attack and extent of the explosives to be used are known, mitigation, detection, and standoff measures would be determined to impede access to the bridge(s) and theoretically reduce the explosive yield that could be more easily carried without detection. Once the explosive yield is reduced to the maximum extent possible, by restricting unfettered access by the attackers, engineers would redesign the critical member to withstand the explosive yield coupled with mitigation and standoff measures (e.g., barriers at the bridge abutments) to protect the bridge(s).

---

[6] According to the American Association of Highway and Transportation Officials or AASHTO, critical or fracture critical members of a bridge are the primary steel members, or portions thereof, whose failure would likely cause the entire or a portion of bridge to fail and possibly collapse.

Hardening software and technological systems means protecting said systems from unauthorized access by potential hackers, attackers, or intruders gaining access. There are many steps that can be taken to secure and harden a facility's operating systems (OS) and software. In practice, this includes removing all nonessential software programs from computers/other components, patching all OS software and hardware, and adding protections such as firewalls and software intrusion detection (Weijdema, 2017). Further steps that can be taken to secure and harden technological/software infrastructure is to develop a strict access control policy and having a strong password management policy (Weijdema, 2017). As technology continues to evolve and change the security and protection sphere, the hardening of all software infrastructure will become even more important over the coming years, as potential attacks could be network based.

CPTED considerations can also play an important role in hardening and protecting infrastructure. Fennelly and Crowe detail that the traditional hardening approach based on physical measures such as fence and barriers leads to constraints on use and access to the environment hardened, and that the traditional approach tends to overlook opportunities for natural access control and surveillance (Fennelly and Crowe, 2013). For hardening, a CPTED design strategy attempts to derive access control and surveillance results as a by-product of the normal and routine uses of the environment. While CPTED still takes advantage of traditional hardening measures, it is possible to adapt normal and natural uses of the environment to accomplish the effects of artificial or mechanical hardening and surveillance (Fennelly and Crowe, 2013). Depending on the port and its natural environment, port officials could take advantage of a CPTED design strategy, consistent with all of the traditional hardening measures previously discussed, to effectively protect and harden physical and technological infrastructure against potential adversaries and attacks.

Technological security measures

Technology plays a critical role in securing ports of entry from all possible threats. DHS, CBP, and other security personnel utilize a range of technological security measures and equipment to secure US ports of entry. Following 9/11, DHS has mainly concentrated its maritime security technological efforts on developing and deploying equipment that can nonintrusively scan containers for nuclear materials or certain other dangerous contents, such as hazardous materials (hazmat), weapons, and people (Johnstone, 2015). Some of the technology that is in use by DHS and CBP to accomplish this goal includes handheld devices that can detect human occupancy in a container by measuring carbon dioxide levels, truck-mounted nonintrusive gamma ray imaging systems that produce radiographic images of container contents, and radiation portal monitors (RPMs) to detect radiation sources (Johnstone, 2015).

As was touched upon earlier, technology plays a significant role in access control systems and IDS. For IDS, technology such as the different cameras (infrared, CCTV, etc.), all the different sensor systems, and the data fusion, display and control system are critical to ensuring adequate and effective intrusion detection for public transportation facilities and ports of entry. Depending on the sensitivity of the infrastructure being protected, access control systems can also be highly technical. Electronic keypads are a simple technological measure involved with access control systems, but also the different biometric systems/technologies used for access control systems are an important measure in port security. Programs like TWIC or other biometric credential systems provide an added layer of security to access control, and as technology continues to develop, access control and IDS will also evolve to utilize these technological developments.

A significant aspect of technological security measures in ports is the scanning of incoming container shipments. An integral part of the CBP comprehensive strategy to combat nuclear and radiological terrorism is the scanning of all arriving conveyances and containers with radiation detection equipment prior to their release from a port of entry (DHS/CBP/PIA-031, 2016). DHS and CBP Radiation Detection Systems comprise the Port-Radiation Inspection, Detection, and Evaluation (PRIDE) System and the Automated Radiation Portal Monitor Data Integration System (ARDIS) (DHS/CBP/PIA-031, 2016). These systems work in tandem: PRIDE connects radiation scanning devices to the CBP network to monitor, assess, and respond to immediate radiation threats, while ARDIS automatically transmits RPM status and scanned data from the PRIDE system to the ARDIS Data Analysis Center-Threat Evaluation and Reduction Database (DAC-TER) for statistical analysis to produce intelligence and near real-time insight at all ports of entry throughout the country (DHS/CBP/PIA-031, 2016). The RPM is the most important piece of equipment when it comes to scanning cargo containers for radiation and is shown in Fig. 8.6. The RPM does not produce images, but rather is a passive system that captures and alerts to energy emitted by radioactive sources that happen to pass near it (Pike, 2011). If the RPM alerts, it is important to understand that an alert by itself does not indicate the presence of a nuclear weapon/material, as there are many legitimate sources of radiation that could set off the alarm like various medical isotopes. After an alarm is triggered during a primary RPM scan, CBP officers will subject the vehicle to a secondary screening either through another RPM or Radioisotope Identification Devices (RIID) inspection (DHS/CBP/PIA-031, 2016). The following identifies the different radiation detection equipment used by CBP and DHS officers (EPA, 2019):

- **Radiation portal monitors:** Drive-through monitoring stations that scan vehicles and their cargo. Portal monitors can detect radiation hidden inside shipping containers.
- **Personal radiation detectors:** Small, highly sensitive devices that sound an alarm when radiation is detected. Many federal officers and agents use these at ports and highway checkpoints in the United States.
- **Radiation isotope identifiers:** Handheld instruments that identify specific radionuclides, including nuclear weapon, medical and industrial radioactive materials. Security officers use these devices to identify the type of radionuclide that triggered an alarm.
- **Large-scale gamma ray/x-ray imaging systems:** These systems use radiation to show images of the contents of cargo containers, rail cars, vehicles, or trailer trucks.

Figure 8.6
A radiation portal monitor in use. *McCormick, L., July 2005. Radiation safety for Customs & Border protection officers and ports. Presented at the American Association of Port Authorities 2005 Port Security and Safety Seminar, East Rutherford, NJ.*

If a more complete image of the container and its contents are necessary, CBP's VACIS will be used. The VACIS system was introduced after the 9/11 attacks to protect from illegal drugs, weapons, and currency from entering the nation. VACIS is an X-ray system that utilizes gamma ray imaging to authenticate the contents inside the container or package without breaking the container or package seal. This X-ray examination can be accomplished pier side or at the laydown areas and internodal yards. CBP can also deploy truck-mounted VACIS units to any inland location. The scan can either be done when a container is stationary or rolling. Stationary scans require only two operators, while rolling scans require three operators (McCormick, 2005). Initially, the cargo will be scanned whole, and examination is carried out with the images obtained. If CBP is not satisfied, each container will be unloaded and individual items will be scanned thoroughly.

2008 New Orleans North American Leaders Summit and VACIS

On April 21 and 22, 2008, the City of New Orleans hosted the North American Leaders Summit (NALS), which was attended by President Bush, President Calderon of Mexico, and Prime Minister Harper of Canada. As an added security operation, DHS's TSA in partnership with CBP developed, coordinated, and conducted a security operation that focused on railroad operations within close proximity to the summit.

The security operation involved the use of CBP's truck-mounted VACIS units to X-ray the rail cars for WMD or other hazmat, such as toxic inhalation hazards (TIH) or other hazmat, that could be used for terrorist purposes as they traversed and/or were stored in the area determined critical and subject to risk (Fig. 8.7).

Figure 8.7
Truck mounted Vehicle and Cargo Inspection System unit used for the 2008 North American Leaders Summit. *Gary Gordon, 2008.*

This operation was unique, as it was the first known use of the truck-mounted VACIS unit by TSA and CBP in support of a railroad security operation, as the system was developed to inspect containers on a truck chassis. The operation was coordinated with and conducted in conjunction with the security efforts of the US Secret Service and other federal, state, and local agencies.

This innovative approach of using the truck-mounted VACIS unit for a railroad application and in a cooperative and partnered manner is nontraditional. Its design could be used for other transportation mode security operations. For example, truck-mounted permanent VACIS units can be used to inspect containers entering and leaving ports either routinely or for targeted or scheduled operations, such as Multi-Agency Strike Force Operations. As the operation was being conducted, CBP was researching a truck-mounted VACIS unit for railroad cars.

Summary

This chapter examines the physical and technological security measures currently in place to address the known threats and associated vulnerabilities of the operations in ports and from or via the surrounding environment. In the port environment, the threat can be either land-based or come from the waterside. Although the security measures herein are focused on man-made disasters and, in particular, terrorist attacks, the combination of a natural disaster and exploitation by a terrorist cannot be ignored and must be considered. Chapter 9 will examine the vulnerabilities and gaps in the physical and technological security measures employed today and (1) how they are positioned to address the evolution of the threat and ultimately the risk and (2) what research is being conducted and considered and by whom.

With the objective of denying access, and deterring, detecting, and delaying and/or defending against an attack, the physical security measures at ports and other transportation facilities are traditionally access control via barriers and fencing. When combined with technology, and in particular cyber systems, a comprehensive approach to security is sought and, hopefully, achieved. That is why access control also includes human and technological surveillance with the latter via cameras, intrusion detection, motion sensing, and strategic lighting. Infrastructure protection and hardening are ways of strengthening a structure against sabotage and compromise (e.g., by strategically placed explosives) to make it more robust and, thus, leading to the resiliency of the port and its operations.

Technological security measures are also focused on denying access, and deterring, detecting, and defending against an attack, but they also include the cyber systems supporting the vetting process for personnel, cargo, and supply chain partners (e.g., TWIC for port workers, VACIS for cargo inspection, and C-TPAT and CSI for the supply chain). Traditional technological security measures include surveilling, inspecting vehicles and cargo and the cameras used in support of perimeter and internal security, and the related cyber systems. System redundancy is like infrastructure protection and hardening by way of employing cybersecurity measures to either thwart cyberattacks or having backup systems in case of a successful attack. Hacking and other cyberattacks could affect the convergence of the physical and technological security measures and should not be taken lightly.

It is important that the intersection of the physical, technological, and cybersecurity measures and systems is clearly understood. This will ensure that a total security program can be implemented that is adaptable to address the evolving threats and associated risks. While not discussing cybersecurity measures at sea to thwart attacks on the automated identification system (AIS) and navigation, it must be considered as part of the overall security of the intermodal maritime supply chain and the subject of further research. The same applies to vessel operations in straits and canals with the security measures in the latter being similar to that in ports.

References

Bennett, B., 2018. Understanding, Assessing, and Responding to Terrorism: Protecting Critical Infrastructure and Personnel. John Wiley & Sons.

Brown, M., 2006. International port security program: implementation of international regulations. In: Proceedings, U.S. Coast Guard, vol. 63. Spring. Number 1.

Crime Prevention Through Environmental Design Guidebook, 2003. National Crime Prevention Council, Singapore.

Crime prevention through environmental design. In: Fennelly, L., Crowe, T. (Eds.), 2013. Chapter 3, CPTED Concepts and Strategies, third ed. Butterworth-Heinemann. ISBN-13: 978-0124116351.

Delta Scientific, February 23, 2007. U.S. Embassies Upgrading Physical Barriers. https://www.securityinfowatch.com/perimeter-security/physical-hardening/news/10558117/us-embassies-upgrading-physical-barriers.

Edwards, F., Goodrich, D., 2013. Introduction of Transportation Security. CRC Press/Taylor & Francis Group. ISBN-13: 978-1439845769.

EPA, Environmental Protection Agency, March 26, 2019. Radiation and Shipping Port Security. www.epa.gov/radtown/radiation-and-shipping-port-security.

Federal Emergency Management Agency, December 2007. Site and urban design for security: guidance against potential terrorist attacks. Chapter 4, Perimeter Security Design, FEMA 430.

FHWA-HIF-18-054, December 2018. Primer on Impact Protection for Critical Transportation Infrastructure. Federal Highway Administration.

Gordon, G., 2018. Intermodal Maritime Container Security: A Multifactor Framework for Assessing Routing (Doctoral dissertation). University of Massachusetts Lowell.

"Infrared Sensors", Integrated Perimeter Security Solutions, Southwest Microwave. www.southwestmicrowave.com/products/infrared-sensors. (Accessed 15 June 2020).

Johnstone, R.W., 2015. Protecting transportation implementing security policies and programs. In: Chapter 6, Implementing Maritime Security. Elsevier Ltd.

Lewis, T.G., 2020. Critical Infrastructure Protection in Homeland Security: Defending a Networked Nation. John Wiley & Sons Inc.

McCormick, L., July 2005. Radiation safety for Customs & Border Protection officers and ports. In: Presented at the American Association of Port Authorities 2005 Port Security and Safety Seminar, East Rutherford, NJ.

Pete, A., February 2012. Principles for Intrusion Detection. Security Today, 1105 Media Inc. securitytoday.com/Articles/2012/02/01/Principles-for-Intrusion-Detection.aspx?Page=1.

Pike, J., July 13, 2011. Radiation Portal Monitors. Retrieved from: https://www.globalsecurity.org/security/systems/rpm.htm.

Port Security Management, 2015. Chapter 12, Managing Technology Solutions for Port Facility Security. In: Christopher, K. (Ed.), second ed. Routledge/Taylor & Francis Group.

Privacy Impact Assessment for the Radiation Detection Systems, July 11, 2016. U.S. Department of Homeland Security (DHS/CBP/PIA-031).

Rowsham, S., Simonetta, R., 2003. Intrusion Detection for Public Transportation Facilities Handbook, vol. 4. Transportation Research Board. TCRP Report 86, Public Transportation Security.

Rozin, M., October 1, 2012. U.S. Security Shifting to Preventative Methods. Security Magazine. https://www.securitymagazine.com/articles/83537-us-security-shifting-to-preventative-methods.

Unified Facilities Criteria, Security engineering: Waterfront Security (UFC 4-025-01), November 1, 2012. U.S. Department of Defense.

Varghese, R., May 22, 2019. In Middle of Trade War, Port of Los Angeles Terminal Gets Ready for Robots. Bloomberg News. Photo: Fallon, P. T.

Waterside Security., Evans, Dr.G., November 27, 2008. Naval Technology. Verdict Media Limited. www.naval-technology.com/features/feature46248/.

Weijdema, E., May 15, 2017. 5 Tips for Infrastructure Hardening. VMGuru. vmguru.com/2017/05/5-tips-infrastructure-hardening/.

CHAPTER 9

Vulnerabilities, gaps, and the future of physical and technological security measures

Gary A. Gordon, PhD, PE, MEMS, LTC USA (Ret.) [1], **Bennett C. Abrams** [2]

[1]*Department of Civil & Environmental Engineering, University of Massachusetts Lowell, Lowell, MA, United States;* [2]*Tulane University, New Orleans, LA, United States*

This chapter addresses the vulnerabilities and associated gaps of the current physical and technological security measures at and in ports given the current threats, and the research and development in progress by academia, industry and the government and that needed to address the evolving threats and minimize risk.

Vulnerabilities and gaps in security measures

Ever since the 9/11 attacks, leaders in government, as well as security professionals, have focused on the maritime transportation system and international supply chain as a potential vulnerability that could be exploited by terrorists for economic and political goals. The major concern is that terrorists could utilize ships or containers to smuggle persons, weapons of mass destruction (WMD), nuclear material, or other dangerous materials into the United States through a port of entry. On top of that, there is also concern that large commercial cargo ships or cruise ships that are anchored in US ports could be the target of a terrorist attack. Not only would such an attack cause major death and damage, but it could also paralyze global maritime commerce, would be a mass casualty event, and/or cause economic damage and political instability on a global scale (Frittelli, 2005).

Cargo ships carry approximately 80% of world trade by volume, so any disruptions, especially those triggered by a terrorist attack could have an immediate and significant impact on both the US and global economies and possibly sovereignty. A terrorist attack at a port would, of course, also have national security ramifications: The Department of Defense (DOD) and the Department of Transportation (DOT) have designated 17 US seaports, of which 13 are commercial ports, as strategic because they are necessary for use

Intermodal Maritime Security. https://doi.org/10.1016/B978-0-12-819945-9.00013-7

Figure 9.1
Loading military vehicles at port of Beaumont, TX. *"Moving the Army Texas Style" Army Logistician, U.S. Army, July-August, 2004 (Donald J. Japalucci, 842d Transportation Battalion Public Affairs Officer).*

by DOD in the event of a major military deployment (Frittelli, 2005). Fig. 9.1, below, shows a ship being loaded with military vehicles at the Port of Beaumont, Texas.

Further given the dependence of the United States and the global economy on a highly efficient maritime transportation system, many experts acknowledge that slowing the flow of trade (e.g., inspect all inbound containers or at least a statistically significant random sample) would be economically intolerable (Frittelli, 2005). Because scanning all inbound containers is logistically and economically unfeasible, such constraints represent a gap and vulnerability in the security measures protecting US ports.

But what are the threats facing US ports? Of the many threats, whether naturally or intentionally or accidentally caused, terrorism is central to the development of security measures. Government leaders and security experts are concerned about the variety of threats from terrorists facing US ports. They are concerned that, among other things, terrorists could:

- Use commercial cargo containers to smuggle terrorist operatives, nuclear, chemical, or biological weapons, components thereof, or other dangerous materials into the United States;
- Seize control of a large commercial cargo ship and use it as a collision weapon for destroying a bridge or refinery located on the waterfront or port infrastructure itself;

- Sink a large commercial cargo ship in a major shipping channel, thereby blocking all traffic to and from the port;
- Attack a large ship carrying a volatile fuel, such as liquefied natural gas, and detonate the fuel so as to cause a massive in-port explosion and fire;
- Attack an oil tanker in a port or at an offshore discharge facility so as to disrupt the world oil trade and cause large-scale environmental damage;
- Use cyberattacks to compromise physical security measures, vetting processes, and navigation and tracking.

There are also a series of threats that are not directly related to the intermodal maritime supply chain but are nonetheless threats to ports and port facilities, and adjacent waterways. These scenarios, although not focused on the intermodal maritime supply chain, should not be ignored because they could lead to trends and possible avenues of compromise that could be retooled for container ships and/or show heightened geopolitical motivation. These threats are that terrorists could potentially:

- Seize control of a ferry, which can carry hundreds of passengers, or a cruise ship, which can carry several thousand passengers, a majority of which are usually US citizens, and threaten the deaths of the passengers if a demand is not met;
- Attack US or other nations' navy ships in an attempt to kill military personnel, damage or destroy a valuable military asset, such as the attack on the *USS Cole* in 2000, and, in the case of nuclear-powered ships, potentially cause a radiological event;
- Use the land around a port to stage attacks on bridges, tunnels, refineries, etc. located on the waterfront or other port facilities;
- Physically attack the port and its facilities from land by running a gate, crashing through a fence or "piggybacking" or "tailgating."[1]

Security awareness should also include terrorists exploiting natural disasters, such as hurricanes as they make landfall, creating a cascading event.

In examining these different threats facing US ports, there are three types of potential targets that must be secured: the port facilities themselves, the ships coming into port, and the container shipments that they would be carrying.

---

[1] Piggybacking or tailgating is when a person or vehicle, respectively, accesses a secure or restricted area on the "credentials" of the person or vehicle in front without showing his/her credentials. This can occur with or without the first person's or vehicle's permission and can be intentional or unintentional. An example of piggybacking is when one worker uses his/her "credentials" (e.g., TWIC card) to access a secure port operations building and a coworker follows immediately behind using the first person's "credentials" with or without the first person's consent to access the building. Because piggybacking and tailgating are often due to laziness, it does not matter whether the second person has proper credentials or not. Tailgating is the same process as piggybacking, but it is when one vehicle follows another through a gate to a secure or restricted area on the first vehicle's "credentials."

Port facilities and different areas of a port have many vulnerabilities that may be exposed to a potential terrorist attack. Port facilities typically have large landside and waterside perimeters, meaning terrorists or criminals have many potential landside and waterside points of entry. Further, some ports are located immediately adjacent to built-up urban areas, which could give terrorists or criminals a place to hide while approaching or escaping the port (Frittelli, 2005). This threat can, of course, be mitigated by, among other things, good lighting, intrusion detection systems (IDS), fencing and access control systems, but still represents a potential vulnerability in port security. Another vulnerability to ports is trucks. Large numbers of trucks move in and out of ports daily, making them a possible vehicle for terrorists to bring themselves and/or their weapons into the port (Frittelli, 2005). On the waterside, terrorists could utilize small vessels, which could look like regular recreational or fishing boats, to mask their approach into port. The U.S. Coast Guard's (USCG) Maritime Security Risk Assessment Model (MSRAM) categorizes and assesses the risk to port facilities allowing for them (the USCG) to assist in prioritizing and assigning security forces and patrols, as shown in Fig. 9.2, below. This helps secure the port's facilities thereby theoretically and, hopefully, measurably reduces the risk of a terrorist attack.

Figure 9.2
USCG patrol vicinity of port of Los Angeles and Long Beach. *Article "Marine Exchange of Southern California" Capt. Edward H. Lundquist, U.S. Navy (Ret.), Defense Media Network at https://www. defensemedianetwork.com/stories/marine-exchange-southern-california/.*

The ships coming into port and anchoring at a pier or in a harbor also represent a vulnerability and potentially an easy target for terrorists. Large commercial cargo ships at a port are likely to be either stationary or moving through the port at slow speeds making them easy to be intercepted by smaller, fast-moving maneuverable boats, which are commonly utilized by terrorists and pirates. Commercial cargo ships are generally unarmed or minimally armed and have small crews,[2] making them vulnerable to seizure by a small group of armed people, as proven by modern-day pirates (Frittelli, 2005). What about using handheld weapons, such as shoulder mounted rocket launchers from the shore or attack by drones? This essentially expands the need for security measures to areas outside the ports and waterways.

The container shipments themselves are also a major potential vulnerability as they could easily be utilized by terrorists. Because of the complexity involved with completing container shipments and the high number of potential parties involved in any import transaction, the processes and documents involved, container shipments represent a series of potential vulnerabilities. Unlike other cargo ships whose loading process occurs at the port and whose cargo is often owned by a single company, container ships carry cargo from hundreds or even thousands of companies, and a single container might also carry cargo for several customers, thus multiplying the number of parties and documents involved (Frittelli, 2005). The parties involved in a shipment usually include the exporter, the importer, a freight forwarder, a customs broker, a customs inspector, inland transportation provider(s), which may include more than one trucker or railroad, the port operator(s), possibly a feeder ship, and the ocean carrier (Frittelli, 2005; Gordon, 2018). Each transfer involved in this shipment/process is a potential vulnerability in the maritime supply chain. The security of each transfer facility and the trustworthiness of each company are, therefore, critical in the overall security of the shipment, and U.S. Customs and Border Protection (CBP) has developed the Customs-Trade Partnership Against Terrorism (C-TPAT) to address this vulnerability (Frittelli, 2005). C-TPAT is a voluntary program through which CBP works with private companies involved in international trade to review and improve the security of their supply chains while facilitating the flow of legitimate trade (Johnstone, 2015).

The 2000 attack on the *USS Cole* and the seaborne 2008 Mumbai attacks demonstrate a further potential vulnerability to ports by small vessels. The Department of Homeland Security (DHS) has identified four major threats where small vessels could be used: (1) for use in the United States as an improvised explosive device (IED), (2) to smuggle weapons, including a WMD, into the United States, (3) to smuggle terrorists into the United States, and (4) as a waterborne platform to conduct an attack (Johnstone, 2015). DHS published the *Small Vessel Security Implementation Plan Report to the Public* in 2011 to address the

---

[2] Some of the largest container vessels are crewed with less than 20 persons.

threats that small vessels pose to ports (Johnstone, 2015). The report includes steps and recommendations, such as developing a strong relationship with the small vessel community in the United States, leveraging technology to enhance detection and tracking of small vessels, and improving the coordination, cooperation, and communication between federal, state, local, and tribal partners, as well as private sector companies and international partners (Johnstone, 2015).

Because international shipping and port facilities involve so many moving parts, vulnerabilities and gaps exist both in the physical and technological security measures themselves, but also at different points along the international maritime supply chain. There are two main vulnerabilities: that ports or ships within them could be the target of a terrorist attack, or that terrorists could smuggle WMDs, persons, or other dangerous materials through a port of entry into the United States. In terms of a port being the target of an attack, this risk is exacerbated at ports because there is both an extensive landside and a waterside perimeter that increases potential points of access. Small vessels could also be used to conduct an attack, which is why a key mission of DHS and USCG is to develop a better relationship with the small vessel community[3] and develop better tracking and detection technology for small vessels. To better combat the risk of terrorist smuggling, technological, and physical developments to make scanning of cargo containers more efficient will be key to mitigating the risk of illegal smuggling.

Future of physical and technological security measures

Given the physical and technological security measures used and discussed herein, the adage of "they only have to be right once and we have to be right all of the time," one must look at how the threats would evolve and evaluate current security measures and what gaps may exist. The gaps are where we must determine if the known future physical and technological methods are sufficient to address evolving threats and where to look to improve the security posture. Remember that complacency could result in disastrous impacts and consequences.

When looking at the future of physical and technological security measures, government agencies, academia, trade organizations, and the industry itself are the likely entities to address this. Appendix A provides a small but representative list of entities that address terrorism, resiliency, and homeland security issues that provides either direct research or insight into what is involved in "keeping several steps ahead of terrorists" when it comes to physical and technological security needs. The research conducted by these entities,

---

[3] The U.S. Coast Guard developed the America's Waterway Watch to enlist the recreational boater as another set of eyes on the waterfront. Many of its elements appear similar to the Neighborhood Watch initiatives that have been in place for decades.

agencies, and organizations either directly addresses the maritime industry and its supply chain security issues or the application of such research could have benefits or point to additional research that could benefit the maritime supply chain security.

The following sections present examples of programs and/or research that address physical and technological security measures based on the evolving threats. If not specifically conducted for ports and the maritime environment and its supply chain, it can be used as a road map as to where research programs could go.

Access control

The future of access control will be a combination of physical security measures (e.g., barriers and fencing) integrated with infrastructure protection and network-based systems that are able to do credential identification and interact with various types of management systems. In terms of the physical barriers themselves, the US DOD employs international testing standards and testing procedures for different categories of vehicle security barriers that must be met to be approved. Companies such as Southwest Research Institute regularly test different security barriers that meet these standards and provide a road map for future improvements to perimeter fencing and access gates.[4]

The future of the development of security barriers will focus on how to make the barriers themselves more robust and resilient and what types of barriers (e.g., bollards, fencing, net system, and active wedge [see Fig. 9.3, below]) are most effective and safe. A further aspect of the future of physical security barriers is how they can be integrated into more digital security systems. Data and analytics will be a key future of physical security and access control, so developing security barriers that are fully integrated with digital security systems is needed.

There are many in the physical security community that feel that a digital transformation is both needed and inevitable when it comes to the future of access control systems. In 2018, Microsoft and Accenture conducted a "Future of Physical Security" survey where 200 senior physical security leaders across multiple industries participated. One of the key takeaways from this survey was that the future of access control calls for a merging of physical and cybersecurity (Foynes, 2019). One aspect of this unification is dynamic identity management: a digital development that authenticates identity—not just credentials—and eliminates the reliance on access tokens like badges and cards (Foynes, 2019). As an example, Michael Foynes, the senior director of global security operations at Microsoft, observes:

---

[4] See https://www.swri.org/industry/product-assurance/seurity-barrier-testing.

Figure 9.3

Wedge barrier. *Ameristar Perimeter Security. https://www.ameristarsecurity.com/en/products/active-barriers/sentinel-wedge-barrier/. (Accessed 7 6 2020).*

Imagine that a data-center technician enters a data facility and is immediately identified through facial recognition, automatically granting access to authorized areas. As the technician moves through the environment, IoT[5] sensors and devices collect additional intelligence in real time, tracking movement and activity.

The future of access control will depend on the development of these digital security systems and identification systems, and on how quickly and efficiently they can be integrated into existing port physical security systems and facilities.

Lighting

The future of lighting and lighting fixtures focuses on the light fixtures themselves and the overall lighting design in conjunction with the lighting requirements of the different uses in the port environment. The aim is to discover how to promote and ensure safety and security while reducing power demands and costs by lighting areas more uniformly. Uninterrupted power is also an issue to be addressed. The Lighting Research Center

---

[5] The Internet of Things is a system of interrelated computing devices, mechanical and digital machines provided with unique identifiers and the ability to transfer data over a network without requiring human-to-human or human-to-computer interaction.

(LRC) at Rensselaer Polytechnic Institute is an example of an entity that is focused on researching and publishing on the effectiveness of different lighting levels and designs.[6] The future of lighting will be focused on which lighting fixtures provide the best illumination at the lowest cost.

Lighting levels in ports vary based on location and activity—along the perimeter these will likely be of lesser intensity than in working areas along the piers. The future of the required lighting level at a port's perimeter should keep up with or even exceed the evolving or anticipated terrorist threat. In interior operational areas of the port, the future of required lighting will focus on how to provide the required illumination to capture quality video images while decreasing light pollution and glare that could adversely affect persons in the operational areas. Lighting is one piece of a puzzle of the overall physical security system, but it plays a major role in ensuring the effectiveness of other aspects of a port's physical security.

As the use of closed-circuit television (CCTV) and other camera-based systems has become more common and effective in physical security systems, lighting and lighting design takes on a newfound significance. This is because proper illumination, color intensity, reflection, etc. all play a major role in how effective and clear the video captured by cameras will be. Where conventional lighting technologies have shortcomings, mainly the maintenance costs and quality of lighting, new and emerging technologies are making lights more effective and at a reduced cost.

Conventional lighting technologies, such as metal halide lights or high pressure sodium lamps, have clear limitations and drawbacks in the port environment: high maintenance costs, poor color rendering, and poor direct control over the light, leading to considerable light loss (Stephany and Hertel, 2016). Fig. 9.4 shows typical pier side operational lighting. Because of these drawbacks, there has been a shift in ports to light-emitting diode (LED) lighting. LED technology has been around since the 1960s, but recent technological improvements have made the technology more viable in the maritime environment (Stephany and Hertel, 2016). While LED fixtures have higher installation costs than conventional lighting technologies, LED fixtures have much longer lifespans than conventional lighting sources and much lower maintenance costs. LED fixtures also have much better color temperature and color rendering ability, which greatly improves the quality of video that can be captured on security cameras (Stephany and Hertel, 2016). Moreover, LED technology also gives operators greater control over light glare and light spillage/pollution, which can have negative impacts on persons in the operational areas as well as any wildlife surrounding the port. One more benefit of LED lighting is that the fixtures can reach full intensity more or less immediately after being turned on, whereas conventional lighting technologies have significant warm-up and cooldown periods.

---

[6] See https://www.lrc.rpi.edu/researchAreas/securityResources.asp.

Figure 9.4

Conventional dockside lighting. *Stephany, M., Hertel, R., May 2016. Lighting Technologies in Ports and Terminals. Port Equipment Manufacturers Association. Retrieved from: https://www.pema.org/wp-content/uploads/downloads/2016/06/PEMA-IP10-Lighting-Technologies-in-Ports-and-Terminals.pdf.*

The future of lighting in the port environment will revolve around the further development of LED fixtures, potential new technologies, and the ability to program light fixtures. In terms of programming, it is becoming increasingly common in ports to attach floodlights to trolleys and cranes. New technology has now allowed for those lighting fixtures to be remotely programmed to remain off during daytime operations and on for nighttime operations, which reduces energy use and light pollution (Stephany and Hertel, 2016). LED fixtures can also be controlled by a dimming system, which is always useful for areas that do not need 100% illumination. In terms of new lighting technologies, one example is light-emitting plasma or LEPs, which have no electrodes, no glass-to-metal seals, and no secondary materials inside the capsule making them efficient and robust. LEPs also offer a high degree of light output directionality, and the ability to dim instantaneously to around 20% of full power (Stephany and Hertel, 2016). One area where both LED and LEP lighting has proven to be inefficient is reaching the required illumination when mounted at heights over 40 m (131 feet) or when the lights are spaced too far apart (Stephany and Hertel, 2016). Future research and developments in lighting design and fixtures will likely focus on this challenge.

Intrusion detection

The future of intrusion detection for the maritime environment, as with the other security measures, will focus on technological and cyber developments to assure that more security camera footage can be analyzed than is the case today. In terms of physical security measures, the future of perimeter IDS will likely revolve around volumetric systems and planar systems. Volumetric systems are those that detect disturbances of a volume of space, such as microwave systems and electric field systems (USNRC, 2017).[7] Planar systems, such as fence disturbance and infrared systems, detect disturbances of the geometric plane containing the system elements (USNRC, 2017). Fig. 9.5, below, depicts a simple above and below water fiberoptic detection system.

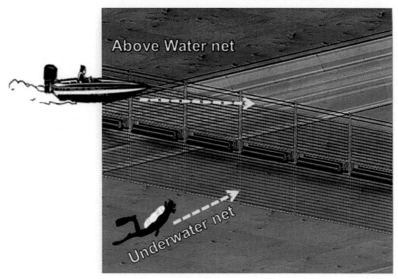

Figure 9.5

Typical above and below water detection system. *Improved Undersea Intrusion Detection Using Raw Optical Fiber, ID# 2015-0910, Invent Penn State. https://invent.psu.edu/ip_item/improved-undersea-intrusion-detection-using-raw-optical-fiber. (Accessed 7 6 2020).*

At present, these physical IDS are combined with an identification system, such as CCTV, to identify, track, and respond to intruders. The monitoring of security footage is an area where the development of digital security systems will have a major effect. The present day viewing of security footage relies heavily on manual processes, and it is difficult for humans to monitor all security content without digitally powered analytics (Foynes, 2019). That is the main reason it is commonly estimated among security professionals that more than 90% of security video footage goes unseen and is typically watched only for reactive investigation (Foynes, 2019). The development of digital systems that can monitor and analyze footage, data, and intelligence in real time will make IDS more effective. These digital systems could also be adapted specifically to the maritime environment and port facilities. The Federal Emergency Management Agency's (FEMA) Port Security Grant Program (PSGP) helps fund the development of port security and, for fiscal year 2020, its top priority is enhancing cybersecurity (FEMA, 2020). The development and unification of physical and cybersecurity systems is the future of IDS, especially in the maritime environment.

---

[7] For a microwave system with separate transmitters and receivers, this space is between the transmitter and the receiver. For an electric field sensor, the space parallels the sensor and generator wires (USNRC, 2017).

Infrastructure protection and hardening

Infrastructure must be protected and hardened from disasters both natural, such as a hurricane, and man-made, such as a terrorist attack. One important development is that infrastructure protection can be addressed as a public and private partnership (PPP). At ports, neither private nor public entities are usually in full control of the security measures in place, so the development of strong partnerships will be key in the future to protect and harden infrastructure (Pomerleau, 2019).

The threat from terrorists is ever-present, and because of the frequency, intensity, and magnitude of natural disasters, the need to harden and protect infrastructure is clear and essential. To address this, DHS's Science and Technology Directorate (S&T) has established a series of "centers of excellence" (COEs); a network of universities conducting groundbreaking research to address homeland security challenges such as these.

One COE that is working on addressing the challenge of natural disasters to infrastructure is the Coastal Resilience Center (CRC) at the University of North Carolina. The CRC developed the Advanced Circulation (ADCIRC) Prediction System (APS) to determine the location and severity of coastal flooding, which can be used to help protect and harden infrastructure (DHS CRC, 2020). The Critical Infrastructure Resilience Institute (CIRI) at the University of Illinois also conducts research to address the challenges of protecting critical infrastructure. In terms of the future, an example of their work is developing new cyber-risk assessment tools to better analyze cyber risks (DHS CIRI, 2020). CIRI has also focused on improving port cybersecurity specifically, working with US port owners and the USCG to develop better port cybersecurity (DHS CIRI, 2020).

The Cross-Border Threat Screening (CBTS) and Supply Chain Defense COE helps DHS S&T research and develop better technologies to secure trade. CBTS specifically focuses on three major areas: technologies to detect biological threats moving through global supply chains, data integration and analytics to support threat detection, and novel methods to minimize risks to DHS operations (DHS S&T COE, 2018). CBTS will also train and educate a highly skilled workforce to prepare for and respond to current and emerging biological threats (DHS S&T COE, 2018). DHS S&T's Maritime Security Center COE provides engineering sensor system applications to: (1) enhance security of the maritime domain, (2) assist decision-makers to enhance US ports to become more resilient to disruption, and (3) build cybersecurity capacity and bolster maritime asset protection. The center utilizes both underwater and aviation technologies, is developing a Port Resiliency Assessment and Planning tool to assess impacts on intermodal networks, supply chains and port communities, and addresses and overcomes cyber threats to vessel navigation, cargo inventory, and port facility systems.

The U.S. DOT 's Volpe National Transportation Systems Center's (VNTSC) Infrastructure Engineering and Deployment Division provides analysis, engineering, and project management to implement operational enhancements and improvements to infrastructure safety and security. This includes surface structures and facilities, systems, vehicles and vessels, and waterways and ports. In a 2013 report, the VNTSC addressed the application of industrial control systems (ICS) security throughout the maritime transportation system. The report identified potential cybersecurity vulnerabilities, and explored possible ICS failures and impacts, and federal policy governing critical infrastructure, cybersecurity, and supply chain resilience (Wallischeck, 2013).

The U.S. Army Corps of Engineers' Protective Design Center (PDC) houses expertise for engineering services related to force protection and protective design for both permanent and expedient applications to protect assets against criminal, terrorist, conventional, nuclear, and special weapons threats. Although much of the research focuses on blast protection, one document addresses vehicle barriers. Given the concern that terrorist attacks have increased, the PDC prepared a maintenance guide for Nuclear Regulatory Commission (NRC)-licensed nuclear power plants for the installation of crash resistant vehicle barriers and their maintenance (PDC-TR 06-03, 2007). This document can provide beneficial guidance for the installation and maintenance of barriers at ports.

The United Nations released a report in 2017 that focuses on how to protect and harden critical infrastructure from terrorists, clearly a different challenge than hardening infrastructure against natural disasters. A fundamental problem when hardening infrastructure against terrorist attacks is that terrorists can adapt their behavior to changes in the security landscape (CTED, 2017). Terrorist threats, therefore, are fundamentally different from safety issues, and there is a limit to the extent to which experience with safety policies can help make better security policies (CTED, 2017). This is particularly important when it comes to hardening port facilities.

Transportation facilities and vehicles are attractive targets for terrorist attacks because of the high concentration of potential victims, and because they also offer the possibility of turning vehicles into weapons with a potentially significant increase in victims (e.g., ships) (CTED, 2017). This also applies to intermodal and other cargo and the potential economic impact. The difficulty of protecting the many potential targets while maintaining smooth transport operations and the difficulty of determining the probability of attack also increase the appeal to terrorists (CTED, 2017). In response to these findings, in 2017, the UN Security Council adopted resolution 2341, which calls on member states to explore ways to assess vulnerabilities, interdependencies, and capabilities of, as well as the cascading effects of, the impacts of terrorist attacks on their critical infrastructure (CTED, 2017). In terms of future development, this resolution is aimed at encouraging member states to strengthen national, regional, and international partnerships, and to find better and more effective ways to share relevant information and communications to better harden infrastructure and facilities against potential terrorist attacks.

Technological security measures

The future of technological security measures, as is interwoven into this chapter, is interrelated with access control, infrastructure protection and hardening, intrusion detection, and lighting. Therefore, and to avoid duplication, this section highlights the issues and programs in general, as they address the evolving cyber threats. Their codependency is evident and important to ensure a holistic and effective approach to security going forward. In addition to the physical environment, technology plays an important role in the intermodal maritime supply chain, vessel navigation and tracking via, among other things, the automatic identification system (AIS).

The future of technological security measures in ports and the maritime environment focuses on cyberattacks, cyber threats, and cybersecurity. As security systems become more digital and make use of more and more different types of technology, the risks and potential damages associated with a cyberattack or cyberterrorism are increased. Potential targets for cyberterrorism at a port and its facilities are potentially the port facility's communication networks, utility systems, surveillance architecture, and information storage and retrieval systems (Christopher, 2015). The often anonymous nature of cyberattacks also makes them an attractive option for terrorists or criminals to employ.

Because of the increased threat of cyberattacks, cyberterrorism has begun to receive a heightened awareness by and focused attention of the US government. The DOD's Defense Advanced Research Projects Agency, also known as DARPA, is focused on developing technologies that can protect computers and networks from attack (Christopher, 2015). The Federal Bureau of Investigation (FBI) has also provided significant funding for a cybersecurity research center, which is focused on developing tools to better detect and investigate cyberattacks (Christopher, 2015). Port facilities, which depend on varying degrees and types of technology, must take advantage of the advancement and development of new systems, and government funding and expertise to best secure their communications networks from the growing risk of cyberattacks. The U.S. Department of Commerce's National Institute of Standards and Technology (NIST) is one of the premier government agencies addressing cybersecurity. Through its "Framework for Improving Critical Infrastructure Cybersecurity," there is a collaborative effort among industry, academia, and the government for improving critical infrastructure cybersecurity (NIST, 2018). These agencies in collaboration with others provide a "whole of government" approach to advances in cyber/technological security.

Summary

The future of port security, both physically and technologically, focuses on the linkage, interrelationships, and unification of existing or newly developed physical security systems with related digital and cybersecurity systems. Fig. 9.6, below, graphically depicts how the NRC envisions facility security as being linked, interrelated and interdependent.

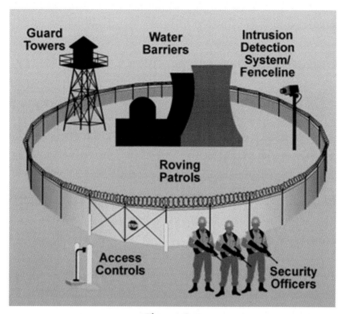

Figure 9.6

Nuclear Regulatory Commission concept of intrusion detection as part of overall security. *Lewis, R., August 23, 2013. Security and Nuclear Power Plants: Robust and Significant. United States Nuclear Regulatory Commission Blog.*

While the impact of cyber systems and cybersecurity will be significant across the entire spectrum of security systems, the cybersecurity systems will be particularly effective in making access control, intrusion detection, and identification more safe and secure. It will also minimize the risk associated with the vetting of cargo, personnel, and transportation providers within the intermodal maritime supply chain.

While the development of digital and cybersecurity systems has many benefits in making ports and security systems more effective, the use of cyber systems also creates new vulnerabilities to terrorists and other bad actors. The risks of cyberattacks/terrorism and other cyber threats must be seriously considered, and steps must be taken in coordination with both private and public entities to make cyber systems as attack proof as they can be. Being like an ostrich with its head in the ground does not make the issue or concern go away nor any better. Ignoring threats and vulnerabilities and resulting risk does not work and could exacerbate the consequences.

It is also important to note that while all of the research and development related to both physical and digital/cybersecurity systems will not be specifically or directly related to ports, the maritime environment, operations and the supply chain, their principles, intent, and certainly some aspects of the newly developed technologies and physical and operational security measures can be adapted for the port and maritime environment. Researchers, practitioners, and government agencies must be diligent in their understanding that developments that are made in security systems both digital and physical in other environments can be modified or adjusted to fit the maritime environment.

Appendix A: University, government agency, and industry research organizations

The following is a partial list of universities, government agencies, and industry organizations that conduct research that addresses terrorism, resilience, and homeland security issues. The research is either directly applicable to maritime and port security or can be used to provide insight into the evolution of the physical and technological security needs.

- The University of Massachusetts Lowell's Center for Terrorism and Security Studies (CTSS) provides a multidisciplinary and collaborative approach to research projects that addresses domestic and foreign security challenges for, among other things, as terrorism, cybersecurity, and WMDs.
- The Maritime Policy and Strategy Research Center at the University of Haifa, Israel, is a leading and unique think tank, both in Israel and internationally, focusing on maritime strategy and research that addresses, among other things, the movement of goods, maritime law, and maritime cyber issues.
- Stevens Institute for Technology is the lead institution for the Maritime Security Center, a DHS S&T COE in port and maritime security conducting research and development of new tools and technologies that provide relevant maritime security-focused programs to enhance our nation's maritime domain awareness and resilience. One area of research is to conduct maritime cybersecurity research for assessing and addressing risks.
- Northeastern University's George J. Kostas Research Institute for Homeland Security advances resilience research, among other things, for critical systems and infrastructure resulting from man-made and natural catastrophes.
- The Rand Corporation's Homeland Security Research Division, under contract with DHS, conducts relevant research that addresses homeland security issues for, among other areas of concern, safeguarding cyberspace and resilience.
- The DHS's Science and Technology Centers of Excellence (DHS S&T COEs) provides relevant research via a partnership with academic institutions, industry, national laboratories, DHS operational components, other federal, state, local, tribal and territorial agencies, state, local, tribal and territorial homeland security agencies, and first responders. (DHS S&T COE, 2020)

- The Transportation Research Board of the National Academy of Sciences, Engineering, and Medicine (TRB) provides transportation improvements and innovation through research and information exchange regarding all modes of transportation. Through its Marine Board, research needs and information relating to new technologies and other issues affecting the marine transportation system and port operations are addressed.
- The International Maritime Organization (IMO) promotes safe and secure shipping through, among other things, international cooperation and the adoption of maritime safety and security standards. Through its international platform, it fosters research that addresses universal physical and technological security measure issues and concerns.
- The USCG's Research and Development Center pursues the application of new scientific technologies for the maritime environment that strategically transforms USCG operations. One such program is the Command, Control, Communications, Computers, Intelligence, Surveillance, and Reconnaissance Program (C4ISR). It is intended to provide interoperability among USCG assets and its partner agencies by acquiring and integrating electronic technology that provides effective situational and communications.
- The Society of American Military Engineers (SAME), through its Resilience Center of Interest promotes the development of policies, development, and implementation of technologies that improve infrastructure resilience and cybersecurity vulnerabilities.

References

Christopher, K., 2015. "Port Security Management", Chapter 12, Managing Technology Solutions for Port Facility Security, second ed. Routledge/Taylor & Francis Group.

Department of Homeland Security, Science and Technology, Critical Infrastructure Resilience Institute (CIRI) Fact Sheet, 2020. https://www.dhs.gov/sites/default/files/publications/coe-ciri-factsheet_190529-508_1.pdf. (Accessed 29 June 2020).

Department of Homeland Security, Science and Technology, Coastal Resilience Center (CRC) Fact Sheet, 2020. https://www.dhs.gov/sites/default/files/publications/oup_coefactsheet_crc_07122019.pdf. (Accessed 29 June 2020).

Federal Emergency Management Agency, 2020. FY 2020 Port Security Grant Program (PSGP) Notice of Funding Opportunity. Retrieved from: https://www.fema.gov/media-library-data/1584730406525-a46c18af6b4ff65ada8668d8044710b0/FY_2020_PSGP_NOFO_FINAL_3.20.20_Strikethru_508AB.pdf.

Framework for Improving Critical Infrastructure Cybersecurity, April 16, 2018. U.S. Department of Commerce, National Institute of Science and Technology. https://www.nist.gov/cyberframework.

Foynes, M., January 15, 2019. The Future of Physical Security. Retrieved from: https://www.accenture.com/us-en/insights/software-platforms/future-of-physical-security.

Frittelli, J.F., May 27, 2005. Port and Maritime Security: Background and Issues for Congress. Federation of American Scientists.

Gordon, G., 2018. "Intermodal Maritime Container Security: A Multifactor Framework for Assessing Routing",. Doctoral Dissertation, Universtiy of Massachusetts Lowell.

Johnstone, R.W., 2015. "Protecting Transportation Implementing Security Policies and Programs", Chapter 6, Implementing Maritime Security. Elsevier Ltd.

News Release: DHS Selects Texas A&M University to Lead Center of Excellence for Cross-Border Threat Screening and Supply Chain Defense, October 1, 2018. Department of Homeland Security, Science and Technology. https://www.dhs.gov/science-and-technology/news/2018/10/01/news-release-dhs-selects-texas-am-lead-cross-border-coe. (Accessed 30 June 2020).

Physical Protection of Critical Infrastructure Against Terrorist Attacks, March 2017. CTED: UN Counter-Terrorism Committee. https://www.un.org/sc/ctc/wp-content/uploads/2017/03/CTED-Trends-Report-March-2017-Final.pdf.

Pomerleau, P.L., 2019. Public-private partnerships: port security. In: Shapiro, L., Maras, M.H. (Eds.), Encyclopedia of Security and Emergency Management. Springer.

Stephany, M., Hertel, R., May 2016. Lighting Technologies in Ports and Terminals. Port Equipment Manufacturers Association. Retrieved from: https://www.pema.org/wp-content/uploads/downloads/2016/06/PEMA-IP10-Lighting-Technologies-in-Ports-and-Terminals.pdf.

Technical Report: Vehicle Barrier Maintenance Guidance, February 24, 2007. U.S. Army Corps of Engineers, Protective Design Center. PDC-TR 06-03.

United States Nuclear Regulatory Commission, August 14, 2017. Intrusion Detection. Retrieved from: https://www.nrc.gov/security/domestic/phys-protect/intrusion.html.

Wallischeck, E., June 2013. ICS Security in Maritime Transportation: A White Paper Examining the Security and Resiliency of Critical Transportation Infrastructure. U.S. Department of Transportation, John A Volpe National Transportation Systems Center.

CHAPTER 10

Information security and cyber threats and vulnerabilities

Andrew B. Morrow

Cybersecurity, School of Business Administration, Capital College, The Pennsylvania State University, Middletown, PA United States

Information security introduction

If there was ever a more compelling case for the application of cyber protections to an industry, one needs only look at some of the current publications emerging from the maritime industry.

Schauer et al. (2017) state:

> For an organization, participating in a maritime supply chain implies not only the need to cooperate with other stakeholders at business level, but due to the ongoing digitalization also to set up interfaces in their information and communication technology (ICT) infrastructure for the ICT systems of their business partners. Hence, these supply chains have become highly interrelated cyber ecosystem, where the complexity and degree of networking of connected digital assets beyond company borders increases. Nevertheless, every data interface also represents a potential threat in form of a possible entry point for unplanned access to the networks and the systems located behind it.

As reported in *The Maritime Executive* (2019):

> Port cybersecurity is a serious consideration, especially for high-productivity, high-automation container terminals. In 2018, a cyberattack affected Chinese ocean carrier Cosco's email and phone systems at several sites in the United States, including its Pier J terminal at the Port of Long Beach. In 2017, the "Not-Petya" cyberattack took down APM Terminals' operations at multiple ports around the world, cutting liftings for Maersk Line by about 20 percent for two weeks and costing an estimated $200−300 million in mitigation and lost business (Port of LA Sets Up New Cybersecurity Coordination Center, 2019).

Intermodal Maritime Security. https://doi.org/10.1016/B978-0-12-819945-9.00010-1

As reported in *The Beacon* (2020):

> *In 2019, the Maritime Exchange processed over 289,000 ocean bills of lading and nearly a half-million container records in Maritime Online, the Delaware River port community intelligence portal, and the system received over 1.8 million cargo status messages from U.S. Customs and Border Protection (CBP) and other federal agencies. The operations staff logged over 13,000 ship movements last year, and Maritime On-Line processed four to five million real-time vessel position reports per month in AIS, the automatic identification system (Tightening up the Code, 2020).*

These publications and numerous others demonstrate the overwhelming requirement of cybersecurity protection for the maritime industry. Never before have more real-time systems been integrated and more data have been available and used to track and secure a tremendous amount of shipments that are constantly in motion. But before we can intelligently discuss specific security systems and mechanisms being utilized by this critical industry, we first need to define some basic tenets.

The topic of information security requires a minimal level of agreement on definitions to begin to understand the nuances of the threats, attacks, and vulnerabilities that arise in any given industry. *Information Security* is defined as "the practice of protecting information by mitigating information risks. It is part of information risk management" (Information Security, n.d.). The following sections concerning basic principles, security controls, defense in depth, security classification, and access control are all located within the Wikipedia.org page for information security (https://en.wikipedia.org/wiki/Information_security).

Basic principles

Key concepts

The CIA triad[1] of *confidentiality*, *integrity*, and *availability* is at the heart of information security (Pennin, 2008). However, debate continues about whether or not this CIA triad is sufficient to address rapidly changing technology and business requirements, with recommendations to consider expanding on the intersections between availability and confidentiality, as well as the relationship between security and privacy (Samonas and Coss, 2014). Other principles such as "accountability" have sometimes been proposed; it has been pointed out that issues such as nonrepudiation do not fit well within the three core concepts (Ross et al., 2019).

In 1992 and revised in 2002, the Organisation for Economic Co-operation and Development (OECD) Guidelines for the Security of Information Systems and Networks

---

[1] The members of the classic InfoSec triad—confidentiality, integrity, and availability—are interchangeably referred to in the literature as security attributes, properties, security goals, fundamental aspects, information criteria, critical information characteristics, and basic building blocks.

(2011) proposed the nine generally accepted principles: awareness, responsibility, response, ethics, democracy, risk assessment, security design and implementation, security management, and reassessment. Building upon those, in 2004, the National Institute for Standards and Technology's (NIST) *Engineering Principles for Information Technology Security* (Ross et al., 2018) proposed 33 principles. From each of these were derived guidelines and practices.

Confidentiality

In information security, *confidentiality* "is the property that information is not made available or disclosed to unauthorized individuals, entities, or processes." While similar to *privacy*, the two words are not interchangeable. Rather, *confidentiality* is a component of *privacy* that implements to protect our data from unauthorized viewers. Examples of confidentiality of electronic data being compromised include laptop theft, password theft, or sensitive emails being sent to the incorrect individuals (Andress, 2014).

Integrity

In information security, *data integrity* means maintaining and assuring the accuracy and completeness of data over its entire lifecycle (Boritz, 2005). This means that data cannot be modified in an unauthorized or undetected manner. This is not the same thing as *referential integrity* in databases, although it can be viewed as a special case of consistency as understood in the classic ACID (atomicity, consistency, isolation, and durability) model of transaction processing.[2] Information security systems typically provide message integrity alongside confidentiality.

Availability

For any information system to serve its purpose, the information must be available when it is needed. This means the computing systems used to store and process the information, the security controls used to protect it, and the communication channels used to access it must be functioning correctly. High availability systems aim to remain available at all times, preventing service disruptions due to power outages, hardware failures, and system upgrades. Ensuring availability also involves preventing denial-of-service attacks, such as a flood of incoming messages to the target system, essentially forcing it to shut down (Loukas and Öke, 2010).

---

[2] The acronym ACID refers to the four key properties of atomicity, consistency, isolation, and durability. Atomicity: all the changes are performed or none of them are. Consistency: data are in a consistent state when a transaction starts and when it ends. Isolation: the intermediate state of a transaction is invisible to other transactions, hence when transactions are run concurrently, they appear to be run serialized. Durability: After a transaction successfully completes, changes to data persist and cannot be undone even in the event of a system failure (https://www.ibm.com/support/knowledgecenter/SSGMCP_5.4.0/product-overview/acid.html).

In the realm of information security, *availability* can often be viewed as one of the most important parts of a successful information security program. Ultimately end users need to be able to perform job functions; by ensuring availability, an organization is able to perform to the standards that an organization's stakeholders expect. This can involve topics such as proxy configurations, outside web access, the ability to access shared drives, and the ability to send emails. Executives oftentimes do not understand the technical side of information security and look at availability as an easy fix, but this often requires collaboration from many different organizational teams, such as network operations, development operations, incident response, and policy/change management. A successful information security team involves many different key roles to mesh and align for the CIA triad to be provided effectively.

Nonrepudiation

In law, *nonrepudiation* implies one's intention to fulfill their obligations to a contract. It also implies that one party of a transaction cannot deny having received a transaction nor can the other party deny having sent a transaction (McCarthy, 2006, pp. 65−66).

It is important to note that while technology such as cryptographic systems can assist in nonrepudiation efforts, the concept is at its core a legal concept transcending the realm of technology. It is not, for instance, sufficient to show that the message matches a digital signature signed with the sender's private key, and, thus, only the sender could have sent the message, and nobody else could have altered it in transit (data integrity). The alleged sender could in return demonstrate that the digital signature algorithm is vulnerable or flawed or allege or prove that his signing key has been compromised. The fault for these violations may or may not lie with the sender, and such assertions may or may not relieve the sender of liability, but the assertion would invalidate the claim that the signature necessarily proves authenticity and integrity. As such, the sender may repudiate the message (because authenticity and integrity are prerequisites for nonrepudiation).

Security controls

Selecting and implementing proper *security controls* will initially help an organization bring down risk to acceptable levels. Control selection should follow and should be based on the risk assessment. Controls can vary in nature, but fundamentally they are ways of protecting the confidentiality, integrity, or availability of information. ISO/IEC 27001[3] has defined controls in different areas. Organizations can implement additional controls according to requirement of the organization (Johnson, 2015, p. 678). ISO/IEC 27002 offers a guideline for organizational information security standards.

---

[3] ISO/TEC is a technical standard of the International Standards Organization for the implementation, management, and maintenance of information security.

Administrative controls

Administrative controls consist of approved written policies, procedures, standards, and guidelines. *Administrative controls* form the framework for running the business and managing people. They inform people on how the business is to be run and how day-to-day operations are to be conducted. Laws and regulations created by government bodies are also a type of administrative control because they inform the business. Some industry sectors have policies, procedures, standards, and guidelines that must be followed—the Payment Card Industry Data Security Standard (PCI DSS) required by Visa and Mastercard is such an example. Other examples of *administrative controls* include the corporate security policy, password policy, hiring policies, and disciplinary policies.

Administrative controls form the basis for the selection and implementation of logical and physical controls. Logical and physical controls are manifestations of administrative controls, which are of paramount importance.

Logical controls

Logical controls (also called technical controls) use software and data to monitor and control access to information and computing systems. Passwords, network and host-based firewalls, network intrusion detection systems, access control lists, and data encryption are examples of logical controls.

An important *logical control* that is frequently overlooked is the principle of least privilege, which requires that an individual, program, or system process not be granted any more access privileges than are necessary to perform the task (Ransome and Misra, 2013). A blatant example of the failure to adhere to the principle of least privilege is logging into Windows as a user Administrator to read email and surf the web. Violations of this principle can also occur when an individual collects additional access privileges over time. This happens when employee job duties change, employees are promoted to a new position, or employees are transferred to another department. The access privileges required by their new duties are frequently added onto their already existing access privileges, which may no longer be necessary or appropriate.

Physical controls

Physical controls monitor and control the environment of the workplace and computing facilities. They also monitor and control access to and from such facilities and include doors, locks, heating and air conditioning, smoke and fire alarms, fire suppression systems, cameras, barricades, fencing, security guards, cable locks, etc. Separating the network and workplace into functional areas are also physical controls.

An important *physical control* that is frequently overlooked is separation of duties, which ensures that an individual cannot complete a critical task by himself. For example, an employee who submits a request for reimbursement should not also be able to authorize payment or print the check. Similarly, an applications programmer should not also be the server administrator or the database administrator; these roles and responsibilities must be separated from one another.

Defense in depth

Information security must protect information throughout its lifespan, from the initial creation of the information on through to the final disposal of the information. The information must be protected while in motion and at rest. During its lifetime, information may pass through many different information processing systems and through many different parts of information processing systems. There are many different ways the information and information systems can be threatened. To fully protect the information during its lifetime, each component of the information processing system must have its own protection mechanisms. The building up, layering on, and overlapping of security measures are called "defense in depth.[4]" In contrast to a metal chain, which is famously only as strong as its weakest link, the defense in depth strategy aims at a structure where, should one defensive measure fail, other measures will continue to provide protection (Kakareka, 2013).

Recall the earlier discussion about administrative controls, logical controls, and physical controls. The three types of controls can be used to form the basis upon which to build a defense in depth strategy. With this approach, defense in depth can be conceptualized as three distinct layers or planes laid one on top of the other. Additional insight into defense in depth can be gained by thinking of it as forming the layers of an onion, with data at the core of the onion, people the next outer layer of the onion, and network security, host-based security, and application security forming the outermost layers of the onion. Both perspectives are equally valid, and each provides valuable insight into the implementation of a good defense in depth strategy.

Security classification for information

An important aspect of information security and risk management is recognizing the value of information and defining appropriate procedures and protection requirements for the information. Not all information is equal and so not all information requires the same degree of protection. This requires information to be assigned a security classification. The first step in information classification is to identify a member of senior management as the

---

[4] In other chapters of this book, there are references to *layered security* or layered defense. The concept is the same.

owner of the particular information to be classified. Next, develop a classification policy; however, some classifications may be mandated as is the case with the U.S. Coast Guard (USCG) or the U.S. Customs and Border Protection (CBP). The policy should describe the different classification labels, define the criteria for information to be assigned a particular label, and list the required security controls for each classification (Bayuk, 2009).

Some factors that influence which classification information should be assigned include how much value that information has to the organization, how old the information is and whether or not the information has become obsolete. Laws and other regulatory requirements are also important considerations when classifying information. The Information Systems Audit and Control Association (ISACA) and its Business Model for Information Security also serve as a tool for security professionals to examine security from a systems perspective, creating an environment where security can be managed holistically, allowing actual risks to be addressed.

The type of information security classification labels selected and used will depend on the nature of the organization, with examples being (Bayuk, 2009):

- In the business sector, labels such as: Public, Sensitive,[5] Private, Confidential.
- In the government sector, labels such as: Unclassified, Unofficial, Protected, Confidential, Secret, Top Secret, and their non-English equivalents.
- In cross-sectoral formations, the Traffic Light Protocol, which consists of: White, Green, Amber, and Red.

All employees in the organization, as well as business partners, must be trained on the classification schema and understand the required security controls and handling procedures for each classification. The classification of a particular information asset that has been assigned should be reviewed periodically to ensure the classification is still appropriate for the information and to ensure the security controls required by the classification are in place and are followed in their right procedures.

Access control

Access to protected information must be restricted to people who are authorized to access the information. The computer programs, and in many cases the computers that process the information, must also be authorized. This requires that mechanisms be in place to control the access to protected information. The sophistication of the access control mechanisms should be in parity with the value of the information being protected; the more sensitive or valuable the information, the stronger the control mechanisms need to be. The foundation on which access control mechanisms are built begin with identification

---

[5] Sensitive Security Information or SSI is a transportation sector protection of sensitive information on, among other things, a need to know basis per 49 CFR 15 (USDOT) and 1520 (DHS).

and authentication. Access control is generally considered in three steps: identification, authentication, and authorization (Andress, 2014).

Identification

Identification is an assertion of who someone is or what something is. For example, if a person makes the statement "Hello, my name is John Doe," they are making a claim of who they are. However, their claim may or may not be true. Before John Doe can be granted access to protected information, it will be necessary to verify that the person claiming to be John Doe really is John Doe. Typically, the claim is in the form of a username. By entering that username you are claiming "I am the person the username belongs to."

Authentication

Authentication is the act of verifying a claim of identity. To continue the example, when John Doe goes into a bank to make a withdrawal, he tells the bank teller he is John Doe, a claim of identity. The bank teller asks to see a photo ID, so he hands the teller his driver's license. The bank teller checks the license to make sure it has John Doe printed on it and compares the photograph on the license against the person claiming to be John Doe. If the photo and name match the person, then the teller has authenticated that John Doe is who he claimed to be. Similarly, by entering the correct password, the user is providing evidence that he/she is the person the username belongs to.

There are three different types of information that can be used for authentication:

- Something you know: things such as a PIN, a password, or your mother's maiden name.
- Something you have: a driver's license or a magnetic swipe card.
- Something you are: biometrics, including palm prints, fingerprints, voice prints, and retina (eye) scans.

Strong authentication requires providing more than one type of authentication information (two-factor authentication). The username is the most common form of identification on computer systems today, and the password is the most common form of authentication. Usernames and passwords are slowly being replaced or supplemented with more sophisticated authentication mechanisms such as Time-based One-time Password algorithms.

Authorization

After a person, program, or computer has successfully been identified and authenticated, then it must be determined what informational resources they are permitted to access and what actions they will be allowed to perform (run, view, create, delete, or change). This is called authorization. Authorization to access information and other computing services begins with administrative policies and procedures. The policies prescribe what information and computing services can be accessed, by whom, and under what conditions. The access control mechanisms are then configured to enforce these policies. Different computing systems are equipped with different kinds of access control mechanisms. Some may even offer a choice of different access control mechanisms. The access control mechanism system offers will be based upon one of three approaches to access control, or it may be derived from a combination of the three approaches (Andress, 2014).

The nondiscretionary approach consolidates all access control under a centralized administration. The access to information and other resources is usually based on the individual's function (role) in the organization or the tasks the individual must perform. The discretionary approach gives the creator or owner of the information resource the ability to control access to those resources. In the mandatory access control approach, access is granted or denied basing upon the security classification assigned to the information resource.

Examples of common access control mechanisms in use today include role-based access control, available in many advanced database management systems; simple file permissions provided in the UNIX and Windows operating systems; Group Policy Objects provided in Windows network systems; and Kerberos, RADIUS, TACACS, and the simple access lists used in many firewalls and routers.

To be effective, policies and other security controls must be enforceable and upheld. Effective policies ensure that people are held accountable for their actions. The U.S. Treasury's guidelines for the systems processing of sensitive or proprietary information, for example, states that all failed and successful authentication and access attempts must be logged, and all access to information must leave some type of audit trail.

Also, the *need-to-know principle* needs to be in effect when talking about access control. This principle gives access rights to a person to perform their job functions. This principle is used in the government when dealing with difference clearances. Even though two employees in different departments have a top-secret clearance, they must have a need-to-know in order for information to be exchanged. Within the need-to-know principle, network administrators grant the employee the least amount of privileges to prevent employees from accessing more than what they are supposed to. Need-to-know helps to enforce the confidentiality-integrity-availability triad. Need-to-know directly impacts the confidential area of the triad.

Auditing concepts
Separation of duties

Separation of duties (SoD), also known as *segregation of duties*, is the concept of having more than one person required to complete a task. In business, the separation by sharing of more than one individual in one single task is an internal control intended to prevent fraud and error. The concept is alternatively called SoD or, in the political realm, separation of powers. In democracies, the separation of legislation from administration serves a similar purpose. The concept is addressed in technical systems and in information technology equivalently and generally addressed as redundancy.

To successfully implement SoD in information systems, a number of concerns need to be addressed:

* The process used to ensure a person's authorization rights in the system is in line with his role in the organization.
* The authentication method used such as knowledge of a password, possession of an object (key, token), or a biometrical characteristic.
* Circumvention of rights in the system can occur through database administration access, user administration access, tools which provide back-door access or supplier installed user accounts. Specific controls such as a review of an activity log may be required to address this specific concern.

Job rotation

Job rotation is a technique used by some employers to change their employees' assigned jobs throughout their employment. Employers practice this technique for a number of reasons. It was designed to promote flexibility of employees and to keep employees interested in staying with the company/organization which employs them. There is also research that shows how job rotations help relieve the stress of employees who work in a job that requires manual labor.

Risk management

Risk management is not a new concept, but a lot of work over the last decade has been concentrated around identifying and managing risk for all organizations. In addition to identifying both assets that need protecting as well as identifying potential threats and vulnerabilities, risk management has become an encompassing term that includes the business impact analyses required for the identification as well as the reactions to achieve an acceptable level of risk that corresponds to the organizational risk appetite. Included in the umbrella of risk management are the concepts of having an incident response plan, a disaster recovery plan, and a business continuity plan. Collectively, these plans are the result of planning how an organization will react to an incident, how it will operate during the recovery period, and ultimately, how it will return to normal operation.

Transportation-related cybersecurity

One of the emerging arenas of maritime risk management is the cybersecurity component of today's infrastructures. This is emphasized the by the numerous stories of attacks on shipment solutions and theft of cargo. Additionally, International Maritime Organization (IMO) Resolution MSC.428(98)—Maritime Cyber Risk Management in Safety Management Systems, issued by the IMO, mandates that vessel administrators are to ensure that cyber risks are appropriately addressed by January 1, 2021 (IMO, 2017a,b, 2020).

The IMO defines maritime cyber risk as "a measure of the extent to which a technology asset could be threatened by a potential circumstance or event, which may result in shipping-related operational, safety, or security failures as a consequence of information or systems being corrupted, lost, or compromised" (IMO, 2020). The IMO also defines cyber risk management as "the process of identifying, analyzing, assessing, and communicating a cyber-related risk and accepting, avoiding, transferring, or mitigating it to an acceptable level, considering costs and benefits of actions taken to stakeholders." The overall goal, as stated by the IMO, is to "support safe and secure shipping, which is operationally resilient to cyber risks."

The IMO has taken the lead on helping organizations meet the ever-present dangers of cyberattacks and threats by issuing MSC-FAL1/Circ.3 Guideline on maritime cyber risk management (IMO, 2017a,b). "The guidelines provide high-level recommendations on maritime cyber risk management to safeguard shipping from current and emerging cyber threats and vulnerabilities and include functional elements that support effective cyber risk management. The recommendations can be incorporated into existing risk management processes and are complementary to the safety and security management practices already established by IMO."

Cybersecurity in the intermodal maritime transportation world is twofold. The threats, vulnerabilities, and risks will be identified and how the organizations and agencies will address them in a virtual and multidimensional approach to security. The first consideration in the twofold process is the security of the cyber and information technology systems that are used to vet and preapprove shippers, freight forwarders, transportation providers, etc. This includes the U.S. Coast Guard/TSA Transportation Worker Identification Credential (TWIC) and CBP programs of Customs-Trade Partnership

Against Terrorism (C-TPAT) and the Container Security Initiative (CSI) that are intended to provide a "TSA PreCheck" for internodal maritime containers destined to the United States.

The second consideration is the cyber-based "industrial controls" and supervisory control and data acquisition (SCADA) processes that are used in port and vessels at sea operations. This includes the U.S. Coast Guard's Automatic Identification System (AIS), CBP vehicle, and cargo inspection system (VACIS) and radiation portals at ports, and port security and surveillance systems.

Inasmuch as supply chain theory embraces the informational and financial flows as well as the physical one, the potential for other vulnerabilities clearly exist. Cyber threats can be trifurcated into those that affect (1) the integrity, which includes the identity, of the cargo; (2) security of landside activities; and (3) the navigation and control of the containership per se.

Moreover, there can always be the potential for cyber threats to incorporate multiple facets simultaneously.

Maritime Transportation Security Act of 2002

The Maritime Transportation Security Act of 2002 (MTSA) (Pub.L. 107−295) was enacted by the 107th United States Congress to address port and waterway security. It was signed into law by President George W. Bush on November 25, 2002 (Maritime Transportation Security Act of 2002, 2020). This law is the US implementation of the International Ship and Port Facility Security Code (ISPS). Its full provisions came into effect on July 1, 2004. It requires vessels and port facilities to conduct vulnerability assessments and develop security plans that may include passenger, vehicle, and baggage screening procedures; security patrols; establishing restricted areas; personnel identification procedures; access control measures; and/or installation of surveillance equipment. The Act creates a consistent security program for all the nation's ports to better identify and deter threats.

Developed using risk-based methodology, the MTSA security regulations focus on those sectors of maritime industry that have a higher risk of involvement in a transportation security incident, including various tank vessels, barges, large passenger vessels, cargo vessels, towing vessels, offshore oil and gas platforms, and port facilities that handle certain kinds of dangerous cargo or service the vessels listed above.

U.S. Coast Guard/TSA Transportation Worker Identification Credential

The TWIC is required by the MTSA for workers who require unescorted access to secure areas of the nation's maritime facilities and vessels. TSA conducts a security threat assessment (background check) to determine a person's eligibility and issues the credential. US citizens and immigrants in certain immigration categories may apply for the credential. Most mariners licensed by the U.S. Coast Guard also require a credential (TWIC, n.d.).

U.S. Customs and Border Protections programs

The following programs are meant to provide a "TSA PreCheck" for internodal maritime containers destined to the United States.

Cargo Systems Messaging Service

Created in the 1990s, the Cargo Systems Messaging Service (CSMS) was developed by CBP to provide timely service messages to automated cargo systems users as well as courtesy messages on related trade processing information. Recently, due to the aging technology currently in use, the CSMS messaging service has become increasingly unstable and poses a risk to CBP's ability to send timely messaging on issues affecting the systems users. After looking into several options for modernizing the technology, CBP's Trade Transformation Office identified a solution that will ensure dependable service. The new technology platform will provide additional benefits, such as the elimination of duplicative messages, improved messaging formats, the ability to embed hyperlinks into messages, etc. CBP will complete the transition to this new technology in September 2020. Overall impacts to end users will be minimal (Cargo Systems Messaging Service, 2020).

Automated Commercial Environment

The Automated Commercial Environment (ACE) is the system through which the trade community reports imports and exports and the government determines admissibility (Automated Commercial Environment (ACE), 2020). ACE became the U.S. Customs' Single Window—the primary system through which the trade community reports imports and exports and the government determines admissibility.

ACE replaces CBP's legacy system, the Automated Commercial System (ACS), for trade processing. Through ACE as the Single Window, manual processes are streamlined and automated, paper is eliminated, and the international trade community is able to more easily and efficiently comply with U.S. laws and regulations. Key elements of ACE include the following:

- It is important to clarify that importers do not file their customs entries directly in ACE.
- The ACE Secure Data Portal does not have entry and entry summary filing capabilities, nor are there plans for building such capabilities.
- The Automated Broker Interface (ABI) continues to be the only approved method available for filing entry and entry summaries in ACE. ACE-certified ABI software is available through a CBP-approved software vendor, such as CustomsNow™ (ACE and Automated Systems, 2020).

Customs-Trade Partnership Against Terrorism

C-TPAT is one layer in CBP's multi-layered cargo enforcement strategy (CTPAT: Customs Trade Partnership Against Terrorism, 2020). Through this program, CBP works with the trade community to strengthen international supply chains and improve United States border security. C-TPAT is a voluntary public—private sector partnership program which recognizes that CBP can provide the highest level of cargo security only through close cooperation with the principle stakeholders of the international supply chain such as importers, carriers, consolidators, licensed customs brokers, and manufacturers. The Security and Accountability for Every Port Act of 2006 provided a statutory framework for the C-TPAT program and imposed strict program oversight requirements.

From its inception in November 2001, C-TPAT continued to grow. Today, more than 11,400 certified partners spanning the gamut of the trade community have been accepted into the program. The partners include US importers/exporters; US/Canada highway carriers; US/Mexico highway carriers; rail and sea carriers; licensed U.S. Customs brokers; U.S. marine port authority/terminal operators; US freight consolidators; ocean transportation intermediaries and nonoperating common carriers; Mexican and Canadian manufacturers; and Mexican long-haul carriers, all of whom account for over 52% (by value) of cargo imported into the United States.

When an entity joins C-TPAT, an agreement is made to work with CBP to protect the supply chain, identify security gaps, and implement specific security measures and best practices. Applicants must address a broad range of security topics and present security profiles that list action plans to align security throughout the supply chain. C-TPAT members are considered to be of low risk and are, therefore, less likely to be examined at a US port of entry.

C-TPAT partners enjoy a variety of benefits, including taking an active role in working closer with the U.S. Government in its war against terrorism. As they do this, partners are able to better identify their own security vulnerabilities and take corrective actions to mitigate risks. Some of the benefits of the program include:

- Reduced number of CBP examinations.
- Front of the line inspections.
- Possible exemption from Stratified Exams.
- Shorter wait times at the border.
- Assignment of a Supply Chain Security Specialist to the company.
- Access to the Free and Secure Trade (FAST) Lanes at the land borders.
- Access to the C-TPAT web-based Portal system and a library of training materials.
- Possibility of enjoying additional benefits by being recognized as a trusted trade partner by foreign customs administrations that have signed Mutual Recognition with the United States.
- Eligibility for other U.S. Government pilot programs, such as the Food and Drug Administration's Secure Supply Chain program.
- Business resumption priority following a natural disaster or terrorist attack.
- Importer eligibility to participate in the Importer Self-Assessment (ISA) Program.
- Priority consideration at CBP's industry-focused Centers of Excellence and Expertise.

Participation in C-TPAT is voluntary, and there are no costs associated with joining the program. Moreover, a company does not need an intermediary in order to apply to the program and work with CBP; the application process is simple to use, and it is done online. The first step is for the company to review the C-TPAT Minimum Security Criteria for their business entity to determine eligibility for the program. The second step is for the company to submit a basic application via the C-TPAT Portal system and to agree to voluntarily participate. The third step is for the company to complete a supply chain security profile. The security profile explains how the company is meeting C-TPAT's minimum security criteria. In order to do this, the company should have already conducted a risk assessment. Upon satisfactory completion of the application and supply chain security profile, the applicant company is assigned a C-TPAT Supply Chain Security Specialist to review the submitted materials and provide program guidance on an ongoing basis. The C-TPAT program will then have up to 90 days to certify the company into the program or to reject the application. If certified, the company will be validated within a year of certification.

Container security initiative

As the single, unified border agency of the United States, CBP's mission is extraordinarily important to the protection of America and the American people (Container Security Initiative, 2020). In the aftermath of the terrorist attacks on September 11, 2001, U.S.

Customs Service began developing antiterrorism programs to help secure the United States. Within months of these attacks, U.S. Customs Service had created the CSI.

CSI addresses the threat to border security and global trade posed by the potential for terrorist use of a maritime container to deliver a weapon. CSI proposes a security regime to ensure all containers that pose a potential risk for terrorism are identified and inspected at foreign ports before they are placed on vessels destined for the United States. CBP has stationed teams of US CBP officers in foreign locations to work together with our host foreign government counterparts. Their mission is to target and prescreen containers and to develop additional investigative leads related to the terrorist threat to cargo destined to the United States.

The three core elements of CSI are:

* Identify high-risk containers. CBP uses automated targeting tools to identify containers that pose a potential risk for terrorism, based on advance information and strategic intelligence.
* Prescreen and evaluate containers before they are shipped. Containers are screened as early in the supply chain as possible, generally at the port of departure.
* Use technology to prescreen high-risk containers to ensure that screening can be done rapidly without slowing down the movement of trade. This technology includes large-scale X-ray and gamma ray machines and radiation detection devices.

Through CSI, CBP officers work with host customs administrations to establish security criteria for identifying high-risk containers. Those administrations use nonintrusive inspection (NII) and radiation detection technology to screen high-risk containers before they are shipped to US ports.

Announced in January 2002, CSI has made great strides since its inception. A significant number of customs administrations have committed to joining CSI and operate at various stages of implementation.

CSI is now operational at ports in North America, Europe, Asia, Africa, the Middle East, and Latin and Central America. CBP's 58 operational CSI ports now prescreen over 80% of all maritime containerized cargo imported into the United States.

Intra-shipment and post-shipment controls
Supervisory control and data acquisition processes

SCADA is a control system architecture comprising computers, networked data communications, and graphical user interfaces (GUI) for high-level process supervisory management, while also comprising other peripheral devices like programmable logic controllers (PLC) and discrete proportional-integral-derivative (PID) controllers to interface with process plant or machinery (SCADA, 2020).

U.S. Coast Guard's Automatic Identification System

Vessel traffic data, or AIS data, are collected by the U.S. Coast Guard through an onboard navigation safety device that transmits the location and characteristics of large vessels for tracking in real time. The MarineCadastre.gov[6] project team has worked with the Coast Guard and National Oceanic and Atmospheric Administration's (NOAA's) Office of Coast Survey to repurpose and make available some of the most important data for use in ocean planning applications (Vessel Tracking Data Used for Ocean Planning, 2020).

CBP vehicle and cargo inspection system

VACIS systems scan cargo containers, trucks, cars, and other vehicles to help authorities search for weapons, nuclear material, narcotics, undeclared goods, and other contraband at cargo terminals, border crossings, military facilities, and other checkpoints (VACIS Cargo and Vehicle Inspection Systems, 2020).

The versatile, compact VACIS M6500 system scans trucks, cargo containers, cars, and other vehicles. The system can scan 150 vehicles per hour or more and can even scan occupied vehicles.

The VACIS IP6500 FullScan system is a powerful, practical solution for scanning cargo containers, trucks, and other vehicles in high-volume operations. Its X-ray imaging and radiation scanning help security personnel intercept weapons, nuclear material, and other contraband hidden in containers. It can scan entire vehicles, bumper to bumper and roof to tires, including occupants. And with its high throughput and small footprint, the system is ideal for seaports and other high-volume cargo facilities.

The VACIS XPL system scans passenger cars and other light vehicles to help security personnel search for weapons, explosives, drugs, and other threats. The system scans entire vehicles bumper to bumper in seconds as they drive through without stopping. Detailed images reveal even small items such as handguns, and color coding highlights explosives, drugs, and other organic materials. The system's low X-ray dose allows drivers and

---

[6] MarineCadastre.gov is a partnered U.S. Department of Commerce's National Oceanic and Atmospheric Administration (NOAA) Office for Coastal Management and U.S. Department of the Interior's Bureau of Ocean Energy Management (BOEM). It is an integrated marine information system that provides data, tools, and technical support for ocean and Great Lakes planning.

passengers to remain in the vehicle while it is scanned, enabling the system to scan 150 vehicles per hour or more in the normal flow of checkpoint traffic.

The VACIS GT system is a rugged, highly mobile system for scanning passenger vehicles, trucks, buses, and other vehicles at remote or ad hoc sites, even in hostile environments.

With its trailer-mounted design, the system can be towed to an inspection site by a light vehicle and readied for use in minutes. The high-throughput system scans vehicles from bumper to bumper and roof to axles in seconds to provide detailed images of their contents.

The Railroad VACIS imaging system helps trained operators see the contents of closed, moving railcars, assisting them in intercepting weapons, contraband, and other items of interest and verifying shipping manifests. The system's rugged design resists corrosion, humidity, rain, and wind, making it an ideal choice for around-the-clock scanning in challenging environments such as remote border crossings.

Radiation portals at ports

All containerized cargo coming into seaports in the United States is scanned by radiation detection equipment. Recently, a new radiation detection system began operating at the Trans-Pacific Container Service Corporation (TraPac) terminal at the Port of Los Angeles in California. The new system automatically scans inbound cargo for nuclear and other radioactive material.

Cargo bound for rail transport is placed on conveyers by automated straddle carriers. The conveyers then move the cargo through Radiation Portal Monitors[7] for scanning. This innovative approach facilitates the flow of trade while protecting the United States from nuclear threats.

The effort to develop this new system was truly collaborative. As TraPac planned to move to an automated terminal, U.S. Customs and Border Protection needed a new method to scan ship-to-rail containers for radioactive material. After TraPac approached DHS with this new scanning concept, DHS worked with the Pacific Northwest National Laboratory (PNNL) to extensively test, evaluate, and approve the systems for live rail operations.

Approximately two million containers are processed through the TraPac terminal every year. This new solution offers a more efficient approach to preventing illicit nuclear and other radioactive materials from entering the United States (Brasure, 2017).

---

[7] More information on other types of radiation portal monitors can be found at https://en.wikipedia.org/wiki/Radiation_Portal_Monitor.

Port security and surveillance systems

Port security is part of a broader definition concerning maritime security (Port security, 2020). It refers to the defense, law and treaty enforcement, and counterterrorism activities that fall within the port and maritime domain. It includes the protection of the seaports themselves and the protection and inspection of the cargo moving through the ports. Security risks related to ports often focus on either the physical security of the port or security risks within the maritime supply chain.

Internationally, port security is governed by rules issued by the IMO and its 2002 International Ship and Port Facility Security Code. Additionally, some US-based programs have become de facto global port security programs, including the CSI and the C-TPAT. However, some businesses argue that port security governance measures are ineffective and costly and that it negatively impacts maritime transport costs.

Physical port security involves the risks to the perimeters of the port. Risks to port security involve natural risks such as hurricanes and flooding, man-made risks such as operator error, and weapon risks such as chemical, biological, and nuclear material. It also involves adequate security systems within the port, such as security guards, video surveillance, and alarm systems.

Physical port security also goes under the umbrella of maritime terrorism. Ports are attractive targets for terrorists because ships and cargoes are fixed in time once they enter the port, which removes the uncertainty in relation to the location of the target.

Apart from physical port security, the port is connected to a larger supply chain. There are various risks along this supply chain that can affect port security, such as explosives attached to the vessel or unwanted passengers on the vessel. Ports are "potential targets of illegal activity which may impact their ability to function as intended, and ports as conduits into and out of national borders and supply chains, which can be exploited in order to introduce or move illegal materials, persons, or activities." That involves increasing the number of vulnerabilities to port security to the supply chain.

Vulnerabilities

Now that the various technologies being used are defined, one can see how the interconnections between them provide a chain where any breach in security weakens the overall shipping strategy.

For example, consider a shipment of foreign-sourced goods requiring intermodal ocean transportation. The shipment utilizes some combination of trucking and railroads to arrive at the originating port, is transferred to one or more ships to convey it to the destination port, where it is unloaded, and finally reaches its final destination using another combination of railroad and trucking to effect inland transportation. Throughout this journey, shipments are constantly monitored via global position satellite (GPS) tracking. Such real-time visibility is valuable to those responsible for the shipment but is equally valuable to potential hijackers for identifying potential targets.

This scenario has other integrated technologies that are valuable targets for cyberattacks whereby to gain intelligence on the shipment. The Automated Manifest System (AMS) messages are derived from bill of lading information and contain specifics regarding the goods contained in the shipment. AIS is a global tracking system that endeavors to know the whereabouts of several hundred vessels transiting the oceans and other principal bodies of water on the planet. While many national governments utilize information from AIS, the USCG is especially interested in those ships destined for US ports as well as the whereabouts of those that are potentially making port calls at embargoed destinations contrary to various presidential directives and treaties where the United States is a signatory.

Once shipments arrive on US shores, the ACE system is the gateway for entry to CBP and contains input from bills of lading, commercial invoices, and related regulations governing specific types of goods.[8] In the aggregate, these systems contain information on the specific nature of the goods such as description, dimensions, country of origin, declared value, and duty classification; the identity of the exporter; the details for the importer including name and location; the name of the arriving vessel along with container number; and the name of the customs broker, if any, along with respective contact information. Figs. 10.1 and 10.2, respectively, depict the physical flow of goods in international trade, and the information flows accommodated by AMS, AIS, and ACE all the while recognizing that GPS is providing visibility data to the transportation services providers (Gordon, 2018).

When considering an international shipment from a cyber perspective, it resembles a complex information network with numerous nodes. Each one of these contact points must be properly secured from attack and access to provide a comprehensive level of CIA; these systems need to ensure that only the proper resources have access to the information contained within them, that only authorized individuals are able to read or update the information, and that the information remains available for the appropriate users at the time when they need to use them.

---

[8] ACE is a central repository for other agencies governing imported goods including Department of Agriculture, Food, and Drug Administration, Environmental Protection Agency for chemicals, and Department of Energy for radioactive materials.

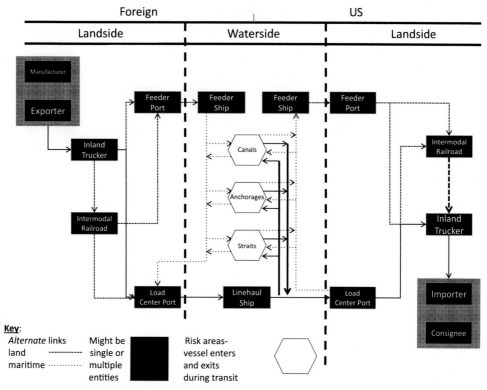

Figure 10.1

Physical flows for imports into the United States. *From Gordon, G., 2018. Intermodal Maritime Transportation Security: A Multifactor Framework for Assessing Routing Risk (Doctoral dissertation). University of Massachusetts Lowell.*

If there is a concern that data in one system can be changed to circumvent observation, compliance, or enforcement, a new development has occurred in the form of blockchain. Originally conceived as a means whereby all trade participants could access the same data and thereby preclude duplication of effort and potential for errors. While not to be totally free of the potential for cyberattack, blockchain poses obstacles because of its distributed nature and the lack of a single central controlling unit. Investopedia (2020) stated the following with regard to decentralized blockchains:

> *Blockchain does not store any of its information in a central location. Instead, the blockchain is copied and spread across a network of computers. Whenever a new block is added to the blockchain, every computer on the network updates its blockchain to reflect the change. By spreading that information across a network, rather than storing it in one central database, blockchain becomes more difficult to tamper with. If a copy of the blockchain fell into the hands of a hacker, only a single copy of the information, rather than the entire network, would be compromised.*

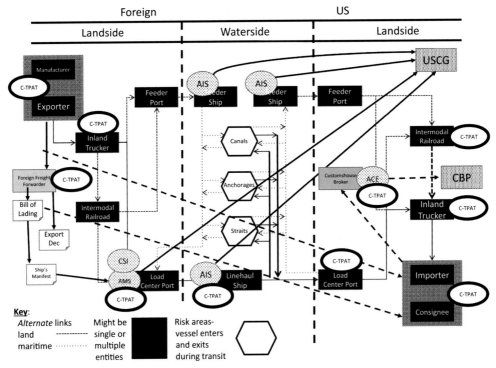

Figure 10.2

Physical flows and information flows plus CSI + C-TPAT nodes. *Adapted from Gordon, G., 2018. Intermodal Maritime Transportation Security: A Multifactor Framework for Assessing Routing Risk (Doctoral dissertation). University of Massachusetts—Lowell.*

Once a transaction is recorded, its authenticity must be verified by the blockchain network. Thousands or even millions of computers on the blockchain rush to confirm that the details of the purchase are correct. After a computer has validated the transaction, it is added to the blockchain in the form of a block. Each block on the blockchain contains its own unique hash, along with the unique hash of the block before it. When the information on a block is edited in any way, that block's hash code changes—however, the hash code on the block after it would not. This discrepancy makes it extremely difficult for information on the blockchain to be changed without notice.

Now, return to the previous discussion about the number of participants in international trade and the types of data that need to be accommodated by multiple information systems. The what, who, where, when, and how data elements are often keyed and rekeyed numerous times, but also a shipment file with that many variables becomes incredibly unique. A. P. Moller Maersk, the Danish shipping line that also happens to be the world's largest, has embarked on a blockchain project with IBM, a pioneer, and early advocate of the advantages of the technology. While no technology is totally immune from cyberattack, blockchain may have some advantages that at least will slow down the advance of cybercriminals and any of their allies who are bent on compromising international trade.

Summary

In this chapter, we have discussed the concepts of information security in general as well as some of the technologies and systems that are directly applicable to intermodal shipments in the maritime supply chain environment. While no single chapter can cover all of the aspects of this complex topic, the information covered provides a solid foundation of both the core concepts as well as the specific systems designed to aid in the protection of cargo and shipments as they may transit the oceans and seas of the planet. This field is ever-changing, and cybersecurity professionals need to be ever vigilant in keeping themselves current with both the technologies being used and the associated threats that accompany their use.

There is a clear interdependency between the physical, informational, and financial flows of the supply chain. While those who work in international trade have largely focused on the physical flow, namely getting their goods from the point of origin to their intended destination, the information flow is now recognized as the key enabler. When information flows are impeded through systems failure or inaccurate data entry, the physical flows may not grind to a halt, but may be seriously slowed. Any malevolent actor can attempt to compromise an international trade-related system for either pecuniary gain or for the intention of smuggling contraband or tainting legitimate cargo. Moreover, compromising such systems also has the potential of affecting the financial flow, or the third flow described in the supply chain literature.

CSI and C-TPAT are not systems per se, but rather databases containing details of supply chains. Those details are critical for vetting shipments to determine which may have elements of interest that make them suspect. Conversely, AMS and ACE are transaction-based systems that contain all of the shipment particulars described above but may, in fact, offer many opportunities to be compromised. Finally, there is AIS, which recent news accounts have detailed as having the potential to be circumvented thereby hiding the true location of a vessel—it is suspected that such has been the case with ships engaged in trade, for example, with North Korea in violation of United Nations sanctions.

If there are several messages that this chapter endeavors to deliver, it would be the following:

- International trade depends on information as a key enabler of both its physical and financial flows;[9]

---

[9] Financial flows, in particular international banking systems, have been purposely excluded from this chapter. While linked to international trade, the complexity of that topic is so extensive as to perhaps warrant a separate book on the topic.

- The number of systems that are developed for commercial activities as well as regulatory initiatives continues to grow in both numbers and complexity;
- With systems comes cyberattacks, whether as criminal or as terrorist acts; and
- There will be efforts to neutralize such efforts, but any such gains may be transitory as the battle of technology continues to be waged.

References

ACE and Automated Systems, January 16, 2020. Retrieved from U.S. Customs and Border Patrol. https://www.cbp.gov/trade/automated.

Andress, J., 2014. The Basics of Information Security: Understanding the Fundamentals of Information Security, second ed. Syngress, Hoboken, NJ.

Automated Commercial Environment (ACE), January 16, 2020. Retrieved from CustomsNow.com. https://www.customsnow.com/resources/automated_commercial_environment.php.

Bayuk, J., 2009. Chapter 4: Information Classification. In: Axelrod, C.W, Bayuk, J.L., Schutzer, D. (Eds.), Enterprise Information Security and Privacy. Artech House, Boston, pp. 59–70. In press.

Boritz, J.E., 2005. IS Practitioners' Views on Core Concepts of Information Integrity. International Journal of Accounting Information Systems 6 (4), 260–279. https://doi.org/10.1016/j.accinf.2005.07.001. In press.

Brasure, L.W., April 6, 2017. New Radiation Detection System Operational at Major U.S. Port. Retrieved from Department of Homeland Security. https://www.dhs.gov/blog/2017/04/06/new-radiation-detection-system-operational-major-us-port.

Cargo Systems Messaging Service, January 16, 2020. Retrieved from U.S. Customs and Border Protection. https://www.cbp.gov/trade/automated/cargo-systems-messaging-service.

CSI: Container Security Initiative, January 16, 2020. Retrieved from U.S. Customs and Border Patrol. https://www.cbp.gov/border-security/ports-entry/cargo-security/csi/csi-brief.

CTPAT: Customs Trade Partnership Against Terrorism, January 16, 2020. Retrieved from U.S. Customs and Border Patrol. https://www.cbp.gov/border-security/ports-entry/cargo-security/ctpat.

Gordon, G., 2018. Intermodal Maritime Transportation Security: A Multifactor Framework for Assessing Routing Risk (Doctoral dissertation). University of Massachusetts–Lowell.

IMO, July 5, 2017. MSC-FAL.1-Circ.3 - Guidelines on Maritime Cyber Risk Management (Secretariat).pdf. Retrieved from International Maritime Organization. http://www.imo.org/en/OurWork/Security/Guide_to_Maritime_Security/Documents/MSC-FAL.1-Circ.3%20-%20Guidelines%20On%20Maritime%20Cyber%20Risk%20Management%20(Secretariat).pdf.

IMO, June 16, 2017. Resolution MSC.428(98) - Maritime Cyber Risk Management in Safety Management Systems.pdf. Retrieved from International Maritme Organization. http://www.imo.org/en/OurWork/Security/WestAfrica/Documents/Resolution%20MSC.428(98)%20-%20Maritime%20Cyber%20Risk%20Management%20in%20Safety%20Management%20Systems.pdf.

IMO, January 5, 2020. Maritime Cyber Risk. Retrieved from International Maritime Organization. http://www.imo.org/en/OurWork/Security/Guide_to_Maritime_Security/Pages/Cyber-security.aspx.

Information Security, n.d. Retrieved from Wikipedia.org: https://en.wikipedia.org/wiki/Information_security.

Investopedia, 2020. Blockchain Explained. https://www.investopedia.com/terms/b/blockchain.asp. (Accessed 29 June 2020).

Johnson, L., 2015. Security Controls Evaluation, Testing, and Assessment Handbook. Syngress, Waltham, MA.

Kakareka, A., 2013. Chapter 31: What is Vulnerability Assessment? In: Vacca, J. (Ed.), Computer and Information Security Handbook, 2nd. Elsevier, Waltham, MA, pp. 541–552. In press.

Loukas, Georgios, Öke, Gülay, 2010. Protection Against Denial of Service Attacks: A Survey. The Computer Journal 53 (7), 1020–1037. https://doi.org/10.1093/comjnl/bxp078. In press.

Maritime Transportation Security Act of 2002, January 21, 2020. Retrieved from Wikipedia.org. https://en.
wikipedia.org/wiki/Maritime_Transportation_Security_Act_of_2002.

McCarthy, C., 2006. Digital libraries: security and preservation considerations. In: Bidgoli, H. (Ed.), Handbook
of Information Security, Threats, Vulnerabilities, Prevention, Detection, and Management. John Wiley &
Sons, Hoboken, NJ.

OECD Guidelines for the Security of Information Systems and Networks: Towards a Culture of Security, May
16, 2011. Retrieved from OECD.org. http://www.oecd.org/internet/ieconomy/15582260.pdf.

Pennin, C., June 30, 2008. The CIA Triad. Retrieved from TechRepublic. https://www.techrepublic.com/blog/it-
security/the-cia-triad/.

Port Security, January 16, 2020. Retrieved from Wikipedia.org. https://en.wikipedia.org/wiki/Port_security.

Port of LA Sets Up New Cybersecurity Coordination Center, July 25, 2019. Retrieved from The Maritime
Executive. https://maritime-executive.com/article/port-of-la-stands-up-cybersecurity-coordination-center

Ransome, J., Misra, A., 2013. Core Software Security: Security at the Source. CRC Press, pp. 40–41.

Ross, R., McEvilley, M., Oren, J., March 21, 2018. Systems Security Engineering: Considerations for a
Multidisciplinary Approach in the Engineering of Trustworthy Secure Systems. https://doi.org/10.6028/
NIST.SP.800-160v1.

Ross, R., Pillitteri, V., Graubart, R., Bodeay, D., McQuaid, R., November 27, 2019. NIST Special Publication
800-160 Volume 2. https://doi.org/10.6028/NIST.SP.800-160v2.

Samonas, S., Coss, D., 2014. The CIA strikes back: redefining confidentiality, integrity and availability in
security. J. Inf. Syst. Sec. 10 (3), 21–45.

SCADA, January 16, 2020. Retrieved from Wikipedia.org. https://en.wikipedia.org/wiki/SCADA.

Schauer, S., Stamer, M., Bosse, C., Pavlidis, M., Mouratidis, H., König, S., Papastergiou, S., 2017. An
Adaptive Supply Chain Cyber Risk Management Methodology. https://doi.org/10.15480/882.1491.

Tightening up the code, 2020. Beacon 30 (1), 1.

TWIC, n.d. Retrieved from TSA.gov: https://www.tsa.gov/for-industry/twic.

VACIS® Cargo and Vehicle Inspection Systems, January 16, 2020. Retrieved from Leidos.com. https://www.
leidos.com/products/vacis.

Vessel Tracking Data Used for Ocean Planning, January 16, 2020. Retrieved from NOAA DigitalCoast. https://
coast.noaa.gov/digitalcoast/training/ais.html.

PART IV

Security measures and public policy

CHAPTER 11

Multilateral trading partner policies

Matthew R. Peterson[1], Richard R. Young[2]
[1]Supply Chain Solutions, LMI, Mechanicsburg, PA, United States; [2]School of Business Administration, Capital College, The Pennsylvania State University, Middletown, PA, United States

While the attacks of September 11, 2001 all occurred within the United States, that day was a game changer for all supply chains, whether they were contained solely within the United States or were global. In the months following that fateful day, the United States passed a series of laws that sought to make global supply chains more secure. Although there was myriad new legislation, most consider the cornerstones to be the Customs-Trade Partnership Against Terrorism (C-TPAT) and the Container Security Initiative (CSI). Both pieces of legislation were designed to curtail the potential for weapons, in particular weapons of mass destruction, from entering the United States where various scenarios posited by RAND Corporation stated that direct and collateral damage within a major US port could be as high as to be in the hundreds of billions of dollars when both direct and indirect costs are considered (Greenberg et al., 2006, p. 125).

This chapter endeavors to explain how the various regulatory initiatives that have been implemented by the major trading nations have attempted to complement one another as well as having been replicated by some of the developing countries. As the chapter unfolds, it will become increasingly obvious that these regulations have serious gaps remaining for several reasons: (1) not all nations, including many of the developing nations, participate; (2) the regulatory structure is not able to capture all situations, including the potential for cargo to be compromised while on the high seas; and (3) the information technology required to support the transactional data that the regulatory structure requires is not sufficiently developed by many nations thereby presenting serious voids where the intended integrity can be compromised.

Why the focus on intermodal transportation?

Of all the goods transported by sea, intermodal transport plays a less significant role than does bulk transport when one considers the volume of grain, oil, compressed gases, chemicals, coal, and building materials such as sand, cement, and aggregates. The total

Intermodal Maritime Security. https://doi.org/10.1016/B978-0-12-819945-9.00006-X

global maritime trade is 11 billion metric tons with 1.8 billion being containerized (Statista, 2018).

Intermodal is the focus of this book because of its heterogeneity, namely the vast array of products and materials moved in the millions of containers arriving in the United States annually. The intermodal container not only protects its goods from potential loss and damage but also from curious eyes as well. The loading and unloading of bulk materials is a rough operation where smuggled goods could easily be damaged. Moreover, liquid bulk cargoes pose difficulties for effectively concealing contraband let alone retrieving it at the receiving end. Moreover, the permutations representing the types of goods carried by container annually can be estimated to number in the tens of thousands.

Taxonomy of intermodal threats

Since the early days of maritime trade, the major concern had been protecting goods from loss and damage. In an earlier era, theft of goods was foremost on the minds of shipowners although enslavement of crews by other nations was also ever-present. In the mid-20th century with the advent of the Cold War where battles were increasingly fought by proxies, the potential movement of materiel with potential security concerns increased. Still, the major threat was perceived to be shipments by state actors. This is not to say that the security and safety of traded goods was in any way diminished, but it is noted that maritime containerization was just in its infancy and that materiel moved on military vessels is out of scope for this discussion. Since intermodal maritime trade is the focus of this book, the discussion of trade security insofar as other nations is concerned, will be essentially limited to the time period beginning with the second half of the 20th century. For ease of discussion, the initiatives for countering threats, as shown in Fig. 11.1, are contained within the immediate post-World War II era, the late 20th century, and the post-9/11 era. Table 11.1 provides a basic description of each initiative to control trade and is a useful primer prior for the following detailed section.

Immediate post-world war II

After the war, global trade experienced explosive growth, especially with the flow of goods needed for rebuilding war devastated areas. With that growth came the realization that such trade would be regulated by individual nations, but if one's export is another's import then some ability to coordinate would be needed. Founded in 1952 and originally known as the Customs Cooperation Council, the World Customs Organization (WCO) had three objectives: (1) be a facilitator of international trade, (2) be a forum for the exchange of experiences as well as a platform for mutual technical assistance, and (3) be an advocate for fighting fraudulent practices among those engaged in international trade (World Customs Organization).

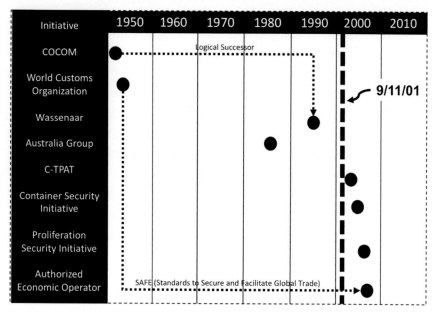

Figure 11.1
Timeline of trade control initiatives.

Table 11.1: Taxonomy of trade control initiatives.

Initiative title	Members	Import or export	Key focus	Structure	Notes
World Customs Organization	183	Both	World trade; legitimate trade		Origin was Western Europe
Coordinating Committee for Multilateral Export Controls (CoCom)	17	Export	Weapons trade	Not a treaty	Now defunct
Wassenaar Arrangement	42	Export	Weapons trade	Not a treaty	Successor to CoCom
Australia Group	43	Export	Chemical weapons; components	Not a treaty	
Customs-Trade Partnership Against Terrorism	United States only	Import	Engage private sector		Secure entire supply chain
Container Security Initiative	60+ bilateral agreements	Import	Extend zone of security	Bilateral	Reciprocity opportunity
Proliferation Security Initiative	105	Export	Weapons; components	Not a treaty	Emphasis on interdiction

Ultimately having 183 members, WCO lists securing international trade as one of its objectives. The organization is noted here because it remains an important information exchange regarding regulation formulation, enforcement practices, and information exchange meaning that nations do not exist as individual silos whereby wrongdoers may be able to leverage the space between governments.

With the creation of the North Atlantic Treaty Organization (NATO) being the intent of containing the spread of communism through the actions of the Soviet Union and its client states (Warsaw Pact aka Comecon[1]), NATO's member nations plus Japan and Australia established the Coordination Committee for Multilateral Export Controls, generally referred to by its acronym CoCom, with the intent of embargoing those goods having a potential military application (World Customs Organization).

CoCom endeavored to control the spread of arms through the establishment of restricted goods lists, mechanisms for allowing exceptions, and the means of national enforcement. Not surprisingly, the major emphasis was placed on the transfer of technology. Unlike NATO, CoCom was not a treaty-type organization, but rather depended upon each of its member nations to enact their own respective legislation for controlling exports. Recall that such unilateral actions were not just the establishment of lists of items prohibited from trade, but also mechanisms for enforcement, a matter that could and did conflict with some members' national policies. Note, too, that any actions of CoCom had to be unanimously approved by all of the members (Crenshaw, 1993, p. iv).

There were three lists of export categories within CoCom: the International Atomic Energy List, the International Munitions List, and the International Industrial List. While the first two lists were relatively straightforward with respect to the items contained, the last list was far more problematic given that these goods were also known to be dual use, meaning that they had both peaceful as well as potentially military-related applications. The latter were described as those materials, equipment, and technology that could potentially allow another nation (read Comecon country) to make significant advances to its military capabilities (Crenshaw, 1993, p. 5).

Whereas CoCom provided for exceptions where nations could engage in trade of otherwise restricted merchandise, it nevertheless required adherence to one of five increasingly stringent limitations that spanned the low-level administrative exception to the all-encompassing embargo. CoCom had experienced the most difficulty when its employees had to perform a specific sign-off for an export and as exceptions became increasingly common, the administrative workload increased commensurately.

---

[1] Acronym for Council for Mutual Economic Assistance. Established in 1949, it was intended to "establish wider economic cooperation between Warsaw Pact nations for the purpose of exchanging economic experience, extending technological aid to one another, and rendering mutual assistance."

As for enforcement, CoCom was an instrument of economic warfare. Clearly, the member nations were in general agreement, but to assert further deprivation of technology by nonmember nations required member nations to impose economic sanctions, specifically as trade restrictions. As the world became more economically interdependent since the inception of CoCom and the Comecon nations gained technological prowess, the ability to wage significant economic warfare became more limited. In the early 1990s, it was determined that much of the technology being employed by Saddam Hussein's Iraq was obtained from other nations, whether they be Comecon or even member states operating under CoCom exception protocols (Crenshaw, 1993, p. 7).

It is not surprising, therefore, that by the mid-1990s CoCom had become obsolete. Nations began seeking other avenues for limiting the trade in military-related merchandise that could be used to arm nations engaged in regional conflicts. Proliferation would remain a problem, and the burden of impeding if not curtailing it fell upon the developed nations, most notably those of the West.

Developed nations expand global oversight

Beginning in the mid-1980s, there was increased concern that many nations were increasing the amount of technology in their military capabilities that was not indigenous to their own industrial base. As advances in biological, chemical, and nuclear arms continued to advance, the Australia Group was formed with many developed nations signing on. In the mid-1990s just as CoCom was appearing to become less effective, the Wassenaar Arrangement (WA) emerged with an emphasis that somewhat mirrored that of CoCom, but with a far more detailed proscription listing and a significantly longer list of participating nations.

Australia group

Stemming from the Iran–Iraq War Saddam Hussein in violation of the 1925 Geneva Convention was found to have used chemical weapons that were believed to be based on materials obtained from other nations. Such chemical precursors were found to be sourced from legitimate international suppliers, which resulted in several nations instituting export controls on those chemicals known to have uses for producing chemical weapons (Australia Group, 2019).

Not surprisingly those various export controls did not possess any uniformity thereby providing an opportunity for such regulations to be circumvented. In 1985, Australia, one of the nations that supplied the chemicals, took the initiative of calling for a meeting of chemical exporting nations with the objective of harmonizing controls. From its foundation with 15 members, the Australia Group (AG) now has 42 participants. Note that the Australia Group is an agreement among participating nations and does not comprise a treaty. Moreover, much like the format used by CoCom, it seeks to restrict trade based on lists of materials, equipment, technology, and software whereby the production of chemical and biological weapons may be fashioned.

Three important factors are derived from the Australia Group effort with regard to parties of interest: (1) terrorist and nonstate actors are within scope; (2) the supply chain with its various participants including manufacturers, distributors, and agents have traditionally been means to disguise diversion; and (3) it is the end use as well as the use for producing intermediate components that are in scope (Australia Group, 2019).

The following guidelines for the issuance of export licenses as stated on the Australia Group's website are both instructive and useful in their endeavor to be as comprehensive and inclusive as possible:

1. Information about proliferation and terrorism involving chemical and biological warfare (CBW), including any proliferation or terrorism-related activity, or about involvement in clandestine or illegal procurement activities, of the parties to the transaction;
2. The capabilities and objectives of the chemical and biological activities of the recipient state;
3. The significance of the transfer in terms of: (1) the appropriateness of the stated end use, including any relevant assurances submitted by the recipient state or end user, and (2) the potential development of CBW;
4. The role of distributors, brokers, or other intermediaries in the transfer, including, where appropriate, their ability to provide an authenticated end-user certificate specifying both the importer and ultimate end user of the item to be transferred, as well as the credibility of assurances that the item will reach the stated end user;
5. The assessment of the end use of the transfer, including whether a transfer has been previously denied to the end user, whether the end user has diverted for unauthorized purposes any transfer previously authorized, and, to the extent possible, whether the end user is capable of securely handling and storing the item transferred;
6. The extent and effectiveness of the export control system in the recipient state as well as any intermediary states;
7. The applicability of relevant multilateral agreements, including the Biological and Toxin Weapons Convention (BTWC) and Chemical Weapons Convention (CWC);
8. The risk of controlled items falling into the hands of terrorist groups and individuals (Australia Group, Guidelines).

Wassenaar arrangement

Fig. 11.1 shows a dashed line from CoCom to the WA not only for the chronology of one's ending more or less coinciding with the other's beginning, but that one really is the successor to the former. A key similarity to CoCom is that the WA publishes annual lists of dual-use goods and technologies, and munitions. On the list of the former can be found special materials, related equipment, and materials processes for a range of goods that include electronics, computers, telecommunications network components, information security protocols, sensors and lasers, navigation and avionics equipment and their components, marine items, and aerospace and aviation materiel. The munitions list, which grows with the advance of technology, can now be found unmanned airborne vehicles among other items (Wassenaar, Homepage).

Of particular note with regard to WA is the inclusion of checklists that pertain to the seller of the goods and the degree to which they have specific knowledge concerning the goods per se as well as knowledge of the customer and their intended use. These checklists may be found in Appendices A and B to this chapter.

Inasmuch as this book concerns transportation issues, the WA also has established guidelines for the transit and transshipment of goods insofar as nations may endeavor to regulate such actions. Note that the focus here is with the nation-state and not the industry that has commercial interests related to the goods to be transported. Appendix B to this chapter provides these guidelines in summary form.

If the WA was to be viewed as CoCom plus provisions for CoCom's shortcomings, it would have to be found in the guidelines for enforcement, which are far more granular than the economic sanctions that were its norm. For example, WA provides for preventative enforcement, effective penalties, investigations, and cooperative information exchanges.

The following is a summary list of the factors that WA addresses when examining a particular export transaction. Note especially that many of these actions are not after-the-fact and may involve detaining shipments, examination of documents prior to shipment, and even face-to-face contact with interested parties such as shippers, consignees, and various participating intermediaries.

1. Evaluate the various parties involved in a proposed export transaction, paying particular attention to those considered to be suspicious, unreliable, or presenting a high-risk of diversion.
2. Create and maintain a database of consignees, end users, and other parties of concern to identify export transactions and related activities deserving closer scrutiny.
3. Confirm all particulars regarding the export license including stated consignee, end user, and end use of items to be exported through review of documentation and/or on-premise checks of the parties to the transaction.
4. Obtain assurances regarding the end use and the nontransfer/reexport of licensed items, as appropriate.
5. Inspect the items and examine the respective documentation that is required to be presented at point of export.

6. Detain suspect shipments and seize unauthorized or illegal exports including items that are passing in transit or being transshipped.

7. Confirm that exported items have reached their intended destinations by either reviewing documentation or on-site verification.

8. Conduct educational outreach programs for export controls.

9. Promote compliance by all relevant parties in export transactions. As appropriate, encourage implementation of internal compliance programmes and voluntary self-disclosures of violations discovered.

10. Inform relevant parties apprised of penalties for failure to comply with the regulations. Cite examples of past criminal prosecution or other civil or administrative enforcement actions.

11. Establish policies for protecting unauthorized disclosure of sensitive data (Wassenaar, Homepage).

The implementation of export controls to be effective need to have penalties articulated for those situations of noncompliance. The WA states that member nations shall have laws, regulations, and policies that provide for the detection and prosecution of those committing violations. Moreover, from an organizational perspective, administrative, civil, and criminal enforcement personnel are retained, trained, and empowered to detect, prevent, and punish violations of export control regulations.

Concomitant member nations need to have investigatory capabilities that include the necessary resources and training to maintain effective enforcement personnel who have the power and the ability to coordinate with other regulatory authorities to identify questionable transactions. For example, the United States has working relationships between the Department of Commerce, Customs and Border Protection (CBP, 2019), the Coast Guard (USCG), Treasury Department, and Food and Drug Administration (FDA) among others in a concerted effort where money laundering, fraudulent transactions, and other business irregularities may be present.

Inasmuch as global trade has grown at prodigious levels during the past half century so has the willingness of nations to become active members in multilateral endeavors to regulate it, especially where the movement of weapons or dual-use merchandise may be concerned. Table 11.2 shows how the growth of memberships in such initiatives has grown; however, the next section of this chapter will address the fallout from the events of 9/11, one of which is a further growth in international cooperation.

The post-9/11 era

The three-pronged terrorist attack on the United States on September 11, 2001 changed the transportation industry forever. But how has it changed? Clearly international

Table 11.2: Participating nations in late 20th century initiatives.

Europe	A	B	C	The Americas	A	B	C	Asia, Africa, and Oceania	A	B	C
Austria		•	•	Argentina		•	•	Australia		•	•
Belgium	•	•	•	Canada		•	•	India		•	•
Bulgaria		•	•	Mexico		•	•	Japan	•	•	•
Croatia		•	•	United States	•	•	•	New Zealand		•	•
Cyprus		•						South Africa			•
Czech Republic		•	•					South Korea		•	•
Denmark	•	•	•								
Estonia		•	•								
Finland		•	•								
France	•	•	•								
Germany	•	•	•								
Greece	•	•	•								
Hungary		•	•								
Iceland		•									
Ireland		•	•								
Italy	•	•	•								
Latvia		•	•								
Lithuania		•	•								
Luxemburg	•	•	•								
Malta		•	•								
Netherlands	•	•	•								
Norway	•	•	•								
Poland		•	•								
Portugal	•	•	•								
Romania		•	•								
Russia			•					Key:			
Slovakia		•	•					CoCom			A
Slovenia		•	•					Australia Group, 2019			B
Spain	•	•	•					Wassenaar arrangement			C
Sweden		•	•								
Switzerland		•	•								
Turkey	•	•	•								
Ukraine		•	•								
United Kingdom	•	•	•								

transportation would become far more scrutinized than any of the initiatives already discussed in this chapter ever envisaged. Information concerning all aspects of global shipments would be subject to review, the private and public sectors would partner in order that a more comprehensive view of supply chains would result, and shipments destined for the United States could be potentially physically inspected by US international partner agencies before being loaded aboard ship. The following provides the details contained in the most significant actions undertaken by the U.S. Congress in controlling the flows of international trade that touch the United States.

National Maritime Intelligence-Integration Office

An organization established following 9/11, the little known National Maritime Intelligence-Integration Office (NMIO) is in part a result of the Intelligence Reform and Terror Prevention Act (IRTPA) and several Presidential directives. Its goal is to support national policymakers and decision-makers on maritime issues and perform actions to create unity of effort and position leaders for efficient and effective decision-making. A key part of NMIO is also an intelligence gathering unit that leverages the efforts of multiple stakeholders at the federal, state, local, and tribal government levels, the private sector, and various unnamed international partners—many of these can be assumed to be agencies found within WA member states. The NMIO collects significant detailed information on the cargoes being transported on all of the oceans of the globe.[2]

Customs-trade partnership against terrorism

With the realization that government alone did not have sufficient resources to vet all of the cargo arriving on US shores annually, the C-TPAT was founded on the premise that it is the private sector—the importers—who possess the most knowledge of what is being imported, who is shipping it, and how it is being transported. In concept, it made a lot of sense, but in reality, it turned out that many importers, both large and small, were lacking significant information about their trading partners (DHS/CBP/PIA, 2013).

In the case of the small importer, they often did not have the resources to finance the international travel necessary for being able to document the chain of custody from the point of origin to that point when they took delivery in the United States. But rather than level an indictment solely at the small importers, there is ample evidence to suggest that many large corporations had for years sourced goods from suppliers that they had never visited and in too many instances knew very little about the respective chain of custody. C-TPAT was designed to overcome that shortcoming and in exchange for expeditious processing of imports through Customs upon arrival importers were to undertake a comprehensive analysis of their foreign suppliers and agree to have CBP certify the documentation. While this was an expensive process for the large importers to perform, there was clear value to be found in not delaying goods upon arrival at a US port—entries for the cargo of the certified importers would normally clear with minimal delay and seldom receive a physical examination. Where Customs found value in engaging the major importers was in having detailed knowledge of a large number of import entries.

---

[2] For many purposes, the National Maritime Intelligence-Integration Office may be considered a maritime fusion center.

The imports of the smaller firms were likely more suspect for several reasons and as would be expected few such firms ever investigated C-TPAT certification. It was a true application of the Pareto Principle where CBP's focus would now be on those 20% of the imports that potentially represented 80% of the problems. CBP would do some random checks of the certified importers and if errors would frequently occur the importer risked the loss of continuing C-TPAT certification.

Container security initiative

In the aftermath of 9/11, CBP faced the realization that the ocean container represented an excellent vehicle for delivering a weapon. As noted earlier, a RAND analysis estimated the economic damage that a variety of weapons could inflict on a US port. However, the task of inspecting the millions of containers reaching US shores annually was a daunting one (Romero, 2003). Moreover, inspecting those containers at US ports meant that screening was being done at the last point of defense whereas the foreign ports of loading actually represented the first line. Thus, was born the CSI where U.S. personnel working closely with their foreign counterparts in-country would vet US-bound containers far earlier in the supply chain. CSI was, therefore, based on three premises:

- The ability to identify high-risk containers. Using automated targeting tools, suspect containers that may pose a risk of terrorism are targeted for inspection. While CBP will not reveal the factors that go into such selection, it can be assumed that C-TPAT would play a role.
- Screen containers, including physical inspection, prior to their being loaded aboard a ship destined for the United States.
- Apply technology for screening high-risk containers expeditiously without unduly slowing down the pace of global trade. The preferred methods are noninvasive such as radiation detection devices and large-scale X-ray (CBP, 2019; Singla, 2019).

As of this writing, CSI is now operational in approximately 60 ports worldwide with representation on every continent. The initiative screens more than 80% of all containerized cargo coming to the United States.

Authorized economic operator credential

On Fig. 11.1, there is a dotted line from the WCO to the Authorized Economic Operator (AEO) that is also marked SAFE (Standards to Secure and Facilitate Global Trade). Established in 2005, AEO is a cornerstone of SAFE and among its many members each has a program with its own particular name, such as the US C-TPAT as discussed earlier; Singapore has the Secure Trade Partnership, or STP, and Australia has the Australian Trusted Partner or ATT. No matter the name, the intended outcome is the same: certifying member firms regarding the integrity of their respective chains of custody in exchange for more expeditious processing that serves to improve the efficiency of supply chains (Noah, 2018).

Economic operators are firms that are part of the supply chain meaning importers, exporters, transport service providers, and a broad range of intermediaries. Any firm is only permitted to have one AEO registration, a designation that is achieved through being able to document and certify its respective segment of the supply chain, but with other requirements attached, including:

- Compliance with customs legislation and taxation rules and the absence of any criminal offenses related to economic activity;
- Accurate recordkeeping:
- Financial solvency;
- Proven practical standards of competence or professional qualifications;
- Appropriate security and safety measures (WCO, 2019).

An AEO designation granted by one state is recognized by the Customs organizations of all member states because they are considered as a safe and secure business partner. With this comes improved relationships with Customs and other government agencies. Firms that are considered business partners are required to implement internal controls that also have the serendipitous effect of reducing theft and losses, fewer delayed shipments, and better customer service (WCO, 2019).

Inasmuch as all of the benefits that were discussed in the above section on C-TPAT are common to AEO, that will not be repeated here. The principal value to AEO is that it is now a worldwide initiative; however, that is not to imply that every WCO member nation has at this point implemented such provisions. Nevertheless, a very significant portion of global trade is now facilitated by participating firms.

The proliferation security initiative

A global effort that aims to stop the trafficking in weapons of mass destruction (WMD), their component materials, and delivery systems between state and nonstate actors, Proliferation Security Initiative (PSI) was found in 2003. Its membership currently stands at 105 nations as shown in Fig. 11.2.

At the outset, membership appeared to mirror that of CoCom with the addition of Poland, but where PSI differs is with the addition of the Statement of Interdiction Principles. Interdiction means the ability to stop or otherwise impede those shipments of WMD-related goods between parties considered to be of proliferation concern. The provision also calls for any action to be consistent with national legal authorities, international law and United Nations Security Council circumstances. It is noted that since its founding, PSI has

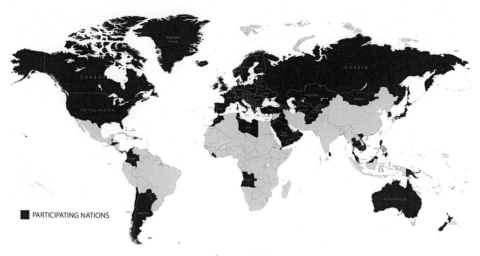

Figure 11.2
Current members of the proliferation security initiative. *U.S. Department of Defense.*

expanded its reach and now embraces a much wider array of proliferation security issues, such as customs enforcement, export controls, proliferation finance, and intangible transfers of technology. Given its broad and flexible mandate, the PSI now plays a vital role in advancing proliferation security norms and standards of practice (Nitkin, 2018).

Multilayered defenses still leave gaps

When taken together, one could conclude that the AG, WA, AEO,[3] CSI, and PSI employ significant resources to establish a comprehensive intelligence picture of the cargo being transported by maritime transportation. Certainly, these represent a multilayered defense where the nature of the goods, the producer, the shipper, the consignee, and the myriad trade intermediaries are not only known, but in many instances active participants in protecting global trade. Nevertheless, there are gaps that remain and as witnessed by the seizure of nearly 20 tons of cocaine in the Port of Philadelphia in June 2019 where small boats rendezvoused with a large containership off the west coast of South America, those gaps do not necessarily need to be small ones.

Information technology plays a very significant role in cargo security because most trade documentation is either online or otherwise electronically captured prior to shipment. That, however, is not a global practice inasmuch as some developing nations still depend

---

[3] From a definition standpoint, Customs-Trade Partnership Against Terrorism can be considered the US-specific version of Authorized Economic Operator.

on manually prepared documents meaning that any ability to intercept shipments is precluded because the goods are long gone before any information details can be reviewed. Finally, there is the matter of cybersecurity, the risks, and vulnerabilities for which are discussed in greater detail in other chapters of this book.

This chapter has laid out the evolution of international cooperation from a WCO where Customs agencies could exchange best practices and inform one another of potential enforcement issues to the nearly concurrent creation of CoCom with its lists of proscribed arms-related goods. As technology advanced, the Australia Group was founded to stem trade in chemical and biological agents, several of its provisions later being adopted within the WA, that was in actuality the successor to CoCom.

The global effort to deprive terrorists of their desired weapons could have ended with Wassenaar, but the events of 9/11 assured that such would not be the case. Almost immediately plans were implemented to enlist the multiple members of global supply chains to protect shipments. The result was C-TPAT and CSI, the former of which became the model from which the AEO as a major component of the WCO's SAFE was derived. The one missing element, interdiction, was provided by the PSI. Interdiction represents a drastic step because it can be deemed an act of war, but it is also the obvious missing element from the CoCom initiative.

Global supply chains are not foolproof or watertight entities. The multilateral attempts to stem the trade in weapons, whether between state or nonstate actors can be logically layered onto the Supply Chain Operational Reference Model, as was described in an earlier chapter. Clearly, efforts have focused on the physical, information, and financial flows; however, gaps do remain.

Appendix A: Wassenaar checklist for international sellers

Your product

1. Is your product still being developed or has it not yet found many customers in your domestic market?
2. Are the characteristics of your product technically superior to those of established competitors?
3. Has your customer requested any unusual customization of a standard product, or do any modification requests raise concerns about potential applications of the customized product?
4. Have you sought an export control classification or self-classification of the item?
5. Does your product have a known dual-use, military, or sensitive application?

End user and end use

6. Is the customer new to your company and is your knowledge about the customer incomplete or inconsistent?
7. Is it difficult to find information about the customer in open sources?
8. Does the customer seem unfamiliar with the product and its performance characteristics (an unreasonable lack of technical knowledge)?
9. Does the customer request a product that seems overly capable for the intended application?
10. Does the customer provide inadequate responses when your sales staff suggests another product might suit the application at a lower cost?
11. Is the customer unable to provide details about the requested product or their technical requirements?
12. Is the stated contact information (e.g., telephone, email, address) of the customer directed to a third party in another country?
13. Does the customer have a foreign company name (e.g., in a language that is unexpected for the country where the headquarters are located)?
14. Is the stated end user a trading company, distributor, or based in a free-trade zone?
15. Is the stated end user more traditionally a freight forwarder?
16. Is the end user connected to the military, the defense industry, or a governmental research facility despite the stated end user being civilian?
17. Is the customer reluctant to provide information about the end use of the product, or to provide clear answers to routine commercial and/or technical questions?
18. Is the customer reluctant to provide an end-user statement or other supporting documentation?
19. Do the products appear to be irrelevant for the customer's stated business activities?
20. Doe the given end use diverge significantly from the end use indicated by the manufacturer?
21. Is the customer forgoing service instructions or warranty usually provided for this product?
22. Is the customer calling in intermediaries for no apparent reason?

Shipment

23. Is the requested shipping route unusual?
24. Are the requested packaging or labeling arrangements unusual?
25. Does the customer want to collect the product in person?
26. Is the collection of the product(s) handled by a party other than the stated customer or intermediaries?

Finance and contract conditions

27. Is the customer offering unusual and/or unreasonably profitable term?

28. Is the customer offering a full payment in advance or an immediate cash payment upon receipt of the products?

29. Is the payment handled by a party other than the stated customer or intermediaries?

30. Does the payment follow another route than the products (e.g., via another country)?

31. Does the customer decline reasonable and practically feasible routine installation, training, or maintenance services in the country of destination and/or suggests that his own personnel is trained for such in the exporting country?

32. Is the installation site in an area with strict security control to which access is severely limited?

33. Is the installation site in any other way unusual in respect to the product being installed?

34. Does the customer have unusual requirements for excessive confidentiality about final destinations, customers, or specifications of products?

35. Is the customer requesting an excessive amount of spare parts or other items related to the product, not correlating with the stated end use?

Note: In the case of doubt regarding a certain enquiry, consult with the competent authority in your country. Sharing information on suspicious inquiries with them is highly recommended.

Appendix B: Wassenaar checklist for transit and transshipment

1. Establish and apply a transparent legal and regulatory system that allows, where appropriate, the authority to control items in transit or transshipment, including the authority to, where necessary and appropriate, stop, inspect, and seize a shipment, as well as legal grounds to dispose of a seized shipment when law enforcement activities are completed.2 This authority should extend fully to activities taking place in special Customs areas located within a sovereign state's territory, such as free-trade zones, foreign trade zones, and export processing zones.

2. Require, where appropriate, authorizations in accordance with national law for the transit or transshipment of listed munitions and dual-use items, as well as for unlisted items (i.e., catch-all authority controls), where there is reliable information that the items are intended to be used in prohibited military or terrorist uses, or that otherwise pose a security concern. Coordination and communication with exporting and importing countries may be required, as appropriate, to ensure that listed items intended for transit or transshipment have been properly authorized for export or import.

3. Utilize an intelligence-led, risk-based approach to identifying cargoes and known end users of concern, including through the use of internationally endorsed requirements for manifest collections in advance of the arrival of all controlled goods. This approach should enable the identification of inconsistencies that raise suspicion, in time to stop and seize items where necessary and appropriate, while taking into account increasing trade volumes and complexities of supply chains, so that available resources can be deployed in an efficient and targeted manner.

4. Conduct focused outreach to manufacturers, distributors, brokers, and freight forwarders to raise awareness of export control obligations, as well as potential penalties for noncompliance, and encourage industry to develop internal compliance programs.

5. Provide training for Customs and enforcement officers, by competent authorities so that they can identify items of concern and increase cooperation between enforcement agencies and licensing authorities.

6. Adopt and deploy appropriate screening technologies and practices and other sources of technical assistance, such as risk-based evaluation of data.

7. Exchange information on policies and practices with respect to transit and transshipment including, where appropriate, any enforcement actions taken, with WA partners.

References

(The) Australia Group, 2019. The Australia Group Homepage. https://australiagroup.net/en/index.html. (Accessed 20 January 2020).

Crenshaw, J., 1993. The Origins of CoCom: Lessons for Contemporary Proliferation Control Regimes. Report No. 7. The Stimson Center, Washington, DC.

Customs and Border Protection, 2019. CSI: Container Security Initiative. https://www.cbp.gov/border-security/ports-entry/cargo-security/csi/csi-brief#wcm-survey-target-id. (Accessed 19 January 2020).

DHS/CBP/PIA, 2013. Privacy Impact Statement for the Customs-Trade Partnership Against Terrorism. Department of Homeland Security, Washington, DC.

Greenberg, M., Chalk, P., Willis, H., Khilko, I., Ortiz, D., 2006. Maritime Terrorism: Risk and Liability. The RAND Center for Terrorism Risk Management Policy (CTRMP), Arlington, VA.

Nitkin, M.B., 2018. Proliferation Security Initiative (PSI). Congressional Research Service, Washington, DC.

Noah, D., 2018. What Is an Authorized Economic Operator? International Trade Blog at. https://www.shippingsolutions.com/blog/authorized-economic-operator. (Accessed 1 February 2020).

Romero, J., 2003. Prevention of maritime terrorism: the container security initiative. Chicago J. Int. Law 597−605.

Singla, S., 2019. What Is the Container Security Initiative and How Does It Work? Marine Insight. https://www.marineinsight.com/marine-safety/what-is-container-security-initiative-csi-and-how-does-it-work/. (Accessed 15 January 2020).

Statista, 2018. Quantity of Loaded Freight in International Maritime Trade from 1970 to 2018. https://www.statista.com/statistics/234698/loaded-freight-in-international-maritime-trade-since-1970/. (Accessed 1 February 2020).

Wassenaar, (n.d.). (The) Wassenaar Arrangement On Export Controls for Conventional Arms and Dual-use Goods and Technologies. https://www.wassenaar.org/home/. (Accessed 23 January 2020).

World Customs Organization, 2019. Compendium of Authorized Economic Operator Programmes. World Customs Organization, Paris.

CHAPTER 12

Intermodal transport security—the Israeli perspective

Aleksander Gerson, Tomer May
Wydra Division for Shipping and Ports Research, Maritime Policy & Strategy Research Center, University of Haifa, Haifa, Israel

Part I - Overview of maritime security

"Without dominion of the sea, the State of Israel would become "A City under Siege"; as we must make the Negev Desert bloom, so we must conquer the expanses of the sea; … the country's security depends on the sea; our commodities and trade are carried by the waves; without naval mastery and force, no land or air forces can ensure our security. However, the importance of the sea is not just political or military: our economic future depends on it"

David Ben-Gurion, Israel's first Prime Minister, 1950

Introduction

Israel is located in the geographical hub of the Middle East, at the crossroads of three continents. Terrestrial transport between Egypt, Syria, Iraq, and Lebanon is possible only via Israel, while Jordan has no direct access to the Mediterranean Sea, except through Israel. Despite what may appear as a desirable strategic position, Israel is, in fact, a geopolitical island surrounded by countries which are mostly hostile or impose severe land trade restrictions (Egypt). The long-standing and ongoing Israeli–Palestinian conflict significantly enhances security threats posed by terrorist activities of organizations such as Hamas (in Gaza) and Hezbollah (in Lebanon), both sponsored by Iran, which aspires to control one of the Syrian ports as its own. The wider circle of threats includes the Houthis in Yemen, Islamic State of Iraq and Syria (ISIS), and Al-Qaeda (Fig. 12.1).

In this geopolitical background, Israel's maritime trade amounts to 98%−99% by volume (Port Development) of its import/export and is, therefore, an economic lifeline. Recently discovered rich gas fields in the Israeli Exclusive Economic Zone (EEZ) offer a significant

Intermodal Maritime Security. https://doi.org/10.1016/B978-0-12-819945-9.00011-3

THREATS FACING ISRAEL

ONGOING TERRORIST ATTACKS   CALLS FOR ITS ANNIHILATION
180,000 ROCKETS ON ITS BORDERS   ISRAELI CITIZENS TARGETED

LEBANON

The Hezbollah terrorist organization, an Iranian proxy, is engaged in worldwide terrorist activity

Over 70,000 rockets, capable of striking the entire state of Israel, many of which are hidden within civilian infrastructure, are aimed at Israeli cities

It is aggressively involved in the Syrian civil war providing troops, training and arms to the barbaric Assad regime, and trying to acquire strategic weapons from Syria

Terrorists launched rockets towards northern Israel (August 2013)

GAZA

The Hamas terrorist organization, an Iranian proxy, has wielded authority over the Palestinian territory of the Gaza Strip since 2007, and holds over 10,000 rockets

Hamas' charter rejects a two-state solution and the legitimacy of a Jewish state, and calls for Israel's complete annihilation

Gaza is also home to Islamic Jihad and Al-Aqsa Martyrs Brigade terrorist organizations, in addition to Global Jihad cells

Since Israeli disengagement in 2005, Hamas has launched continued attacks against Israel, launching over 8,000 rockets and mortars

SINAI

Increased lawlessness in Sinai provides a home for Global Jihad and other terrorists, and has resulted in rocket attacks, and multiple cross-border raids

Multiple terrorist infiltrations of Sinai border, incl. August 2011 attack that killed eight Israelis

Multiple rockets launched towards southern Israel, including the resort city of Eilat

SYRIA

Chemical weapons have been used in a brutal and bloody civil war that has claimed the lives of over 100,000 people

The Assad regime's cache of game-changing weapons, including chemical weapons and ballistic missiles, poses an extraordinary threat

A growing population of Jihadist and other terror cells are amassing in Syria

WEST BANK

Radical forces opposing the Palestinian Authority and a culture of conflict generate strong anti-Israel incitement and hatred

ISRAEL

IRAN

Iran's pursuit of nuclear weapons combined with extremist cries for annihilation translate into an unprecedented threat

Its accelerating enrichment program has amassed roughly 400 pounds of 20% uranium, sufficient for several nuclear bombs

The Iranian-sponsored global terror campaign, through its proxy Hezbollah, spans 24 countries, including the United States and European Union

Iranian leaders call Israel a "cancerous tumor" and threaten to "wipe Israel off the map"

KEY
Incidents   Threats

EMBASSY OF
ISRAEL
TO THE UNITED STATES

August 27, 2013

Figure 12.1

Threats facing Israel from its neighbors (Embassies). Source: Consulate General of Israel in Houston, https://embassies.gov.il/houston/News/CurrentAffairs/Pages/Threats-Facing-Israel-Map.aspx.

economic promise, but simultaneously pose an additional security problem and a potential source of political discord with Turkey and Lebanon.

This chapter aims to portray how Israel's maritime trade operates on the background of the country's unique security problems, and the measures taken to ensure the vital supply chain during peace and in times of hostilities.

The vital role of ports and shipping of Israel

Despite Israel's pivotal geographic location bridging east and west, Israel is surrounded by hostile countries, some directly bordering it, others in the second or third circle. This renders commerce between Israel and its neighboring countries negligible or in some cases impossible. Disparity of economies (GDP per capita in thousands of USD in 2018: Israel—41,700; Syria—2000; Jordan—4200; Lebanon—8270 and Egypt—2500)

(World Bank) and the nondemocratic political regimes explain the paucity of commerce even with neighbors with which Israel has signed a peace treaty. Hence, the majority of Israel's markets are geographically distant and dependent on maritime trade (Port Development).

Israeli airborne commerce is restricted in its volume (less than 2%); however, Israel has alternative routes for international trade, via the Mediterranean and the Red Sea. The vast majority of goods and all raw materials (liquid and solid bulk) are carried by sea in view of the obvious advantage in carrying capacity and cost (economies of scale). Consequently, the importance of maritime trade (shipping and ports) for Israel is paramount.

Any disruption in the maritime supply chain might prove damaging to Israeli national trade. In times of hostilities, foreign crews are reluctant or refuse to sail ships to Israeli ports. Even during routine times, Israeli territorial waters are considered a "War Zone Area" by all major insurance firms. This in turn steeply increases insurance fees and places Israeli ports at a competitive disadvantage.

In times of military conflict, Israel's lack of natural resources such as oil, chemicals, animal feed, and military hardware renders it highly dependent on foreign trade.

The number of Israeli merchant marine ships, which traditionally imported vital commodities during times of hostilities, and Israel's marine manpower and know-how have been severely depleted since the 1990's. This underscores the necessity of keeping Israel's navigational routes open and secure at all times.

Israel's ports

Israel has five major sea ports—three commercial ports (Haifa, Ashdod, and Eilat) and two energy ports (Hadera and Ashkelon), as shown in Fig. 12.2. Ashkelon connects with the Gulf of Eilat via the Ashkelon—Eilat Pipeline, which was laid following the closure of the Suez Canal in 1967—75. Haifa and Ashdod are the only major container ports, and are in the final phase of a major expansion which will enable them to serve Very Large Container Ships. The geographic distance from major shipping routes, as well as the isolation from its trading partners, prevents Israeli ports from becoming important hubs of global transshipment.

A 2018 government plan for building a railway between Oman and the Saudi Arabian Peninsula through the port of Eilat to Mediterranean ports, as an alternative to the Suez Canal, aimed to transform these ports into regional hubs of commerce. This project, which aimed to bypass the straits of Bab-el-Mandeb, which are compromised by the Iran sponsored Houthis, has not materialized due to excessive cost and lack of international support (Fig. 12.3).

Figure 12.2
Ports of Israel. Source: Adapted from Israeli Ministry of Foreign Affairs (MFA.gov.il) map.

The chain of supply which begins at the loading port, progresses through maritime transport by ships and is completed at the discharge port. Safety and security at any stage of the process are vital, especially at the port of destination, where the authenticity and security of the cargo must be ensured. Any disruption, at any stage of loading, transport,

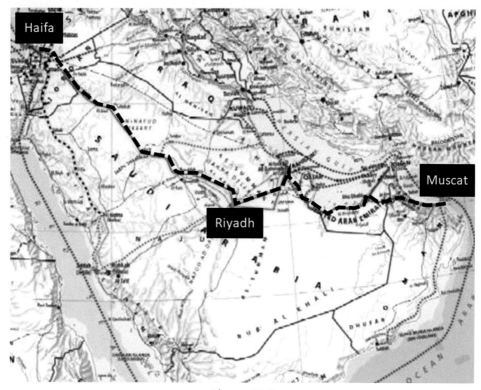

Figure 12.3
Planned railway from Haifa to Oman. Adapted for map from Israeli Ministry of Intelligence.

or safe discharge, equals a breakdown of the supply chain. This risk is increased in times of crisis or military conflict.

Threats to maritime transport to and from Israel

Dangers to maritime transport are numerous: explosives smuggled on board and timed to explode at sea or in discharge port, hijacking of a merchant ship at sea, attack on a ship (by shooting at or using an explosives-loaded small boat) when navigating too close to a hostile shore, or sabotaging the ship during stay at a loading port (by diverse explosive devices). These scenarios are only too real for Israeli flagged ships. Israeli discharge ports are also not immune to armed attacks by Katyusha rockets, long and medium range rockets (Israel—Iraq conflict, 1991, and the second Lebanon war with Hezbollah (2006) (Ch-Strategy; Port2port)) and Hamas rockets from Gaza (2014).

Modern commercial ports are a vital link, serving as an interface between maritime and land transport. Efficient port operations should be seamless in order to prevent bottleneck formation in the supply chain. A well-developed infrastructure of hinterland, road, and rail is required for efficient transport of goods. Ports in Israel are vital to urban development and the national economy, and therefore, in many respects, determine the resilience of Israeli economy (Dalit Kaspi-Shechner; DMAG).

In the current geopolitical reality where most of Israel's area is within range of missiles, the country is compelled to exercise tight control on land, air, and mainly at sea in order to ensure safe passage and access to all commercial and energy ports.

Israel trades mainly with Western Europe, Asia, and North America. The route to these destinations must traverse the Straits of Gibraltar, the Suez Canal, Straits of Tiran, Bab-el-Mandeb, or the Malacca Straits. Each of these is a potential "choke point", blockade of which would deprive Israel of its vital commercial link (Lorentz). Historically, Israel has been subjected to attempts of maritime blockade: in 1956 during the Anglo-French-Israeli conflict with Egypt over control of the Suez Canal; in 1967 the Straits of Tiran in the Red Sea, were blockaded by Egypt; during the "Yom Kippur War" (1973), Egypt proclaimed a maritime blockade for Israeli ships at the Bab-el-Mandeb Strait (the entrance to the Red Sea) (Walker), and also mined Jubal Straits in the Gulf of Suez (at least one Israeli oil tanker was sunk by an Egyptian mine, another was damaged) (Fig. 12.4).

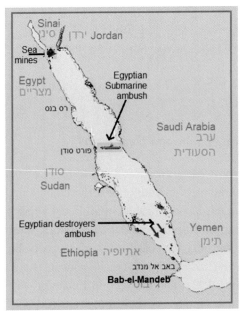

Figure 12.4
Attempt to blockade Israeli shipping in the Red Sea, 1973 (Amutayam). Adapted from Israel Navy website: http://www.amutayam.org.il/?CategoryID=580&ArticleID=1380.

A recent (November 2019) bilateral agreement between Turkey and Libya to create an EEZ, although not recognized by any other country, still constitutes a potential threat to freedom of navigation in the eastern Mediterranean (Dalit Kaspi-Shechner) (Fig. 12.5).

Maritime transport—a vector for smuggling of military hardware

The Palestinian—Israeli conflict which spans some 100 years has experienced many terrorist activities against the State of Israel which were supported by terror sponsoring countries such as Iran, Iraq, Syria, Libya, and others. Smuggling of military hardware which fuels terrorist activities against Israel has always been a major concern.

The carrying capacity and the ease of concealing the real owners/charterers of a vessel offer a perfect platform for smuggling. Despite modern technologies and security measures imposed by the international community, smuggling of military hardware in containers poses a challenge.

Containers may be used for smuggling of:

- Military hardware;
- Dual-use goods;
- Illicit goods and drugs to finance terror activities;
- Containers can be used as a direct vector for terrorist attacks.

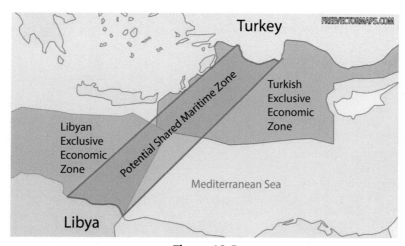

Figure 12.5
Turkish—Libyan Memorandum of Understanding for Exclusive Economic Zone in East Mediterranean. Map modified by Jerusalem Center for Public Affairs, April 2019. Base map source: FreeVectorMaps.com.

Smuggling of military hardware

In 2002, a small freighter "Karin A" loaded in the Iranian port of Kish was intercepted by the Israeli Navy. On board the vessel, 54 tons of ordnance were found which were destined for Hamas and Islamic Jihad in Gaza. This cargo was dispatched directly from Iran by the so-called "Al-Quds", an Iranian "Revolutionary Guards" spearhead. It is interesting to note that the Muslims of Iran are Shiites, while the Hamas and Islamic Jihad are Sunnis, who usually oppose one another, but are united in their declared hostility toward Israel.

In 2009, the Container Vessel "Francop" loaded with 540 Tons (10 times that of the "Karin A") of medium range rockets, sophisticated explosives (C4), land mines, and other weapons, all destined for Syria and Hezbollah in Lebanon, was intercepted in the Mediterranean Sea (MFA). In 2011 and 2014, two other ships—the "Victoria" and "Klos C" (near the Sudan coast) (Fleetmon; Jpost)—were intercepted by Israeli Navy. The latter vessel carried Shore-Sea (C-802) missiles, torpedoes, and radars, all user manuals were written in Farsi (Fig. 12.6). The support for Iranian sponsored terror against Israel had clearly entered the maritime domain. The success of intercepting these ships far from the Israeli coast demonstrates the capacity of the outermost security ring of Israel, and its far-reaching intelligence capabilities.

Figure 12.6
Rockets discovered on board the cargo vessel "Klos C" (Israel Defense). Source: Israel Defense Force, https://www.israeldefense.co.il/en/content/weapons-seizure-photos.

Dual-purpose materials

In 1994, the Israel-PLO (Palestinian Liberation Organization) Economic Agreement, Paris (Foreign Policy), was signed between Israel and the Palestinian Authority. The agreement aimed to join Israel and the Palestinian Authority under a single customs and excise system. Namely, all goods destined for the Palestinians undergo inspection by Israeli customs. One of the most contentious issues was that of dual-use goods. This was already resolved within the "Wassenaar Arrangement" (Wassenaar), an agreement to contribute to regional and international security and stability by promoting transparency in the transfer of conventional arms and dual-use goods and technologies. The Israeli Ministry of Defense issued a statute to enforce the "Arrangement" as an additional measure for preventing the use of certain goods for terrorist activity.

Smuggling illicit goods and drugs to sponsor terror activities

There are different means of sponsoring and financing terror. One of these methods is transfer of funds from abroad through supply of goods. The goods are purchased by Islamic organizations from international firms and transferred to Palestinian controlled areas. The profit from the sale of goods is transferred to terror organizations such as Hamas or the Islamic Jihad in Gaza, masquerading as humanitarian aid. Some of the goods are fake labeled goods manufactured in developing countries and sold in markets and/or dedicated shops and stalls. These profits too are transferred to terrorist organizations.

Utilizing such methods, terror organizations are able to evade customs inspection and deliver hundreds of thousands of dollars to fuel their terror activity. Israeli security and custom authorities go to great lengths to prevent such attempts.

Containers as a direct vector for terrorist attack

On March 14, 2004, 10 port of Ashdod employees were murdered and another 16 wounded in a terror attack (Bombing). Two 18-year-old suicide terrorists were hidden in a double-walled container, which enabled them to evade the tight port security. They were strapped with explosive devices, entered the port, and triggered the explosive device in two different locations, aiming to maximize the damage.

In this case, the terrorists were smuggled into Israel through a land checkpoint without being detected. However, containers are frequently used by illegal migrants and stowaways, and similar acts of terrorism could be perpetrated directly on a short sea voyage.

Thwarting threats to freedom of navigation—Israeli national doctrine

- Israel does not have substantial international terrestrial trade and is, therefore, a geopolitical island;
- In order to ensure Israel's economic resilience, the maritime supply chain must be safeguarded in times of peace or military conflict;
- Israeli commercial ports may be compromised by naval blockade and are within rocket range of hostile terrorist groups in the north (Haifa and Hadera) and in the south (Ashdod and Ashkelon). The southern-most port of Eilat (Gulf of Aqaba) is directly threatened by Al-Qaeda and ISIS sympathizers in the Sinai Desert;
- The recent emergence of cyber terrorism which might affect ships and port controls requires technological developments to counter these threats.

Safety of navigation and safety of Israeli ports are evidently intertwined and must be ensured at all times.

How are these goals achievable?

Israeli port authorities, which are responsible for the security of ships and their cargoes, receive instruction and guidance from the Police, the General Security Services (GSS—"Shin Bet") and Israeli Navy.

Security services are responsible for obtaining early data regarding cargo which is shipped to Israel from a foreign port, in order to classify and categorize it prior to loading. Following a government decision, a National Cargo Assessment Center for Security, Information, and Cyber was founded (March 2014) to liaise, improve, and coordinate data between various authorities in Israel. The Institute for Intelligence and Special Operations (The "Mossad") was formed in December 1949. It is a major stakeholder in Israeli security affairs by gathering intelligence, secret diplomacy, and prevention of terrorist activities against Israel. Among its varied roles, it provides invaluable assistance in optimization and profiling of import cargoes such as military hardware and drugs, and intelligence associated with money-laundering schemes.

All navigational routes, harbor roads, and commercial ports' basins are continually patrolled and guarded by the Israeli Navy, which is also authorized to board ships prior to their entrance into Israeli territorial waters in case of any suspicion of illegality. Israel has no Coast Guard, however units of Maritime Police fulfill a similar role.

For obvious reasons, it is beyond the scope of this chapter to elaborate on intelligence gathering methods. Nevertheless, a major apprehension of containers transporting drugs in a foreign port highlights that movements of goods within the international chain supply are closely monitored by custom authorities in Israel and around the world (Times Of Israel; Global news; Sea-Transport; Nuclear-Material).

Securing Israeli commercial ports

Security of ports in Israel operates in accordance with relevant governmental directives (Public Organizations, 1998) and falls under the auspices of:

- Physical security (armed police officers) at all port gates for persons entering ports, "clever" electronic gates for trucks and other vehicles (Megaport—see Part II);
- Scrutiny of all personnel (GSS "Shin Bet"), ships' crew members or passengers entering or leaving Israel;
- Custom authority's involvement in approving merchandise for export/import and other covert activities to prevent contraband and/or any illegal activities.

Conclusion

Although many of the security measures employed by Israel closely resemble means used by many other countries, there are some distinct differences:

- Israel is a geopolitical island surrounded by hostile countries;
- Navigational routes to and from Israel are under continuous potential threat;
- Israel is under constant threat of military conflict, and its ports are easily targeted by medium and long range enemy weapons;
- Over 98% of transport of goods to and from Israel is by the maritime route, which, therefore, constitutes the country's economic lifeline;
- The recently discovered gas fields in the Economic Waters of Israel are also potential targets for terrorist attacks, and considerable protective means must be allocated to ensure their security;
- In order to offset the numerical population inferiority relative to countries surrounding Israel (9 million vs. approximately 350 million) (World Population Review), Israel must possess the ability to constantly develop superior intelligence capabilities and remain at the forefront of newest technologies, thus maintaining a qualitative edge.

Part II—implementation of security
Introduction

Israel is a narrow strip of land ($\sim$22,000 km^2) and one of the most densely populated countries in the world. Its coastal cities are located within easy reach of the eastern border (at the narrowest point $\sim$20 km), a situation which deprives Israel of strategic depth. Free access to the Mediterranean is, therefore, vital to the State of Israel. The discovery of gas fields in Israel's Mediterranean EEZ, which have the potential to ensure Israel's energy independence, poses an additional challenge to Israel's defense needs in the maritime arena. Israel's southern-most port of Eilat, which is the country's only portal of access to the Red Sea and Far East, is sandwiched between Jordan and the Sinai Desert, and is in close proximity to Saudi Arabia. Egypt's 1967 blockade of the Straits of Tiran became a "casus belli" for the State of Israel, resulting in the 6-Day War.

The sea holds numerous threats for the State of Israel, from targeting of Israeli vessels and strategic installations, through disruption of maritime trade to blockade and isolation. The expansion and modernization of the fleets of Egypt and Turkey, and increasing involvement of the fleets of Russia and China in the Eastern Mediterranean are potential challenges to the technological and qualitative superiority of the Israeli Navy (Chorev). The evolution of maritime terrorism against the State of Israel has been well documented by A. Lorentz (Lorentz).

Since the 1948 foundation of the State of Israel, the Middle East and the world have undergone changes such as: globalization and technological communication advances on the one hand and cyber warfare on the other. Israel's original security doctrine was defined by its first Prime Minister, David Ben-Gurion, in the 1950s. It has largely withstood the test of time until recently, and parts of it are still valid. However, the 21st century has brought with it new and complex security threats, which require amendments and adaptations to the doctrine, in particular with respect to the maritime domain.

Israel's security model

Israel's strategic location is focal for the international community for several reasons:

- The eastern Mediterranean is a source of production and export of oil and gas;
- Approximately 25% of maritime traffic converges in eastern Mediterranean passages (Suez Canal and the Bosporus); therefore, its security is of major interest to global economy;
- The area's political volatility can potentially destabilize the entire region;
- Israel shares democratic and cultural values of the west. As such, it is considered a valuable commodity to the international community.

The Israeli security system is organized in three constructs, each comprised of three circles:

1. The first construct is the physical or perimetric circle—all security events occur outside this circle.
   - The "walled circle"—security events occur on the walls, fences, gates, doors etc.
   - The inner circle—security events occur within.
2. The second construct is the Proactive Construct which includes:
   - The "alert circle" is designed to alert against any suspicious act or danger.
   - The second circle is the deterrent circle, designed to redirect or mislead any potential perpetrator.

- The third circle is aimed at thwarting and aborting the enemy's mission.
3. The Continuous Construct operates on a time line and encompasses:
    - Prevention—all activities which aim to minimize or prevent the threat.
    - Endurance—managing the threat when it materializes.
    - Restoration—all activities which enable restoring the functional routine or creating an improved functionality against hostile activities.

The maritime arena

Israel's EEZ is larger (27,346 km^2) than the area of the State of Israel. Israel's strategic maritime zone has increased in importance with the finding of rich gas fields within the EEZ. Existing Israeli legislation regarding maritime borders and their security has not been finalized by the Israeli Knesset. The statutes and regulations regarding security of shipping and ports (2008) require updating and adaptation, as at present they do not cover all maritime security risks (Fig. 12.7).

Israeli ships and ports conform fully to the International Maritime Organization (IMO) Security Conventions (SOLAS—the ISPS Code, SUA (IMO)). Israeli port security is maintained using advanced technological means (e.g., screening of containers for smuggling of radioactive materials or explosives) and is rigidly supervised by Israeli security services.

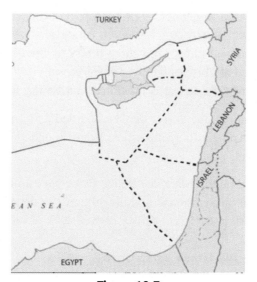

Figure 12.7

Exclusive Economic Zone of Israel and neighboring countries (JISS). Source: The Jerusalem Institute of Strategy and Security/PRIO Cypress Centre, https://jiss.org.il/en/yanarocak-turkey-at-the-eastern-mediterranean-crossroads/.

The Israeli Navy

Most of Israel's western border is coastal. It accommodates Israel's major commercial and energy ports and constitutes Israel's main portal for international trade. The coastal line hosts various strategic installations, such as commercial ports, power stations, desalination plants, and naval bases. The Israeli Navy is charged with protection of the coastline territorial waters and the EEZ (including exploration and production oil and gas platforms). It is also charged with securing navigational routes throughout the Mediterranean and the Red Sea. Achieving optimal security of the maritime domain requires cooperation between the Israeli Navy, Israeli civil authorities, and those of other countries (BlobFolder). Since Israel does not have a Coast Guard, the Israeli Navy assumes the role of securing the territorial adjacent waters and EEZ. It operates advanced technologies utilizing satellites, autonomous vessels, and underwater listening devices.

The Israeli Navy operates a liaison desk for commercial shipping. In order to optimize control of vessel movements toward Israel, a graded reporting system has been devised, which is capable of accurately verifying any vessel, its cargo, and crew.

- Any vessel carrying dangerous goods, anticipating arrival at Israeli port within 48 hours (Unishipping) is required to notify the arrival port and the shipping agency.
- Following this, any vessel at a distance of 100 nautical miles (NM) from the Israeli coast is required to send an IMOT (Israeli Ministry of Transport) Report (MOT; Findaport) notifying RCC (Rescue Coordination Center), Israeli Navy, Border Police, etc.
- At 25 NM or at very high frequency (VHF) reception distance, a vessel is interrogated verbally by Israeli Navy.
- At a distance of 12 nautical miles from shore (entry to Territorial Waters), all vessels are visually ascertained at close range by a naval vessel.
- From this point onwards, the vessel is monitored until entry to an Israeli port.

If at any stage suspicion arises, the vessel may be boarded and inspected by the Navy jointly with other appropriate civilian authorities. If any concerns remain, the vessel may be denied entry to an Israeli port.

The Navy is supplemented by the Maritime Police Force for enforcing the law for small craft, including prevention of contraband and illegal entry or departure of vessels (at marinas and pleasure craft).

Freedom of navigation—the Israeli perspective

In view of Israel's absolute economic dependence on free navigational routes in times of peace and conflict, freedom of navigation is one of its vital interests. Israel's Emergency Administration (Ministry of Economy and Industry) (Emergency Division) defines the nation's ability to import vital commodities during hostilities, but does not adequately cover Israel's national commercial needs and is in need of expansion. The Israeli perspective (Dalit Kaspi-Shechner) is that "Freedom of Navigation is the ability to operate at sea without restrictions and to maintain the continuity of the supply chain to and from Israel. Freedom of navigation requires three elements: (1) delivery of goods from country of origin; (2) maritime transport through navigational routes; (3) security of ports of destination."

Israel has on two occasions been forced to go to war over its freedom of navigation (Suez Crisis, 1956; Six-Day War, 1967). These events triggered investment in and reinforcement of the Israeli Navy, especially with respect to the ability to operate far from Israeli borders in the southern maritime arena of the Red Sea.

Intermodal transport

Intermodal transport in the Israeli reality is largely restricted to container trade (annual movement of containers in Haifa and Ashdod ports amounts to three million twenty-foot equivalent units (TEU) (CARGO), which includes: goods transported by road and rail from Israeli manufacturers to sea ports; goods discharged in Israeli ports and distributed by road and rail to Israeli consumers; transshipment of containers within Israeli ports and hinterland. Transshipment via Israel to neighboring countries is very limited, due to the geopolitical situation (BOI). Movement of goods from Israel to the Gaza Strip was previously comprised of essentials (food, medicines, and gas oil for power and lighting), for the relief of living conditions of the Gaza population. Currently, Israel allows the entrance of all civilian goods into the Gaza Strip, with the exception of a list of materials defined as "dual-use," which, according to Israel, can be used for military purposes. Israel purchases a limited quantity of agricultural products from Gaza. Security measures at the border between Gaza and Israel is very tight, the details of which are beyond the scope of this chapter. Trade between Israel and the Palestinian Authority is regulated by COGAT (Coordination of Government Activities in the Territories) (Cogat). Trade between Israel and the West Bank is substantial and estimated at several billion USD. However, since the terrorist attack at Ashdod Port in 2004, security of containers entering and leaving the West Bank has been upgraded and new technologies were introduced.

The international community largely depends on free maritime trade and safe maritime routes. However, terror or revolutionary organizations attempt to utilize these routes for transport of illegal substances and military hardware for fueling and sustaining their activity. All stakeholders strive to devise security counter measures to eliminate, or at least minimize, such activities (Israports). The State of Israel participates in the joint efforts by programs such as:

- WCO SAFE (Framework of Standards to Secure and Facilitate Trade (Unece Contents));
- C-TPAT (U.S. Customs-Trade Partnership Against Terrorism (CTPAT);

- AEO (Authorized Economic Operator (Unece);
- ICS—Import Control System (ICS);
- Megaports (Port Technology)—cybersecurity;
- CSI (Container Security Initiative) (Congress).

Following the September 11, 2001 attack on the World Trade Center, the United States initiated a security program (CBP) for inspecting containers. This was the trigger for international collaboration for carrying out security inspections of containers in the loading port, prior to their loading on board vessels. In Israel, this program has been activated in the ports of Haifa and Ashdod, where each container destined to the United States is subject to profiling by US Authorities (Congress; CBP; EPA), namely screening and physical inspection. High-risk containers (with potential for misuse by terrorist groups) are targeted using obtained strategic intelligence and complex algorithms. Such containers are also subject to screening for nuclear radiation (EPA) (Fig. 12.8).

Following a Government decision in 2014, a National Cargo Profiling Center was established, which aims to facilitate collaboration between the various security authorities in Israel. A complementary security system "World Gate" was established by the Israeli Customs Authority, which is a technological platform for electronic international trade utilized by all firms within the Israeli maritime commerce community. This system provides services to all stakeholders in the logistic chain of maritime commerce (sea ports, customs, shipping agents, international shipment, importers, exporters, etc.), including

Figure 12.8
Container being screened at Haifa Port. Source: Tomer May, 2020.

security authorities. The system is operated jointly by the IMOT, Administration of Shipping and Ports, and the Customs Administration (within the Ministry of Finance). Participation in this program is voluntary and aims to conform to the requirements of international bodies such as the IMO and WCO (World Customs Organization) and the WTO (World Trade Organization) (Unctad).

Complementary physical measures such as single-use electronic seals provide the recipient of the container with full disclosure regarding the contents of the container and confirmation of approval by the appropriate authorities in Israel, while the container can be monitored via Global Positioning System (GPS) to ensure it has not been tampered with throughout the voyage (Fig. 12.9).

The use of technological devices not only serves to enhance security but also facilitates port system efficiency, including shortening ships' stay in port.

The main entrance to Haifa's container port operates a smart gate system, with 17 entry lanes for container trucks. This system is equipped with electronic and biometric identification technology. Each such lane has a truck's LPR (License Plate Recognition) reading system, RFID (Radio Frequency Identification) reading of the driver's license, and driver face recognition and finger prints. The information obtained from this system provides the port's operation management with cross-verification of the entering vehicle data (Fig. 12.10).

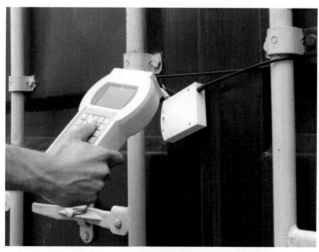

Figure 12.9
Electronic seal (Europa). Source: EU Science Hub, https://ec.europa.eu/jrc/en/patent/2818-electronic-active-seal-containers.

Figure 12.10
Electronic gates at Haifa Port. Source: Leviton & Shumny Architects Ltd., 2020.

All Israeli ports gates and entrances are manned by well-trained ex-special-units personnel of the Israeli Defense Force. The combination of advanced technology and highly trained security manpower is the backbone of Israel's security on all fronts, including sea and air ports.

Summary

Despite peace accords with Egypt and Jordan, Israel's terrestrial borders are all troubled, in parts hostile and in parts disputed. Therefore, Israel's Mediterranean coastline is the only true opening for international trade, which is the country's lifeline. Navigational routes to Israel have in the past been compromised; therefore, Israel must ensure its permanent freedom of navigation. Israeli ports through which all vital commodities pass must maintain very high standards of security at all times. Israel invests heavily in the latest technology and manpower to ensure free and secure transport of goods to and from the country. Israel's energy independence and its economic future rely on its ability to develop, sustain, and secure its maritime borders.

Acknowledgments

Mr. Moshe Zalmenson, for sharing his experience of many years as a security officer for the Israeli Ministry of Transport and for his useful advice.

References

https://www.alaraby.co.uk/english/indepth/2019/12/10/turkish-libyan-alliance-in-eastern-mediterranean-a-game-changer.

http://www.amutayam.org.il/?CategoryID=580&ArticleID=1380.

https://www.gov.il/BlobFolder/guide/current_situation_policy/he/Report_1.pdf.

https://www.boi.org.il/he/NewsAndPublications/PressReleases/Documents/Israel-Palestinian%20trade.pdf.

https://mfa.gov.il/MFA/MFA-Archive/2004/Pages/Suicide%20bombing%20at%20Ashdod%20Port%2014-Mar-2004.aspx.

http://asp.mot.gov.il/SPA_HE/CARGO/TrafficContainersTEU2019.pdf.

https://www.cbp.gov/border-security/ports-entry/cargo-security/csi/csi-brief.

Chorev, S. Interview in: https://www.makorrishon.co.il/news/202451/. Hebrew).

https://ch-strategy.hevra.haifa.ac.il/images/books/2018/011118-7.pdf.

http://www.cogat.mod.gov.il/en/Our_Activities/Pages/default.aspx.

https://www.congress.gov/109/plaws/publ347/PLAW-109publ347.htm.

CTPAT.cdp.dhs.gov.

Dalit Kaspi-Shechner. The Threat of Maritime Blockade. At: http://maarachot.idf.il/PDF/FILES/6/112436.pdf.

https://www.dmag.co.il/pub/paprica/galim2019/8. (Hebrew).

https://embassies.gov.il/houston/News/CurrentAffairs/Pages/Threats-Facing-Israel-Map.aspx.

https://www.gov.il/en/departments/Units/emergency_division.

https://www.epa.gov/radtown/radiation-and-shipping-port-security.

https://ec.europa.eu/jrc/en/patent/2818-electronic-active-seal-containers.

https://www.findaport.com/country/israel.

https://www.fleetmon.com/maritime-news/2014/3257/klos-c-syrian-missiles-intercepted-red-sea/.

https://mfa.gov.il/MFA/ForeignPolicy/MFADocuments/Yearbook9/Pages/181%20Israel-PLO%20Economic%20Agreement-%20Paris-%2029%20April.aspx.

https://globalnews.ca/news/4864862/cocaine-seizure-port-of-halifax/.

http://www.ics-import-control-system.net/.

www.IMO.org.

https://www.israeldefense.co.il/en/content/weapons-seizure-photos.

http://www.israports.org.il/he/TaskYam/Pages/IndexTermsAndProcesses/avtachathasachrhabeinleumi.aspx.

https://jiss.org.il/en/yanarocak-turkey-at-the-eastern-mediterranean-crossroads/.

https://www.jpost.com/Defense/Final-inventory-of-Iran-arms-ship-40-rockets-180-mortars-400000-bullets-344797.

Lorentz, A. The threat of maritime terrorism to Israel. At https://www.ict.org.il/Article.aspx?ID=983#gsc.tab=0.

https://mfa.gov.il/MFA/ForeignPolicy/Iran/SupportTerror/Pages/nava-force-intercepts-Iranian-weapon-ship-4-Nov-2009.aspx.

http://asp.mot.gov.il/media/com_form2content/documents/c5/a557/f49/SN-RAD17(o).pdf.

http://www.port2port.com/article/Sea-Transport/U-S-and-Israel-to-Cooperate-on-Detecting-Illicit-Shipments-of-Nuclear-Material/.

http://www.israports.org.il/en/PortDevelopment/Pages/default.aspx.

https://www.porttechnology.org/editions/megaports_megaterminals/.

http://www.port2port.com/article/Sea-Transport/Haifa-Port-NIS-113m-profit-was-made-in-2006/.

Public Organizations, 1998. Law for Regulation of Security in Public Organizations. Hebrew. http://m.knesset. gov.il/Activity/committees/ForeignAffairs/LegislationDocs/sedef7.pdf.

http://www.port2port.com/article/Sea-Transport/Huge-ecstasy-smuggling-attempt-foiled-in-Haifa-port/.

https://www.thetimes.co.uk/article/israel-builds-railway-to-forge-new-alliance-p6drwjh56.

https://www.timesofisrael.com/canada-says-israel-bound-cocaine-shipment-intercepted/.

https://unctad.org/en/Docs/sdtetlb20041_en.pdf.

http://tfig.unece.org/contents/wco-safe.htm.

http://tfig.unece.org/contents/authorized-economic-operators.htm.

https://www.unishipping.co.il/israeliports.html.

Walker, G.K. State practice following world war II, 1945—1990. In: Grunawalt, R.J. (Eds.), International Law Studies — 1993 — Targeting Enemy Merchant Shipping, vol. 65. Naval War College, Newport, Rhode Island, pp. 137.

https://www.wassenaar.org/.

https://data.worldbank.org/indicator/NY.GDP.MKTP.CD?locations=ZQ.

http://worldpopulationreview.com/continents/the-middle-east-population/.

PART V

Risk mitigation approach

CHAPTER 13

Loading at a foreign port

Richard R. Young Ph.D., FCILT [1], Gary A. Gordon Ph.D., PE, MEMS, LTC USA (Ret.) [2], Bennett C. Abrams [3]

[1]School of Business Administration, Capital College, The Pennsylvania State University, Middletown, PA, United States; [2]Department of Civil & Environmental Engineering, University of Massachusetts Lowell, Lowell, MA, United States; [3]Tulane University, New Orleans, LA, United States

To follow the flow of information and the movements of physical goods in the supply chain is a complex and often convoluted process. A useful mechanism for explaining this along with the regulatory initiatives is through the use of a case study written with the sole purpose of placing the reader in the midst of the action. In the following case, we endeavor to follow three import shipments, all of which are related to the same firm, but several key variables have been introduced: (1) a shipment with a U.S. Customs and Border Protection (CBP) Customs-Trade Partnership Against Terrorism (C-TPAT) certified supply chain, (2) one with a new supplier that is virtually unknown to the importer, and (3) a less than container load being handled by a Nonvessel Operating Common Carrier (NVOCC). To add to the complexity of the case, one of these shipments is comingled with a household goods move from a higher-risk country of origin and another is transloaded from a feeder ship.

Illustrative case: Ready-Tech, Inc.

This case is a detailed account of the firm, Ready-Tech, Inc.,[1] a medium size online distributor of electronic communications equipment and accessories such as antennas, mounting hardware, connecting cables, and related instrumentation. Approximately 12 years ago, Ready-Tech had made a strategic decision to invest in undertaking the necessary vetting of its supply chains to become certified under the C-TPAT initiative. Their calculations suggested that the savings in inventory holding costs due to reduced Customs clearance time would easily pay back the outlays.

---

[1] The shipping firms of Hapag-Lloyd, NYK Lines, and Yang Ming are real; however, all other firms, locations, and dates are fictitious. Any likeness to actual events and entities are, therefore, purely coincidental. This case was written for illustrative purposes only and is not intended to represent either appropriate or inappropriate administrative practices.

Intermodal Maritime Security. https://doi.org/10.1016/B978-0-12-819945-9.00013-7

Three shipments and their particulars

During September 2019, Ready-Tech had prepared three orders, the details of each are quite unique other than that all were destined to arrive at the Port of Charleston, South Carolina, before being trucked inland to its distribution center near Atlanta.

The first, containing cable and connectors, was part of a regular monthly order from Endau Electric in Malaysia. Ready-Tech had been doing business with Endau for more than 15 years, never had any quality issues, and about 10 years ago had gone from letter of credit payment terms to open account. On average, Ready-Tech orders two or three 20-foot ocean containers per month with the value of the goods being approximately $25,000 per container. Endau Electric, being a family-owned firm, has some international logistics capabilities such as preparing documentation and arranging for inland transportation. Conversely, all ocean particulars had been delegated to GB&R Forwarding. In this case, particulars are deemed to mean negotiating for and booking of ocean freight, obtaining marine insurance coverage, preparation of an ocean bill of lading and the Malaysian export declaration.

The second was a trial order of hardware components from a new supplier, Ng Industrial, in Vietnam. With an unknown relationship, this order for a full 20-foot container was on a letter of credit basis with Ng handling all transportation particulars with its forwarder, South Seas Shipping. Other than Ng making a single phone call, South Seas handles virtually every aspect of inland and ocean transportation. All documentation, ocean carrier negotiations and booking of the shipment, and the relationship with the Vietnamese authorities are completely delegated. Moreover, South Seas is shown as the exporter of record for all of Ng's international shipments.

The final order to consider was for seven gross of embroidered golf shirts from Abbas Textile in Pakistan. These were intended to be given away by Ready-Tech's salesforce at trade shows, golf outings, and other customer-related events. Abbas was an unknown entity to Ready-Tech but nevertheless came recommended by a major customer. Since the quantity was relatively small and hardly being able to fill a 20-foot container, the shipment was to be handled by the NVOCC division of the forwarder, Dyna Shipping (Pvt) Ltd. When the shipment arrived in Karachi, the most convenient container with sufficient available space also held the household goods of a Pakistani national who was moving to the United States. Moreover, with a value approximating US$5000, the transaction was arranged through Abbas's bank, Askari Bank which handled it as cash against documents[2] in order to lower administrative overhead costs for both buyer and seller.

---

[2] Cash against documents is a simple process whereby the seller has the negotiable bill of lading together with its commercial invoice sent to a commercial bank. The buyer pays the bank, and the bank pays the seller. While the bank collects a modest fee for the service, it contains far less detail concerning the performance of the importer or the exporter.

Specific logistics arrangements

The shipment of Malaysian connectors moved by road from Endau, which is located on the east coast, to Singapore where its clearance by Singaporean authorities was a simple process given that GB&R designated the shipment as moving in bond and destined only for export. Land transportation between Endau and the Port of Singapore was effected by C.K. Port Trucking, Ltd., a family-owned firm that has provided services to Endau for over 10 years, has an enviable performance record, and all of their vehicles are equipped with the tracking device mandated by the Port of Singapore Authority (PSA). GB&R Forwarding also has a long track record and had achieved Authorized Economic Operator (AEO) status.

Upon arrival within the area operated by PSA, the container was logged in by NYK Line, operator of the vessel of the intended voyage. The shipment particulars were reviewed by Singaporean Customs as per the arrangement made for Singapore's participation in the CBP's Container Security Initiative (CSI). With a C-TPAT certified supply chain and a verified exporter and freight forwarder, the review was routine. Every container was submitted to radiation scanning by the Singaporeans. The container was then run past a vehicle and cargo inspection system (VACIS) unit operated in conjunction with CBP and no anomalies were found. Without any further delay, the shipment was cleared and added to the ship's manifest[3] which was submitted to U.S. Customs at least 24 hours prior to being loaded aboard the NYK Hawk. There being no concerns over hazardous material content or weight considerations, the container was added to the stow plan and assigned to a ship's location that optimized convenience at other ports of call. Not quite a month later some 96 hours prior to the NYK Hawk's arrival at the first U.S. port of call, her manifest was electronically submitted to the U.S. Coast Guard.

Ng Industrial was located near the former huge U.S. airbase at Da Nang. The container holding its shipment to Ready-Tech was loaded aboard a coastal feeder ship for transit to the Port of Vung Tau, Vietnam's principal container port, located a relatively short drive from Ho Chi Minh City. Vung Tau is not among the overseas ports where there is a CSI presence. Still, Hapag-Lloyd, operator of the vessel on which the voyage was booked required that the ship's manifest, a compendium made front data contained on the bills of lading, was provided at least 24 hours prior to loading. At this point, the process will

---

[3] Since the earliest days of shipping, whether international or purely domestic, cargo and passenger manifests have been submitted to ship captains for approval. The captain has the right to refuse the loading of anything that could be deemed potentially injurious to the ship, its crew, passengers, or other cargo. In recent times, the 24- hours rule has been entered into regulations, and more recently, US law requires that the cargo manifest be submitted to the U.S. Coast Guard 96 hours prior to arrival at the first US port of call. There are a general cargo manifest and a separate hazardous goods manifest. Examples of each are found in Appendix A to this chapter.

mirror that of the Singapore originating container by having it listed on a manifest to be transmitted to the U.S. Coast Guard at least 96 hours prior to arrival. Because this container was not sufficiently scrutinized at Vung Tau, it will be more carefully inspected upon arrival in Charleston.

The final container of interest is the consolidated shipment consisting of the golf shirts from Abbas and the household effects of the Pakistani family moving to the United States. While the container was first stuffed with the family's goods at their residence, the golf shirts, after being picked up at Abbas by a Dyna Shipping Company vehicle, were added by the container freight station personnel at the Port Muhammad Bin Qasim, the principal seaport serving Karachi. As it turns out, Qasim is the busiest seaport of Pakistan and has been a CSI port since 2006. The container in question, being a consolidated shipment, received more attention than most shipper-loaded containers because household effects potentially covers a wide range of items, but has also historically been a common source for smuggling. Not unlike other CSI ports, containers entering the port destined for the United States pass through a radiation detector and then subjected to examination by a VACIS unit. Not completely satisfied with the contents as shown by electronic examination, the container was sidelined and opened for human physical inspection.[4] With nothing untoward discovered, it was restuffed, new seals were applied, and its data were entered into the manifest system for the feeder vessel that would transport it from Qasim to the Port of Nhava Sheva, India, the load center port where it would meet the Yang Ming[5] vessel that will convey it to North America. Since the container was already vetted at Qasim, it would not need to repeat that process during the transfer process.

Information flows at port of loading

In addition to importers, exporters, and shipping lines, there are myriad others who are party to the information pertaining to a given shipment. Termed as "intermediaries" these include freight forwarders, NVOCCs/consolidators, customs brokers, initiating and corresponding banks, insurance underwriters, terminal operators, and export packers. Taking each of the scenarios as contained in the Ready-Tech Case, it becomes obvious that the particulars for any transaction in legitimate trade can possess, or likely possess, a few secrets.

---

[4] Physical customs inspections are either pier view or pier strip. The former is when the container is opened, and the load viewed without removal from the container. A pier strip requires each parcel to be removed and potentially opened for closer examination.

[5] Vessel sharing is common in containerized shipping because competing lines can establish agreements to use each other's vessels thereby improving service and reducing the sailing of half empty ships. It is akin to the code sharing agreements that airlines use.

The Endau purchase

In this scenario, the exporter is also the manufacturer, and they possess the most knowledge of the nature of the goods involved. As shown in Fig. 13.1, *some time prior to the goods being completed in production, Endau sent a forwarder's instruction to GB&R detailing the weight, the number of parcels, Ready-Tech as the importer, C.K. Port Trucking as the inland carrier, destination port (Charleston), value of the shipment, and date that the goods will be ready. GB&R made a booking with NYK Line and arranged for an empty container to be picked up by C.K. Port Trucking. The forwarder also added this shipment to the blanket marine insurance policy that it maintained with a local Singaporean underwriter and in due time prepared the ocean bill of lading and the dock receipt that will be used to acknowledge the receipt of the container by PSA. Moving in bond also meant that GB&R prepared a Malaysian export declaration, which essentially served as input for Malaysian trade statistics and to inform the authorities of what precisely was being shipped.*

Because GB&R Forwarding, C.K. Port Trucking, and Ready-Tech have had longstanding relationships, this transaction is a relatively simple one. No complex banking arrangements were necessary, and everyone privy to the transaction found nothing unusual about the nature of the goods including their weight, description, and value. Moreover, Ready-Tech is C-TPAT certified, and GB&R is AEO certified.

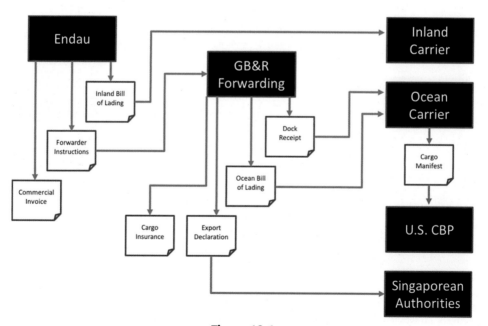

Figure 13.1
Document flows for the order from Endau.

The Ng industrial order

This scenario is nearly the exact opposite of the Endau situation because the exporter was South Seas Forwarding whereas the manufacturer was Ng Industrial. All logistics and trade details were arranged by South Seas Forwarding. The major details that Ng had to arrange were the compliance with the letter of credit[6] that Ready-Tech had opened with the international department of SunTrust Bank in Atlanta and confirmed through the Asia Commercial Bank in Ho Chi Minh City. As shown in Fig. 13.2, *other than being informed of the intended shipping date and being furnished with copies of the purchase order and letter of credit, everything else was arranged by South Seas including preparation of all documentation. While South Seas was known to the Vietnamese authorities, to Hapag-Lloyd, the local trucker, and the container terminal operator, no one else had any*

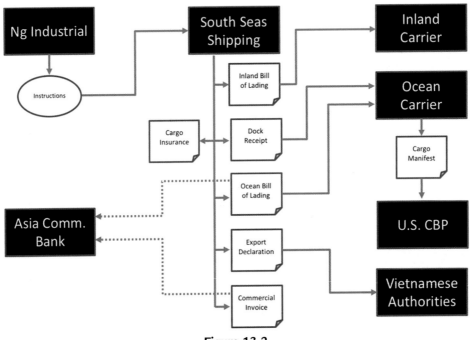

Figure 13.2
Document flows for Ng industrial example.

---

[6] Letters of credit utilize the services of an initiating bank and a confirming bank, each of which serves to respectively protect the interests of the importer and the exporter. Letters of credit are specific documents that detail the performance required of each party with respect to quality, quantity, timely performance, price, and shipping instructions.

appreciable knowledge concerning the transaction, the seller, the US importer, or the nature of the goods. Provided that the goods of this trial shipment are found acceptable, there may be a future relationship, but this is not known.

The golf shirts scenario

Small international shipments are usually of little interest to shipping companies, international banks, insurance underwriters, and other intermediaries. While the costs for these services are disproportionately high in relation to the value of the goods, they provide little profit and little to no opportunity for repeat business. Dyna Shipping had some prior business with Abbas Textiles, but the firm was little known by the shipping line, the port operator, and the Pakistani authorities. Upon receipt of a simple email from Abbas describing the particulars of the sale, Dyna, as per Fig. 13.3, *attended to all shipment details including insurance coverage, arranging for consolidation, booking the container, arranging for shipment pickup, preparation of the Pakistan export declaration, and issuance of their house bill of lading.*[7]

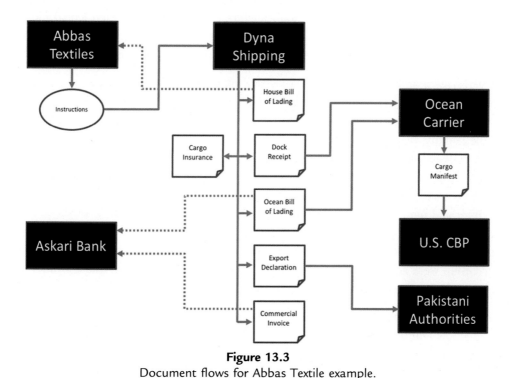

Figure 13.3
Document flows for Abbas Textile example.

---

[7] A house bill of lading is issued by the consolidator to the shipper of a less than full container load.

As is now obvious from decomposing the administrative elements of three different import scenarios all with the same importer, international trade depends heavily on relationships. The longer the relationship and the greater the volume at stake, the higher the confidence that the respective shipments are legitimate. This is in part because the potential for future business is omnipresent meaning that anything that would threaten such would be most unwelcome. Finally, there is the matter of the relationship between regulators and trade participants. C-TPAT and AEO initiatives have strengthened the public–private partnerships by offering the quid pro quo of expeditious handling of those shipments transacted by knowledgeable and verified firms. The concept of dealing with known entities, therefore, has great value.

Comparing the processes: maintaining the flow of commerce and protecting supply chains

In earlier times, Customs, as a unit within the U.S. Treasury Department, had its primary mission as revenue collection in the form of duties and tariffs. During the 1980s, Customs began taking on an increasing law enforcement role as the nation sought to curtail the influx of illicit drugs, much sourced in Latin America. Since 2001 when it was merged with the Border Patrol, renamed CBP and transferred to the newly created Department of Homeland Security, its focus has become twofold: preventing the importation of harmful and prohibited substances and as an enabler of international commerce.

The 1980s saw a dramatic increase in computer applications devoted to the processing of import entries. At the same time, customs brokers and freight forwarders also began making heavy investments in information technology. Processing time for entries, which could be lengthy, began to shorten. Brokers and forwarders that refused to embrace technology were increasingly bypassed by the major importers who realized that entry clearance time was an important component in overall lead time and that inventory in transit bore a carrying cost. Those small brokers and forwarders were either acquired by their larger and more capable competitors or simply went out of business. In short, the industry underwent a dramatic consolidation. Moreover, the larger firms became significantly more international in representation as firms such as Fritz Companies and the Tower Group were acquired. Federal Express, UPS, and DHL, all with transportation assets as well, became global logistics providers.

The large firms catered to the largest importers and exporters that would likely include names such as DuPont, IBM, BASF, Siemens, Van Munching (Heineken Brewing), PPG, and Procter and Gamble. Nevertheless, there were many firms that needed service plus there were those firms endeavoring to conduct business in third world nations that had remained relatively untouched by the technology advances that had transformed the global logistics practices of the developing world. While international trade was conducted by those firms from American, European, and leading Asian nations as a high-tech endeavor, many third world countries still issued manually prepared documentation.

In the next section, the case study will be discussed with regard to what is: (1) required by the United States, (2) required by international law (e.g., IMO: International Maritime Organization), and (3) what ports may employ that centuries old maritime practices. Then, the vulnerabilities and gaps on security of the physical and documentation flow and how risk evolves for arrival at US ports will be discussed.

Manifests: types and uses

There are several types of manifests: cargo, freight, dangerous cargo, out of gauge, and refrigerated (or reefer). Of these, those that are of particular interest to CBP and the United States Coast Guard (USCG), respectively, are the cargo and dangerous goods manifests. The cargo manifest is in essence the cover sheet for all of the bills of lading for which goods are to be conveyed on a particular voyage. Clearly, the line is interested in this, and it is the basis for which the master of the vessel or their representatives makes the determination as to what will be carried or excluded on a particular voyage. Note that the master has the authority to deny loading anything that they do not want on board. The second use of the *cargo manifest* is that it notifies CBP what is heading to the United States on a particular voyage. The USCG receives both the *cargo* and the *dangerous goods manifests* 96 hours in advance of the ship's arrival at the first US port thereby serving notice and allowing a determination for what may be denied entry.

The other types of manifest are strictly for use by the shipping line. A *freight manifest* contains all of the information found on the *cargo manifest* plus all of the freight charges and whether these are to be paid by the shipper or the consignee. The *out of gauge manifest* identifies cargo of abnormal dimensions that may require special stowage arrangements while the *reefer manifest* states which containers must be stowed in specific locations where electrical connections are available in order that refrigeration equipment can be made operable during the voyage.

Physical flows

The basic physical flow for foreign sourced merchandise begins with a seller, who may or may not be the manufacturer of the goods. After loading, the container is sent to the port, transferred to a vessel, and sent to its destination. However, there are several permutations possible when one considers the variables (1) a full container or a partial that needs to be consolidated; (2) direct sailing to destination or is a feeder vessel needed to convey the container to a load center port; (3) transport to the port of loading whether by road or rail, the latter may require draying for access; and (4) upon arrival at the port of unloading are the same issues as in item 3. Moreover, whenever there are handoffs between modes or within modes or between vessels, containers are at rest, a condition that makes them most vulnerable.

Whether at the port of loading or the port of discharge, authorities employ a hierarchy of examination processes as shown in Table 13.1 below.

U.S. customs presence

As mentioned in the case, both the Port of Muhammad bin Qasim and Singapore were some of the early participants in CSI; however, Vung Tau despite having major shipping lines carrying US-bound cargo does not. With the growth of exports originating in Vietnam, it is entirely possible that Vung Tau will become a member in the future, but for the moment those cargoes receive extra scrutiny upon arrival in the United States. C-TPAT is not an initiative where CBP has a presence at foreign ports, but rather where importers have had their supply chains documented and vetted by CBP agents, which includes onsite visits to offshore suppliers, prior to certification being granted.

Information and documentation

The documentation requirements for each of the various scenarios presented in the case are as provided above, but also previously illustrated in Figs. 13.1−13.3. The information

Table 13.1: Container examination hierarchy.

Examination type	Process considers	Conditions
• Administrative review	• Documentation is accurate. • Known shippers. • Goods described not suspect. • Recognized intermediaries. • No anomalies.	• If acceptable, physical inspection not required. This is the typical process employed; however, authorities may randomly escalate on a sampling basis.
• Pier view	• Container is opened, but contents not removed.	• May resolve a simple document error.
• Pier strip	• Container is opened, contents removed, but packages not opened.	• May resolve an item count error or goods description question.
• Extensive examination	• Container is opened, contents removed, and individual packages weighed and/or opened.	• Typically employed when probable cause exists such as the presence of contraband.

concerning the status of an individual container is maintained in several systems including those of the freight forwarder, the container line, the terminal operator, and the regulatory agency responsible for clearing export shipments.

In the case presented, shipments are through two ports, specifically Muhammad bin Qasim and Singapore where there is a CSI presence, but also where there is sufficient information technology to expeditiously process the necessary documentation. The case does need to be made; however, that many ports located in third world nations have documentation prepared manually. This leaves the potential for administrative errors as well as delays often meaning that any regulatory review of a shipment's particulars may not actually occur until sometime after the shipment has departed. It may also be likely that the shipment may have already arrived and been received by the consignee before regulators catch up with it.

Physical and technological security measures

Because of the complexity of the international intermodal maritime supply chain, the security of the US ports relies on the security and inspection capabilities of foreign ports where the cargo and shipments that are bound for the US originate. In the case of Ready-Tech, the overall security of the shipment is dependent on the security capabilities and measures at the Port of Singapore, Port Muhammad Bin Qasim in Pakistan, and the Port of Vung Tau in Vietnam. The less secure these ports are, the higher the overall risk associated.

In general security terms, it is important to know whether an international port is compliant or in line with the IMO International Ship and Port Facility Security (ISPS) Code. ISPS is a comprehensive set of measures to enhance the security of ships and port facilities, and was developed in response to the perceived threats in the wake of the 9/11 attacks in the United States (Blümel et al., 2008). The Code has two parts: one describing mandatory requirements; one in the form of guidelines. The purpose of the Code is to provide a standardized, consistent framework for evaluating risk, enabling governments to offset changes in threats with changes in vulnerability for ships and port facilities through determination of appropriate security levels and corresponding security measures (Blümel et al., 2008). Countries of final destination can also have their own national regulations. For example, in the United States, the USCG requires that any vessel traveling to the United States from a foreign port on a voyage of over 96 hours must file their cargo manifest with the USCG at least 96 hours prior to the vessel arrival.

The Port of Singapore is the busiest container transshipment hub and the largest publicly owned-port in the world and offers connectivity to more than 600 ports in 123 countries

(Ship-Technology, 2020). The port is owned by the Maritime and Port Authority of Singapore (MPA). Because of the port's economic importance to Singapore and the international maritime supply chain as a whole, it has very robust physical and technological security measures and can be considered one of the most secure ports in the world. The port is compliant with ISPS Code in order to improve and maintain the security of both ships and port facilities.

To make sure that foreign ports are compliant with ISPS, the USCG's International Port Security Program (IPSP) seeks to reduce risk to US maritime interests by ensuring that international ports have effectively implemented ISPS. Through reciprocal port visits, the discussion and sharing of port security best practices, and the development of mutual interests in securing ships coming to the United States, both domestic port security and the security of the global maritime transport system are enhanced through IPSP and gives the USCG, confidence in foreign countries/ports implementation of the ISPS Code (USCG, 2020). While many of the physical and technological security measures found in the port may be similar or identical to those found in US ports, some aspects may differ. This is because the ISPS Code does not require that specific types of physical security measures be imposed on ports, but that nations, ports, and facilities are permitted to decide the best combination of security measures to meet their needs, while ensuring that the purposes of the ISPS Code are achieved (Brown, 2006).

According to Brown, writing in the USCG *Proceedings of the Marine Safety and Security Council*: "The U.S. government and Coast Guard fully respect that various nations and ports will implement innovative and locally useful practices to meet these security goals" (Brown, 2006). The Port of Singapore has six different terminals, so coordinating security measures is a large but also an achievable mission. The Terminals Security Department maintains high levels of security in cooperation with the MPA, the Police Coast Guard, the Republic of Singapore Navy, and the Singapore Civil Defense Force (Ship-Technology, 2020). The port's physical and technological security measures include an armed auxiliary police force, perimeter fencing, manned gates, 24-hour closed circuit television (CCTV) surveillance system and metal detectors for people and cargo (Ship-Technology, 2020). The police conduct regular patrols and checks to control threats from external sources, and furthermore, other security procedures include security pass system for staff, temporary passes for visitors, and an IT system to track the movement/location of all containers within the terminal (Ship-Technology, 2020).

Another important security aspect of the Port of Singapore is that it is a National Targeting Center for Cargo (NTC-C) supported targeting approach CSI port, meaning it targets higher-risk containers and conducts prescreening of these containers in partnership with CBP.[8] In-person inspectors in Singapore work in coordination with CBP's NTC-C in Virginia to review shipments and analyze data. The NTC-C targeting approach relies on in-country CBP inspectors to review higher-risk shipments and US-based CBP inspectors to review lower-risk shipments. NTC-C analyzes advance cargo information before shipments reach the United States (GAO, 2013).

The second port involved with Ready-Tech's shipments is Port Qasim located on 12,000 acres on the coast of the Arabian Sea near Karachi, the commercial capital of Pakistan. The port is not only accessible by sea but is also well connected to Pakistani road and railway networks (CBP, 2007). The security of foreign ports is very reliant on relationships, especially the relationship between the port and the U.S. Department of Homeland Security (DHS). Port Qasim is a remote target approach CSI port and is one of the first ports to become so (GAO, 2013). Shortly after, Port Qasim was designated a Secure Freight Initiative (SFI) Phase 1 port in December 2006, and construction of the Secure Freight Facilities began in 2007 (CBP, 2007).[9] Further, the SFI International Container Security (ICS) system was installed in February 2007 (CBP, 2007). This allows for Port Qasim to scan 100% of the shipments to the United States, not just those deemed high risk (as required by CSI), for nuclear and radiological materials. Similar to US ports, Port Qasim uses radiation portal monitor (RPM) systems, non-intrusive inspection (NII) equipment for imaging, and hand-held Radiation Isotope Identification Devices (RIIDs), as well as other technologies to ensure the integrity of the scanning process. Data are transmitted to the United States for review and analysis (CBP, 2007). Port Qasim was selected as an initial SFI port because of the strong political will of the host nation, the unique nature of its operation in a strategic location, and its processing of a significant number of transshipments (CBP, 2007). This is indicative of the strong relationship that DHS/CBP has with the Port Qasim and provides confidence that shipments from Port Qasim have been scanned and are secure.

The Port of Vung Tau in Vietnam appears to be the least secure of the three ports originating Ready-Tech's shipments, and, therefore, presents the most risk. Vung Tau is not a major port, but is a smaller port involved in transshipment of containers. The Vietnam Port Association (VPA) states that 80% of container exports and imports go

---

[8]   There are 61 foreign ports that participate directly in the Container Security Initiative program or where U.S. Customs and Border Protection (CBP) coordinates with to evaluate and secure US-bound cargo container shipments (GAO-13-764, 2013). CBP's targeting approach ranges from in-country CBP inspection through via regional hubs to National Targeting Center for Cargo targeting relying on in-country CBP inspectors for high-risk shipments and US-based CBP inspectors for low-risk shipments.

[9]   The Secure Freight Initiative (SFI) is a DHS program and is part of the SAFE Port Act of 2006. It uses non-intrusive Inspection (NII) and radiation detection technology, and the goal is to scan 100% of incoming containers to the United States for nuclear or other radiological materials. Data from these systems are then provided to US officials at U.S. Customs and Border Protection's National Targeting Center for analysis.

through smaller ports (Das, 2019). One aspect that makes Vung Tau less secure than the other ports is the risk of piracy. In 2015, there were at least nine successful piracy boardings in the Vung Tau region, many of which occurred in broad daylight (Allmode, 2015). This is indicative of an ongoing problem and makes Vung Tau a high-risk/alert area for piracy, and any shipment going through the area will have to take considerable security measures and remain on high alert. Another aspect that makes the shipment through the Vung Tau riskier than the other two ports is the lack of a relationship with DHS. While the USCG did find in a 2006 assessment that Vietnam and its ports were generally in compliance with ISPS, Vung Tau is not a CSI port or involved in any other DHS program to secure/target high-risk containers before their arrival in the United States (USCG, 2006). Because Vung Tau is not a major port, it is unclear what kind of scanning technology and inspection ability the port has, thereby making it, in theory, less secure. Because of the lack of available information on Vung Tau's physical and human security measures, the cargo through Vung Tau is the riskiest of Ready-Tech's shipments.

The security of container shipments is heavily influenced by the relationships and level of trust between all of the parties involved in the shipment. When talking specifically about the safety and security of foreign ports, it is important to understand what kind of relationship that port/nation has with the United States and DHS. The Port of Singapore, which is owned and backed by the legitimacy of the Singaporean Government, has a very strong relationship with DHS which is evident by the fact that it is a CSI port. Port Qasim, despite the fact that the United States and Pakistan have had at times an uncertain relationship, is also a CSI port, which: (1) is indicative of a relatively trusted relationship with DHS and (2) provides added security to shipments coming the Port of Qasim. Vung Tau lacks an established relationship the with DHS given that it is not a CSI port and its physical, technological, and human capabilities being less known.

Cyber issues

When considering cyber issues at United States and foreign ports, it must be recognized that cyber is an overarching system used in conjunction with and to process information and required documentation, the physical flows and the physical and technological security measures. They all require a level of protection to drive, accommodate, and enhance security and risk mitigation and are used to, among other things:

- Vet supply chain partners under programs like C-TPAT;
- Target and vet containers and their contents under CBP's CSI program;
- Manage access or perimeter control systems, such as at gates, shorelines, and biometric identification for workers;

- Manage technological surveillance methods, such as CCTV, including infrared and motion sensing cameras, and intrusion detection; and
- Manage systems that support the operations within the port, such as lighting and crane movements.

The questions that must be addressed are (1) what level of cyber sophistication does the foreign port have? and (2) how do they compare to those at US ports and foreign ports that are closely partnered with the United States in cargo security programs and measures? This includes the vetting processes used for containers (CSI) and supply chain and service providers entering the port (C-TPAT). Consistency, capabilities, and creditability of the systems are important, as is integrity and redundancy or backup systems.

It is evident that the procedures, practices, and security measures in this chapter, as well as throughout this book, are cyber reliant and present an attractive target of compromise by a terrorist or criminal. This vulnerability must be addressed in relation to, among other things:

- The extent that containers are inspected at the port;
- The dependence, reliance, and level of sophistication of the foreign port cyber systems;
- The extent to which the cyber systems are linked to documentation, physical, and technological security measures and operations;
- Where the port is located; and
- The geopolitical environment of the region in which the port is located.

These issues are covered in the case that began this chapter. Depending on the specific port, these will have differing levels of cyber sophistication and, thus, vulnerability and associated risk. For the ports, commodities shipped, and supply chain partners, the following section address the anticipated risk of a cyber compromise that could impact the "cleanliness" of the container when they reach US shores.

Physical, technological, and cyber impacts on risk

What does this all meant with regard to physically and technologically securing the intermodal maritime supply chain to and at the ports? Let us look at each of the three supply chain scenarios and ports used.

Port of Singapore

In the first scenario, the history of the supply chain partners and capability in international logistics, associated documentation, and arranging for inland transportation suggest a trusted and capable supply chain. The Port of Singapore being a CBP CSI port and the supply chain C-TPAT certified shows that port operations and security is consistent with that in US ports. This is further evidenced by the CBP radiation screening and VACIS inspection at the port, and along with the proper documentation allows the containers to be added to the ship's manifest and loaded in accordance with U.S. Customs 24-hour rule. This is further enhanced by the manifest being transmitted to the U.S. Coast Guard in accordance with its 96-hour notice of arrival rule.

Singapore is one of the safest ports with regard to intermodal supply chain risk management. There is a risk, however, because the security measures are cyber dependent (e.g., CSI and C-TPAT vetting) and the ever-present potential for hacking, which could result in a container with a weapon of mass destruction (WMD), its components, or other contraband being cleared. Also, and with regard to C-TPAT, a supply chain partner that should not be vetted and become a trusted partner in the supply chain could be surreptitiously cleared. Consequently, this requires a cyber security plan that addresses possible attacks and required protection measures, improper vetting or clearing a partner or container in the supply chain and the possibility of an insider threat.

Port of Vung Tau

In this scenario, hardware components were to be shipped from a new supplier in Vietnam. With this unproven relationship, all transportation matters are handled by its forwarder, including documentation, ocean carrier negotiations and booking, and the relationship with the Vietnamese authorities. The container holding the hardware components was loaded onto a coastal feeder ship for transit to the Vung Tau. Despite this, the vessel's operator requires that the bills of lading be provided at least 24 hours in advance so that ship's manifest can be prepared, and container(s) can be loaded consistent with the U.S. Customs 24-hour requirement. From this point on, the process is similar to that of the containers loaded in Singapore in that the manifest can be transmitted to the U.S. Coast Guard at least 96 hours prior to arrival.

Vang Tau is, at least in theory, not as secure as Singapore in that it is not a CSI port, the extent of C-TPAT vetting of the supply chain partners is not known, and the exact physical and technological security measures in place are not clearly defined. The combination of the new supplier and supply chain relationships adds to the anticipated risk as does exposure with the handling of the container(s) to/from the coastal feeder ships. All of this can result in a level of risk that is linked to the cyber systems used to document the container contents, establish chain of custody of the containers, knowing the container's location and tracking its drayage and the coastal voyage to the Vung Tau. Although possibly less dependent on cyber systems than Singapore and US ports, its vulnerability to hacking and insider threats still exists and the perception of less robust cyber security measures in place provides a vehicle that bad actors could use to sabotage or compromise a container or its contents. Therefore, the port should have a cyber security plan that addresses the threats and vulnerabilities and security measures in place, and closing the gaps that may exist.

Port Muhammad Bin Qasim

In this scenario, a small shipment from an unknown but recommended supplier is consolidated in an ocean-going container with household goods upon arrival at Port Qasim. Being a CSI port, containers entering the port destined for the United States go through radiation scanning and VACIS inspection. Containers with contents in question from the technological evaluations are physically inspected. After the physical inspection and assuming all is in order, the container would be resealed, new seals applied. The documentation would then be updated to reflect the physical inspection and entered into manifest for the feeder vessel that would transport it to Nhava Sheva, India (GAO-13-764, 2013).

Port Qasim can be considered safe as it utilizes a CSI remote targeting approach relying on host nation container inspections and electronically providing results to CBP. This is supplemented by what appears to be robust physical and technological security measures, as evidenced by a strong relationship with DHS. The shipment in the scenario, however, may be riskier because of its nature and by its transloading from a feeder to ocean-going vessel. The risk associated with the reliance on cyber systems for vetting and tracking at both ports is likely attributable to the importance of information flow regarding the vetting of cargo and the intermodal maritime supply chain partners, chain of custody, and container location. Hacking and/or insider threats could result in the container being cleared when it clearly should not be. This would also apply to any C-TPAT supply chain partners that are not property vetted and, thus, should not be trusted. This requires the implementation of a cyber security plan that addresses possible compromises and required protective measures.

In this section, the importance and dependency of the linkage among physical, technological, and process (e.g., financial and physical flow) and cyber systems and risk was discussed. Virtually all physical or administrative processes rely on the cyber systems, which is a conduit for the flow of information, is the enabler of the financial and physical flows and could be compromised allowing for weapons or other unwanted and improperly marked goods or contraband to be cleared, loaded on the ship and offloaded in the United States. This includes the vetting of supply chain partners under C-TPAT. The physical and technological security measures in place and in particular the camera systems could be hacked to either not work or provide false images. Perimeter fencing and access control could be compromised to allow unwanted access through the gates or via the fence line plus the shoreline provides further intrusion opportunities. Finally, to further document the linkage and importance, the 16 DHS critical infrastructure sectors, two of which information technologically and communications are enabling functions meaning that other sectors, such as transportation and critical manufacturing, are dependent on them in order to function. This relationship is evidenced in the complexity and cyber dependence of the processes and related security measures.

How does this tie together?

This chapter has focused on the issue of complexity and how the various participants from both the private and public sectors function in order to address it. The chapter opened with a theoretical case that provided three scenarios for imports originating in different ports. Ports employ different technologies to managing intermodal maritime trade, but their governments will also have different approaches to regulations. Some choose to participate in bilateral initiatives such as CSI. In the case of load center ports, shipping lines serving the United States may make direct calls; other instances, feeder vessels need to be employed. Finally, every supply chain is different even when established by the same importer. Intermediaries play a major role in facilitating trade and the combinations of firms, the services that they may provide, their reputations, and whether or not they participate in any form of vetting or certification process makes for an environment where public and private organizations need to collaborate to protect mutual self-interests.

The foregoing paragraph leaves the reader feeling left with the challenge of how to effect global supply chains that are both efficient and resilient. If trade is to become more secure, more and not less high-quality information will need to be exchanged between the various participants. International organizations, such as the World Customs Organization and the IMO have engaged in this for many years, but so has the trade organizations, whether they are collectives of shipping companies, importers and exporters, or intermediaries. Within the United States, there are consortia of government agencies that have the moniker of *fusion centers*. The same concept is being applied internationally with through two noteworthy information sharing and analysis centers (ISACs): the Maritime ISAC and the Maritime Transportation Systems ISAC[10]. These are just two of 26 industry sector-related organizations that not only share security information between members but also participate with government-run fusion centers.

---

[10] See maritimesecurity.org and mtsisac.org to find their homepages.

Appendix A

SHIPPING MANIFEST TEMPLATE

1. VESSEL NAME		6. HEAVY LIFTS			OCEAN CARGO MANIFEST
2. STATUS		7. OUTSIZE DIMENSION			RECAPITULATION OR SUMMARY
3. VOY DOC NO.					
4. DATE YYYY/MM/DD		Indicate Recapitulation or Summary	RECAPITULATION Line a applicable		
5. LOADING PORT			SUMMARY Line b applicable		

				ORIGINAL		PAGE NO.	
				REVISED		NO. OF PAGES	

8. DESCRIPTION AND LOCATION OF HEAVY LIFTS AND OTHER SPECIAL DATA

9. TOTAL CARGO LOADED

	(1) DESTINATION PORT	(2) DESCRIPTION	(3) LENGTH-WIDTH-HEIGHT	(4) SELF SUS	(5) NON S.S.	(6) VES	(7) CGO	(8) STOW LOCATION	(9) LONG TONS	(1) DESTINATION PORT	(4) SELF SUS	(5) NON S.S.	(6) VES	(7) CGO
a.														
b.	(1) DESTINATION PORT	(2) COMMODITY CATEGORY	(3) FOR MSC USE					(4) TRANSPORTATION ACCT CODE	(5) ON DECK	(1) NO. OF UNITS POV'S/ MAIL OR OTHER				

10. I HEREBY CERTIFY THAT THE ARTICLES LISTED HEREON HAVE BEEN PLACED ABOARD IN APPARENT GOOD ORDER AND CONDITION.

12. NAME AND MAILING ADDRESS OF PREPARING ACTIVITY

a. SIGNATURE	b. GRADE/RANK	c. TITLE

11. I HEREBY ACKNOWLEDGE HAVING RECEIVED THE CARGO MANIFESTED HEREON IN APPARENT GOOD ORDER AND CONDITION FOR DELIVERY AS INDICATED, EXCEPT AS OTHERWISE SPECIFICALLY NOTED.

MASTER OF VESSEL (Signature)

IMO DANGEROUS GOODS MANIFEST

(IMO FAL Form 7)

(As required by SOLAS 74, chapter VII, regulations 4.5 and 7-2.2, MARPOL 73/78, Annex III, regulation 4.3 and chapter 5.4, paragraph 5.4.3.1 of the IMDG Code)

			Page Number

1.1 Name of ship	1.2 IMO number	1.3 Call sign	

1.4 Voyage number	2. Flag State of ship	3. Port of loading	4. Port of discharge

5. Booking/ Reference Number	6. Marks & Numbers Container Id. No(s). Vehicle Reg. No(s).	7. Number and kind of packages	8. Proper Shipping Name	9. Class	10. UN No.	11. Packing Group	12. Subsidiary Risk(s)	13. Flashpoint (in °C.c.c.)	14. Marine Pollutant	15. Mass (kg) Gross/Net	16. EmS	17. Stowage position on board

Additional information

18.1 Name of master	19.1 Shipping Agent

18.2 Place and date	19.2 Place and date

Signature of master	Signature of Agent

References

Allmode, 24 Sept. 2015. Piracy Incident Report: Vietnam. OnboardOnline. OnboardOnline. www.onboardonline.com/superyacht-news/operations/piracy-reports/piracy-incident-report-vietnam/.

Blümel, E., et al., 2008. Ship, port and supply chain security concepts interlinking maritime with hinterland transport chains. WMU J. Maritime Aff. 7 (1), 205–225. https://doi.org/10.1007/bf03195132.

International port security program: implementation of international regulations. In: Brown, M. (Ed.), 2006. Proceedings, U.S. Coast Guard, vol. 63. Spring. Number 1.

Das, K., 6 August 2019. Port Infrastructure in Vietnam 3 Regional Hubs for Importers and Exporters. Vietnam Briefing News, Dezan Shira & Associates. www.vietnam-briefing.com/news/port-infrastructure-vietnam-3-hubs-for-importers-exporters.html/.

Supply Chain Security: DHS Could Improve Cargo Security by Periodically Assessing Risks from Foreign Ports, (GAO-13-764), 2013. U.S. Government Accountability Office.

Port of Singapore, 2020. Ship Technology, Verdict Media Limited. www.ship-technology.com/projects/portofsingapore/.

United States Coast Guard, 2020. International Port Security Frequently Asked Questions. United States Coast Guard (USCG) Atlantic Area, U.S. Department of Homeland Security. www.atlanticarea.uscg.mil/Our-Organization/Area-Units/Activities-Europe/Maritime-Security/IPS-Program-FAQ/.

U.S. Coast Guard, 2006. U.S. Coast Guard Assessment Team Finds Vietnam in Compliance with International Ship and Port Security Code. Wikileaks. Accessed 7/11/20. https://wikileaks.org/plusd/cables/06HANOI2161_a.html.

U.S. Customs and Border Protection, October 2007. Fact Sheet: Port at a Glance, Port Qasim, Karachi, Pakistan. Homeland Security Digital Library, U.S. Customs and Border Protection. www.hsdl.org/?view&did=29185.

CHAPTER 14

In-transit threats and risk management

Jon S. Helmick[a]

Maritime Logistics & Security Program, United States Merchant Marine Academy, Kings Point, NY, United States

13.06.2020: 0042 UTC: Posn [Position]: 04:05.62N - 005:44.52E, Around 19nm SW of Bayelsa, Nigeria.

Shortly after deck officers discovered that the vessel was far off course as the result of GPS positioning error, around 15 armed men boarded a container ship underway. Most of the crew managed to retreat into the citadel. Head count in the citadel indicated that two members of the crew were missing. When the crew emerged from the citadel they found the Chief Mate had been killed and the second Assistant Engineer had serious injuries. The vessel headed towards Lagos.

Having conveyed the injured engineer to a hospital and transferred the body of the deceased Chief Mate to authorities ashore, the vessel resumed her voyage. 12 days later, not long after partial cargo discharge and the ship's departure from the Port of New York and New Jersey, a massive explosion occurred in the container terminal. Shortly thereafter, radiation detectors carried by government officers in the port began to alert. An emergency was declared and a large area was evacuated.

Subsequent investigation determined that the "pirates" who boarded the vessel off Africa had in fact been terrorists, who brought the ship close to land by interfering with the GPS signal on which navigation depends, and who inserted a Radiological Dispersal Device (RDD) (commonly known as a "dirty bomb") into one of the containers on deck before allowing the ship to continue her voyage. Remote detonation was apparently accomplished by means of a cell phone attached to the explosive device. Numerous injuries and several fatalities resulted from the attack, the port was shut down for several days, and a sizeable urban area was contaminated and required costly cleanup.

---

[a] NOTE: The opinions expressed in this chapter are those of the author alone and do not necessarily represent the views of the U.S. Department of Transportation, the Maritime Administration, or the U.S. Merchant Marine Academy.

Intermodal Maritime Security. https://doi.org/10.1016/B978-0-12-819945-9.00014-9

Introduction

The above incident report is fictional. However, it illustrates a feasible, high-consequence attack upon an underway cargo ship.

This chapter considers security threats to merchant ships that are in transit between ports and the risk management approaches that can be employed to address them. Because such transits often involve periods of time spent at anchor (typically waiting for a berth), security risks associated with these intervals are included in the discussion.

Merchant vessels in transit from one port to another and those at anchor are vulnerable to several types of security threats. The most significant of these are piracy and armed robbery, terrorism, and cyberattack. Other security issues include smuggling, stowaways, and human trafficking, but because these are typically not initiated while a ship is in transit, they are not discussed here.

The age-old scourge of maritime piracy waxes and wanes and the geographic epicenter of concern shifts frequently. But even in this era of fast, high-tech ships, a handful of pirates in an outboard-powered skiff are too often able to breach vessel security and hijack a ship; hold the vessel, her crew, and cargo for ransom; or otherwise dramatically disrupt the intermodal supply chain.

Terrorism and the threat it poses to marine transportation have been the subject of multiple international conventions and the promulgation of extensive national regulations. Merchant ships underway can be both the target of terrorist violence and the means of conveyance for attacks.

Cybersecurity is of increasing concern in the maritime sphere. There have been multiple incidents in which the Global Positioning System (GPS) signals upon which modern ships rely for navigation have been jammed or spoofed in attempts to bring vessels off their intended tracks and potentially into danger. Modern shipping, highly dependent on the internet, e-mail, and other forms of electronic communication, has proven vulnerable to attacks designed to compromise business and cargo operations. Entire shipping companies and their operations have been paralyzed by cyberattacks.

These security threats and their management are discussed in turn in the pages that follow.

Threats and consequences
Piracy and armed robbery

Piracy directed at modern ships can disrupt intermodal movements of cargo and the supply chains in which they are embedded. Piracy may involve cargo theft and crew abduction for ransom. It can result in the payment of large ransoms, increased insurance premiums, diversion from intended routes, and—most significantly—injury and death for merchant vessel personnel.

"Piracy" is defined in article 101 of the 1982 United Nations Convention on the Law of the Sea (UNCLOS) as follows:

Piracy consists of any of the following acts:

(a)   Any illegal acts of violence or detention, or any act of depredation, committed for private ends by the crew or the passengers of a private ship or a private aircraft, and directed:
   (i)   On the high seas, against another ship or aircraft, or against persons or property on board such ship or aircraft;
   (ii)   Against a ship, aircraft, persons, or property in a place outside the jurisdiction of any state.
(b)   Any act of voluntary participation in the operation of a ship or of an aircraft with knowledge of facts making it a pirate ship or aircraft;
(c)   Any act inciting or of intentionally facilitating an act described in subparagraph (a) or (b).

Maritime and international law generally defines the term "high seas" with reference to areas outside the national jurisdiction of coastal states. For coastal states that claim an Exclusive Economic Zone (EEZ), some degree of national jurisdiction may extend up to 200 miles off the coastline. Piracy provisions in the UNCLOS Convention encompass the EEZ beyond the territorial waters of littoral countries (International Maritime Organization, 2011).

Attacks on merchant ships that take place inside the territorial or internal waters of a coastal state may be characterized as "armed robbery," "maritime crime," or "piracy," depending on the agency or entity that is compiling or reporting statistics on such incidents.

The International Maritime Organization (IMO) defines armed robbery as follows:

"Armed robbery against ships" means any of the following acts:

1   Any illegal act of violence or detention or any act of depredation, or threat thereof, other than an act of piracy, committed for private ends and directed against a ship or against persons or property on board such a ship, within a state's internal waters, archipelagic waters, and territorial sea;
2   Any act of inciting or of intentionally facilitating an act described above.

The International Maritime Bureau's Piracy Reporting Centre (PRC) indicates that there were 162 incidents of maritime piracy and armed robbery worldwide in 2019, down from 201 in 2018. Worldwide, 130 vessels were boarded by pirates, four ships were hijacked, 17 attempted attacks occurred, and 11 vessels were fired on. The human cost to vessel personnel in these incidents was substantial. Fifty-nine crew members were taken hostage, 134 were kidnapped, one was killed, and seven were injured (International Maritime Bureau, 2019).

The geographic distribution of piracy and armed robbery attacks changes somewhat from year to year, but certain piracy hotspots are well established. Ten years ago, the focus of pirate attacks was off the Horn of Africa and the western Indian Ocean. In 2010, almost 700 mariners were being held hostage off the coast of Somalia aboard 30 merchant ships. The objective of Somali pirates has been the hijacking of ships, their cargo, and their crews, in order to secure ransom for their release. In 2019, the waters off Nigeria accounted for the largest number of actual and attempted attacks worldwide, with 35 such incidents. Twenty-five attacks were reported in Indonesian waters in 2019. Other areas with a high number of attacks included the Straits of Singapore with 12 incidents, Malaysia with 11, and Peru with 10 (International Maritime Bureau, 2019).

Cargo theft is one aspect of the piracy problem. Even ships underway are vulnerable to this problem; there have been a number of cases in which vessels have been hijacked for the specific purpose of the stealing and reselling of the cargo. Such incidents have predominantly involved petroleum cargoes.

Terrorism

Merchant ships have in the past been the targets of terrorist activity. Notable examples include the 1985 takeover of the cruise ship *Achille Lauro* in the Mediterranean, the 2004 bombing of the *SuperFerry 14* in the Philippines, and the 2013 attack on the *Cosco Asia* off Egypt.

In the case of the *Achille Lauro,* four militants affiliated with the Palestinian Liberation Front and posing as passengers hijacked the ship while on a cruise itinerary in Egypt. Their motivation was to secure the release of 50 Palestinian prisoners being held by Israel. Israel did not respond to this demand, and the terrorists then shot and killed a disabled American passenger and threw his body overboard. The ship, then steaming in the Mediterranean, was denied entry to ports in Syria and Cyprus, but the terrorists negotiated safe passage for themselves into Egypt in exchange for the safety of the remaining passengers and crew members. Ultimately, the hijackers were captured, tried, and incarcerated in Italy (Pallardy, 2010).

On the evening of February 27, 2004, the 10,192-ton *SuperFerry 14* departed from Manila with 899 passengers and crew aboard. Approximately 1 h after the ship got underway for Cagayan de Oro City, an explosion occurred, which turned into a catastrophic fire that caused the master to order the ship be abandoned. The *SuperFerry 14* ultimately sank. A total of 114 passengers and two crew members were lost in the casualty. Subsequent investigations determined that the explosion resulted from detonation of a bomb that had been concealed inside a television and placed in a passenger berth. The perpetrator and six others were arrested and were found to be members of the Al-Qaeda linked Abu Sayyaf group (Safety4Sea, 2019). Cruise ships and ferries, given their large numbers of passengers and crew members, are clearly rich targets for terrorists (Fig. 14.1).

Figure 14.1
Passenger ships represent particularly attractive targets for terrorists, with the largest carrying over 5000 guests. *Photo by Jon S. Helmick.*

On August 31, 2013, the 10,061-TEU (twenty-foot equivalent unit) container ship *Cosco Asia* was attacked by terrorists with rocket-propelled grenade (RPG) launchers as she departed the northern end of the Suez Canal. Two shells were reported to hit the vessel, causing an explosion and fire in one container. After stopping briefly to conduct a damage survey, the *Cosco Asia* proceeded on her voyage. There were no injuries among the crew (SeaNews, 2013). A container struck by one of the rockets was found to contain USD 5.8 million worth of smuggled cigarettes (JOC, 2013).

Cyberattack

Ships and the maritime industry as a whole are increasingly reliant on computerized and internet-connected technology. At the same time, criminals, state actors, and terrorists are becoming more skilled and sophisticated in their ability to compromise these systems for nefarious purposes.

The maritime industry uses computers and cyber-dependent technologies for navigation, communications, ship systems monitoring and control, cargo transfers, access control, passenger and cargo screening, fire detection, financial and other business transactions, and other purposes. Attacks on these systems can result in such consequences as groundings, collisions, cargo loss, environmental pollution, disruption of trade, and human injuries and fatalities.

In the past few years, a number of significant cyberattacks in this sector have occurred. In June 2017, approximately 20 ships in the Black Sea reported that their GPS equipment and the navigation systems showed that the vessels were miles away from their actual positions. The electronic chart display systems aboard these ships showed that they were miles inland at an airport. This appears to have been a case of large-scale misdirection, or "spoofing," of GPS satellite signals; Russia is believed to have been the perpetrator (Galileo, 2017). Similar occurrences have taken place off Korea near the North Korean border. North Korea was found to have committed three GPS jamming attacks against South Korea from 2010 to 2012. The attack in August 2010 was of 4 days' duration. The final attack in the series in 2012 lasted for 16 days, causing 1016 aircraft and 254 vessels to experience GPS signal interruption. These attacks caused large disruptions in navigation and timing, and made necessary the emergency landing of a U.S. military reconnaissance aircraft during an exercise in South Korea (Thompson, 2015). Given the extent to which modern shipping and transportation in general are dependent on GPS to function, the apparent ease with which GPS satellite signals can be jammed or spoofed over a large geographic area is concerning.

Phishing and spear phishing of vessels at sea via e-mail communications have become increasingly common. The U.S. Coast Guard issued advisories on this subject in July 2019, warning that e-mails impersonating U.S. Port State Control authorities and containing malware were being sent to ships. The Coast Guard warnings highlighted the fact that a merchant vessel inbound for the Port of New York suffered a cyber incident that affected its onboard network. The malware significantly degraded the functionality of the onboard computer system, but essential vessel control systems were not compromised. It was noted that the vessel was "operating without effective cybersecurity measures in place, exposing critical vessel control systems to significant vulnerabilities" (Rider, 2019).

The worldwide operations of container carrier A.P. Møller–Maersk were brought to a near-total standstill in June 2017 by the lightning-fast spread through its IT systems of the NotPetya worm. Maersk was not specifically targeted in this attack but, according to some experts, was collateral damage in a cyberattack by Russia on Ukrainian entities. The NotPetya worm, riding on a penetration tool known as EternalBlue that was stolen from the U.S. National Security Agency, spread after the update servers of a Ukrainian accounting software company were hacked. Maersk was one of the companies using that software. In the end, it was necessary for the firm to rebuild its entire network of 4000 servers and 45,000 PCs. The estimated financial impact of this cyberattack for Maersk was $300 million, while the aggregate cost to the many multinational companies that were affected by the NotPetya worm, such as FedEx and Merck, was on the order of $10 billion (Greenberg, 2018).

Risk management strategies
Risk-based decision-making

Governmental organizations, ship operators, insurers, and other participants in the intermodal maritime transportation system must ultimately determine what constitutes acceptable risk for a given threat to security, but to minimize risk effectively requires more than regulation and corporate concern. A coherent risk management strategy is needed. This strategy should emphasize the human element in the prevention of security incidents. It is also desirable that an "all-hazards" approach be adopted, in which efforts to prevent and mitigate safety and environmental casualties are leveraged in security risk management. Conversely, security management strategies and practices can often be used to address marine safety and environmental risks. It has also been suggested that a comprehensive maritime risk management program should focus on the interaction between management, the work environment, human behavior, and technology (Abernathy and Speakman, 2007).

The U. S. Coast Guard identifies the following risk management strategies (Myers, 2007):

- **Spread out:** Spread the loss exposure responsibility out among different entities, across operations, or across time.
- **Transfer:** Make others accept loss exposure responsibility.
- **Accept:** Live with the current loss exposure level or responsibility.
- **Avoid:** Cancel or delay the activity that involves the risk, or do not operate equipment that involves the risk.
- **Reduce:** Do something to reduce the accident potential.

Along with the quantification of risk and the measurement of outcomes, a philosophy of continuous improvement rounds out what are considered the important elements of any effective risk management program. The inclusion of feedback loops that allow managers to gather data and information on the effectiveness of the program and a system that requires them to take corrective action based on the feedback received is essential to the success of all risk management programs.

Risk-Based Decision-Making (RBDM) is a systematic process that provides a framework for acquiring, analyzing, and acting upon risk-related information, monitoring the impacts of risk management decisions, and communicating the results to stakeholders (Myers,

2007). It is suitable for application by both government agencies and entities in the private sector.

RBDM consists of the following components:

1. Establish the decision structure.
2. Perform the risk assessment.
3. Apply the results to risk management decision-making.
4. Monitor effectiveness through impact assessment.
5. Facilitate risk communication.

Establish the decision structure means determining what decisions need to be made, who should be involved in making the decisions, identifying alternatives for decision-making, determining factors that will affect decisions, and assessing the considerations that will influence stakeholders in the decision-making process.

Perform the risk assessment means deciding what questions regarding risk need to be addressed, identifying the data and information that must be acquired in order to answer those questions; choosing the methodologies that will be used to address risk-related problems; determining the appropriate scope of the analysis; and applying risk analysis tools and methods to identify hazards, evaluate their consequences, and estimate their probabilities of occurrence.

Apply the results to risk management decision-making means evaluating how to best manage risks using the available information and options and selecting one or more of these alternatives.

Monitor effectiveness through impact assessment means quantifying and tracking the outcomes of the preceding decision processes and modifying risk management approaches based on actual results.

Facilitate risk communication means ensuring, throughout the RBDM process, that guidance, input, and relevant information flow between those who can contribute to the process and those who are affected by it.

RBDM supports the all-hazards approach to maritime security and also has the endorsement of the U.S. Coast Guard.

Conventions, codes, and regulations

Certain international conventions and codes support the preservation and enhancement of maritime security. These instruments have been developed mainly by the IMO, a unit of the United Nations whose members include 174 different countries registering the vast majority of ships in the world fleet.

Central among these instruments is the ***International Ship and Port Facility Security (ISPS) Code***. The ISPS Code was adopted by the IMO at a diplomatic conference in London in December 2002. It is incorporated into the International Convention for the Safety of Life at Sea (SOLAS) Convention by reference in Chapter XI-2, which is titled "Special Measures to Enhance Maritime Security." The primary goal of the Code is to form an "international framework through which ships and port facilities can cooperate to detect and deter acts which threaten security in the maritime transport sector" (International Maritime Organization, 2003).

The ISPS Code is divided into Part A, which contains mandatory provisions, and Part B, which sets forth guidance for the implementation of Part A. Some countries and regional bodies—the EU, for example—have made mandatory certain sections of Part B.

The functional requirements of the Code include:

- Gathering and assessing information concerning security threats and exchanging such information with appropriate Contracting Governments;
- Requiring the maintenance of communication protocols for ships and port facilities;
- Preventing unauthorized access to ships, port facilities, and their restricted areas;
- Preventing the introduction of unauthorized weapons, incendiary devices, or explosives to ships or port facilities;
- Providing means for raising the alarm in reaction to security threats or security incidents;
- Requiring ship and port facility security plans (PFSPs) based upon security assessments; and
- Mandating training, drills, and exercises to ensure familiarity with security plans and procedures.

Among other provisions, the ISPS Code requires the issuance of an International Ship Security Certificate (ISSC) by flag states or their designated Recognized Security Organizations (RSOs) to ships that are found to be compliant with the Code. Each vessel must now carry a trained Ship Security Officer (SSO) who is responsible for security aboard the ship. The Company Security Officer (CSO) is responsible for overseeing the development and implementation of a Ship Security Plan (SSP) for each vessel in the company's fleet. The Port Facility Security Officer (PFSO) is charged with duties similar to those of the CSO with respect to the PFSP. The ISPS Code establishes three security levels for various threat conditions (known in the United States as "MARSEC Levels"), which may vary at any given time for specific ships and port facilities depending on circumstances.

Another IMO instrument of significance in this context is the ***International Convention on Standards of Training, Certification, and Watchkeeping (STCW) for Seafarers***, 1978, as amended. The STCW Convention and its associated Code were established by IMO member nations as a global framework for the development and enhancement of merchant mariner competence. The 2010 Amendments ("Manila Amendments") to the STCW Convention and Code included new requirements for security-related training of vessel personnel, especially antipiracy training. The Manila Amendments entered into force on January 1, 2012 (International Maritime Organization, 2017a).

In the context of cybersecurity, the IMO adopted **Resolution MSC.428(98) Maritime Cyber Risk Management in Safety Management System (SMS)**. In essence, the resolution mandates that vessel operators incorporate cyber risk management strategies into the SMS required under the IMO **International Safety Management (ISM) Code.** Flag states are expected to accomplish this no later than the first annual verification of the company's Document of Compliance after January 1, 2021 (International Maritime Organization, 2017b).

In the United States, major legislation on maritime security is contained in the **Maritime Transportation Security Act of 2002** (P L. 107–295), known as the MTSA. To a large degree, the MTSA mirrors the ISPS Code. It contains the following key provisions and requirements (U.S. Congress, 2002):

- Vessel and facility vulnerability assessments;
- National and area maritime security plans;
- Security plans for certain facilities and vessels;
- Transportation Security Cards;
- Grant program;
- Assessment of security at foreign ports;
- Enhanced foreign seafarer identification;
- Maritime Security Advisory Committees;
- Implementation of vessel Automatic Identification Systems (AIS);
- Enhanced intermodal security;
- Provision of civil penalties for violations;
- Codification of the USCG Sea Marshal program;
- Electronic transmission of shipment data;
- Development of standards and curriculum for maritime security professional training.

Governmental initiatives, policies, and guidance

At the national level, a number of security-related initiatives, policies, and guidance documents have been developed by governments involved in shipping and international trade. Some representative examples from the United States are discussed here.

A U.S. Customs and Border Protection (CBP) initiative that is relevant to vessel in-transit security is the ***Customs Trade Partnership Against Terrorism (C-TPAT)***. C-TPAT, begun in 2001, involves partnerships between CBP and the trade community that are meant to enhance international supply chain and US border security. Participants in this voluntary program currently include more than 11,400 certified partners, including US importers/exporters, US/Canada highway carriers, US/Mexico highway carriers, rail and ocean carriers, licensed US Customs brokers, US marine port authority/terminal operators, US freight consolidators, ocean transportation intermediaries, nonvessel operating common carriers, Mexican and Canadian manufacturers, and Mexican long-haul carriers. The ***Security and Accountability for Every Port (SAFE Port) Act of 2006*** provided legislative support and structure for the C-TPAT program and imposed strict program oversight requirements (U.S. Customs and Border Protection, 2020a).

Industry participants agree to cooperate with CBP to assess their supply chains, identify security vulnerabilities, and implement security measures to enhance security and remedy deficiencies.

Once certified, C-TPAT members accrue several benefits, the most important of which is a reduction in cargo and container inspections upon arrival at U.S. ports of entry.

Another CBP initiative that is intended to prevent high-risk containers from being loaded aboard ships headed for the United States is the ***Container Security Initiative (CSI)***. The central objective of CSI is to screen and identify containers that pose a potential terrorism risk before they are loaded in foreign ports. U.S. CBP Officers collaborate with their foreign counterparts to ensure that containers destined for the United States do not contain materials or persons that are a threat to security.

CBP employs automated targeting tools to identify containers that may pose a security risk, based on advance information and strategic intelligence. Containers are screened as early in the supply chain as possible, generally at the port of departure. This technology includes large-scale X-ray and gamma ray machines and radiation detection devices. CBP collaborates with host customs administrations to establish security criteria for identifying high-risk containers.

CSI is now operational at major container ports around the world. The 58 CSI ports that participate in the program now prescreen over 80% of the containerized cargo that enters the United States by sea (U.S. Customs and Border Protection, 2020b).

Industry guidelines

Where maritime piracy is concerned, an established blueprint for strengthening shipboard defenses and responding to pirate attacks is the ***Best Management Practices (BMP)*** series. The most recently released version of the publication, ***Best Management Practices to***

Enhance Maritime Security for Vessels and Mariners Operating Off the Coast of West Africa including the Gulf of Guinea (BMP WA), was prepared in recognition of the alarming increase in attacks off West Africa. Previous editions dealt primarily with Somali piracy. The BMP series is prepared by industry associations such as BIMCO and SIGTTO, in cooperation with government, military, and law enforcement organizations (Maritime Executive, 2020).

In response to the accelerating challenges associated with maritime cybersecurity, the industry has generated *The Guidelines on Cyber Security Onboard Ships.* Developed through a collaboration involving BIMCO, CLIA, ICS, INTERCARGO, InterManager, INTERTANKO, IUMI, OCIMF, and the World Shipping Council, the Guidelines are intended to "offer guidance to shipowners and operators on procedures and actions to maintain the security of cyber systems in the company and onboard the ships. The guidelines are not intended to provide a basis for, and should not be interpreted as, calling for external auditing or vetting the individual company's and ship's approach to cyber risk management" (BIMCO et al., 2018).

Training, drills, and exercises

Merchant mariners have been characterized as the "front line of defense" in maritime security. For ships in transit, this is especially true. The extent and quality of seafarer training and preparedness is critically important in the effort to prevent, detect, defend against, and mitigate security threats to vessels underway.

The ISPS Code stipulates specific training requirements for seafarers aboard commercial ships. By way of support for member states, the IMO publishes a series of "model courses" for global implementation that set forth the learning objectives and content for the training of vessel personnel in maritime security and antipiracy subjects. In 2003, on behalf of the United States and in partnership with the government of India, the U.S. Merchant Marine Academy developed model courses for SSO, PFSO, and CSO. In 2011, the Academy prepared additional courses for vessel and facility personnel in other categories and revised the existing IMO maritime security curriculum to address the mandates contained in the 2010 STCW Manila Amendments to provide (among other enhancements) increased antipiracy competences for merchant vessel personnel worldwide. The courses in this series that are focused on vessel personnel are: (1) SSO, (2) Security Training for Seafarers with Designated Security Duties, and (3) Security Awareness Training for All Seafarers.

While the specific training requirements vary depending on which category of personnel is involved, the Code intends for trainees to develop knowledge, skill, and proficiency in:

- Developing, and/or maintaining, and/or supervising the implementation of an SSP;
- Assessing security risk, threat, and vulnerability;

- Undertaking regular inspections of the vessel to ensure that appropriate security measures are implemented and maintained;
- Ensuring that security equipment and systems, if any, are properly operated, tested, and calibrated; and
- Encouraging security awareness and vigilance.

Security drills and exercises must be conducted at intervals specified by the ISPS Code. Drills, which involve a test of individual elements of the SSP, must be conducted at least every 3 months, with limited exceptions. Exercises, which are meant to be a broad test of the SSP, must be held at least once per calendar year, but not more than 18 months apart. Exercises may involve port facilities, government agencies, and other entities.

Carriers and ships with proactive security postures will usually be found to engage in more frequent drills and exercises than the minimum required by convention and regulation. In addition, they will likely pay particular attention to the importance of lessons learned in each such event. A "hot wash" at the conclusion of each drill or exercise, in which participants discuss what went well and what could have been improved, is the best way to identify these lessons learned.

Vessel security assessments and vessel security plans

The cornerstone of ship security under the ISPS Code and implementing national regulation is the SSP (in the United States., termed Vessel Security Plan, or VSP). The SSP/VSP is intended to "ensure the application of measures on board the ship designed to protect persons on board, cargo, cargo transport units, ships' stores or the ship from the risks of a security incident" (International Maritime Organization, 2003).

Title 33 of the U.S. Code of Federal Regulations (CFR) Section 104.405 defines the content of the VSP:

(1) Security organization of the vessel;
(2) Personnel training;
(3) Drills and exercises;
(4) Records and documentation;
(5) Response to changes in MARSEC Level;
(6) Procedures for interfacing with facilities and other vessels;
(7) Declarations of Security (DoS);
(8) Communications;
(9) Security systems and equipment maintenance;
(10) Security measures for access control;
(11) Security measures for restricted areas;
(12) Security measures for handling cargo;
(13) Security measures for delivery of vessel stores and bunkers;
(14) Security measures for monitoring;

(15)   Security incident procedures;

(16)   Audits and VSP amendments; and

(17)   Vessel Security Assessment (VSA) Report.

The VSA is the foundation for development of the VSP. The VSA involves collection of background information and a careful and systematic evaluation of conditions and vulnerabilities aboard the ship, based in part on an "on-scene survey" in which relevant dimensions of security are physically investigated. 33 CFR 104.305 contains the following requirements for the VSA Report that is intended to document the results of these efforts:

The vessel owner or operator must ensure that a written VSA report is prepared and included as part of the VSP. The VSA report must contain:

- A summary of how the on-scene survey was conducted;
- Existing security measures, procedures, and operations;
- A description of each vulnerability found during the assessment;
- A description of security countermeasures that could be used to address each vulnerability;
- A list of the key vessel operations that are important to protect;
- The likelihood of possible threats to key vessel operations; and
- A list of identified weaknesses, including human factors, in the infrastructure, policies, and procedures of the vessel.

The VSA report must address the following elements on board or within the vessel:

- Physical security;
- Structural integrity;
- Personnel protection systems;
- Procedural policies;
- Radio and telecommunication systems, including computer systems and networks; and
- Other areas that may, if damaged or used illicitly, pose a risk to people, property, or operations on board the vessel or within a facility.

The VSA report must list the persons, activities, services, and operations that are important to protect, in each of the following categories:

- Vessel personnel;
- Passengers, visitors, vendors, repair technicians, facility personnel, etc.;
- Capacity to maintain safe navigation and emergency response;
- Cargo, particularly dangerous goods and hazardous substances;
- Vessel stores;
- Any vessel security communication and surveillance systems; and
- Any other vessel security systems, if any.

The VSA report must account for any vulnerabilities in the following areas:

- Conflicts between safety and security measures;
- Conflicts between vessel duties and security assignments;
- The impact of watchkeeping duties and risk of fatigue on vessel personnel alertness and performance;
- Security training deficiencies; and
- Security equipment and systems, including communication systems.

The VSA report must discuss and evaluate key vessel measures and operations, including:

- Ensuring performance of all security duties;
- Controlling access to the vessel, through the use of identification systems or otherwise;
- Controlling the embarkation of vessel personnel and other persons and their effects (including personal effects and baggage whether accompanied or unaccompanied);
- Supervising the handling of cargo and the delivery of vessel stores;
- Monitoring restricted areas to ensure that only authorized persons have access;
- Monitoring deck areas and areas surrounding the vessel; and
- The ready availability of security communications, information, and equipment.

The VSA must be documented, and the VSA report must be retained by the vessel owner or operator along with the VSP. The VSA, the VSA report, and the VSP are Sensitive Security Information (SSI) and must be protected from unauthorized access or disclosure.

The VSP, properly prepared, provides a blueprint for ongoing efforts to secure the ship against threats of all kinds and a response plan for security contingencies that may arise. It is the responsibility of the CSO to develop the plan with appropriate expert assistance. It is the duty of the SSO to supervise the implementation of the plan and the task of all members of the crew to assist in executing it. The plan must undergo an annual audit to ensure that it remains current and that new vulnerabilities and emerging threats are fully addressed.

Voyage planning

Merchant ships operate in an environment that, even in favorable times, involves a variety of risks. Traffic, weather, hazards to navigation, pirates, terrorist threats, and other concerns must be addressed in a thorough and systematic way if a ship is to complete her voyage safely, efficiently, and without negative environmental impact. By carefully ascertaining as many of the hazards and contingencies associated with a planned passage as possible, they may be avoided or at least mitigated.

The collection of relevant data, the evaluation of proposed routes, the identification of known and potential hazards, and the development of contingency plans are key activities in managing the risks that are inherent in passage making by sea. Although it is impossible to anticipate every detail of a voyage, an organized approach is essential in identifying areas unsafe for navigation, environmental protection zones, security zones, areas of potential low visibility, port and terminal facilities en route, regions of military conflict, areas presenting a high risk of piracy or armed robbery, and similar hazards. Large ships and those carrying hazardous cargoes may be required to consider additional factors. Just as important is the need to establish the location and capability of rescue installations, medical facilities, and other emergency services that may be needed during the voyage.

Best practice in voyage planning and management consists of the following elements:

- Appraising all relevant information;
- Planning the intended voyage;
- Executing the plan, taking prevailing conditions into account;
- Monitoring the ship's progress against the plan on a continuous basis;
- Reviewing the effectiveness of the plan following the voyage.

These elements are generally undertaken in a linear and sequential manner.

Security-related information that needs to be considered in the appraisal stage of voyage planning includes risk of terrorist activity, statistics and projections on pirate attacks, the problem of stowaways in port, restrictions concerning shore leave for vessel personnel, reports on incidents of armed robbery in ports and anchorages, and related concerns.

Information should also be acquired concerning regulatory restrictions and the potential political implications of use of and the carriage of weapons, the use of armed and unarmed onboard security teams, and related issues specific to the coastal zones and ports to be visited on the voyage.

Generally speaking, the objective should be to plot a track that will keep the ship well clear of all hazards. Areas of danger should be clearly marked, recognizing that these may be of different size and configuration depending on the weather, the stage of the tide, and the ship's loaded or ballasted condition. Such areas should include known High-Risk Areas (HRAs) for piracy and locations within coastal zones where known security threats exist. The determination of what constitutes an appropriate margin of safety will depend on factors such as tide and current conditions, the ship's maneuvering characteristics, the time of transit in darkness or daylight, weather, draft, alternative tracks available, and so on. In some cases, the company will specify a minimum standard for the closest point of approach to dangers and how far the ship's track should be offshore.

It is also important to note on the charts that will be used for the voyage the location of security zones, such as those that national administrations may designate around power plants, military facilities, and passenger ship terminals. Similarly, the existence of firing ranges in which weapons may be discharged or where military aircraft may drop bombs must be highlighted.

Rerouting and risk avoidance

Where the geographic location of known security risks can be determined, as is often the case where maritime piracy is concerned, modifying the usual track of the ship to minimize exposure or to avoid the threat entirely may be considered. This option may range from a minimal deviation to a drastic reconfiguration of the vessel's route.

Factors that must be considered in rerouting decisions include longer voyages, increased crew costs, higher fuel costs, escalation of other operating costs, and larger in-transit inventory costs. Delayed cargo delivery stemming from increased transit time may become problematic. According to the U.S. Maritime Administration, rerouting a tanker departing from Saudi Arabia to the United States around the Cape of Good Hope instead of through the Suez Canal and Gulf of Aden to avoid HRAs adds approximately 2700 miles to the voyage. This reduces the number of voyages the ship can make in a year from about six to five. This reduces the effective capacity of the particular supply chain of which that vessel is a part. Routing via the Cape of Good Hope in this example would incur additional costs of about $3.5 million annually (Maritime Administration, 2010).

Military and paramilitary intervention

Where HRAs are established as a result of piracy or other criminal activity in the maritime sphere, one possible response is the deployment of naval and other military forces with the goal of protecting merchant vessels.

At the height of attacks by Somali pirates against merchant ships off the Horn of Africa, multiple UN Security Council resolutions authorized international naval forces to "enter the territorial waters of Somalia" and to operate ashore "in Somalia for the purpose of suppressing acts of piracy and armed robbery at sea." Naval operations in the region included "Operation Atalanta" overseen by the European Union Naval Force (EUNAVFOR), the multinational "Combined Task Force 151 (CTF-151)" led by the United States, and "Operation Ocean Shield" under the NATO umbrella. During the years of highest incidence of Somali piracy, some 40 naval vessels were engaged in counter-piracy missions in the Western Indian Ocean, Gulf of Aden, and off the Horn of Africa (Stockbruegger, 2010).

While naval forces can provide an important deterrent effect against certain security threats, there is a major physical challenge inherent in attempts to police large areas of the ocean in order to protect or rescue individual ships from attack. Nonetheless, this approach has proven to be successful in reducing the incidence of pirate attacks in some regions (Fig. 14.2).

Figure 14.2
Members of a joint U.S. Navy/U.S. Coast Guard Visit, Board, Search, and Seizure (VBSS) team operating as part of Combined task force (CTF) 151 capture suspected pirates after responding to a merchant vessel distress signal. *U.S. Navy photo by Mass Communication Specialist First Class Eric L. Beauregard.*

The carriage of embarked security teams aboard ships that must transit HRAs is another option to preserve security, especially where piracy is the concern. Privately Contracted Armed Security Personnel (PCASP), who are often former military or law enforcement personnel, have been shown to be highly effective in deterring pirate attacks. Embarked security teams typically board the ship prior to the beginning of the passage through areas of pirate activity, disembarking once the vessel clears the area of high risk. The use of embarked security teams has generated concern about topics including command and control, liability, firearms management, applicable law, use of force, and insurance. Many coastal states will not allow merchant ships carrying weapons into their coastal zones, a situation that has forced some PCASP operations to deploy floating armories on the high seas to hold weapons near the origins and terminations of high-risk transits. Further, some countries restrict the use of PCASP teams in their coastal waters. Nigeria, for example, prohibits armed guards aboard ships in its territorial waters, which effectively prohibits their use in the Gulf of Guinea.

The absence of worldwide regulations and standards for the training and operation of embarked security teams has resulted in the development of certification programs by organizations such as BIMCO and the Security Association for the Maritime Industry

(SAMI). The goal of these initiatives is to provide carriers with a degree of assurance regarding the quality and reliability of the companies and embarked security teams they hire (Yanchunas, 2014).

Variations on this approach include Vessel Protection Detachments, which are active-duty military personnel carried aboard a ship with explicit approval of the vessel's country of registry, and Coastal State Embarked Personnel, which are embarked armed personnel originating from the coastal state whose waters this ship is transiting, based on arrangements between ship operators and the providing national authorities (Oceans Beyond Piracy).

The question of whether or not to arm merchant ship crews is the focus of significant disagreement. On the one hand, it can be argued that merchant vessel personnel should be able to defend themselves directly and that they should have available at all times the means to do so. On the other hand, many experts maintain that merchant ship crews lack the training needed to effectively engage armed adversaries, and that vessel personnel who are given weapons are more like to cause an escalation of life-threatening combat than not. The IMO recommends strongly that merchant vessel personnel not be armed (International Maritime Organization, 2015).

Security systems and equipment

Merchant vessels can deploy and use to their advantage certain security systems and individual items of security equipment. These include the following:

- AIS;
- Ship Security Alert System (SSAS);
- Locks;
- Lighting;
- Handheld radios;
- Global Maritime Distress and Safety System (GMDSS) equipment;
- Closed Circuit Televisions (CCTV);
- Automatic Intrusion Detection Device (Burglar Alarm);
- Metal detectors;
- Explosive detectors;
- Baggage screening equipment;
- Container X-ray devices;
- General alarm;
- Transportation Worker Identification Card (TWIC) readers;
- Long Range Acoustic Device (LRAD);
- Razor wire;

- Electric fencing;
- Yacht radar;
- Netting;
- Slippery foam;
- Security glass film;
- Water and foam monitors;
- Other antipiracy devices.

Under the ISPS Code and flag state regulations, vessel personnel are required to be familiar with the operation, limitations, and calibration and maintenance requirements of security equipment carried onboard. They are not expected to acquire in-depth knowledge of the technical and scientific bases underlying its functioning. Approved training focuses on developing in trainees an understanding of the appropriate deployment of security equipment and the extent to which the use of such equipment may expose seafarers to personal danger, escalate conflict with hostile boarders, or compromise the safety of the ship and/or cargo (Fig. 14.3).

Figure 14.3
A crew member aims a Long Range Acoustic Device (LRAD) at an incoming small craft off the starboard bridge wing during a small boat attack drill. An LRAD directs intolerably intense beams of sound at a target to deter approach and can also be used as a loud hailer. *U.S. Navy photo by Photographer's Mate Third Class Tucker M. Yates.*

Conclusion

Merchant ships face a variety of security threats while underway. Keys among these are piracy and armed robbery, terrorism, and cyberattacks. If not successfully avoided or deterred, these threats can result in injury and loss of life of vessel personnel, damage to and loss of ships and cargoes, and disruption of the intermodal supply chain, related business, and economies.

Approaches to minimizing and mitigating these threats include international conventions and codes; national regulations; governmental initiatives, policies, and guidance; industry guidelines; formal risk-management systems; VSPs and assessments; training, drills, and exercises; voyage planning; rerouting; military and paramilitary intervention; and security systems and equipment. These strategies and methodologies are not mutually exclusive; in fact, they are often synergistic and mutually reinforcing.

Current challenges to the security of ships underway exist against a backdrop of reduced crew sizes and a trend toward the development and deployment of autonomous ships, which must inevitably weaken deterrence capabilities and may invite new forms of security risk. The newest container ships in the world fleet have reached astonishing size and, simultaneously, have decreased crew size to previously unimaginable levels through increasingly sophisticated automated systems and equipment. The largest container ship in service today, the *MSC Gülsün,* can carry 23,756 Twenty-foot Equivalent Units (TEUs, a standardized measure of ship cargo capacity). The vessel is 400 m (1312 feet) long and more than 60 m wide (Logistics Manager, 2019). But, *MSC Gülsün* and the other ships in her class carry only 25 or 26 crew members—about one-half of the number needed aboard a small cargo ship 50 years ago.

At the time of this writing, news is emerging of a possible cyberattack against Mediterranean Shipping Company, the owners of *MSC Gülsün*. The company's websites have been shut down.

References

Abernathy, W.J., Spearman, S.S., 2007. Spring PTP: a pound of cure. Oil spills: risk management and the human element. Proc. Marine Safe. Sec. Coun. 64 (1), 93—95.

BIMCO, C.L.I.A., et al., 2018. The Guidelines on Cyber Security Onboard Ships, Version 3. Retrieved from: https://www.ics-shipping.org/docs/default-source/resources/safety-security-and-operations/guidelines-on-cyber-security-onboard-ships.pdf?sfvrsn=20.

Galileo, G.N.S.S., September 21, 2017. Mass GPS Spoofing Attack in Black Sea? Retrieved from: https://galileognss.eu/mass-gps-spoofing-attack-in-black-sea.

Greenberg, A., August 22, 2018. The Untold Story of NotPetya, the Most Devastating Cyberattack in History. Wired. Retrieved from: https://www.wired.com/story/notpetya-cyberattack-ukraine-russia-code-crashed-the-world/.

International Maritime Bureau, January 16, 2019. IMB Piracy Report 2018: Attacks Multiply in the Gulf of Guinea. Retrieved from: https://www.icc-ccs.org/index.php/1259-imb-piracy-report-2018-attacks-multiply-in-the-gulf-of-guinea.

International Maritime Organization, 2003. International Ship & Port Facility Security (ISPS) Code, 2003 and December 2002 Amendments to SOLAS. IMO, London. IMO-I116E.

International Maritime Organization, 2011. Circular Letter Concerning Information and Guidance on Elements of International Law Relating to Piracy. Circular Letter No, p. 3180.

International Maritime Organization, 2015. Recommendations to Governments for Preventing and Suppressing Piracy and Armed Robbery against Ships. MSC.1/Circ.1333/Rev.1.

International Maritime Organization, 2017a. STCW. IMO, London. IMO-ID938E.

International Maritime Organization, 2017b. Maritime Cyber Risk Management in Safety Management Systems. MSC 98/23/Add.1, Annex 10.

JOC, October 2, 2013. Rocket Attack on Cosco Ship Hit Container of Smuggled Cigarettes. Retrieved from: https://www.joc.com/maritime-news/container-lines/cosco/rocket-attack-cosco-ship-hit-container-smuggled-cigarettes_20131002.html.

Logistics Manager, August 23, 2019. World's Biggest Container Ship Completes Maiden Voyage. Retrieved from: https://www.logisticsmanager.com/worlds-biggest-container-ship-completes-maiden-voyage.

Maritime Administration, 2010. Economic Impact of Piracy in the Gulf of Aden on Global Trade. Homeland Security Digital Library. Retrieved from: https://www.hsdl.org/?abstract&did=232008.

Maritime Executive, March 31, 2020. Security Guidance Updated for Gulf of Guinea. Retrieved from: https://maritime-executive.com/article/security-guidance-updated-for-gulf-of-guinea.

Myers, J., 2007. Risk based decision making. Proc. Marine Safe. Sec. Coun. 64 (1), 6—9.

Oceans Beyond Piracy. Issue Paper: Privately Contracted Armed Maritime Security. Retrieved from: http://oceansbeyondpiracy.org/sites/default/files/attachments/Privately_Contracted_Armed_Maritime_Security_IssuePaper.pdf.

Pallardy, R., October 6, 2010. Achille Lauro Hijacking. Encyclopedia Britannica. Retrieved from: https://www.britannica.com/event/Achille-Lauro-hijacking.

Rider, D., October 16, 2019. Maritime Meets Cyber Security. Maritime Executive. Retrieved from: https://www.maritime-executive.com/blog/maritime-meets-cyber-security.

Safety4Sea, February 27, 2019. Superferry14: The World's Deadliest Terrorist Attack at Sea. Retrieved from: https://safety4sea.com/cm-superferry14-the-worlds-deadliest-terrorist-attack-at-sea/.

SeaNews, September 20, 2013. Fire, Explosion Aboard 10,061-TEU Cosco Asia in Suez Terror Attack. Retrieved from: https://www.seanews.com.tr/fire-explosion-aboard-10-061-teu-cosco-asia-in-suez-terror-attack/110977/.

Stockbruegger, J., 2010. Somali Piracy and the International Response: Trends in 2009 and Prospects for 2010. *Piracy Studies: Research Portal for Maritime Security*. Retrieved from: http://piracy-studies.org/2010/somali-piracy-and-the-international-response-trends-in-2009-and-prospects-for-2010/.

Thompson, B., 2015. GPS spoofing and jamming: a global concern for all vessels. Proc. Marine Safe. Sec. Coun. 71 (4), 50—51.

U.S. Customs and Border Protection, 2020. CTPAT: Customs Trade Partnership against Terrorism. Retrieved from: https://www.cbp.gov/border-security/ports-entry/cargo-security/ctpat.

U.S. Customs and Border Protection, 2020. CSI: Container Security Initiative. Retrieved from: https://www.cbp.gov/border-security/ports-entry/cargo-security/csi/csi-brief.

U.S. Congress, November 25, 2002. Maritime Transportation Security Act of 2002 (Public Law 107—295). Retrieved from: https://www.congress.gov/107/plaws/publ295/PLAW-107publ295.pdf.

Yanchunas, D., June/July, 2014. Masters, Shipowners Face Liability Risk from Armed Guards' Mistakes. Professional Mariner, pp. 41—44.

CHAPTER 15

At US ports*

Ports illustrated

An old maritime adage holds that "if you've seen one port, you've seen one port." In essence, each port, even individual terminals within a given port, is unique. As a result, a solution to a problem at one port will not necessarily suit the needs of any other, even if the problem is common to all. Not only are all ports different, but the terms used to describe them are nearly as varied as their operations. For this discussion, "port" and "seaport" refer to "A place for the lading and unlading of the cargoes of vessels, and the collection of duties or customs upon imports and exports... either on the seacoast or on a river, where ships stop for the purpose of loading and unloading, from whence they depart, and where they finish their voyages" (Black's Law Dictionary). This is not to be confused with a terminal, which is a "single man-made facility that may have several berths, that handles vessels and possibly more than one type of vessel or cargo," (Barnes, 2013). So, if it fits within a port, it is a terminal. That said, the terms "port" and "terminal" are also frequently interchanged, as are "facility" and "marine terminal." Perhaps confusing at first, but ascertaining meaning through context becomes increasingly easy.

Comparisons reveal contrasts

While all ports concern themselves with ensuring as timely vessel and cargo turnaround as possible, a diverse array of factors serves to differentiate them. Public or private ownership is foremost among these. Public ports have the benefit of government subsidies for capital investments, including security devices and equipment. On the other hand, public facilities can be hampered by extremely rigid procurement requirements that can cause lengthy delays when implementing critical projects. Public ports are often focused on economic impact and may sacrifice profit for job creation; thus they may be more apt to invest in non-revenue producing assets, such as those associated with physical and logical security. Private ports, conversely, generally target the bottom line as a fundamental goal, establishing spending and operating parameters like any other business. Most US ports

---

* *Anonymous This chapter is provider with the understanding that neither the author nor their organization is identified. The editors do assure the reader, however, that the author is a high-profile individual who has a substantial grounding in the subject matter.*

Intermodal Maritime Security. https://doi.org/10.1016/B978-0-12-819945-9.00007-1

comprise both public and private facilities, often leading to tension among their owners and operators. Multi-state port systems, such as the tristate Delaware River area, further complicate port priorities. Consider, for example, an automatic identification system (AIS), which tracks ship locations in real time. If Philadelphia terminals decide to invest in this technology but those in Delaware do not, a 60-mile gap may exist in the common operating picture.

Individuating ports by the level of security risk generally hinges on the cargo handled. Break-bulk ports, those moving goods shipped separately (think automobiles or steel slabs) or in nonstandard packaging (like cocoa beans), present the least exposure. Oil terminals bring their own risks, such the potential to target a tanker in an effort to cause a spill, close the waterway, and cause significant environmental and economic damage. Passenger terminals, where the cargo is people, are also very high risk and require security measures well beyond those of other facilities. Of equal risk are ports that handle containers.

By their very nature, shipping containers hide their contents, providing ample opportunity for malicious actors to cause harm. These include housing stowaways, smuggling drugs or counterfeit goods, human trafficking, and CBRNE (chemical, biological, radiological, nuclear, explosive) weapons. While cargo manifest data are sent to government officials and marine terminal operators in advance of each container ship arrival, security practitioners can never be certain that the containers hold only that which is manifested. Witness the June 2019 seizure of over 16 tons of cocaine stowed within seven containers laden aboard a Mediterranean Shipping Company (MSC) vessel (Dienst, 2019). MSC is a regular caller at US ports, a member of the Customs-Trade Partnership Against Terrorism (C-TPAT), and, thus, considered a trusted partner. Despite this, MSC was responsible for the largest cocaine seizure in US history ("U.S. Customs and Border Protection Seizes, 2019").

Finally, in this day and age, the level of automation deployed at marine terminals must be considered when assessing port differences. Unautomated or semiautomated ports require human action to load, unload, move, and store cargo; this provides substantial opportunity to introduce contraband or weapons into the supply chain, and it can also decelerate cargo delivery. Thus, container loading and discharging require speed not only to meet customer needs but also to strengthen terminal security. As port security professionals know, a moving target is clearly harder to hit. Automated ports, on the other hand, require little to no human-cargo interaction. However, they are likelier to exchange and store large amounts of data, leading to increased cyber risks. Marine terminal owners and operators must base their security investments on measures which best meet their own operations, including the type of cargoes handle and level of automation, as well as the security posture of the overall port region in which they operate.

Common carriage

What often unites terminal owners and operators are the security-driven laws and regulations governing their operations. Many US regulations are designed to comply with international mandates, such as the International Ship and Port Facility Code, the "basis for a comprehensive mandatory security regime for international shipping" ("The International Ship") established by the International Maritime Organization. In this way, US ports are at parity with those in other ratifying nations and, thus, not priced out of consumer goods markets due to more restrictive, more costly, security protocols.

US cargo terminals are governed by the Maritime Transportation Security Act of 2002 (Pub.L. 107—295). Known as MTSA, the law and its implementing regulations dictate activities ranging from access control, to security training and exercises, to communication with ships while at dock. Regulations require that facilities designate security officers, establish procedures for the various MARSEC (maritime security) levels, and develop facility security plans. Not surprising given that the rules were promulgated in 2005, however, is that MTSA does not address cybersecurity, other than to require restricted access to sensitive computer and telecommunications systems. In fact, while the Coast Guard has considered the need to develop maritime cybersecurity regulations, it has not yet done so. Some in industry argue that the Coast Guard has no place in this realm, as there are no uniquely maritime cybersecurity risks.

The Security and Accountability For Every Port Act of 2006 (Pub.L. 109—347), or SAFE Port, amended MTSA to add numerous requirements for seaport security. Among many other mandates, SAFE Port included new access requirements for individuals engaged in the surface transportation of intermodal containers in and out of a facility (i.e., truck drivers and rail crews). It required additional Coast Guard facility inspections, US citizenship for individuals involved in MARSEC, and distribution of port security grants based on the level of port risk.

While the Coast Guard is responsible for overseeing terminal and vessel security, Customs and Border Protection (CBP) enforces regulations pertaining to international cargoes arriving at US ports. CBP has always had to find the delicate balance between its often competing missions of enforcement and trade facilitation, which has only become more challenging with the advent of e-commerce and ultralarge container vessels (ULCVs). Prior to 9/11, CBP's primary security concerns were drug interdiction, cargo theft, and the import of counterfeit goods. Despite the evolving threats and increased risks over the last 2 decades, for the most part, the pre-9/11 customs regime for container examinations has been sufficient to meet 21st-century security needs. The most notable post-9/11 CBP mandate at marine terminals has been to require that port operators verify cargo release directly with CBP rather than relying on information from the ship or its agent. Allowing a container out of a port's custody without proper release is known as a "gate-out," and CBP may issue a fine and/or require that the container be returned to the terminal.

The mandates considered here have resulted in exponentially enhanced security measures at US ports. Without them, it is highly unlikely facility operators would have invested in security at the levels currently seen. The reality is that nonrevenue producing activities like security simply do not get the financial attention they may deserve unless there is a compelling reason to do so. Regulatory compliance is just such a compelling reason.

Roadblocks at ports

As can be seen by some of the examples above, ports face unique security challenges compared to other industry sectors. The direct threats include, among many others: stowing CBRNE weapons aboard containers; cargo tampering, such as introducing noxious chemicals into the food supply at agriculture ports; stowaways; and using vessels as bombs to injure humans, the environment, and the economy. Yet because marine terminals are peppered in among places where humans gather, especially at river ports, numerous indirect threats exist that can cause massive human injury and loss of life. For example, cargo terminals in Camden, New Jersey, are directly adjacent to an aquarium, a park, an amphitheater, and the tourist-attracting battleship "USS New Jersey." A mile across the river is Penn's Landing in Philadelphia, which hosts outdoor festivals all summer and is home to the Independence Seaport Museum. And above it all are the Ben Franklin and Walt Whitman Bridges, carrying nearly 215,000 vehicles a day (The DRPA family of sites). The destruction of these critical transportation arteries would cause economic chaos for the entire mid-Atlantic region and beyond. So though facility security plans can generally disregard mass evacuations or vessel-bridge allisions, region-wide MARSEC plans must take threats to human life and the economy very seriously.

As discussed in this section, port security planners must overcome numerous barriers to effective incident prevention and response.

Information Sharing/Communication: Like their counterparts in other industries, port security professionals rely on timely, accurate, and actionable information. While the Coast Guard requires facilities to report security breaches, port professionals lament the fact that the information flow is mainly one way. For instance, when a facility security officer reports an individual taking unauthorized photographs, the National Response Center does not share its findings or report back any action taken. Nor is the information shared with security personnel at nearby facilities so they can watch for the same person or other pattern. Equally distressing is the lack of information provided by CBP when crew guards are required. Each vessel must electronically file a crew manifest prior to arrival. Based on its analysis, CBP may require that one or more guards, and in some cases armed guards, be placed on watch to prevent crew from leaving the ship (at least from the land side). However, CBP will not provide any reason for this requirement, even if the ship is arriving directly from another US port where no guards were deemed necessary. Finally, facility personnel who attend an Area MARSEC Committee meeting might receive an intelligence briefing, but these are not always offered. When they are, information is not shared with those unable to attend. These are just a few examples to illustrate one of the foremost challenges to improving security at US ports.

Container Visibility: Simply stated, there is almost none. Terminal operators and government inspectors rely on the manifest description of cargo stowed within containers. The ship operator will not know if a container has been compromised when filing data, or if the operator does know of contraband or weapons stowed aboard, clearly he will not report it. Further, not all containers take advantage of RFID (radio-frequency identification) technology, which tracks tags adhered to containers. Among those that do, not all are tracked from origin to destination, and some terminals lack the infrastructure to utilize it. In general, when shippers use RFID to track containers, they are looking to ensure if the goods arrive when they are supposed to arrive; they are not analyzing anomalies in the schedule with an eye toward extraordinary delays that might reveal the introduction of contraband. Interestingly, the federal government plays its own role in obfuscating container security. As it is packed, each container is sealed, and that seal number is included on documents transmitted to CBP, the marine terminal operator, and others. When CBP inspects a container at a US port, of necessity the officer breaks the seal. After completing the inspection, CBP will reseal the box, but the officer does not update the data system or other documents to reflect the new number. Clearly, verifying container integrity further down the transportation chain then becomes increasingly problematic.

Limited Technology Infrastructure: Some terminals may spend heavily on video cameras, biometric sensors for access, RFID, and other security equipment. More often, facilities lack at least some desired equipment. From a big-picture perspective, security infrastructure can be sorely wanting. For example, terminals generally face cameras inward (towards land), so who is watching the water? And were facilities to face cameras outward, substantial gaps in coverage would likely exist. Further, camera feeds are not shared, so if terminals grant video access to law enforcement, those users must maintain separate accounts for each facility. Clearly not an ideal situation during a security response operation. The same is true for transportation management system data, which partners in the transportation chain use to track goods movement. Lastly, some ports have no region-wide AIS systems, and other have systems that include commercial vessels but not blue force (e.g. friendly military vessels).

Law Enforcement Familiarity: Better said, a lack thereof. When police enter a jewelry store to stop a robbery, officers have an idea of the possible store layout, the type of merchandise on sale, and the number of people who may be working there. At a marine terminal, responders may have no comprehension of its size, scope, or operation. They may not understand the inherent risks or challenges that may impede response, such as forklifts zipping by or that the person hiding behind a wall of containers is a longshore worker, not a criminal (or vice versa). Compounding the problem is that multiple jurisdictions (e.g., federal agents, or state, municipal, and port authority police) might respond to a single incident, without benefit of interoperable communications and a not necessarily clear line of authority. Coupling all this with the lack of visibility into containers, any one of which might harbor a CBRNE weapon, for example, creates a recipe for disaster.

Cybercrime: This is one area where ports may have an advantage over other industry sectors, for now. Though significant volumes of electronic data accompany the ship and cargo along their journey, in the ocean cargo environment, much data exchange still takes place on paper. Today, a data system breach may not prevent some port facilities from conducting business on paper, albeit at a slower pace. That said, a bad actor who accesses port facility data can cause substantial harm beyond the economic losses usually associated with a data breach. For instance, accessing a cargo manifest might reveal that certain chemicals are laden within a container—chemicals that might very well release deadly particles into the air for miles if exploded.

This discussion encompasses only a few of the challenges security professionals at US ports face, though it does touch on some threats common to container terminals. But all is not lost. Several measures to combat these threats are available to maritime stakeholders.

Preparedness is paramount

Just as information is key to effective security management at the terminal level, collaboration is essential at the port level. Port stakeholders work together to prevent, plan for, respond to, and recover from transportation security incidents through their local Area Maritime Security Committees (AMSCs). Typically comprised of law enforcement, first responders, emergency management officials, port and vessel operators, and service providers such as pilots and longshore workers, AMSCs are the umbrella under which port community members develop protocols for addressing their greatest risks at the macro level. Perhaps even more importantly, AMSCs are also extremely effective at helping people who must work together during a security incident, develop the relationships, and build the level of trust among partners so critical to a safe, speedy response, and recovery. Further, to the extent that "lessons learned" and "best practices" are shared among port security professionals, AMSCs serve as the venue for that communication.

Beyond the AMSCs, numerous federal programs exist to help harden marine terminals against attack.

Among the most beneficial initiatives has been the Port Security Grant Program. According to the Federal Emergency Management Agency, which administers the program, "The [PSGP] plays an important role in the implementation of the National Preparedness System by supporting the building, sustainment, and delivery of core capabilities essential to achieving the National Preparedness Goal of a secure and resilient nation" ("Port Security Grant"). The PSGP has helped facility owners/operators acquire fencing, lighting, cameras, access control systems, and other assets. It has funded law enforcement patrol and response boats and firefighting apparatus. The PSGP has also supported security training, and it has been used to launch fusion centers and deploy multiagency data systems. Yet even good programs usually have room for improvement, and the PSGP is no exception. While the program began in 2002, it switched to a "fiduciary agent" model for high-risk ports in 2007. Under this model, grant applications were made to and approval decisions were made by the AMSC and the Captain of the Port (COTP). The local fiduciary agent, also selected by the AMSC, managed the funds for the region, and the number and nature of security assets available locally were transparent to the entire port community. For reasons never made entirely clear, Federal Emergency Management Agency (FEMA) discontinued the fiduciary agent model after 2011 in favor of direct competition, despite the fact that other homeland security grant programs are still managed through fiduciaries. The result? Fewer dollars available to many regions, and no local accountability for grant recipients or visibility into the success or failure of their projects.

Today, in order to decide which grant applications to fund, FEMA uses, among other criteria, another post-9/11 program known as MSRAM, the Maritime Security Risk Analysis Model, developed by the Coast Guard to mitigate the risk of terrorist attacks at US ports. MSRAM houses infrastructure data (e.g., number and type of cargo terminals) that allow for "risk-informed approaches to prioritize its investments, and for developing plans and allocating resources that balance security and the flow of commerce" (General Accountability Office, 2011). MSRAM is a valuable decision-support tool, but many maritime stakeholders recognize that it cannot take the place of local knowledge, experience, and analysis.

Other federal tools for detecting anomalies are improving every year. For example, CBP officers wear personal radiation detectors when they are aboard maritime terminals. Also available are radiation portal monitors, which scan entire containers either as they are unloaded or outbound at the facility gates. When first deployed, radiation portal monitor (RPM) alarms would sound with every shipment of bananas and other harmless cargoes that emit natural radiation, greatly impeding operations and slowing cargo flow; though today they operate much more effectively, they can still cause backups at facility exits. Another boon to the trade community and to CBP is VACIS (Vehicle and Cargo Inspection System), essentially machines that conduct nonintrusive "X-ray" inspections of containers or chassis. According to CBP, VACIS has decreased wait time "by 58,000 h per year valued at a gross domestic product of nearly $1.9 million" (Non-Intrusive Inspection Systems, 2016). Contrast this with the requirement to dray containers to an offsite container examination station, which costs several days and hundreds of dollars per container. In ports handling large volumes of perishable products, lengthy delays for container inspections can result in the loss of entire shipments due to spoilage.

Another set of federal program has also increased cargo throughput at US ports while concurrently enhancing the nation's security posture: increased advance data reporting. When filers submit data electronically prior to arrival, CBP systems analyze the bill of lading and entry information to look for red flags, such as first-time shippers or whether a food importer is registered. In fact, the system will flag some containers as "Do Not Load" before they have even departed the foreign port of loading, keeping threats well away from US borders. These advance targeting systems greatly minimize the number of physical exams necessary on arriving containers, greatly improving supply chain velocity. The Advance Notice of Arrival/Departure system allows the Coast Guard to consider the security regimes of each vessel's last five ports of call, among other factors, as it evaluates whether a security boarding is necessary upon arrival in the United States. In essence, these and other data systems help federal officials find the needle in the haystack. They also pave the way for expedited clearance of ships and cargoes through programs like C-TPATand AQUA Lane, the Advanced Qualified Unlading Approval. While electronic data reporting has necessitated significant capital expenditures by port owners and operators and radically changed business processes, if it can speed cargo throughput, it is a cost industry is ultimately willing to bear.

No discussion of federal security programs at US ports is complete without considering the Transportation Worker Identification Credential (TWIC). The TWIC was mandated through MTSA and other legislation, and its original goal was to provide a standard ID for workers in all commercial transportation modes: air, rail, ocean, mass transit, and pipeline. Port stakeholders initially supported the TWIC program wholeheartedly, as in the immediate aftermath of 9/11, many terminals issued site-specific IDs. TWIC would prevent those who need to access multiple facilities—such as pilots, truck drivers, railroad employees, and longshore laborers—from having to obtain, and sometimes pay for, multiple ID cards. The Transportation Security Administration (TSA) began work on TWIC in 2002, and by 2008, the agency was issuing TWIC cards to maritime workers. The program has not realized its full potential, however, as Coast Guard has yet to finalize regulations for TWIC readers at marine terminals. It is important to note that industry is no longer as enthusiastic about the program or its utility as a tool to combat terrorism.

Among the concerns are that the biometric component will not be used at any but the highest-risk terminals (i.e., those handling passengers and certain dangerous cargoes) and even if it were used at all terminals, stakeholders are unsure that the card and the readers could withstand the harsh outdoor environments prevalent at port facilities. Even as a flash pass, TWIC has already committed the mortal sin of slowing commerce at port facilities; introducing biometric readers at facility access points will only exacerbate the problem.

Terminal owners and operators have also developed programs to boost preparedness. Some facility security officers have undergone law enforcement training, and private-sector personnel in some areas may have opportunities to embed themselves on a regular basis within local or regional fusion centers. Different facility operators share radios, and in one interesting project, two oil terminals, a container facility, and a general cargo facility partnered in the development of their business continuity plans. Private sector organizations also share video, AIS vessel tracking feeds, advance vessel schedules, and a host of other information with port partners. Most notable, however, are the numerous drills and exercises involving facility personnel and multiple response agencies that take place several times a year at each port. These cover everything from active-shooter response, an Improvised Explosive Device (IED) attack on a bridge, a bomb in a container, and nearly any scenario someone can plan. Mandated by MTSA and often funded via port security grants, these exercises have afforded numerous benefits. Chiefly, they familiarize port security personnel with the National Incident Command System, provide a venue for partners to meet and work together in advance of an actual incident, and most importantly, they allow all the players to test unforeseen aspects of their plans.

Though faced with often conflicting priorities, local governments have made strides to combat port security issues as well. State and municipal police have increased waterway patrols, and interagency collaboration has resulted in sharing of information, assets, resources, and training among and across departments. Ports may not receive the same attention as perhaps schools and hospitals when it comes to investing limited public resources, but they are certainly on the radar, which may not have been the case before 9/11. However, despite the many noteworthy gains in preparedness, much more can be done.

Opportunities abound

Attempting to determine the success or cost-benefit ratio of security initiatives is hopeless. Security practitioners would have to demonstrate that something did not happen as a result of some process or asset, an obvious impossibility. Nonetheless, that there are opportunities to improve MARSEC at US ports is undeniable. Most of the following discussion will simply reflect the converse of some of the shortcomings described earlier. Many of the programs will require little investment beyond additional personnel time, and all will benefit facility owners and operators as well as the government agencies charged with safeguarding the nation's ports and waterways.

The obvious first place to look is to eliminate duplicative or wasteful activity. Consider, for example, container inspection processes. Shortly after the Department of Homeland Security was created, officials touted and industry applauded the new One Face at the Border initiative; the idea was that personnel responsible to inspect vessels, cargoes, and crews would wear the same uniform, follow consistent procedures, and be thoroughly crosstrained. The program would "eliminate the previous separation of immigration, customs, and agriculture functions at U.S. air, land, and seaports of entry, and institute a unified border inspection process" (Myers, 2005). While combining legacy immigration and customs services has engendered some efficiencies, the One Face dream unfortunately never materialized. Similarly, in October 2001, CBP decided it would no longer conduct in-stream boardings, citing officer safety (despite the fact that Coast Guard and private-sector personnel regularly board ships while at anchorage or underway). Rather than boarding vessel at the port entrance, officers now wait for ships to dock. While this can increase costs by delaying cargo operations, in its extreme, it can unnecessarily cost thousands of dollars to a ship owner. In one example, a ship arrived at the Delaware Breakwater (about 120 miles from the Customhouse in Philadelphia), discharged cargo onto a barge for upriver transit, after which it was scheduled to depart. Because the ship had technically entered US waters and notwithstanding that it would be sailing without docking, CBP decided it must inspect the crew. Yet rather than CBP officers making the 2-hour drive to Delaware Bay, the agency required the crew be brought to the officers in Philadelphia. Because a certain number of crew must remain aboard ship at all times to meet safety requirements, the owner had to hire a launch to pick up and deliver three small groups of crew members to/from the ship and had to hire transport for each group to Philadelphia and back. The round-trip for each group was 5 to 6 h or more. In the end, what might have taken a total of 5- hours cost the ship owner nearly 40- hours and thousands of dollars in transport services. We can only ask, was this really necessary to safeguard the United States from crew members who would never land on US soil?

In lieu of physical vessel boardings to interview crew, CBP should consider using video. As described earlier, CBP successfully introduced nonintrusive container screening to aid its security mission, but it will not avail itself of modern methods for crew screening. While CBP attempts to meet ships on arrival, schedules sometimes prevent timely boarding, impeding cargo operations, which can cause thousands in stand-by labor charges, delay cargo delivery, and potentially jeopardize the ship schedule for the remainder of the voyage. Clearly CBP officers could better use the time normally spent unproductively in travel, as well as expedite cargo flow, by inspecting via video. Quite possibly, however, CBP rejects the technology as it does not want to be seen as taking steps that might appear to be softening the security regimen for processing foreign nationals.

Video has other benefits at US ports as well. Adding video to monitor the waterways could, at fairly low cost, dramatically aid a port's security posture by providing visibility to the Coast Guard and others where none currently exists and by linking existing video into a common operating picture. Port-wide efforts to link feeds and provide new views would improve both prevention and response efforts. Beyond providing a common portal, a region-wide video system could minimize the need for physical waterway patrols, freeing resources to conduct other activities. While historically ports were concerned primarily with oil tankers and chemical ships as targets, today's ULCVs, which can block an entire waterway if damaged, present a new set of challenges for security professionals. Early detection of threats via video can certainly help mitigate this risk.

Another opportunity lies with unmanned vehicles, which are only just beginning to find their way into the MARSEC realm. Marine terminal operators can use unmanned aerial vehicles to help patrol areas not otherwise accessible, and drones can also check for container seal integrity, and provide X-ray imaging. In November of 2019, the Borders, Trade, and Immigration Institute at the University of Houston announced an initiative to study whether using unmanned systems in MARSEC can help detect radiation, human trafficking, and drug smuggling. Similarly, unmanned underwater vehicles can also be used to patrol under ships while docked or anchored within US ports, as can sonar devices. Expanding the use of these systems could greatly improve security at US ports.

The burgeoning smartphone-as-desktop trend has a powerful potential to enhance MARSEC. Smartphone apps could be used for everything from checking access badges to verifying CBP release status, to container bar code/RFID scanning, and a host of other critical functions. However, the maritime industry will undoubtedly be challenged in this regard in the near term, as its aging workforce (Sasseen, 2017) may be less likely to adopt such technology.

Yet numerous initiatives beyond deploying more gadgets stand ready to aid in the fight to make US ports more secure. Expanding electronic data exchange would go a long way toward enhancing security—at the same time it would increase efficiencies and decrease waste. While some data are filed electronically, many processes are still conducted on paper. These include filing a request to enter a port, requesting permission to unlade cargo, reporting ships' stores, and paying vessel tonnage tax, to name a few. Not only is requiring so much paper anachronistic, some required data are simply irrelevant today. Federal agencies should modernize processes, assess data needs, and complete the transition to a paperless environment. This would improve security by providing more advance information, eliminate wasted time processing unneeded data and forms, and decrease the costs of printing, delivering, processing, and storing paper documents.

Finally, port professionals would realize substantial benefit from two-way communications. If an ocean carrier data system is breached, someone spoofs a vessel's navigation system, or a marine terminal is targeted, and port security professionals do not generally hear about it other than through media reports. As mentioned earlier in this chapter, facility security should be informed of the disposition of cases when they file reports, and upriver ports need to know when a breach occurs at one of their downriver neighbors. The government-endorsed Maritime ISAC (information sharing and analysis center) has not proven to be successful. Rather, an electronic information portal to share this type of information would go a long way toward improving preparedness. Individuals requesting access would be vetted, but the goal should be to share information as soon as it is available and with as many people who have a right and a need to know.

The bottom line

A shipping container changes custody many times as it makes its way from far-off growers, manufacturers, and sellers to the US heartland, and it is vulnerable to tampering at each transition. No stage of its journey presents such abundant opportunity for malfeasance than at seaports, where offloading, moving, storing, and ultimate transfer to inland drayage are choreographed among numerous hands. Port operators and the government agencies which regulate—and support—them must, therefore, be ever diligent, using all available tools to overcome the numerous challenges to keeping those ports safe that they collectively face. Beyond that, port stakeholders can work together to develop processes to more effectively capitalize on limited security resources and improve the system as a whole. Finally, policymakers at all levels must be mindful that any attempt to develop a one-size-fits-all comparison is meaningless. At the end of the day, "when you've seen one port, you've seen one port."

References

Barnes, M., September 17, 2013. Port, Harbour or Terminal. What's the Difference? Shipping Guides LTD. www.portinfo.co.uk/port-information/our-blog/247-what-s-the-difference-between-a-port-harbour-and-terminal. (Accessed 8 November 2019).

Black's Law Dictionary Free second ed. "What is PORT?" <https://thelawdictionary.org/port/> (Accessed 12.03.2019).

Dienst, J., June 18, 2019. More than 16 Tons of Cocaine Worth up to $1B Seized in Massive Bust in Philadelphia. NBC News. www.nbcnews.com/news/us-news/over-16-tons-cocaine-seven-shipping-containers-seized-massive-bust-n1019021. (Accessed 11 November 2019).

General Accountability Office, November 17, 2011. Security Risk Model Meets DHS Criteria, But More Training Could Enhance its Use for Managing Programs and Operations. https://www.gao.gov/products/GAO-12-14. (Accessed 12 November 2019).

Myers, D., July 1, 2005. "One Face at the Border" — Is it Working?" Migration Policy Institute. https://www.migrationpolicy.org/article/one-face-border-it-working. (Accessed 12 November 2019).

Non-Intrusive Inspection Systems & Radiation Detection Equipment, May 2016. Customs & Border Protection Publication No. 00506-0506. www.cbp.gov/sites/default/files/assets/documents/2016-May/nii-radiation-detection-fy15-review_0.pdf. (Accessed 12 November 2019).

"Port Security Grant Program." Federal Emergency Management Agency. <https://www.fema.gov/port-security-grant-program> (Accessed 12 May 2019).

Sasseen, J., August 23, 2017. Maritime Industry Is Growing, But the Workforce Is Aging. HeraldNet. https://www.heraldnet.com/business/maritime-industry-in-washington-faces-aging-crisis/. (Accessed 13 December 2019).

The DRPA family of sites. Delaware River Port Authority. www.drpa.org. (Accessed 11.11.2019).

The International Ship and Port Facility (ISPS) Code. International Maritime Organization. <www.imo.org/en/OurWork/Security/Guide_to_Maritime_Security/Pages/SOLAS-XI-2%20ISPS%20Code.aspx> (Accessed 12.11.2019).

U.S. Customs and Border Protection Seizes MSC Gayane following Record Cocaine Seizure, July 8, 2019. U.S. Customs and Border Protection. www.cbp.gov/newsroom/local-media-release/us-customs-and-border-protection-seizes-msc-gayane-following-record. (Accessed 11 November 2019).

CHAPTER 16

Routing analysis, risk, and resiliency*

Gary A. Gordon PhD, P.E., MEMS, LTC USA (Ret.)
Department of Civil & Environmental Engineering, University of Massachusetts Lowell, Lowell, MA, United States

A container ship of an unnamed line is destined to Haifa, Israel form Pusan, South Korea. The voyage will traverse the Strait of Malacca and Suez Canal; both constricted waterways. Prior to loading at Hanjin Center Terminal in Pusan, the containers and their contents have been properly vetted. Before departing, the ship's Captain assessed the risk of the chosen route and found it to be acceptable. The assessment was based on, among other things, the safety and security of the route.

Three days into the voyage, the Captain learned of unrest in and around the Strait of Malacca with an advisory to not pass through the strait until informed otherwise by authorities. The Captain had two options. The first was to slow down and wait for the authorities to advise that the unrest in the Strait of Malacca had subsided. The second was to reroute the voyage south to pass between Indonesia and Australia, which would add many additional days and cost to the voyage. The question is which of the two options would be both safe and as cost effective as possible? The decision the Captain made was by the "seat of the pants."

The Captain was still nevertheless somewhat relieved because of not having the issues in and around the Strait of Hormuz like he had had on a voyage a couple of years prior. At least, he thought, when heading into the Persian Gulf he knew who the threats were, where they would likely be coming from, and that the United States and Royal Navies were being alert to possible developments. With pirates, however, the predictability factor was almost completely gone. A rerouting would require a major extended voyage or transloading at a port to rail and/or truck. Thinking of this, the Captain wished that a simple risk assessment model was available to help him/her in the decision-making process. It would allow him/her to make a decision empirically supplemented by intuition, rather than by the "seat of the pants."

Introduction

Routing risk analysis looks at the operational, physical, and procedural security measures of the intermodal maritime supply chain and how they can mitigate risk. The question is

---

* Much of this chapter is taken from the author's doctoral dissertation entitled "Intermodal Maritime Container Security: A Multifactor Framework for Assessing Routing Risk".

Intermodal Maritime Security. https://doi.org/10.1016/B978-0-12-819945-9.00001-0

how can the risk of the intermodal maritime container supply chain be determined? There are many ways of doing this, but the majority of the methods are data-intensive, analytically driven, complicated and burdensome to operate, use, and interpret. Therefore, and in response to this, a simplified and practitioner-focused routing risk assessment framework has been developed that utilizes the principles of the US Army CARVER (Criticality, Accessibility, Recuperability, Vulnerability, Effect, and Recognizability) model that is used to assess mission validity and requirements (Joint Publication 3-05.2, 2003; FM 34-36, 1991). The simplified route assessment framework is focused on the intermodal maritime container supply chain being targeted, rather than the targeting approach and perspective of the US Army CARVER model. The model would allow any of the stakeholders in the intermodal maritime container supply chain to change course and reroute a ship or container creating resilience in it (supply chain) while reducing risk (Gordon, 2018).

This chapter will look at risk assessment models and processes that are applicable to transportation and, in particular, the maritime environment. These models will provide an understanding of risk and its components and a framework for assessing routing risk and route selection. Note that analytic risk assessment models are often data intensive and process oriented and not "user-friendly" and not an expedient assessment of risk that can be run and rerun as the threat profile changes (Gordon, 2018).

General discussion of risk assessment models

Risk assessments are part of the risk management process (Vellani and Butterworth, 2007). The process assesses and derives risk as a function of threat, vulnerabilities, and consequences, determines the appropriate security measures, and implements and monitors the selected security measures. Risk assessments can be either subjective or quantitative. Qualitative or subjective risk assessments are usually used for "low value" assets or when historical data and metrics are not available precluding a quantitative approach. A quantitative risk assessment is a metric-based process and assigns values to risk levels. It is the premise of this chapter that a simplified and expedient risk assessment method or framework that is supply chain stakeholder and practitioner-focused lends to addressing risk in a qualitative or subjective manner.

The history and discussion of risk assessment is long and involves many focal points, such as finances and infrastructure (Lewis, 2015). In recent history, risk assessment approaches have been used to look at terrorist intent, what is to be protected, and cost effectiveness of protective measures (Schnaubelt et al., 2014). Over the years, the probabilistic risk analysis or PRA has become the method of assessing risk to critical infrastructure. The foundation of homeland security risk assessments has evolved from Bernoulli's expected utility theory (EUT) through and combined with the principles of Bayesian's belief networks, probable maximum loss (PML) theory, and game theory (Lewis, 2015). These methods morphed and evolved and led to the simplistic approach to risk analysis of:

$$R = T \times V \times C \tag{16.1}$$

As briefly discussed in Chapter 4, risk is determined by threats (T) involved, vulnerabilities (V) caused by the gaps in the security measures in place, and consequences (C) resulting from the threats and vulnerabilities. This can be quantified, but the principles and relationships provide a basis and understanding of the correlation among the components.

There are many risk assessment models used for various purposes. The CARVER + Shock and Operations Risk Management (ORM) methods have been used for military applications, and the Risk Analysis and Vulnerability Assessment (RAVA) is used for federal government nonmilitary uses. Given the rise in cyber hacking, the Threat, Vulnerability, Risk model (TVR) is a method that has an application to the computer industry. As protective measures increase the robustness in and resilience of security measures and hardening targets, softer targets (e.g., commercial uses) that have the potential of impacting the economy and instilling fear become attractive (Cupp and Spight, 2007). The underlying premises of these models could be used as guiding principles to assess the risk of a terrorist placing a weapon of mass destruction (WMD) in a container destined to the United States to impact mainstream America (Gordon, 2018).

The PRA was originally used to assess the risk to the nuclear power industry for a range of events, to include equipment failure and terrorist attack. For the nuclear power industry, the threat is the probability of an attack, vulnerability is the probability of the attack being successful, and the consequences of an attack can have varied units of measure (Lewis, 2015). Threat-asset pairs are used in this technique because different assets have different threats and vulnerabilities and, thus, consequences. For example, a vehicle borne improvised explosive device (VBIED) would likely have different consequences when employed in a tunnel than if deployed in a port intermodal container yard. In a tunnel, the consequences could include significant casualties, extensive damage, and possible long-term denial of an important transportation node. In a port intermodal container yard, the impact would likely be limited to damage, minor casualties, and economic loss. Just think of a VBIED attack in the Ted Williams Tunnel under Boston Harbor versus at the Conley Intermodal Terminal nearby.

Risk assessment models are essentially focused on analytically or subjectively determining risk. A method or framework whereby minimizing and mitigating risk is determined on a "real-time" basis is what would benefit the transportation industry. As discussed previously, cost, resource availability, data intensiveness, and computer and analytical expertise are just a few of the reasons the industry would benefit from a simple "user-friendly" model (Gordon, 2018).

Many assessment approaches and models appear to be more focused on the process and analytics, rather than the risk and minimizing and mitigating it on a "real-time" basis.

Models are often complex, data and resource intensive and cumbersome to run. Therefore, the industry appears to be hesitant to use many of them. For example, the rail corridor risk management system (RCRMS) is one of them. A prior literature search on risk assessment models substantiates the tendency for complicated analytical models and, thus, the need for a simple risk model. The beneficiaries would be the industry the model is focused on and, for transportation, the expertise and institutional knowledge of the practitioner and partners in the supply chain (Gordon, 2018).

We discussed previously that the US Army's CARVER model is a targeting method and an acronym for Criticality, Accessibility, Recuperability, Vulnerability, Effect, and Recognizability, which are the factors in target selection in the analysis. It is a subjective analysis based on experience that utilizes values from 1 to 10 to determine effectiveness (Gordon, 2018). The principles of the CARVER model have been adapted for civilian and government use to protect assets and determine vulnerability. The U.S. Department of Agriculture and U.S. Food and Drug Administration, for example, adapted the CARVER model for assessing the risk and determining vulnerabilities in the Department of Homeland Security (DHS) food and agriculture critical infrastructure sector to address possible terrorist desires to inflict mass casualties and/or resulting psychological impacts, and adversely affect the economy (Bennett, 2018). Given the wide adaptation of the US Army CARVER model and its principles and simplicity, it will be used as a basis to assess risk and determine mitigation and protective measures for the intermodal maritime supply chain to reduce the risk associated with the delivery of a WMD or its components to US shores.

Risk analysis and assessments are more developed in the insurance and financial industries and less in homeland security. The dynamic nature of terrorism and lack of a historical database are major reasons for this. Therefore, and through 2007, homeland security risk analysis methods have mainly been probabilistic in nature relying on intelligence (Masse et al., 2007). The DHS approaches risk analysis and assessments holistically with the intent of implementing mitigation measures to "buy down" risk. DHS looks at this process as part of its Homeland Security Grant Program (HSGP) to understand the return on investment (ROI) of prioritizing protective measures, risk allocation, and developing strategies for assessing, mitigating, and managing risk. The approach is general in nature and focused on phased funding, and is built upon the relationship among risk, threats, vulnerabilities, and consequences.

The question is how do general risk assessment methods apply to transportation industry? Recognizing that critical infrastructure and associated risks are important in and to and from ports, a risk analysis, such as the Blue Ribbon Panel Method for tunnels, could provide a "bridge" to a transportation focused risk assessment (U.S., 2003).

Transportation risk assessment models

When looking at the application of risk assessment models to transportation, there is a wide range of models. Brian Bennett discussed the CARVER model as a method of looking at the interrelationships among assets, threat, vulnerabilities, and protection measures (Bennett, 2018). The threats and vulnerabilities, as they apply to the port environment, were previously discussed in Chapter 4.

Rutgers University developed a PRA to quantify the likelihood and consequences of a crude oil release accounting for route and train-specific characteristics based on the 2013 Lac-Megantic Bakken crude oil train derailment and resulting Federal Railroad Administration's (FRA) rule (Liu, 2016). In a book on transportation security utilizing intelligent transportation systems, several methods of assessing risk critical to transportation infrastructure were discussed (Fries et al., 2009). The approach to the Blue Ribbon Panel Method is based on probability, occurrence, vulnerability, and asset importance. A fault-tree analysis was also discussed, which can be both quantitative and qualitative, and focused on infrastructure failure resulting from a deliberate attack. The Monte Carlo method of analysis is also introduced in the book to establish mathematical solutions where there are multiple dynamic factors. Finally, the Weibull Hazard Model discussed in the book is based on the statistical distribution of the variables as a means of assessing changing hazards based over time. These analysis methods are not simple and require complex analyses (Gordon, 2018).

Many models on aviation risk found are focused on the risk at Transportation Security Administration (TSA) checkpoints. The TSA Risk Management Analysis Tool or RMAT is a simulation model that looks at adversary and defender roles and actions to address the risk to commercial aviation. The model is data intensive with about 4300 input variables and a reliance on a large number of uncertain parameters (Morrall et al., 2012). The data intensiveness makes the model framework unsuitable for a practitioner-focused risk assessment framework or model. On the landside of transportation, the mandated FRA's RCRMS was developed to evaluate routing alternatives for hazmat and reduce the risk of a major incident (49 CFR 172.820, 2008). RCRMS was built around rail risk analysis factors found in 49 CFR 172.820, Appendix D, and includes 27 factors to be considered in the analysis of routing risk. The factors are centered around the physical characteristics of the route(s), operations, safety measures, regulatory and procedural measures, and threats and vulnerabilities (Gordon and Young, 2016). Because of the cost and complexities associated with RCRMS, the railroads were "handcuffed" by the process with, among other things, limited routing options, and was viewed as another "unfunded mandate" by the federal government.

Maritime risk assessment models

Risk in the maritime security (MARSEC) context involves issues, threats, and disciplines all of which are interrelated (Edgerton et al., 2019). They include terrorism against ships and ports, supply chain security, human smuggling, contraband, cargo theft, hijacking and kidnapping, and piracy. Different solutions are required for the threats identified. The solutions range from international governmental treaties and codes to a greater maritime domain awareness. This can be accomplished by way of: (1) technology, (2) seagoing forces, such as navies and coast guards, (3) command and control, and (4) private sector programs to promote effective security management. These factors should be considered, as risk assessment methods are studied, and new approaches developed. Addressing supply chain security is important, as a simple risk assessment framework will require an in-depth knowledge of the maritime intermodal container supply chain and risk associated with it.

When looking at risk assessment models for the maritime environment and especially ports, one just has to look at the U.S. Coast Guard's (USCG's) Maritime Security Risk Assessment Method or MSRAM for a starting point (Brady, 2007). The benefit of MSRAM to the thesis of this chapter is the expected surety that the physical security measures in place at United States and foreign ports are effective, similar and verified, and that comparable risk assessment models are used. A disadvantage of MSRAM is much like that of RCRMS in that it is not readily available to industry, as the results are classified or sensitive security information (SSI), respectively. The concept of MSRAM is an adjunct to the USCG International Port Security Program in that it can be used to assesses security of foreign ports. MSRAM allows the USCG to prioritize its limited resources in protecting the ports and responding to evolving threats. Through MSRAM, the risk to, from, and within the ports can be determined.

In a paper on the vulnerability of the maritime transportation system (MTS), it was determined that there were no methods that specifically assessed MTS risk (Berle et al., 2011). It was further stated that supply chain risk assessment models only considered anticipated threats. The concept of the paper transferred the principles of a safety-oriented assessment to a maritime supply chain vulnerability assessment. This was based on the MTS's ability to withstand and recover from a disruption and most importantly to cope with low probability, high impact occurrences. The framework looked at failure modes across the MTS impacted by such failures. This included at terminals and intermodal connections. The paper indicated that there is limited research on maritime supply chain vulnerability. It further suggests that future research consider vulnerability of critical infrastructure in ports. The assessment approach, like that of CARVER and the focus of a simple model or framework, is subjective in nature relying on subject-matter experts (SME), experiential information and data, and that quantification is by way of subjectively assessing the impact basically as major or minor.

After the 1989 Exxon Valdez oil spill, there was concern among the USCG and stakeholders in Prince William Sound regarding the risk associated with the transportation of crude oil in the sound (Merrick et al., 2000). A probabilistic model was developed that addressed the risk to develop mitigation measures. Input to this probabilistic model was based on a simulation of oil transportation in Prince William Sound, data analysis, and SME assessments. This model, as discussed, loosely parallels the subjectivity of the U.S. Army CARVER model, but with more complex analyses and numeric outcomes.

In 2012, an analysis of security risks in the global container supply chain (GCSC) was conducted using the analytical hierarchy process or AHP (Bachkar et al., 2013). The research objective was to formulate a framework to address, mitigate, prioritize and evaluate risk, and validate the assumptions based on SME input. The paper cited that previous research identified six criteria associated with GCSC risk: measurement, environment, personnel, material, method, and machine. There are five steps in the assessment. They are structuring the decision problem, collecting input data, calculating priorities of the decision elements, deriving alternative values for decision-making, and validating the decision process. The assessment process is subjective with a measurement scale to evaluate the six criteria much like a decision matrix. The results of the analysis showed that the findings were consistent with previous studies on container security and that all security measures are understood by all of the participants and stakeholders in the supply chain and that they (the personnel) can be trusted.

In a 2006 report, the United Nations (UN) introduced a risk assessment and management framework that shifted the focus of maritime security from facilities to the supply chain, and reflect the global nature of the transportation network (United Nations, 2006). The assessment document examined the current layered approach to security and advocated for alternative risk assessment methods to reflect the complexity and integrated nature of the global transportation network. It was recognized that the complex regulatory environment and operating scenarios are key considerations and challenges, as well as being able to secure the supply chain. The assessment document cites a number of US and international regulations and programs and part of the process, to include the:

- International Maritime Organization's (IMO) International Ship and Port Facility Security (ISPS)[1] Code and its automated identification system (AIS) requirement;
- U.S. Customs and Border Protection's (CBP's) Container Security Initiative (CSI);
- U.S. CBP's Customs-Trade Partnership Against Terrorism (C-TPAT);
- USCG's MARSEC level and Maritime Transportation Security Act (MTSA) requirements.

---

[1] The International Ship and Port Facility Security Code is an amendment to the Safety of Life at Sea Convention and addresses minimum security requirements for ships, ports, and government agencies.

Also discussed are event and fault-tree analyses as ways of identifying and assessing the risk consistent with the ISPS Code accepted MARSEC levels as rating values. The UN in its research observed a number of issues regarding regulatory risk that could affect the assessment framework and include regulatory risk being reactive, that there is no real framework for nongovernmental risk assessments and that not many countries have taken on comprehensive regulatory assessments. When looking at the current risk environment, several things stood out to the UN and includes the understanding of the effect terrorists could have on the supply chain, shortcomings of traditional approaches to modeling threats, vulnerabilities and risk (e.g., probabilistic), and enumerating the cost/benefit among the supply chain participants. The UN report framework considers three components of risk: the environment, which addresses external sources (e.g., terrorists); organizational, which addresses supply chain uncertainty; and network-related, which addresses interactions between the stakeholders and the supply chain, which includes the uncertainties associated with trading with noncomplaint partners. In a deregulated environment, a balanced approach is essential to the efficiency of security requirements from an increasingly regulated environment.

Maritime security, whether at sea, in ports and connecting to and from ports, is a major concern. How to enhance security while not adversely affecting effectiveness and efficiency is a central issue. When addressing security and management, there are three foundational elements to ensure efficient and effective maritime security management: quality, risk, and business continuity. The major objective of the empirical research conducted by the Australian Maritime College was to identify factors important to effective maritime security (Thai, 2009). The model as developed had 13 dimensions, including security policy structure and stakeholder communications, and 24 associated factors, such as clear definition of risk levels, available resources, and contingency planning. The model's findings supported the validity of the 24 factors and that the handling and response to the incident are regarded as the most important part of the process, along with risk assessment, risk-based security mitigation strategies and plans, and management commitment. The model was detailed and statistical and difficult to present the research results in a "user-friendly" manner. This model along with the others discussed herein are not simple, are resource intensive requiring extensive data, and does not appear to be able to provide the practitioner and industry with a "hip pocket" assessment than can be used anywhere at any time to address threats and vulnerabilities to protect the supply chain.

What can be concluded from reviewing the risk assessment models presented herein? Although only a few are discussed, it can be concluded that a practitioner-focused model that is easy to use reflects the knowledge of and intuition from the practitioners, is not data intensive, process oriented, and analytically cumbersome would be the most useful. A model that looks at the entire supply chain is also desirable, as risk does not end when the ship is at sea. The risks also include the manufacturing process and "stuffing" the intermodal containers, the loading and landside movement from the manufacturer, vetting process, security at the foreign port, unloading at the US port and, then, the inland movement. All provide the opportunity for tampering.

Maritime CARVER framework

A Maritime CARVER routing risk assessment framework was developed from the concept and principles of the U.S. Army CARVER risk assessment method and developed and adapted to address the security of transporting intermodal maritime containers (Gordon, 2018). The difference between the U.S. Army and Maritime CARVER risk assessment frameworks is that the U.S. Army CARVER looks at the risk of attacking a target and the Maritime CARVER looks at the intermodal maritime container as being targeted for tampering particularly by smuggling a WMD or WMD component material in a container into the United States. The Maritime CARVER will identify the assets involved, physical security measures to and at the foreign port, the vetting of the manufacturer and exporter, nature of cargo, country of origin, and US government and international security measures employed at foreign ports and at sea. The potential points where risk could be heightened (e.g., Malacca Strait) or mitigated were also used in the framework development. Note that the greater likelihood of placing a WMD or WMD material in a container is prior to entering the foreign port and when being loaded on the ship.

The Maritime CARVER framework, as developed, uses a simple and subjective approach that is based on practitioner and subject matter expertise, such as port operators, ship captains, and freight forwarders, as input for the assessment. As discussed previously, traditional risk assessment methods are often data intensive focusing on severity and probability and, although beneficial, often result in modeling methods that are burdensome, which is not the objective of the framework. The Maritime CARVER framework uses minimal data, which are readily available as part of the intermodal maritime container supply chain. Probability consequence severity is introduced subjectively and based on the experience of the practitioners as to likelihood of occurrence. Numeric values are assigned, based on conditions associated with the input factors, which are intuitive in nature, manageable and not data intensive, and focused on assessing risk from the practitioner's perspective and is not analytically and theoretically driven.

The Maritime CARVER factors address the shipment of intermodal maritime containers to the United States recognizing the potential of how, when, or where risk could be heightened or mitigated. The framework approach is based on a targeted perspective, rather than targeting as in the U.S. Army's CARVER model. The factors are based on a given capability and resolve of terrorists to compromise an intermodal maritime container from the foreign manufacturer to its inland destination in the United States, and U.S., international and host nation measures to thwart the terrorist. The components of the model are:

- Chain of custody;
- Approach to targeting and monitoring;
- Routing;
- Vetting;
- Exposure;
- Regulatory.

The chain of custody factor or condition involves the surface transportation from the foreign manufacturer to the load center port, including via feeder ports, to the first or subsequent US ports. The principle of chain of custody, as with the TSA's regulation on chain of custody (49 CFR 1580), is that the more times a container is handled, the greater the risk. The risk extends from loading at the manufacturer to the surface modes to the handling of the intermodal maritime containers to and from ships and, to a lesser degree, on the voyage itself. Since intermodal maritime containers are not easily compromised at sea and the security measures in place prior to arriving at a US port, this factor will be limited to the landside transport from the foreign manufacturer to the port.

Approach to targeting and monitoring is focused on operations to and through the originating ports and is focused on the examination of container shipments based on participation in the U.S. CBP's targeting programs via in-country personnel, regional hubs, remotely relying on host governments, as well as other US government and international procedural security measures. This includes CBP's Container Security Initiative (CSI) and NTC-C (National Targeting Center-Cargo), and relying on in-country personnel for high risk shipments and US-based personnel for low risk shipments (GAO-13-764, 2013). This factor or condition is, in principle, based on governments partnering and participating in these programs and accompanying targeting measures, and is an indication of the involvement of CBP in inspecting and vetting the intermodal maritime containers.

Routing is the next factor and is the ocean voyage and its remoteness. The proximity of ships to land, especially in known areas of piracy (e.g., off the shores of Somalia), is another consideration, as the environs around straits and canals, and how they could contribute to the ease of boarding ships. On the other hand, canals and straits make monitoring and observing ship activity somewhat easy. Although a remotely feasible possibility, the method of connected or underway replenishment could provide an opportunity to tamper with an intermodal maritime container while at sea by way of smuggling a terrorist or WMD material onto a ship.[2]

Vetting is the screening of the manufacturer, exporter, shipping line(s), surface transportation providers, and cargo in the supply chain. The thoroughness of the vetting to include the strength and weakness of CBP's CSI, C-TPAT and 24-hour Advance Cargo Manifest Declaration Rule will be a consideration. At sea, US and international rules and regulations, which includes the USCG's AIS and 96-hour advanced notice of arrival (NOA) regulation (33 CFR 160.212), and CBP's Smart Box Initiative and Automated Targeting System (ATS) will also be considered in the subjective assessment. Cyber threats could also compromise the vetting process, as would insider threats involving personnel involved in the process.

The exposure factor focuses on the vulnerability of the physical facilities, to include ports and intermodal yards and terminals, based on the physical, to include perimeter and access control, intrusion detection, cameras, lighting, terrain and geographic features, and associated human elements. Cyber security for tracking vessels and its contents, at sea, in harbors, and ports, and managing container seals are also components of exposure. Insider threats are also a contributing factor to exposure via the ability to compromise the physical and human security measures in place.

The last factor, regulatory, involves US international and host nation or state regulatory processes governing port and maritime security, and the transportation of intermodal maritime containers. While each nation or state has its own regulations governing maritime transportation and operations, the IMO has enacted conventions and treaties that embrace those of the individual nations (International Maritime Organisation, 2020). When looking at intermodal maritime containers, IMO's Safety of Life at Sea (SOLAS) convention and its ISPS Code are particularly relevant. State signatories to IMO conventions and treaties, such as the Mutual Recognition Agreement (MRA), are compliant with US regulations governing maritime facilities, transportation, and operations. Therefore, this factor addresses host nation or state compliance with IMO conventions and treaties on the transportation of intermodal maritime containers.

For the purpose of building the framework, the analysis of a simulated route was used. It was based on a route from Shanghai, China though Pusan, South Korea to Houston, TX via the Panama Canal. Validation was via a case study for a route from a chemical manufacturer in Frankfurt, Germany, through the Port of Hamburg to Oakland, CA via the

---

[2] This occurred in June 2019 when cocaine was loaded aboard an MSC (Mediterranean Shipping Company) containership off the west coast of South America. It was interdicted by Customs and Border Protection and the United States Coast Guard in the Port of Philadelphia.

Ports of New York/New Jersey, Norfolk, NJ, and Charleston, SC, and Panama Canal. Both were based on actual routes and are depicted graphically in the figures, below - Fig. 16.1 for the simulated route and Fig. 16.2 for the case study.

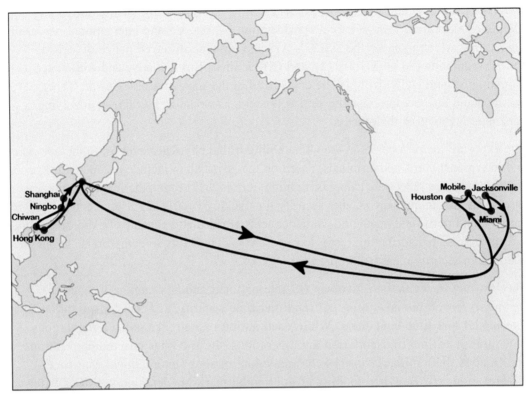

Figure 16.1
Simulation routing map (Gordon, 2018).

The Maritime CARVER framework utilizes tables of input criteria and conditions, much like that of the U.S. Army CARVER Method, to assign numeric values to reflect the risk associated with the specific condition. Based on a subjective assessment by expert practitioners, a maximum value of 10 can be assigned to each factor. A value of 10 equates to the riskiest condition for that factor. Since there are six factors, a maximum score of 60 is possible and reflects the riskiest condition, as the higher the value, the riskier the factor. The combined values of the factors can be used to evaluate different routes and conditions. The following table presents the chain of custody conditions and corresponding numeric values (Table 16.1).

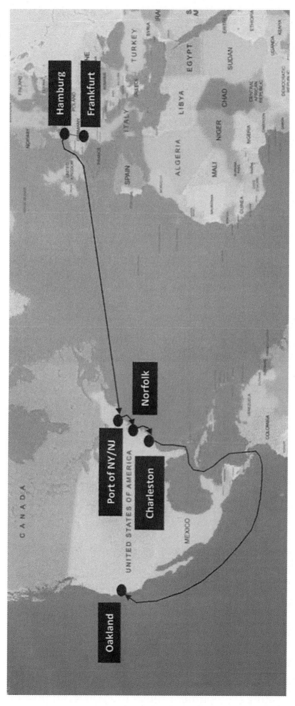

Figure 16.2
Case study routing map (Gordon, 2018).

Table 16.1: Chain of custody conditions and values.

Condition	Value
Combined rail and truck to feeder port via intermodal yards	9–10
Combined rail and truck to load center port via multiple intermodal yards	7–8
Combined rail and truck to load center port via intermodal yard	5–6
Direct rail or truck to feeder port from foreign manufacturer	3–4
Direct rail or truck to load center port from foreign manufacturer	1–2

In theory, once a ship is loaded, the container will not be handled and the chain of custody will be via the ship's officers and company officials. That is why chain of custody is limited to the land transportation to the port. The assessment of the routing risk from Frankfurt, Germany to Oakland, CA, is summarized in Table 16.2, below. The bold values in the table indicate the average risk numbers for (1) each risk component and (2) the entire route. Note that the route segment from the Port of New York/New Jersey to Norfolk, VA, and Charleston, SC, is not included. This is because the route segment is within US territorial waters, thus, exposure to risk is minimal.

Table 16.2: Maritime CARVER risk matrix for frankfurt to oakland route.

Frankfurt via ports of NY/NJ, Norfolk, and Charleston to Oakland							
Route segment	C	A	R	V	E	R	Risk no.
Manufacturer in frankfurt to port of Hamburg	2	4	8	2	2	2	20
Port of Hamburg to port of NY/NJ	2	2	4	2	2	4	16
Port of NY/NJ to Panama canal	4	4	6	2	2	2	20
Transiting Panama canal	2	2	8	2	6	2	22
Panama canal to Oakland	2	2	2	2	2	2	12
Component risk number	**2.4**	**2.8**	**5.6**	**2.0**	**2.8**	**2.4**	
Combined route risk number							**18.0**

The Maritime CARVER framework process starts with the development of the input information for the route segment and condition observed and ends with the selection and implementation of the best routing option. The steps are:

- Develop the input data from information obtained from importer, container line, or other supply chain partner, as appropriate.
- Determine the validity of the input data from the supply chain partners given the expertise of the provider(s) and source.
- Conduct the assessment using the validated information and input data.
- Rerun the assessment should a changed condition be encountered by any supply chain partner using the data and information reflecting the changed condition.
- Select lowest risk routing option based on security, although other factors could be considered in selecting the optimum route, to include supply chain duration and cost.

Note that multiple alternate routes could be run to plan for anticipated situations or conditions affecting the preferred route. Fig. 16.3, below, graphically depicts the assessment process.

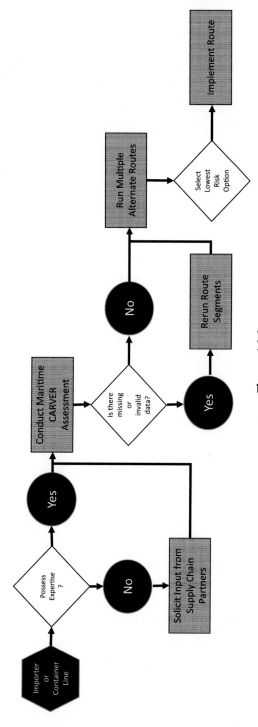

Figure 16.3

Maritime CARVER framework process (Gordon, 2018).

Other than the importer and container shipping line, other entities that may be involved in the assessment process, include, but are not limited to:

- Port authorities and operators;
- Land and maritime transportation providers;
- Manufacturers and suppliers;
- Exporters and freight forwarders.

Although not part of the supply chain, government agencies, such as CBP and the USCG, would be logical agencies to monitor the assessment process and be part of the vetting process. The IMO could also be a partner via their policies and expertise. These partners would help ensure that the assessment process is proper and the information used is valid.

How does this benefit the industry?

What does assessing the risk to the intermodal maritime container supply chain and, in particular the ease and user friendliness of the model or framework, mean to the industry?

The Maritime CARVER framework is intended to be used to determine the riskiness of a route to ensure that the industry partners in the supply chain (manufactures, transportation companies, and exporters/importers) are properly vetted. It is also intended to be an aid to helping the supply chain partners select ports based on physical, human, and cyber security measures that are robust and resilient and consistent with US and international maritime security programs.

How can the industry use the framework and what benefits will have? The framework is designed to reflect how the supply chain partners choose and government organizations protect the supply chain with the goal of minimizing the risk of a WMD landing on US shores for onward movement inland. The framework can be adapted, and provides value added to minimize the risk of smuggling contraband or a range of criminal activities associated with maritime intermodal containers. Specifically, the following will be considered as they apply to the supply chain:

- Route selection to identify and avoid, when and where possible, areas of known threats, such as piracy, and where constraints exist, such as through canals and straits.
- Selecting ports that are secure, to include the land and maritime transportation to them from the manufacturers.
- Selecting manufacturers, exporters, and freight forwarders, based on geographic location and trustworthiness with regard to security.

- Selecting land transportation routes and carriers that minimize the handling of the containers, are trustworthy and provide the most direct routes to the port. This also applies to coastal routes from feeder to load center ports.
- How the framework can be used to complement US government and the intermodal maritime security community practices and programs, as a tool to address security gaps.
- How, unlike the railroad's RCRMS and other complicated analytical and objective risk assessment models, this framework would be easy to operate and used in a timely manner and not be resource intensive and cost prohibitive.
- Although a factor in route selection, cost is not addressed in the framework because it (the framework) is focused on security and the impact of deterring WMDs landing on US shores.

The goal of the Maritime CARVER routing risk assessment framework is to develop a simple methodology that addresses and minimizes the risk of a WMD, drugs, and other contraband landing on US shores. Further and as a value added of this framework to the industry, it could be extended to detect tainted foodstuffs (e.g., produce from South America) and, thus, the potential to "weaponize" items in the food supply chain.

Where do we go from here?

The benefits of the Maritime CARVER routing risk framework are simple. It provides a simple and user-friendly process that a ship's captain, manufacturer's distribution manager, consignee, CBP Port Director, etc. can use to assess the risk of the supply chain and its segments. It would allow for a "mid-course" adjustment should an incident require diverting any part of the supply chain and its transportation network. It allows the supply chain partners to work with regulators on risk and "game" alternate routes early in the process, in a timely and cost-effective manner in support of decision-making and as part of route selection.

Understanding the risk associated with the maritime intermodal container supply chain and available alternatives and their advantages and disadvantages is important. What else would benefit the United States and the world as a whole? Although there are many avenues for additional research and study, several can be considered as important, based on today's risk environment. They include:

- The cost and economic impacts and how they influence route and supply chain partner selection to mitigate the risk. This includes consumer impacts and insurance, which are a consideration when evaluating the viability of a supply chain partner or route.

- Technology and cyber based systems are an important adjunct to vetting, security measures, and monitoring and navigation. Research into how cyber attacks and compromises impact the risk associated with the maritime intermodal container supply chain and security measures to be employed should be considered.

- This framework is not exclusive to deterring WMDs from being smuggled into the United States. It could be used to deter and detect drugs or other contraband. Future investigation should look at the particulars of drugs and other contraband and ways of detecting them, as well as the associated vetting processes. Either a separate framework, based on the Maritime CARVER model, or combining the two into one application is a possibility that should be explored. However, the differences between the uses (WMDs vs. drugs and contraband) must be clearly understood when considering a uniform approach to the framework. This is because the approach(es) and method(s) may not be as similar or different as anticipated.

- Further research by the industry could look at more and diverse routes to provide a more global perspective. This would bring into play the areas and conditions in the framework allowing for the diverse conditions and global issues.

- Data obtained from the Maritime CARVER could be compiled to establish patterns, trends, and databases to be used as a foundation for intermodal maritime container routing and supply chain analyses, assessment frameworks, and techniques.

- Consideration should be given to developing the framework for a dashboard application to be used on PCs and tablets for easy use in the field and at sea to provide "field expedient" assessments.

The framework discussed herein is fundamentally theory building, rather than theory testing. Having established the Maritime CARVER framework for selecting service providers, ports, and routes, the next step would be to assess what methodologies are being employed under various scenarios. To effectively do this, a survey methodology could be developed to: (1) assess the policies and procedures and efficacy of the chain of custody for the supply chains, (2) determine how the selection of ports of loading can be accomplished, and (3) engage trade and selecting providers of transportation services. The assessment of risk of international trade is a significant undertaking in that there are a numerous importers, exporters, and combinations of transportation providers and trade intermediaries. The way these are aligned will remain problematic, both for the managers of the respective supply chains and the government regulatory authorities.

References

49 CFR 172.820, 2008. Additional Planning Requirements for Transportation by Rail.

Bachkar, K., Won, K., Szmerekovsku, J., 2013. An analytical hierarchy process framework to mitigate security risk in the global container supply chain. J. Manage. Eng. Integrat. 30–42.

Bennett, B.Z., 2018. Understanding, Assessing, and Responding to Terrorism: Protecting Critical Infrastructure and Personnel, second ed. Wiley Publishing.

Berle, O., Asbjornslett, B., Rice, J., 2011. Formal Vulnerability Assessment of a maritime transportation system. J. Reliab. Eng. Syst. Safe.

Brady, B., 2007. The maritime security risk analysis model. Coast Guard J. Safe. Sec. 64 (1).

Cupp, S., Spight, M., 2007. A homeland security model for assessing US domestic threats. In: Center for Homeland Defense and Security. Naval Postgraduate School.

Edgerton, M., Shapiro, L., Maras, M., 2019. "Maritime Security: Acceptable Risks", *Encyclopedia Of Security And Emergency Management*. Springer.

FM 34-36, 1991. "Special Operations Forces Intelligence and Electronic Warfare Operations", Appendix D, Target Analysis Process, U.S. Army.

Fries, R., Chowdhury, M., Brummond, J., 2009. Transportation Infrastructure Security: Utilizing Intelligent Transportation Systems. Wiley Publishing.

GAO-13-764, 2013. Supply Chain Security: DHS Could Improve Cargo Security by Periodically Assessing Risks from Foreign Ports. Government Accountability Office.

Gordon, G., 2018. "Intermodal Maritime Container Security: A Multifactor Framework for Assessing Routing Risk". University of Massachusetts Lowell.

Gordon, G., Young, R.R., 2016. Hazmat routing: alternate routing risk analysis. In: Joint Rail Conference. American Society of Mechanical Engineers and Mineta Transportation Institute.

International Maritime Organization, June 6, 2020. Introduction (To Conventions). http://www.imo.org/en/About/Conventions/Pages/Home.aspx.

Joint Publication 3-05.2, 2003. Joint Tactics, Techniques, and Procedures for Special Operations Targeting and Mission Planning, Appendix A, Target Analysis Methodology, Section 3, CARVER Evaluation Criteria, Pages A-2 to A-6.

Lewis, T., 2015. Critical Infrastructure Protection in Homeland Security: Defending a Networked Nation, second ed. -13: 978-1118817636.

Liu, X., 2016. Development of a Risk Assessment Tool for Rail Transport of Flammable Energy Resources. Rutgers, The State University of New Jersey, USDOT. Report CAIT-UTC-NC16.

Masse, T., O'Neil, S., Rollins, J., 2007. The Department of Homeland Security's Risk Assessment Methodology: Evolution, Issues, and Options for Congress. Congressional Research Service.

Merrick, J., van Dorp, J., Harrald, J., Mazzuchi, T., Spahn, J., 2000. A systems approach to managing oil transportation risk in Prince William sound. Syst. Eng. 3 (3).

Morral, A.R., et al., 2012. Modeling Terrorism Risk to the Air Transportation System. RAND Corporation.

Schnaubelt, C., Larson, E., Boyer, M., 2014. Vulnerability Assessment Method Pocket Guide, A Tool for Gravity Analysis. RAND Corporation Arroyo Center.

Thai, V., 2009. Effective maritime security: conceptual model and empirical evidence. Marit. Pol. Manag. 36 (2), 147−163.

United Nations, 2006. Maritime Security: Elements of an Analytical Framework for Compliance Measurement and Risk Assessment, UNCTAD/SDTW/TLB/2005/4.

U.S. Department of Transportation, Federal Highway Administration, 2003. Recommendations for Bridge and Tunnel Security.

Vellani, K., Butterworth, H., 2007. "Strategic Security Management: A Risk Assessment Guide for Decision Makers", Chapter 6 − Risk Assessments.

PART VI

The way forward: Recommendations

CHAPTER 17

Systems considerations for Intermodal Maritime Security operations

James H. Schreiner

Department of Systems Engineering, United States Military Academy, West Point, NY, United States

"Systems Thinking is a discipline for seeing wholes. It is framework for seeing interrelationships rather than things, for seeing patterns of change rather than static snapshots".
—Peter Senge, The Fifth Discipline (Seng, 2006).

"A System is a network of interdependent components that work together to try to accomplish the aim of system. A system must have an aim. A system must be managed. The secret is cooperation between components toward the aim of the organization".
—W. Edwards Deming, The New Economics (Deming, 2018).

The Maritime Domain and its associated operations challenge governance and oversight by their ever-evolving layers of domestic and international complexity. The first chapter in this book described intermodal transfer, buyer and seller exchanges, global location, and the speed of technology advancement. The chapter described these elements of a global maritime system in the context of trade goods and policies which are led and managed by a multitude of professional stakeholders across the supply chain. Shared *Situational Awareness* of the domain by these individuals to capture this dynamic complexity is only as good as the frequency in which information and intelligence are gathered, analyzed, and presented. This assumes that intelligence is in usable form to both practitioners within the network and those who design and implement ways and means to achieve objectives. Intermodal Maritime Security can, therefore, be described as a complex system of many stakeholders and nodes operating in a changing environment, and as such, reflection and consideration of concepts in Systems Theory can be helpful. This chapter will present principles in *Systems Theory* which might assist in simplifying the "so what" of the complex system so that innovative design and continuous improvement might be realized.

Intermodal Maritime Security. https://doi.org/10.1016/B978-0-12-819945-9.00017-4

Descriptions and definitions of System Theory, referred to as system science at times, are plentiful and slightly vary based on the domain, or type of system under examination by the practitioner who wrote about it. A useful description for the Maritime Security System could begin as an "interdisciplinary study of interrelated systems across multiple domains which results in knowledgeable action, and is governed by models, principles, and laws" (Von Bertalanffy and Sutherland, 1974). The typical strategic planner or practitioner might not find this definition overtly helpful, but the dissection of its components and definitions might be. Defining the key concepts of Systems Theory better allows for ideation in "next steps" for improving future Maritime Risk Mitigation strategies and enabling models. This chapter focuses on the concepts and disciplines behind Systems Theory, thus highlighting a method of thinking about and designing enhancements for the future system.

System definitions and key concepts

To begin, a *system* is defined by the International Council on Systems Engineering (INCOSE) as "an integrated set of elements that accomplishes a defined objective" (Sebok, 2020). Inherent to this definition is the idea of an "element." Elements can include products, processes, people (or stakeholders), information (data), techniques, facilities, services, and other support or enabling. Several models have been presented including the supply-chain operations reference (SCOR) model which allows visibility of "types" of stakeholders relative to tasks which overlap along the supply chain in the physical, informational, and financial "flows" (Reference Figs. 17.1 and 17.2). The Global Maritime Intelligence Integration Plan (IIP) for example captures the complexity associated with the informational flows as an enabler to understanding risk and enabling the construction of a layered defense. Each of the flows and each of their elements form subsystems within the overarching system of Maritime Security, and each subsystem evolves or learns as a result of changing conditions around, and interactions with adjacent systems.

This Maritime Security System of Systems (SoS) is dynamic in nature. *Complex Adaptive Systems (CAS)* can learn from their environment and adapt to changing conditions. Intelligence teams working in the Maritime Security Environment are representative of a CAS as they are inherently one entity within the composite of the complete system which must adapt within its ecosystem. In essence, the ability to understand and control a system is difficult due to the evolution in how it performs given the changing environment and adjacent systems (Holland, 1992). *Environmental factors* influencing change include but are not limited to technological, economic, political, legal, health and safety, social, security, ecological, cultural, historical, moral/ethical, organizational, and emotional factors directly or indirectly interconnected to the system (Parnell et al., 2011a—e). In Maritime Security, the global economy itself represents a CAS as the US government must acknowledge mutual dependence with changing nation-state policies so that exchanges are topical and relevant for consistent and effective implementation of security policy strategy.

The *stakeholders* who influence the environment and have a role in designing and managing systems require defining as well. Stakeholders vary in the power they wield to influence, their legitimacy to make claims, and their urgency to affect the present or future aspects of a system (Parnell et al., 2011a—e). Making distinctions about the taxonomy in which they fit guides efforts to gather insights into the system and manage relational risk. Stakeholder types include decision authorities, clients, owners, users, consumers, and interconnected persons or organizations (Parnell et al., 2011a—e). Aggregating these stakeholders into the larger categories of manufacturers, importers, exporters, Maritime Security Policymakers, and/or agencies could be helpful.

Systems Thinking (ST) is the discipline which provides an iterative mental framework allowing the individual to "think" through how a complex or CAS interacts with the environment and other adjacent systems under uncertain, complex, and ambiguous conditions (Cabrera and Cabrera, 2015a,b). ST begins prior to defining the problem and endures throughout the system life cycle. While the global supply chain and security systems could conceivably trace back to WWII, the exponential growth in complexity of the global marketplace led to the formal need for the 2002 Maritime Domain Awareness (MDA) program as the catalyst for an ST approach (NSMS, 2005g). In the ST definition, an "iterative mental framework" calls for a *mental model* creation which captures an approximation of reality and allows for real-world *feedback* to inform the model (Fig. 17.1). In essence, this simple ST model allows for system design and adaptation for security strategy ways and means to be assessed through shared awareness of the system and its dynamics.

Maritime domain awareness using systems thinking

Acknowledging that the Intermodal Maritime Security System is at least complex as, but often takes on the attributes of a CAS, it can be difficult to understand where to begin in developing a mental model approximation. Because a system is complex does not mean that its analysis is incapable of adherence to simple rules and graphical portrayals. Application of soft-systems methodologies and tools are extremely helpful in capturing a mental model which in turn allow for shared situational awareness and understanding of the complex system.

The Cabrera Research Laboratory at Cornell University has developed four basic rules—Distinctions, Systems, Relationships, and Perspectives or DSRP which can help the Maritime professional think about the mental model structure (Cabrera and Cabrera, 2015a,b). The four rules (below bullet definitions and descriptions) allow for the system to be thoroughly captured utilizing ST principles thus enabling a most accurate representation of reality in the form of a mental model. To examine each rule:

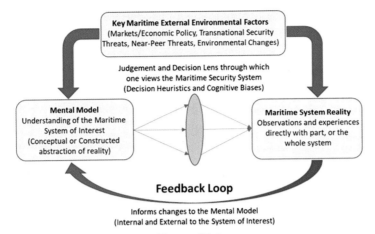

Figure 17.1

Mental models approximate the real world; feedback loops and the environment.

- (D) *Distinction Rule: Any idea or thing that can be distinguished from the other ideas or things it is with.* A key element when analyzing a system or a system need resides with an understanding of its *system boundary* as shown in Fig. 17.2. What is the system of interest (SoI) being looked at, and what is external of it? In order to enhance the system, one must understand its boundary to avoid uncontrollable complexity. The system boundary allows for proper defining of inputs, outputs, mechanisms, and controls thus supporting system design and development (Parnell et al., 2011a–e). An example of using boundary distinctions would be in alignment of ways and means for the US Maritime Security Program versus what actions international partners might pursue. International partner policy and actions might become inputs into the SoI for the United States, and, thus, reinforce the need for a feedback loop to update mental models which capture the system in its natural environment.

- (S) *Systems Rule: Any idea or thing can be split into parts or lumped into a whole.* This rule acknowledges that no complex system exists in isolation, but that by understanding the higher, adjacent, and subsystems of the SoI, the thinker can understand implications of design or strategy on others. An example of this would be in the establishment of a Maritime Operational Threat Response Plan in which both state and the federal interagency would have to nest actions alongside legal jurisdictions and technology. Most organizations retain what is known as a organizational hierarchy chart to show relative positions of units or individuals. The Systems Rule asks for a similar understanding of systems.

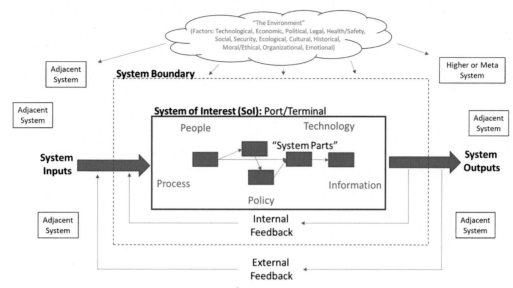

Figure 17.2

System of Interest in relation to the system boundary, feedback loops, adjacent systems, and the environment.

- (R) *Relationships Rule: Any idea or thing can relate to other things or ideas.* Beyond understand the fit of a SoI relative to other systems, the nature of the relationship to other systems is critical. Are there lines of authority or simply lines of influence? Can cognitive thoughts or motivation be understood? The Domestic Maritime Outreach Plan represents why one would want to understand relationships so that ways and means can once again be properly aligned to achieving the system aim.
- (P) *Perspectives Rule: Any thing or idea can be the point of view of a perspective.* Development of system boundaries, understanding relationships, and capturing all systems typically provide one point of view. Investments in stakeholder research to the extent possible can ensure that relationships between nodes in a system are not ill-informed but offer diversity of perspective. For example, gaining the perspectives of the customers in the SCOR model would help to inform the system design for delivery and return processes and policy.

The DSRP framework rules allow for thorough understanding of systems as a foundation of mental models, avoiding bias, and describing logic which could influence new system design or continuous improvement of existing systems. While there is a tie to a visual representation in the Cabrera Research Laboratory using Plectica[1] software, a second methodology provides a complementary approach to dissecting the SoI.

Representing the Maritime SoI could be accomplished through Boardman's Soft Systems Methodology and its systems-diagrams or "system-i-grams" (Blair et al., 2007). System-i-grams assist in the analysis of interdependencies and relationships between functions and actors. They provide "a basis for systems architecting, in terms of both enterprise integration (reliant on business process architecting) and technology systems development (reliant on requirements management)" (Gorod et al., 2008).The tool shown generically in captures a series of function and actor nodes (represented in the ovals) and actions/relationships links (represented by the lines and action descriptors). The visual provides a mental model for understanding the 'fit' and relationship of the System of Interest (SoI), highlighted in Fig. 17.3 relative to other systems, and could become an enabling model which drives research and the pursuit of alternative perspectives if a relationship is not well understood. The system-i-gram also can benefit future efforts to model causal loops through System Dynamics approaches.

The clarity of the relationships captured in the actions word 'links', and the complexity of these models can quickly complicate understanding for the Systems Thinker. In Fig. 17.3, an initial model presents a system-i-gram representation of the combined financial, informational, and physical flows between major actor nodes in the intermodal maritime supply chain. The flows in this figure capture only the exporter to importer perspective, or from the global market into the U.S. market system. It may be helpful for analysis to have one overarching system-i-gram, and then a series of complementary system-i-grams to dive deeply into the nuanced inputs and outputs for the SoI. For purposes of this model, one can quickly see how the 'layers', or sub-systems within the U.S. government can be captured to generalize so that the System of Interest, or Local Port Authorities can be examined in the context of the 'meta-system', or the Maritime Transportation Security System.

Considerations for the intermodal Maritime Security System

The United States' position in the global marketplace demands systems which are sensitive and agile to addressing its growing magnitude and complexity. As presented in

---

[1] https://www.plectica.com/publications. Plectica allows you to create visual maps. The core unit of a map is a card, which can represent people, tasks, objects, or ideas. These cards can exist on their own or be nested inside another card. A card can be connected to any other card with one or more relationship lines, and those relationships can be defined through a relationship card. A map can be viewed and edited by multiple people at the same time.

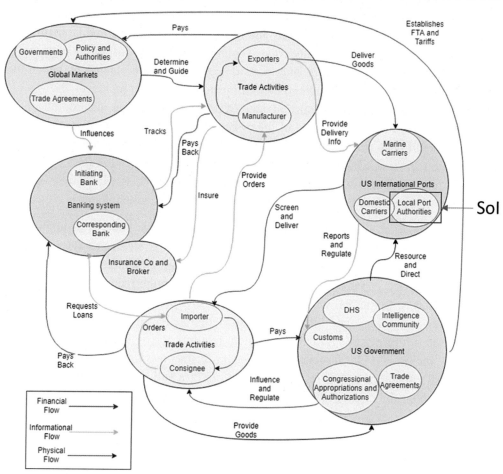

Figure 17.3
Example System-i-Gram with system of interest to study for Maritime Security.

Appendix A of Chapter 1, 95 percent of overseas US trade, which is expected to double within 20 years, transit across its 361 public ports of entry including 113,000,000 passengers and 32,000,000 vehicles each year (MTS Section). Comprehending the emergent qualities of this complex adaptive system will change yearly, monthly, and perhaps even daily without a systems approach to assessing the current state and designing future solutions. ST approaches represent the foundation by which analytical approaches and applications of system dynamics, system engineering, data science, and basic security strategy can best serve the decision-making organization. The following paragraphs simply represent some of the considerations for the Maritime Security Professional or Executive who is in search of improvements.

Defining the System Problem: Systems Theory and Systems Thinking—The brief exploration in Sections System definitions and key concepts and Maritime Domain Awareness using systems thinking into what is a large and diverse discipline of systems theory and ST concepts, approaches, and methodologies provide a manner by which the Maritime system can be understood and communicated. They also represent an opportunity to clearly baseline the current state of the systems so that ideation efforts can seek to improve portions or the whole of the system under examination. Adoption of these approaches should be at the forefront and nested within future methodologies as a foundational effort from which all discussions are facilitated. The Intermodal Maritime Security System itself, and systems within, require this step or design improvements to the system will risk missing the strategy's objective or serving its stakeholders.

Achieving alignment in Ends-Ways-Means—A strategy is only as good as its alignment of resources (means) enabled by a series of methods, tactics, or strategies (ways) to achieve strategic means (ends). Alignment of the strategy requires an understanding of the system and all its complexity, captured in a model, and updated through measurements by iterative exposure with the real world. How does the alignment of "means" such as people, process, policy, technology, and information/knowledge deliver the system from current state to a desired future state? Strategy alignment requires active ST approaches and should be all inclusive. Peter Drucker's *The Theory of Business* describes elements of ST and strategy alignment of means in his "specification of a valid theory of the business." Assumptions about the environment, mission, and core competencies must fit reality.

1. Assumptions in all three areas have to fit one another.
2. The theory of the business must be known and understood throughout the organization.
3. The theory of the business has to be tested constantly.

A portion of defining and analyzing the problem statement using ST should also include the capture of the future state including a measurement and data strategy. Measurement of the "future state" (Strategic Objective) requires metrics, ideally binary in nature (Cabrera and Cabrera, 2018). In the Department of Defense (DoD) Joint community, JP5-0, Joint Planning (June 16, 2017) presents a structured look into the development of strategy through operational designs and approaches including the importance of measurement. Generically, Key Performance Parameters/Indicators (KPP/KPIs) in Fig. 17.4 measure characteristics and attributes of a system; Measures of Effectiveness (MoEs) looks to track how well a system carries out the overall goals for the customer (Shah and Nowicin, 2020).

An example of this might be with emergent nonintrusive inspection technologies. KPP/KPIs could represent the system's reliability and affordability in detection of radiological or chemical threats while MoEs could represent detection rates or time to employ.

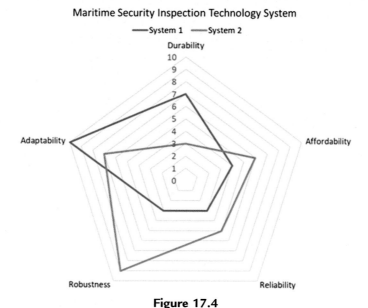

Figure 17.4

Kiviat chart for visualizing key performance parameters/indicators. *Source: Shah, Nowicin, 2020. A Guide to the Engineering Management Body of Knowledge, fifth ed. Domain 9. pp. 227.*

The KPP/KPIs and MoEs then allow for comparison to other systems through metrics such as weight, speed of inspection scan, and data transfer rates. The purpose of employing metrics is rooted in tracking progress toward achievement of objectives, and at the same time understanding trade-offs of system designs to support decision-making and resourcing of new systems.

Employing Value-Focused Thinking to achieve Decision Quality—CAS and their components (flows) can evolve with pace. In the design of systems to support Maritime Security, it is, therefore, imperative to use ST theory to develop system solutions which might exist in some form, while also imagining systems which might be. If a Port for example is looking to develop an Information and Knowledge Management (IKM) System to track physical commodity flow, it might be simple to begin my looking at Commercial Off-the-Shelf (COTS) technologies first to determine how each alternative might meet the need. This represents an "Alternative Focused Thinking" (AFT) approach and is naturally how we might frame a decision problem (Keeney, 1996). Values represent "principles" used for evaluation of action/inaction and alternatives about our system (Keeney, 1996). A Value-Focused Thinking (VFT) approach builds off of an ST rooted, strategy enabled approach to designing or improving a Maritime Security System. Table 17.1 provides just one example of thinking through values prior to any design and evaluation efforts of a new IKM system. The value categories are comprehensive, but not all inclusive. Dependent on

Table 17.1: Value Categories for use in Developing Maritime Security Systems.

Examples of a value system in maritime security	
Values	**Examples**
Ethics	Does not compromise the completeness of data capture of commodities through the port.
Traits	Must be useful, easy to use, and intuitive to all within the port from executives to operators.
Characteristics	Desire a highly scalable Information and Knowledge Management (IKM) system with cloud storage capacity to grow as inputs/outputs to the port ebb/flow.
Priorities	Interoperability of the port IKM system with other systems in the Maritime Security System takes priority over cost considerations.
Value trade-offs	System usability of interface design and storage capacity will require testing and evaluation of prototypes.
Attitude toward risk	The risks are spending time thoroughly migrating data from legacy systems outweigh loss in training of current staff.

the nature of the system being developed, so long as the values afford the decision-maker and team the ability to think about solutions to the problem in a constraint-free manner, then VFT is being achieved.

The ability to achieve decision quality in the choice of a new system incorporates a VFT approach and clarity of thought in a moment of time which can be guided by six elements as seen in Fig. 17.5. Decision quality is the quality of a decision at the moment a decision is made, regardless of its outcome (Howard, 1988). Quality of a decision is a direct function of how informed the decision maker is in an uncertain environment. An Intermodal Maritime Security system decision ought to ensure System Thinking and VFT are inherent to the process of evaluating candidate system solutions, and each of these are integrated parts of assessing decision quality.

Employing the right system "means" to understand and improve your system—This chapter began by revealing that systems theory approaches ultimately result in "knowledgeable action" for the system. That action resides in the decisions to design and implement solutions for the system. At the same time, alignment of the "right" human skills and enabling technologies play critical roles in the decision-making experience, and these capabilities may or may not be inherent to the Maritime Security Organization conducting the analysis, design, or implementation. There are many applications or

Figure 17.5

Decision quality framework for system evaluation. *Source: Abbas, A.E., Howard, R.A., 2015. Foundations of Decision Analysis. Pearson Higher Ed.*

disciplines which might be useful for the Maritime Security System community including:

- System Dynamics (SD) is a study to look at the behavior of a complex system using stocks, flows, feedback loops, and time delays (Sterman, 2010). The SD model can help decision-makers understand behaviors within the SCOR model given a changing environment in which the supply chain and three parallel flows reside. "Scoring" candidate solutions on their performance in a current or future environment is powerful in testing assumptions, and ensuring decision quality is achieved for decisions are made. Human dynamics can be modeled in this approach which could enhance understanding of outreach and coordination strategies.

- Systems Engineering (SE) is an interdisciplinary approach and means to enable the realization of successful systems which focuses on problem definition, customer needs, functionality early in the development cycle, requirements generation, design synthesis, and system validation (Parnell et al., 2011a–e). Providing clarity of what the system shall do (requirements) in the context of its life cycle ensures that they perform well, and ST is inherent throughout the life cycle. Most life cycle models include similar steps in establishing the system need, developing the systems concept, design and development, deployment, operation, and retirement of the system. Each of these steps can incorporate a host of subdiscipline means for delivery. The "VEE" model of SE as captured by the U.S. Department of Transportation in Fig. 17.6 receives use across most federal organizations (FHWA, 2003). The "VEE" model represents the key steps in the systems life cycle from problem definition (left side) through the system design, implementation, testing, and integration (right side).

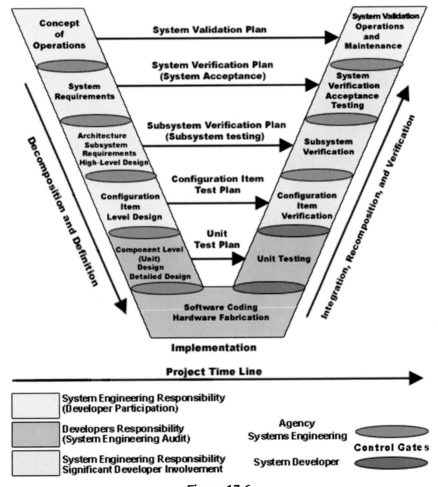

Figure 17.6

United States Department of Transportation (USDOT) systems engineering "VEE". *Source: https:// ops.fhwa.dot.gov/freewaymgmt/publications/cm/handbook/chapter7.htm.*

- Data Science and Data Analytics represent fields which are foundational to all organizations as the amount of big data grows exponentially, and in particular across the rapidly expanding global supply chain. Data Science works with the cleaning and preparation of structured and unstructured data while Data Analytics examines that data to draw insights and meaningful conclusions. The MTS Section 101 findings to Congress from Appendix A in Chapter 1 describe a complex system capable of producing extremely large data sets, or "Big Data,"[2] across the system requiring analytical support for assessment, design, and improvements in the Maritime Security System. Employment of these disciplines will assist in understanding the state of the system better (ST) and assist in the decision worthy nature of the data for new system design or improvements.

Summary

The Intermodal Maritime domain and its security systems are CAS by nature, and further complicated by the rapidly changing global environment. Looking across this system as a whole and all its parts requires shared situational awareness which benefits from regular feedback loops to ensure the model approximates reality. The use of an ST approach provides the foundation to consider how an entity in the system defines the problem, develops a traceable and measurable strategy which is aligned, is focused on value creation and decision quality, and ultimately choses the right "means" to improve the system. Each consideration presented merely skims the surface of its discipline, but is meant to highlight that the volatile, uncertain, complex, and ambiguous global risk to the supply chain can be somewhat tamed through the application of systems theory and the many complementary disciplines and concepts. Every aspect of maritime transportation and security might benefit or be enhanced as MDA effects not only the United States but also the global community.

References

Abbas, A.E., Howard, R.A., 2015. Foundations of Decision Analysis. Pearson Higher.

Blair, C.D., Boardman, J.T., Sauser, B.J., 2007. Communicating strategic intent with systemigrams: application to the network-enabled challenge. Syst. Eng. 10 (4), 309—322.

Cabrera, D., Cabrera, L., 2015a. Systems Thinking Made Simple, p. 31.

Cabrera, D., Cabrera, L., 2015b. Systems Thinking Made Simple, p. 45.

Cabrera, D., Cabrera, L., 2018. Flock Not Clock: Align People Processes and Systems to Achieve Your Vision, pp. 44—48.

Deming, W.E., 2018. The New Economics for Industry, Government, Education. MIT Press.

Gorod, A., Gandhi, S.J., Sauser, B., Boardman, J., 2008. Flexibility of system of systems. Glob. J. Flex. Syst. Manag. 9 (4), 21—31.

---

[2] Merriam Webster: Big Data—an accumulation of data that is too large and complex for processing by traditional database management tools.

https://ops.fhwa.dot.gov/freewaymgmt/publications/cm/handbook/chapter7.htm.

Holland, J.H., 1992. Complex adaptive systems. Daedalus 121 (1), 17–30.

Howard, R., 1988. Decision analysis: practice and promise. Manag. Sci. 34 (6).

Keeney, R.L., 1996. Value-focused Thinking. Harvard University Press, pp. 6–10.

Reference the MTS Section 101 Findings in Appendix A.

National Strategy for Maritime Security, 2005g. National Plan to Achieve Maritime Domain Awareness. Department of Homeland Security, Washington, DC. https://www.dhs.gov/sites/default/files/publications/HSPD_MDAPlan_0.pdf. (Accessed 14 April 2020).

Parnell, G.S., Driscoll, P.J., Henderson, D.L. (Eds.), 2011a. Decision Making in Systems Engineering and Management, vol. 81. John Wiley & Sons, p. 317.

Parnell, G.S., Driscoll, P.J., Henderson, D.L. (Eds.), 2011b. Decision Making in Systems Engineering and Management, vol. 81. John Wiley & Sons, p. 37.

Parnell, G.S., Driscoll, P.J., Henderson, D.L. (Eds.), 2011c. Decision Making in Systems Engineering and Management, vol. 81. John Wiley & Sons, p. 14.

Parnell, G.S., Driscoll, P.J., Henderson, D.L. (Eds.), 2011d. Decision Making in Systems Engineering and Management, vol. 81. John Wiley & Sons, p. 5.

Parnell, G.S., Driscoll, P.J., Henderson, D.L. (Eds.), 2011e. Decision Making in Systems Engineering and Management, vol. 81. John Wiley & Sons, p. 8.

https://www.sebokwiki.org/wiki/Download_SEBoK_PDF.

Senge, P.M., 2006. The Fifth Discipline: The Art and Practice of the Learning Organization. Currency.

Shah, Nowicin, 2020. A Guide to the Engineering Management Body of Knowledge, fifth ed., p. 227 Domain 9.

Sterman, J., 2010. Business Dynamics. Irwin/McGraw-Hill c2000.

Von Bertalanffy, L., Sutherland, J.W., 1974. General systems theory: foundations, developments, applications. IEEE Trans. Syst. Man Cybern. 6, 592-592.

Wingrove, S., Sauser, B., 2014. Example of Systemigram. Retrieved from: http://www.boardmansauser.com/Worlds_of_Systems/Systemigrams.html.

CHAPTER 18

Public policy and security partnerships

Richard R. Young

School of Business Administration, Capital College, The Pennsylvania State University, Middletown, PA, United States

The United States Coast Guard (USCG) Captain of the Port (COTP) for one of the major US load center ports of arrival for containerized cargo stood next to the bollard securing the stern of the massive containership to the pier. Earlier, multiple gantry cranes had been positioned to reach out across the beam of the vessel and had begun transferring containers from the ship to waiting chasses. In 1985, when this scenario occurred, this containership with its 3000 TEUs (twenty-foot equivalent units) was considered one of the largest afloat but the promise of even larger ships loomed on the horizon as shipyards worldwide had already embarked on plans to build countless fleets for transiting the world's oceans carrying goods of every description.

"How can we assure that none of these containers are transporting quantities of illegal drugs or even worse, weapons of mass destruction or their components?," he asked the Customs inspector standing nearby.

"That would be far too big a task for Customs. The only way we can even think about that level of security is by engaging the shipping companies," came the reply.

"We need to think of the role that responsible importers and exporters can also play!" observed the COTP.

"Maybe so, but as a law enforcement agency that will likely be a very difficult idea for us to sell. I'm not sure that it is about to happen during our lifetime."

What this dialog was hinting at probably some 40 years ago was a partnership between government and the private sector even though one could posit that the devil would be in the details. International trade consists of many participants, and the challenge would be to get the major ones to focus their efforts on more secure supply chains.[1] This begins with

---

[1] The timeframe of the dialog actually precedes the widespread use of the term supply chain, yet the concept was already being applied as such.

Intermodal Maritime Security. https://doi.org/10.1016/B978-0-12-819945-9.00015-0

defining public policy, but then also delving into the topic of partnerships for which when it comes to international trade there are many. This chapter endeavors to examine the types of partnerships that developed, their underlying rationale, and how the experiences from one were leveraged to create newer initiatives.

Public policy is defined as "… simply what government (any public official who influences or determines public policy, including school officials, city council members, county supervisors, etc.) does or does not do about a problem that comes before them for consideration and possible action. Policy is made in response to some sort of issue or problem that requires attention. Policy is what the government chooses to do (actual) or not do (implied) about a particular issue or problem" (Project Citizen, 2020). Moreover, public policy is articulated in legislation or executive order at any level, but then is implemented through specific regulation developed by one or more agencies of the executive branch.

Stemming the tide of drug smuggling

It is instructive to consider those efforts where government and the private sector have collaborated with respect to containerized international trade. This distinction is made because during World War II major US exporters were visited by the Federal Bureau of Investigation which sought their assistance in identifying potentially useful war materiel being diverted by neutral nations to the Axis powers. With containerized shipping facilitating world commerce and the drug boom, particularly that which was originating in South America, the U.S. government forged one of the first cooperative programs—the Carrier Initiative Program (CIP). As shown in Fig. 18.1, below, CIP was developed by the Customs Service[2] and encouraged transportation carriers to assist in detecting and preventing the flows of illicit drugs into the United States. There were separate arrangements developed for each of the three major transportation modes—air, land, and sea.

What the carriers received from this program was twofold: (a) a greater awareness of their potential for enabling drug smuggling and an incentive for improving their security and (b) extensive training resources from Customs. The latter encompassed training carrier personnel in enhanced search techniques, identifying the means for concealing drugs in otherwise legitimate cargo shipments, and conducting risk assessments based on shipment origins and destinations, identity of shippers and consignees, and nature of the goods. Moreover, carrier managements received training on conducting document reviews; improving physical and procedural security of facilities, vessels, and information systems; and identifying opportunities where internal personnel might conceivably participate in smuggling conspiracies (K-Line, 2020; Shapiro, 2020).

---

[2] At the time of Carrier Initiative Program's development, Customs and Border Protection had yet to be established, nor had its parent the Department of Homeland Security—that would not happen for another 17 years.

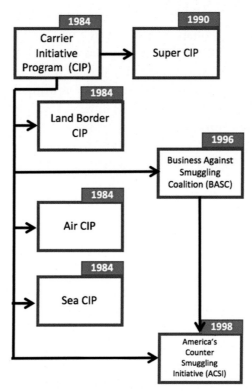

Figure 18.1
Partnerships against drug smuggling.

Across the three modes more than 4000 carriers signed onto CIP and in 1990 based upon what Customs was able to learn about where efforts needed to be focused, implemented the Super Carrier Initiative Program (SCIP) specifically engaging those carriers that were most at risk for potentially transporting illicit drugs, but with a particular emphasis on the transport of cocaine from northwestern South America (Shapiro, 2020).

If CIP and SCIP engaged the transport companies, 1996 witnessed the development of an importer and exporter alliance with the objective of augmenting CIP. Enter the Business Antismuggling Coalition, or BASC, which focused on shipments of goods from Latin America to the United States by examining those entire processes for manufacturing and shipping goods. Member firms were encouraged to establish more security-aware environments whereby manufacturing plants could reduce if not outright eliminate their respective product exposure to drug smuggling. Much akin to CIP and SCIP, BASC was supported by Customs and an extensive training endeavors ensued. As this is written more that 4500 manufacturing firms in Central and South America have become members of BASC. Among these are numerous subsidiaries and affiliates of North American and European multinational companies (K-Line America, 2020; Shapiro, 2020).

A logical extension of BASC occurred just two years later with the founding of the Americas Counter Smuggling Initiative (ACSI) which built upon the CIP and BASC programs and logically linked the manufacturing and distribution activities within the international supply chains. ACSI was likely the first such initiative that articulated the concern that legitimate supply chains could be used to unwittingly facilitate the movement of illegal drugs. In as much as resources needed to be devoted to safeguarding legitimate international trade and, as a consequence, partnerships were not only public and private but also public and public with U.S. Customs building improved relationships with their foreign counterparts that included extensive training activities of their respective officials (Business Alliance for Secure Commerce, 2020).

Terrorism and changing international trade forever

The terrorist attacks of September 11, 2001 as noted in several of the preceding chapters represented a significant game changer for both global trade and the transportation modes that facilitate it. This is a book about intermodal maritime transportation; however, as any traveler or shipping executive will readily attest, the changes to trucking, railroads, and aviation affect both the breadth and depth of carrier operations. With nearly 23 million TEUs of goods arriving in the United States each year plus 2.38 million loaded railcars and 4.55 million loaded trucks (Bureau of Transportation Statistics, 2019), preventing terrorist activity, whether it be transporting weapons or other illicit goods, tampering with cargo, or inflicting damage, was immediately recognized as a monumental task that easily outstripped government resources for both surveillance and interdiction.

With too large a task to assign to one or more government agencies, the logical solution was to develop multiple partnerships that would include: (1) government and the private sector, the proverbial public–private partnership; (2) U.S. government to foreign government partnerships, the end result being a plethora of bilateral arrangements that are working agreements rather than treaties per se; and (3) an underlying reliance on private to private partnerships suggesting that stronger ties between firms engaged in international trade would provide some information links that may not have been realized formerly.

Fig. 18.2, below, illustrates how those lessons learned from CIP, BASC, and ACSI were applied to the post–September 11 environment to reduce if not eliminate the international transport of weapons of mass destruction, weapons components, and those items having both commercial and military applications, notably the dual use items.

The Customs-Trade Partnership Against Terrorism (C-TPAT) came about with the realization that every member of the supply chain plus the government had to cooperatively engage if there was any hope of preventing future acts of terrorism. Drawing

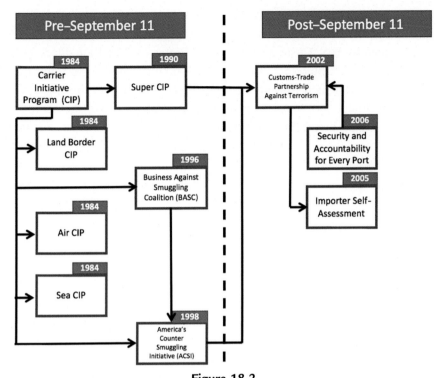

Figure 18.2

Creating partnerships to stem terrorism—part 1.

from the lessons learned from BASC and later ACSI, the primary responsibility for both (a) identifying every member of the supply chain beginning with the manufacturer of the goods and (b) documenting their respective security arrangements by necessity would fall on the importer. Drawing from the experience gained with the CIP, the carriers were obviously important members of any supply chain; hence, their membership in C-TPAT was also to be included (Caldwell, 2017; Edmonson, 2003).

Being that the information and financial flows were just as critical to attaining a complete understanding of any supply chain, those trade intermediaries having such responsibility were added as well. Now customs brokers, freight forwarders, non-vessel operating common carriers, air freight consolidators, inland transportation services providers, and cargo terminal operators are eligible for membership. Note that insurance underwriters and banks specializing in facilitating international trade[3] are recognized supply chain participants, but not specified as potential C-TPAT members.

---

[3] Initiating banks open letters of credit for buyers and corresponding banks represent sellers in international transactions.

C-TPAT would contain elements that none of the predecessor alliances employed, namely (a) a certification process whereby an importer's supply chains need be documented and subsequently verified by U.S. Customs and Border Protection (CBP) auditors, (b) a disciplinary process where importers that are found to be in violation of import regulations can be suspended or terminated from the partnership, and (c) a quid pro quo whereby member importers would enjoy more expeditious entry processing of their shipments. The single feature of C-TPAT that differentiated it from all of the previous arrangements was this quid pro quo where the CBP was as much as saying "we need you on board because this task is far to big and complex for government to undertake on its own." At the outset, C-TPAT was both huge and complex; however, all of the advantages of the predecessor programs were realized without imposing the extra administrative requirements of duplicative effort. In short, C-TPAT was useful for continuing to stem the flow of smuggled drugs while at the same time thwarting the efforts of terrorist organizations, whether state-sponsored or not, desiring to bring weapons into the United States.

There were two drawbacks to the successful implementation of C-TPAT: (1) that any relationship between the importers and CBP would be in the form of a partnership given that there were decades of a near adversarial history; and (2) that importers would need to make major investments in being able to provide the required detailed documentation for each of their supply chains.[4] For the latter, the investment meant changing the approaches to global sourcing that would need to include vetting the second, third, and tertiary tiers of the supply chains. Suppliers would need to be visited meaning international travel, which itself represented a sizable expense.

In 2005, CBP added an additional program that complemented C-TPAT, the Importer Self-Assessment, or ISA. Importers that are already members of C-TPAT that have been verified and certified are able to apply for membership in ISA where they assume the responsibility for being proactive in the monitoring of their own activities and how they are in compliance with Customs Law and CBP regulations. They are still subject to random audits, but being able to document their processes, measure their performance, and employ feedback loops whereby their processes can be improved is the key to membership and continuance in the program[5] (Shapiro, 2020).

---

[4] The plural "supply chains" is intentional because each individual supplier in theory represented separate documentation to satisfy the requirements established under Customs-Trade Partnership Against Terrorism.

[5] The elements of Importer Self-Assessment membership appear to closely mirror the requirements for ISO 9000 registration for quality improvement.

Partnerships to the fore

The title of this chapter alludes to public policy, but with an emphasis on partnerships. Much of the effort beginning with CIP in the mid-1980s has been on programs that have some modicum of a quid pro quo. Clearly, the Customs Service and later CBP expended resources up front for the training of private sector participants; however, after a period of time, antismuggling became a mindset that was woven into each firms' culture. As an exemplar, BASC still exists today with an organization of participating companies that has its own governance and information sharing mechanism (Business Alliance for Secure Commerce, 2020).

Where government perhaps benefitted most was with the change in relationships with importers and exporters. In tracing this history, much of the past century had Customs, at the time called the Customs Bureau, seeing itself as a revenue collection agency, which was understandable given that up until the early years of the 20th century most of the revenue for operating the federal government came from duties and excise taxes. During the 1980s when the Customs Bureau changed its name to the Customs Service, there was a drive to make it a trade facilitator. Occurring in part because of the steady slide in tariff rates and simplification of the tariff itself when it was revised to become the Harmonized Tariff Schedule of the United States, there remained the revenue collection element and with it the organizational locus within the Department of the Treasury. At that time, Customs agents were trained alongside of Internal Revenue agents at Quantico, VA; hence, a revenue emphasizing organizational culture was sustained even despite the War on Drugs and the development of laudable programs such as CIP and its various descendants.

Referring to the aforementioned Fig. 18.2, there is a clear division resulting from September 11, 2001. Not only was this the impetus for Congress to create the Department of Homeland Security (DHS), but by merging the Customs Service with the Border Patrol to create CBP such became the driver for cultural change. The revenue collecting culture, nevertheless on the wane during the final years of the last century, was substantially deemphasized as protecting the homeland became the key objective. The metamorphosis was not unlike that experienced by the Coast Guard when it dropped the moniker of Revenue Cutter Service and eventually was moved from the Treasury Department to the Department of Transportation. Its cultural transformation was complete when it, too, was placed under the newly formed DHS and its former commandant became the Deputy Secretary.[6]

---

[6] In 2002 upon the department's establishment, Admiral James Loy became the first Deputy Secretary of the newly created DHS under Secretary Thomas Ridge.

The public–private partnership

The mechanics of establishing partnerships, at least if one subscribes to much of the legal advice of the day, are fraught with problems. For one, there is the problem of quid pro quo, or as the legal profession would ask "Is there consideration here?"—both parties need to have an advantage in entering into the partnership.

In order to attract the participation of the private sector, the consideration would be a matter of importers saving time, which is a logical trade-off since a shorter lead time—that from point of origin to when the goods are finally placed in the hands of the importer (or the importer's customer in many situations) reduces the inventory investment. Importers have for many years endeavored to discover ways to reduce transit time, in particular the time needed for their merchandise to clear CBP by having their entry documentation processed and the goods inspected, if necessary. In the past, it was a common practice for importers to change ports of entry hoping to find those that had the shortest queues and, hence, the most expeditious processing (Edmonson, 2003).

As CBP endeavored to establish an incentive for importing firms to want to participate in any partnership, there were two elements that were the key variables in the trade-offs to be considered: (1) the aforementioned import entry clearance times and (2) the amount of effort necessary to establish validated status in the C-TPAT process. The intent of CBP was to create a sufficiently high barrier to entry whereby the largest, and, thus, the most significant and potentially trustworthy importers would participate—CBP knew who it wanted for partners and structured C-TPAT in such a way that would attract them. Conversely, the barriers could not be so high that any potential benefits were not worth the effort involved in attaining. The record now shows that those importers that were prompted by early participants were exactly those that CBP had hoped would participate with such well-known firms as IBM, PPG, Eastman Kodak, DuPont, and BASF being among the primary examples.[7] The process consisted of three levels, as depicted in Fig. 18.3, below. Signing up and declaring an intent to participate then required extensive documentation by the importer and an equally extensive verification process to be performed by CBP.

Learning to operate in a partnership environment is not a simple endeavor, nevertheless industry was quick to learn of C-TPAT benefits and in 2002, the year that the program was rolled out, 1500 companies had signed on. The following year saw that number double to 3000, and by the third year, it had more than doubled again reaching more than 7000 firms. Membership continued to grow albeit at a decreasing rate and by 2012 reached

---

[7] These firms were members of the Import Processes Benchmarking Consortium facilitated by the Center for Supply Chain Research at Penn State University during the 1990s.

Tier	Name	Qualifications
1	Member	Application completed and submitted
2	Validated	Firm documents supply chain and CBP verifies and certifies
3	High Level	Firm is able to demonstrate that it has developed security processes

Figure 18.3
C-TPAT tiers.

slightly more than 10,000. By 2017, membership plateaued at 11,500. At the outset, the partnership appeared somewhat lopsided as members were realizing benefits, but few had been verified and certified (Caldwell, 2017).

Internationalization of trade partnerships

One characteristic of all partnerships is that they continue to evolve. C-TPAT was authorized by the Security and Accountability for Every (hence, SAFE) Port Act, but this is where the public—private partnerships and the public-public partnerships become intertwined. C-TPAT was the first attempt of a public—private partnership that sought to address the entire supply chain with respect to terrorism. Comprehensive in its approach of engaging importers and requiring their documenting the chain of custody for their globally sourced goods, it became the model for the World Customs Organization (WCO) to emulate as shown in Fig. 18.4 (Kerlikowske, 2016).

In 2005 beginning with the Standards to Secure and Facilitate Trade (aka SAFE, but not to be confused with the U.S. SAFE Port Act) … *the WCO articulated its key elements as*:

- Harmonizing advance cargo information
- Introducing a risk management approach
- Sending country's customs inspection of high-risk containers
- Establishing a benefits program for compliant traders

Moreover, the SAFE Framework of Standards is a set of recommendations to (member) customs organizations that includes issues as:

- Integrated Customs control procedures for integrated supply chain management
- Authority to inspect cargo, and use modern technology in doing so
- Risk management system to identify potentially high-risk shipments
- Identification of high-risk cargo and container shipments
- Advance electronic information on cargo and container shipments
- Joint targeting and screening (European Commission, 2020)

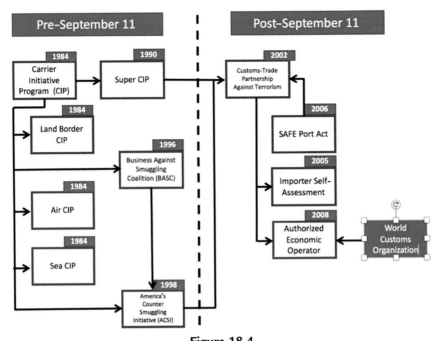

Figure 18.4
Creating partnerships to stem terrorism—part 2.

From these elements came the development of the Authorized Economic Operator (AEO) Program which the European Union defines as a concept based on a Customs-to-Business partnership. Moreover, traders who voluntarily meet a range of criteria work in close cooperation with customs authorities to assure the common objective of supply chain security and entitled to enjoy the benefits throughout the EU. Membership is open to all economic operators that are authorized for customs simplification and/or supply chain security and safety. As of 2019, the WCO states that there included 77 (national) operational AEO programs, 17 programs that are yet to be launched, 31 operational customs compliance programs, and two customs compliance programs yet to be launched (World Customs Organization, 2020).

In addition to those nations where AEO programs are established, there are a number of other nations that participate by means of mutual recognition agreements (MRA). Note that C-TPAT is considered the AEO program of the United States, but add to the list are the European Union, Canada, New Zealand, Jordan, Japan, South Korea, Taiwan, Israel, Mexico, Singapore, Dominican Republic, and Peru. Moreover, there are over 50 bilateral AEO MRAs that include members other than the United States (World Customs Organization, 2019).

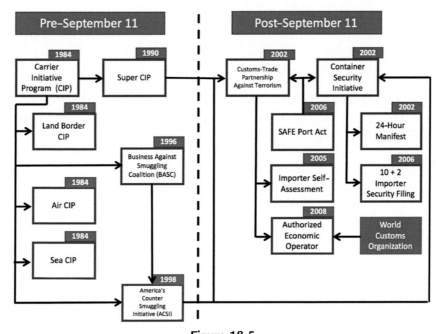

Figure 18.5

Creating partnerships to stem terrorism—part 3.

Prior reference was made to the SAFE Port Act and its authorization of C-TPAT, but as shown in Fig. 18.5, SAFE was also the basis for the Container Security Initiative (CSI) being authorized. The advent of CSI can be seen to be based upon the public-public partnerships established by a series of bilateral agreements between the United States and 35 other nations that in the aggregate represent a more than 80% of the containerized global trade destined for the United States. CSI operates with CBP officers being located at foreign ports of loading and works in close collaboration with their counterparts from the host nation to establish security criteria for identifying high-risk containers. As with those lessons learned with the initiatives operating in Latin America, a key element of CSI lies with CBP's training of customs officials from other nations. Currently, 60 foreign ports of loading participate and are mostly load centers where not only land-based cargo enters maritime transportation, but also transshipment ports where feeder vessels from smaller ports meet US bound vessels (Customs and Border Protection, 2020).

Closely related to CSI is the 24-Hour Manifest Rule. Not so much a partnership as a regulation that when coupled with other initiatives makes for a significantly more transparent supply chain. All cargo, whether being unloaded at a US port or on board a vessel making at a US port call, is now reported as a detailed manifest at least 24 hours prior to be loaded on board a vessel at the foreign port. This requirement applies to all ocean carriers, whether they are handling full container loads or break-bulk cargo, or if they happen to be nonvessel operating common carriers (NVOCC).

Although the quid quo pro is clearly skewed in favor of CBP under this regulation, there is an advantage accruing to the shipping line in the form of better information concerning the nature of those cargoes being loaded aboard their vessels. Such knowledge provides for more informed decisions regarding container stow plans, but also more accurate description of the goods, the weights, and whether the correct rates are being charged (19 CFR § 4.7).

A final element that the SAFE Act provides in relation to CSI is the $10 + 2$ Importer Security Filing (ISF). ISF refers to 10 data elements that importers must provide to CBP 24 h prior to a container being loaded at the foreign port. Related to the Manifest Rule explained above, the $+2$ element refers to the two additional electronically supplied data elements that are added by the carriers (Shapiro, 2020).

Summary

This chapter began with a fictitious yet highly plausible conversation between a U.S. Coast Guard officer and a senior Customs agent where there was a concern that despite the efficiencies inherent with the use of intermodal containers, that they also had the potential for smuggling all sorts of contraband into the United States. While not articulated as such, both knew that 100% physical inspection of the millions of TEUs[8] was not a practical solution, yet protecting the nation was a very real challenge. Both also knew that policing intermodal traffic was too big of a task for either government or industry acting alone and that the solution likely was to be found in some form of partnership.

Dividing the time period since 1984 into two eras: pre–September 11 and post–September 11, the emphasis is preventing drug smuggling and preventing terrorist activity, respectively. CBP (nee Customs) implemented its first partnership with importers with CIP, the key lesson learned was that of the quid pro quo—CBP had to move away from the law enforcement emphasis to that of providing training for industry to be good partners. If CIP engaged the carriers in a partnership, it was BASC and later ACSI that sought to enlist the support of the offshore manufacturers—now the lesson learned was that they had to engage the multiple parties within the supply chain. These lessons proved to be even more valuable in the post–September 11 era.

---

[8] In 2018 there were 20+ million twenty-foot equivalent units arriving on US shores. If the combination of 20-foot and 40-foot units is split evenly, this approximates 13.4 million boxes.

It is suggested that readers refer to Chapter 10 which provides useful detail about how international organizations evolved after World War II, but in particular the role of the WCO, which plays heavily in the development of the AEO Program. Note, too, how, public—private partnerships are central to the functioning of C-TPAT and how public-public partnerships, particularly of an international type, are the basis for the effective functioning of CSI.

Protecting nations from either smuggling of illegal drugs or preventing the proliferation of weapons of mass destruction is a dynamic environment meaning that perpetrators continue to evolve with their tactics, and legitimate entities continue to develop new approaches to thwart them. New tactics may often mean the employment of new technologies but may also be in the form of new elements of interorganizational cooperation where levels of trust have evolved to facilitate greater information exchange as well as improved tactics and levels of cooperation.

One topic that this chapter has not addressed is the crisis in global human trafficking. Better knowledge of international supply chains by importers, exporters, transportation services providers, and intermediaries has the serendipitous effect of while not making human trafficking impossible, making it potentially yet more difficult to execute.

Finally, this chapter contained the terms "public policy" and "partnerships" in its title, which until recent years the latter could have been seen as antithetical to the former. Getting public policy to embrace the private sector has not been an easy task to undertake given the substantial institutional memory of both the public as well as the private sectors. The historical adversarial relationship had to be overcome and if it was not for those initial efforts beginning with the CIP and incrementally augmented with other measures implanting C-TPAT and its global equivalent, the AEO would not have been possible.

References

19 CFR § 4.7, 2005. Inward Foreign Manifest; Production on Demand; Contents and Form; Advance Filing of Cargo Declaration. Retrieved April 21, 2020. https://www.law.cornell.edu/cfr/text/19/4.7.

Bureau of Transportation Statistics, 2019. Transportation Statistics Annual Report 2019: The State of Statistics.

Business Alliance for Secure Commerce, 2020. https://www.wbasco.org/en. (Accessed 15 May 2020).

Caldwell, S.L., August 12, 2017. Can C-TPAT be fixed? The Maritime Executive. Retrieved April 21, 2020. https://www.maritime-executive.com/magazine/can-c-tpat-be-fixed/.

Edmonson, R.G., June 15, 2003. Next step for C-TPAT? J. Commer.

European Commission, 2020. Authorized Economic Operator (AEO). Retrieved March 29, 2020. https://ec.europa.eu/taxation_customs/general-information-customs/customs-security/authorised-economic-operator-aeo/authorised-economic-operator-aeo_en#what_is.

K-Line America, 2020. Customs-Trade Partnership Against Terrorism (C-TPAT). Retrieved April 21, 2020. https://kline.com/compliance-security/K-Line-Security-Initiatives.

Kerlikowske, G., 2016. Tenth Anniversary of SAFE Port Act. Retrieved March 2, 2020. https://cbp.gov/newsroom/blogs/tenth-anniversary-safe-port-act.

Project Citizen, 2020. Center for Civic Education. https://www.civiced.org/pc-program/instructional-component/public-policy. (Accessed 20 April 2020).

Shapiro, 2020. Common Terminology: Government Sponsored Security/Compliance Programs and Initiatives. Retrieved April 21, 2020. https://www.shapiro.com/resources/common-terminology-government-sponsored-security-compliance-programs-initiatives/.

U.S. Customs and Border Protection, 2020. CSI: Container Security Initiative. Retrieved May 2, 2020. https://www.cbp.gov/border-security/ports-entry/cargo-security/csi/csi-brief#wcm-survey-target.

World Customs Organization, 2019. Compendium of Authorized Economic Operator Programmes. WCO, Brussels.

World Customs Organization, 2020. WCO in Brief. Retrieved May 1, 2020. https://www.wecoomd.org/en/about-us/what-is-the-wco.aspx.

Further reading

Smita, S., November 19, 2019. What is Container Security Initiative (CSI) and How Does it Work? The Maritime Executive.

CHAPTER 19

Intermodal maritime security: where do we go from here?

Gary A. Gordon, PhD, PE, MEMS, LTC USA (Ret.) [1],
Richard R. Young, PhD, FCILT [2]

[1]*Department of Civil & Environmental Engineering, University of Massachusetts Lowell, Lowell, MA, United States;* [2]*School of Business Administration, Capital College, The Pennsylvania State University, Middletown, PA, United States*

Ms. Hanna Yen, Director of Supply Chain Management at Coastal Pharmatech[1], sat in her office pondering the email that she had just received informing her that Coastal had just received Food and Drug Administration (FDA) approval to market garric hydrochloride, a new product for treating a major infection. Having been working to develop the necessary supply chain network that would convey the active ingredient from the supplier located in Sri Lanka, Yen remained most concerned that Coastal is able to maintain continuity of supply. She looked back at the notes she had taken at the various management meetings and from prior emails and realized that it would require taking unprecedented measures to assure that the material would not: (1) have its quality compromised in any way during transit, (2) that the refrigerated 20-foot ocean containers maintain their temperature and humidity requirements, and (3) that delays from origin to destination be minimized given that the material was sole sourced and the supply chain from Sri Lanka to northern New Jersey was a long one. One action that she had taken early in the process was to engage the appropriate personnel from the procurement and logistics organizations in order that Coastal' s arrangements were sufficiently comprehensive and that the network functioned as a coordinated system and that suboptimization could be avoided.

Supplier: Dahliwal Organics Ltd., was a known supplier having furnished other bulk materials to Coastal in the past. Coastal had a good relationship with Dahliwal and the end-to-end supply chain had been vetted and certified years ago under Customs-Trade Partnership Against Terrorism (C-TPAT). Moreover, Dahliwal's process for engaging its suppliers of both goods as well as services was appropriately documented.

---

[1] Coastal Pharmatech and Dahliwal Organics are fictional companies devised for the purpose of this case. Mediterranean Shipping and the Port of Colombo, Sri Lanka are real; however, all other elements of this case including names of materials and products, dates and times, and locations are strictly fictional and intended for instructional use one.

Intermodal Maritime Security. https://doi.org/10.1016/B978-0-12-819945-9.00019-8

Packaging: The active ingredient was a dry white crystalline powder packaged in fiber drums having a polyethylene liner. A 20-foot container ideally held 40 such drums arranged four to a pallet.

Shipping: The most direct route utilized Mediterranean Shipping Company (MSC) sailing from Colombo to New York via the Suez Canal. MSC also had the advantage of having vessels on this route equipped with sufficient electrical power connections to operate the refrigeration or reefer unit of the containers. Moreover, Colombo was a Cargo Security Initiative (CSI) port having been the 40th such port to join in 2005.

Shipping Terms: FOB[2] Colombo meaning that Dahliwal would arrange and pay for land transportation to the port. Title would pass once the cargo is on board the vessel, which technically means once the container is lifted and passes beyond the ship's rail.

Customs Formalities: Months prior to FDA approval, Yen had submitted samples to U.S. Customs and Border Protection (CBP) and secured a binding duty rate. This information was subsequently shared with their appointed customshouse broker.

Resilience: If there is one thing about a newly approved drug, it is that a firm cannot endure a supply shortage. Production delays would be unacceptable, hence Yen had begun discussions with FedEx to provide airfreight backup, albeit an expensive option, should it be needed. Fortunately, the material was not hazardous and could airfreighted in any quantity. With near-sourcing becoming more commonplace in the wake of the COVID-19 pandemic, Yen had also begun investigating production in the western hemisphere if a supplier capable of receiving the necessary regulatory approvals could be identified. Unfortunately, those tasks proved to be lengthy ones with estimates being 12 months as the most optimistic.

While Yen knew that she had done just about everything that she could to set the stage and protect the shipments of the critical material, she remained concerned that some vulnerability existed. Two examples immediately came to mind: one concerning drug smuggling; the other, cargo fires aboard ships due to misdeclared freight. In 2019, there had been a highly publicized cocaine seizure in the Port of Philadelphia, a containership was found to have rendezvoused with smaller vessels off the west coast of South America where over US$1.2 billion in contraband was taken aboard. In that case, the vessel had been detained and ultimately seized by the U.S. Coast Guard (USCG). Secondly, when a fire breaks out in a cargo container, it may likely spread to others often meaning that shipments are jettisoned for the sake of safety of the ship. In both cases, cargo was late

---

[2] FOB means *freight on board* and in international use is only applicable to maritime transportation. One of the INCOTerms (or international commercial terms) updated once each decade by the International Chamber of Commerce, Paris, France. It defines where title passes and which charges are attributable to the buyer and the seller.

being discharged and the hundreds if not thousands of containers involved meant numerous disrupted supply chains. Such incidents might be more frequent than originally thought when one watches the news as reported in "American Shipper." Misdeclared freight is estimated by one study to represent nearly 8% of all shipments with a higher incidence when hazardous goods are involved (Dupin, 2019). Finally, there were reports of piracy occurring in narrow straits and canals, where vessels may lie at anchor awaiting dock space, and where shipping lanes are relatively close to shore.

One thought that Yen did not have concerned cybersecurity of the information flows that included potential exposure from email traffic going back and forth between Coastal and Dahliwal to shipping documentation between Coastal, the overseas forwarder, the container line, the truckers, and the customshouse broker. Added to this was the matter of information exchanges between Coastal, the trade intermediaries, CBP, and the FDA, latter named because the material in question is a pharmaceutical component. *Related to cybersecurity was also the matter of tampering with vessel automated identification systems (AIS) where ships can be reported at locations that could differ substantially from their actual positions.*

The above case can serve as an illustration for one of the more comprehensive and well thought through processes that importers might use in constructing a supply chain where an offshore source is being employed. Nevertheless, some discussion of the more prevalent factors needs to be considered as a critical part of thinking about the future of these endeavors. The following sections are an amalgam of the opinions of the editors based upon their collective experiences along with those of the various authors of the preceding chapters.

A high level overview of intermodal maritime security

Security of the intermodal maritime supply chain is complex. There are: many stakeholders and partners; international dynamics and political ideologies; different host nation and international rules, regulations, and policies; and varied levels of physical protective measures and technologies. This makes consistent treatment of security difficult, hence, the challenge. The "state of the industry" regarding intermodal maritime supply chain security and how to accomplish acceptable measures to minimize risk must be addressed and maximize the process and techniques used to the extent possible. It is a delicate balance among national sovereignty, efficiency of the supply chain, risk mitigation, and cost.

Threats and vulnerabilities are not static. As the threats and associated vulnerabilities evolve, the gaps in security must be addressed appropriately to ensure that risk is minimized, and the well-being and economies of the nation and that the people involved are not exposed to undue risk. This chapter will look at the relationship among the components of the intermodal maritime supply chain through the lens of those topics discussed in earlier chapters of the book. From what we have learned from the past and foresee in the future, this chapter will address future threats, vulnerabilities and consequences, and how security measures should be constructed to minimize risk. It will involve procedural, human, physical, and technological security measures, and their evolution to address the changing landscape.

Earlier chapters have highlighted the number of variables involved in intermodal maritime transportation, a factor that makes this chapter one of the most challenging of all to compose. At the outset, one needs to consider the sources of the threats, but then focus on the potential opportunities for addressing these. Since the term *intermodal* implies two or more modes, those activities occurring on land and at sea become key variables. Similarly, revisiting the SCOR Model, as shown earlier in Fig. 3.7, reinforces the need to focus on the three principal flows of *physical*, *information*, and *financial*, but to also consider a heretofore not included activity, namely *plan*.

Thinking about the threats

A documented and vetted global supply chain reduces risk and vulnerability in part because it means that the importer has built relationships with the various supply chain members, which in turn means that variability is also reduced. Although a past practice, the rebidding of contracts with the various participants, of which depending on such factors as terms of sale, origin and destination pairs, relationship between importer and exporter, and the nature of goods themselves, there might be between 10 and 15 for each of an importer's supply chains adds a significant level of complexity. Many firms may have the contractual responsibility divided between several departments often where little coordination may be present. Ostensibly, the rationale for doing this is to keep reducing the price paid for the respective services but doing so has little cognizance of the total cost involved nor for the increased vulnerability incurred by changing participants.

Importing firms need to embrace the concept of resilience and in so doing build alternative courses of action into their supply chain thinking, but these alternatives are engaged with the thorough knowledge of protecting the supply chain and establishing mitigation scenarios that can be exercised when manmade or natural catastrophic events potentially disrupt the continuity of supply.

Physical flows

Bifurcating the physical flow into landside and waterside, when importers vet and document their supply chains they begin with understanding all aspects of their suppliers including their physical security measures, those with whom they engage for providing transportation to the port and the integrity of the port itself, a factor where having a CSI presence comes into play.

This brings us to the problem of the waterside, which from a distance perspective may pose a significant threat potential despite the appearance of a containership being secure. A return to the vignette that opened Chapter 16 may prove instructive.

Information flows

The information flows have been amply discussed in multiple chapters and illustrated with several flow charts. They are admittedly complex, in part because they can have so many variations. Moreover, much of the data shared are repeated often. The two key parties in the information exchange are the buyer and the seller, which may or may not necessarily be the importer and the exporter. Between ocean and land carriers, the various information handling intermediaries, and the government authorities, there are also many exchanges. Chapter 10 introduced the concept of blockchain, a technology that holds much promise for improving the security of trade information but is only now just barely beyond its embryonic state.

Trading between related companies

Without doubt, there is a need for existing partnerships to be strengthened. Chapter 18 discussed three types: (1) public-public, or how governments have begun to cooperate often within the structure of bilateral and multilateral agreements; (2) private-private, as has occurred with the help of industry associations and in particular the formation of Information Sharing and Analysis Centers (ISAC), but also any dyadic arrangements that may be formed between firms; and (3) public–private, as is the case with C-TPAT.

One development that emerged since the end of WWII has been the global corporation where through a network of subsidiaries around the globe, import–export operations increasingly occur between related parties. For example, transactions between the US subsidiary and the Brazilian subsidiary of a German global corporation becomes much less complex because of the use of open accounts using a common currency, the sharing of global transportation agreements, and often common intermediaries. Moreover, large multinational firms have the volume and name recognition that not only provides market leverage but the regulatory leverage that comes with being a known entity. Perhaps, some early pioneers of this structure were the British East India Company, the Dutch East India Company, Hudson Bay Corporation, and the handful of Japanese trading companies such as Marubeni, Mitsui, Sumitomo, Fuji, and Mitsubishi.

As the volume of trade between global companies continues to occupy a larger and larger portion to total activity, enforcement concerns turn toward the small to medium size importers and exporters that have little to no name recognition, but also have minimal expertise for arranging international shipments. Moreover, small size and minimal volumes are also one reason why there is little rationale for them engaging in initiatives such as C-TPAT. This becomes a de facto rationale for enforcement resources to be concentrated where the most risk and vulnerability may lie. If this is one dimension, a second would be shipments originating in third world nations where not only trading entities may be smaller, but (1) where international trade documentation preparation may not be enabled by electronic commerce, (2) documentation accuracy may be in question, (3) the timeliness of the information flow may lag the physical flow, and (4) the potential for corruption and criminal activity could be greater.

Security measures taxonomy

Risks can occur individually or in combination: "piled on top of another." From previous chapters, we have seen that risks are associated with:

- Domestic and international regulatory process and procedures;
- Manual versus automated international trade documentation;
- Physical threats and vulnerabilities resulting from gaps in security measures;
- Technological and cyber threats that impact all aspects of the supply chain;
- Human factors that are country and politically based.

Table 19.1, below, shows the structure of risk and how the security measures could be "piled on top of another." The table provides a template format and structured approach that could provide an understanding of how the security measures are linked and provide a foundation for analysis, comparison, and evaluation.

The rating or evaluation of the security measures and conditions would be made subjectively based on the "boots-on-the-ground" and academic experience of the editors. A simple measure of impact scale gradated by *high, moderate, low,* or *no impac*t is recommended. The subjective analysis used to determine the impacts to populate the table is detailed in Appendix A.

Appendix A looks at the first security measure; *procedural* and how it affects or "piles up on the others" in relative detail to explain the assessment process. The other security measures *documentation, physical flow, physical security, technological and cyber,* and *human* will not be assessed and is left to the reader or practitioner to determine. The evaluation criteria used in the analysis of the security measures as they relate to each other are summarized in the following Table 19.2.

Table 19.1: Security measures taxonomy.

Security measure	Security measure impacted					
	Procedural	Documentation	Physical flow	Physical security	Technological and cyber	Human
Procedural						
Documentation						
Physical flow						
Physical security						
Technological and cyber						
Human						

Table 19.2: Security measures taxonomy evaluation criteria.

Evaluation criteria	Impact on evaluation criteria			
	High (Significantly)	Moderate (Moderately)	Low (Minimally)	No Impact (or not measurable)
Documentation flow	Impedes the timeliness of the documentation flow and associated financial flows and operational aspects.			
Physical flow	Impedes the physical flow to and from the ports and at sea.			
Physical security measures	Diminishes the effectiveness of the physical security measures and in combination with the human security measures.			
Technological and cybersecurity measures	Impacts the ability to effectively operate the technological and cybersecurity measures and the interrelationships with the other security measures (e.g., documentation flow and access control).			
Human	Impacts the ability of security forces, administrative personnel in the supply chain and those involved in operations to properly vet, secure, and operate given security measures and procedures.			

From the assessment in Appendix A, it can be concluded that no one security measure operates individually or in a vacuum. It shows: (1) how the dependency of one security measure implemented on another, (2) how the changes in procedural and/or regulatory matters impact the others, and (3) how the human aspect of security is involved in all. Table 19.A.1 summarizes the impacts of the security measures assessment. It shows that, for the procedural security measures, impacts range from low to high with the impact on technological and cybersecurity measures as high and human as low. Details of the determination of the procedural security measures impacts are presented in the appendix. Although costs are not considered in the assessment, increased costs associated with operational and physical security impacts and are difficult to overlook.

Table 19.A.1: Security measures taxonomy and their impacts.

			Security measure impacted			
Security measure	Procedural	Documentation	Physical flow	Physical security	Technological and cyber	Human
Procedural		Moderate	Moderate	Moderate	High	Low
Documentation	TBD		TBD	TBD	TBD	TBD
Physical flow	TBD	TBD		TBD	TBD	TBD
Physical security	TBD	TBD	TBD		TBD	TBD
Technological and cyber	TBD	TBD	TBD	TBD		TBD
Human	TBD	TBD	TBD	TBD	TBD	

Manual versus automated international trade documentation

The documentation required to effect international trade goes back centuries and can generally be considered slow to undergo change. Where change does occur, an example being updating the standards for assigning responsibility in the event of less, it is affected by international agreement. If one considers the major changes, the first perhaps would be that the shipping industry largely imposed its documentation standards on ports or nation-states and achieved a modicum of standardization. A second era would have been when manual documentation was superseded by some of the first electronic information technology, but that nascent technology was very slow in achieving global acceptance. The third era could arguably be evolving automated documentation onto a network where speed of transmittal and availability across participants becomes commonplace. Note, too, that many locations only recently moved away from manually prepared documentation with some skipping the era of legacy systems altogether.

The addition of government initiatives, whether it is C-TPAT, CSI, or the International Ship and Port Facility Security (ISPS) Code, is a relatively recent phenomenon, but it does serve to foster better cooperation among developed nations. As has been largely the case throughout history, the industry, because it must function within the regulatory frameworks of so many nations, is often the driver of change.

Despite the efforts to make intermodal maritime shipping more secure, there remains an ongoing concern over the occurrence of misdeclared and/or improperly packaged cargo, often involving hazardous goods. In a study conducted by the National Cargo Bureau on containers arriving at US ports, 55% of all containers failed having one or more deficiencies, but 69% of those carrying hazardous materials failed. Approximately 44% failed for poorly secured cargo, 39% for incorrect or missing placards, and 8% for misdeclared cargo (Dupin, 2019). Moreover, the origins of these containers were largely from either Asia or Latin America.

To stem the tide of such issues, the matter has been taken up by the United Nation's International Maritime Organization's Subcommittee on Carriage of Cargo and Containers where there is concern that these are clear violations to the provisions of the International Maritime Dangerous Goods Code. The major container lines have announced significant fines for those shippers who are found to tender containers to commerce in violation (Dupin, 2019).

The overarching concern with the shipment of hazardous cargo is that if this can get past the scrutiny of the current initiatives, then the potential for the movement of illicit goods, whether such contraband is illegal drugs or weapons, is not only real but larger than originally estimated.

Technological and cyber threats that impact all aspects of the supply chain

With the increasing application of information technology across the supply chain, there is an offsetting level of cyber threat potential. One basic differentiation is whether the technology (1) pertains to the vessel, (2) is related to the cargo, (3) may be government systems for regulating trade, or (4) are the systems employed by importers, exporters, and trade intermediaries. Throughout this book, the various authors have emphasized the complexity of the global trading network given the number of participants, hence systems may bridge multiple classifications.

Vessel systems

Often those that immediately come to mind are navigation systems, which include the Global Positioning System (GPS) often linked to both radar and sonar, but also the Automatic Identification System (AIS) which functions for ships in a manner similar to that of an aircraft transponder. AIS has been hacked in order to not reveal the location or proper identity of a vessel whereas compromising GPS could put a vessel into unsafe waters. Ship's controls govern everything from speed to fuel consumption to fire enunciating panels to environmental systems. Containerships have heating and cooling connections with each linked to a central controller.

Cargo systems

Most often related to transaction-oriented applications, all of the documentation including bills of lading as well as respective manifests are maintained digitally. If hacked, a bill of lading could be modified to show a different number of units than what was originally loaded, a different description of the goods, or a different consignee or importer. Such an information anomaly could hide any number of opportunities for illegal actions.

Government trade regulation

All government systems may be vulnerable to hacking. C-TPAT exists as a database containing the certified supply chains of participating firms that includes the names and contacts of its respective partners. Tampering with this information could potentially insert or substitute a new source of supply. Customs entries are processed through the Automated Commercial Environment (ACE) system where there is the potential for a hacker to compromise the system by modifying an existing entry or by creating bogus ones. Likewise, the CSI database may be hacked so as to not flag a container that might otherwise be suspect and would normally be subjected to inspection.

Importers, exporters, and trade intermediaries

As early as the 1980s, large exporters and importers began to develop information systems to support their international business activities. Commercial offerings were few, hence many of these had to be homegrown. As legacy systems, they were indigenous to specific firms, and if there were interfaces, these were solely with internal accounting and procurement functions. Electronic data interchange (EDI) was in its infancy. At that time some larger customs brokers and freight forwarders began developing their own systems, often with primitive connections to major customers. Fast forward to today when importers, exporters, shipping lines, forwarders, and customs brokers all have interconnectivity, much of which has been promulgated by CBP through their Automated Broker Interface and later their ACE system.

At the end of Chapter 10, the discussion of blockchain provided some insight into how international trade transaction systems could be made more secure by creating a trading partner—spanning application that protected data by precluding the hacking of a single participant's inputs. With major firms, such as Maersk Line undertaking a major test, blockchain has the potential of improving data security, but it is unlikely that it will be (1) totally hack free, or (2) the standard for everyone moving forward.

Where do we go from here?

In the case that introduced this chapter, the protagonist, Hanna Yen, had taken notice of how misdeclared and improperly packaged freight could lead to shipboard incidents that in recent years have caused fires and killed or injured crew members. As a shipper of an important material, this problem presented a clear risk to her business.

Misdeclared freight, however, begs the question that when there are major initiatives such as C-TPAT and CSI in place, how can such infractions be so prevalent? Several unsubstantiated answers come to mind: (1) that the misdeclared cargo was tendered by smaller shippers that were not part of C-TPAT, (2) that the cargo was not otherwise suspect and passed through CSI, and (3) that the cargo originated with a large volume valuable customer for whom the line did not wish to anger.

Near-sourcing and crossborder shipments

Already a growing trend, the relocation of suppliers to closer offshore locations has made the headlines. Such moves shorten supply chains which removes some of the variability from transit times, but may also divert present day maritime shipments to overland instead of an ocean voyages. There is more to the story than meets the eye, however, because border crossings can be affected with significantly less complexity. Where there may be three modal legs to an intermodal maritime shipment, there is typically only one for a crossborder one. The documentation is substantially simpler with only a commercial invoice, export declaration, and bill of lading involved. Customs entries for entering the United States remain the same no matter what mode is selected. Finally, trucking is far easier to arrange, and the transit times are significantly shorter.

C-TPAT is still a valuable tool no matter what the mode although the security of trucks on the highway or containers loaded on railcars may have risk factors, there are fewer modal handoffs meaning that cargo does not need to stand idle for long periods and potentially vulnerable. Finally, crossborder transportation is more flexible where alternative routes can be readily taken in order to avoid natural disasters.

Resilience of supply chains

Many supply chain networks were constructed with low cost being the objective function. During normal times when demand is predictable, they deliver as intended. During those times when either there are substantial fluctuations in demand or supply is constrained, hardwired supply chains can fail and potentially threaten the firms that constructed them. Consider some events of the past 10 years. In 2010, Iceland's Eyjafjallajökull volcano erupted causing major disruptions to cross-Atlantic air transportation. Although the eruption only lasted approximately 1 week, flight operations were impacted for over a month and some 20 countries shut down their airspace entirely. The 2011 Tohoku earthquake and tsunami devastated an important coastal region of Japan and disrupted Toyota auto assembly operations worldwide.[3] In 2014, a West Coast labor slowdown, and subsequent dock strike idled operations at 29 ports estimated to represent the movement of US$ 1 trillion of goods annually. Finally, as this book is being written, much of the world is battling the coronavirus. All modes of transportation have been affected, and major

---

[3] The 2011 Tohoku earthquake and tsunami also caused the Fukushima Daiichi Nuclear Power Plant complex disaster.

disruptions have occurred to the supply of lumber, foodstuffs, aluminum, and even (most notably) toilet paper.

Many managements live by the "it can't happen to us" frame of mind instead of weaving contingency plans into the fabric of their supply chain planning. Alternate suppliers, whether of goods or services, need to be arranged before they are needed.

Distributed decision-making, often done in a vacuum

In the case that opened this chapter, Hanna Yen had engaged the various decision-makers when assembling the various components of her new supply chain with the result being a network where members functioned as a coordinated system. Clearly, this is an important element when undertaking new business, but while not addressed in the case, the protocols should be established that call for similar coordination whenever changes need to be made. Fragmented changes are potentially dangerous to the integrity of the network and need to be avoided.

Where research can benefit intermodal maritime security?

The various chapters of this book have emphasized that there are many moving parts that can be assembled into countless combinations all yielding maritime supply chains. Some of these will be more secure than others for a variety of reasons; hence, there is the recommendation that further research can benefit the industry. The disciplines of insurance, homeland security studies, transportation, supply chain management, and law would find the subject to be of interest, but we would advocate a crossdisciplinary approach as well.

There are several methodologies that potentially could add value to the discussion. While not seeking to embark on building a taxonomy of all that could be applied, there are several that are worth mentioning.

- *Data Analytics*: With as many variables as are represented by intermodal maritime transportation, the potential useful data have to be voluminous. The field is generally considered to consist of four types of analysis, all of which have valuable utility.
- *Descriptive Analytics*: Answering the question of *what* has happened, descriptive analytics seeks out the identity of key variables, moderating variables, and the providing of key insights as to what has been a success or a failure.
- *Diagnostic Analytics*: Many consider that doing the deep dive into descriptive analytics potentially can answer the questions of *why* certain results occurred. Several of the authors in this book expressed a concern with the occurrence of anomalies. Diagnostic analytics are used to find relationships and trends that may explain those anomalies.

- *Predictive Analytics*: This methodology is useful when attempting to answer questions of *what is likely to happen* in the future. One potentially useful statistical technique could include data envelopment analysis (DEA), which is essentially nonparametric regression.
- *Prescriptive Analytics*: Prescriptive analytics helps answer questions about *what should be done.* By using insights from predictive analytics, data-driven decisions can be made. This allows businesses to make informed decisions in the face of uncertainty. Prescriptive analytics techniques rely on machine learning strategies that can find patterns in large datasets. By analyzing past decisions and events, the likelihood of different outcomes can be estimated.
- *Artificial Intelligence*: While there are several types, the one that seems to have some promise is evolutionary algorithms, which are a subset of machine learning in that they self-improve over time. These create a population of algorithms and preserve the ones that are most successful at predicting outcomes. Evolutionary algorithms are well suited to optimization tasks where there are many variables and a dynamic environment. Basically: find a way to the best possible result which is a useful application in an endeavor such as securing supply chains.

Systems theory

Chapter 17 addressed the need to adopt systems theory to the problem or to put it into more layman's terms apply a model that embraces all of the variables and thereby can preclude suboptimization. Two tools were previously discussed, the Maritime CARVER Model in Chapter 16 and the fusion centers. While neither are truly new, they are adaptations of other models applied to maritime security.

- *Maritime CARVER model*—User-friendly, subjective, and practitioner-based routing risk assessment model. Based on a US Army model for identifying targets, it has many attributes that commend it for evaluating potential vulnerability in maritime routing. Given that containerized trade is categorized as a liner service with known routes and schedules, Maritime CARVER endeavors to concern itself with threats that may be present along those known itineraries.
- *Fusion centers*—Perhaps with a little oversimplification, fusion centers and ISACs are similar organizations with similar roles but with different memberships. There are numerous fusion centers now established within the United States, each being a merger of law enforcement and other government agencies that share information across organizational boundaries in order to connect the dots from disparate data. In its most basic form, fusion centers are clearing houses for information that link state police, county and local police, Federal Bureau of Investigation, Secret Service, CBP, USCG, and even state conservation officers, the Postal Inspection Service, and others. Perhaps somewhat

of an outlier, but the various railroad police agencies, because of their state charters, are also included in this otherwise public sector activity.

ISACs comprise representatives from specific industry-specific groups, several of which are transportation related. Despite the specific orientation of a group, each is committed to gathering, analyzing, and sharing information: (1) within its own respective group, (2) across group boundaries, such as surface transportation and the oil and gas group should there be threats detected with the petroleum industry, and (3) with the various fusion centers as well as individual private sector agencies.

In closing the question remains as to whether the security gap can indeed be closed. After making substantial investments in technology, human assets, and standing up a plethora of organizations representing nearly every permutation of public and private activity, it is reasonable to conclude that the concept of 100% security is not only beyond reach, but not realistic. While intermodal maritime security can be improved, even substantially so, the volume of 20-foot equivalent units or TEUs transported every year means that the statistical odds are against complete success. Nevertheless, that does not mean that both private and public sectors should stop trying because the means for breaching security will continue to evolve therefore demanding that the means of thwarting them do likewise.

Appendix A—security measures taxonomy assessment

This analysis addresses how the procedural security measures relate to the others and show if and how they could be "piled on top of another." The principles of the assessment for the procedural security measures can be generalized and applied, as appropriate, to the other security measures to determine impacts. They are included in Table 19.A.1 as TBD and left to the reader, practitioner, or supply chain partner and/or as an academic exercise.

Domestic and international procedural processes

For this security measure, consider how the procedural processes affect documentation flow, as well as in-place physical flow, physical security, technological and cyber, and human security measures. The assessment and measures of impact will be summarized in Table 19.A.1, below.

- **Documentation flow**—Documentation flow is challenging and critical to efficient and safe/secure operations, as it could delay loading and possible departure (e.g., 24-h manifest rule). As regulations change, processes and procedures do likewise. What may be acceptable today may not be in the future. Therefore, supply chain partners should: (1) be mindful of that possibility, (2) have systems sufficiently flexible and adaptable so they can react to the changes in a timely manner, and (3) regularly follow and monitor regulatory matters so as not to be caught unaware. Should the supply chain partner not maintain awareness and be forward leaning with regard to regulations and procedural compliance, the impact could be ***high***. Conversely and if they are, it could be ***low***. Also given the reliance of documentation on cyber systems and the inconsistencies among supply chain partners around the world, an impact value of ***moderate*** can be deemed appropriate.

- **Physical flow**—The procedures can impede the physical flow of containers to and from the ports, both for loading at the port and at sea. Changes to the procedures could impact operations by way of timing and/or delayed departures and arrivals. This can occur via changes to the 24-h manifest rule and CSI clearance, both of which could delay vessel loading. Changes to the USCG 96-hour notice of arrival (NOA) rule could impact the arrival and vessel offloading. New or modified regulations or policies could impose changed or additional procedures and processes that could impact operations. As with documentation flow, for supply chain partners that are not sufficiently cognizant of changes to regulations and procedural matters, the impact could be ***high***. If they are aware, it could be ***low***. Similar to documentation flow, an impact value of ***moderate*** can be deemed appropriate.

- **Physical security measures**—The physical security measures are to deter, delay, and/or detect intrusions. They must be intuitive but must be able to evolve to reflect changes in the threat environment and advances in technology. They must also complement the human and operational security measures but be sufficiently flexible to anticipate how threats can evolve and technology advances. This reduces the vulnerabilities and minimizes the gaps between the threat environment and in-place physical security measures. It has been said that we must be correct all of the time, but the terrorist only once. Therefore, physical security must be adaptable to procedural changes (that respond to terrorist activity) to be effective. Not having the flexibility or foresight to adapt to the procedural changes could diminish the effectiveness of the physical in combination with the human security measures. Therefore, when supply chain partners are not aware and flexible with regard to regulations and procedural matters affecting physical security measures, the impact could be ***high***. If they are aware, it could be ***low***. Looking at the global nature of the supply chain and evolving threat environment, an impact value of ***moderate*** can be deemed appropriate.

- **Technological and cybersecurity measures**—Technology and cyber systems are adjuncts to the physical security measures (e.g., intrusion detection systems), "vehicles" for documentation flow (e.g., vetting cargo and supply chain partners), and aids to physical flows (e.g., GPS and AIS). Understanding that procedures must evolve with changing threats, technology, and cyber systems must at least keep pace. Documentation flow is cyber dependent. Hence, technological and (in particular) cybersecurity research and programs must anticipate the evolving threat environment and required regulatory, procedural, and process changes. Similar to physical security measures, the supply chain partners, port operators, and land-based transporters that are not forward leaning and flexible with regard to regulations and procedural matters, the impact could be *high*. If they are, it could be *low*. Considering the extent of the overarching dependence of the procedural and all security and vetting measures on technology and cyber systems, an impact value of *high* can be deemed appropriate.

- **Human security measures**—Documentation and physical flow, and the physical, technological, and cyber system security measures are dependent on its human components. For example, (1) CSI, C-TPAT, and supply chain partner personnel are used to vet cargo and personnel, (2) the Transportation Security Administration (TSA) and USCG Transportation Workers Identification Credential (TWIC) for workers in ports, including ships' crews are vetted and enforced by TSA and USCG personnel, respectively, (3) gates are staffed by security forces and closed-circuit television (CCTV) systems are monitored; the latter requiring response, and (4) technological perimeter control is often supplemented by roving security forces. Therefore, it can be concluded that regulatory or procedural changes will require a change in staffing needs to be properly engaged and respond. Since this is a matter of staffing changes and can be accomplished in a relatively short period of time, an impact value of *low* can be considered appropriate.

It should be noted that there are often cost impacts associated with security measures and adaptability and flexibility to change. Since this assessment is focused solely on security measures, costs are not considered. It should be understood; however, that costs associated with the security measures could be associated with delays, slowing or modifying operations, burdensome and difficult to overlook.

Reference

Dupin, C., September 6, 2019. Container Inspections Reveal Misdeclared Cargo, Poor Stowage. American Shipper.

List of additional readings

Bichou, K., Joseph, S., Zamparini, L., 2013. Maritime Transport Security: Issues, Challenges and National Policies. Edward Elgar Publishing Limited, Cheltenham, UK.

Burns, M., 2015. Logistics and Transportation Security: A Strategic, Tactical and Operational Guide to Resilience. CRC Press, New York.

Christopher, K., 2015. Port Security Management, second ed. CRC Press/Taylor & Francis Group, Boca Raton, FL.

Direnzo III, J., Drumhiller, N., Roberts, F. (Eds.), 2017. Issues in Maritime Cyber Security. Westphalia Press, Washington, DC.

Edwards, F., Goodrich, D., 2013. Introduction to Transportation Security. CRC Press, New York.

Grover, J., 2016. Maritime Security: Progress and Challenges in Implementing Cargo Security Programs. U.S. General Accountability Office, Washington, DC.

Hakim, S., Albert, G., Shiftam, Y. (Eds.), 2016. Securing Transportation Systems. John Wiley and Sons, Hoboken, NJ.

Helmick, J., 2008. Port and maritime security: a research perspective. J. Transp. Secur. 1, 15−28.

Johnstone, R. W, 2015. Protecting Transportation: Implementing Security Policies and Programs. Butterworth-Heineman, Waltham, MA.

Martonosi, S., Ortiz, D., Willis, H., 2005. Evaluating the Viability of 100 Percent Container Inspection at America's Ports. RAND Corp., Pittsburgh, PA.

Meade, C., Molander, R., 2006. Considering the Effects of a Catastrophic Terrorist Attack. Center for Risk Management Policy, RAND Corp., Pittsburgh, PA.

Monacelli, N., January, 2018. Improving maritime transportation security in response to industry consolidation. Homel. Secur. Aff. 14, 2.

Moran, D., Russell, J. (Eds.), 2016. Maritime Strategy and Global Order: Markets, Resources, and Security. Georgetown University Press, Washington, DC.

Paul, S. (Ed.), 2016. Global Responses to Maritime Violence: Cooperation and Collective Action. Stanford University Press, Palo Alto, CA.

Sampson-Wood, T., 2013. The Compromised Cargo Container: Terror in a Box, 15 Florida Coastal Law Review.

Sheffi, Y., 2001. Supply chain management under the threat of international terrorism. Int. J. Logist. Manag. 12, 2.

Tarr, R., McGurk, V., Jones, C., 2005. Intermodal transportation safety and security issues: training against terrorism. J. Pub. Transp. 8, 4.

[The] White House, 2005. The National Strategy for Maritime Security. Department of Homeland Security, Washington, DC.

Index

Note: 'Page numbers followed by "*f*" indicate figures and "*t*" indicate tables.'

Printed in the United States
By Bookmasters